RELIGION IN INDIA

Oxford in India Readings
in Sociology and Social Anthropology
GENERAL EDITOR
T. N. MADAN

RELIGION IN INDIA

Edited by
T. N. MADAN

DELHI
OXFORD UNIVERSITY PRESS
CALCUTTA CHENNAI MUMBAI
1997

Oxford University Press, Great Clarendon Street, Oxford OX2 6DP

Oxford New York
Athens Auckland Bangkok Calcutta
Cape Town Chennai Dar es Salaam Delhi
Florence Hong Kong Istanbul Karachi
Kuala Lumpur Madrid Melbourne Mexico City
Mumbai Nairobi Paris Singapore
Taipei Tokyo Toronto

and associates in
Berlin Ibadan

First published 1991
Second and enlarged edition in Oxford India Paperback 1992
Fourth impression 1997

ISBN 0 19 563092 0

Phototypeset by Imprinter, 89, New Rajdhani Enclave, Delhi 110092
Printed at Rekha Printers Pvt. Ltd., New Delhi 110020
and published by Manzar Khan, Oxford University Press
YMCA Library Building, Jai Singh Road, New Delhi 110 001

To

Kamala

in fond remembrance of a shared childhood

and for

Vandana

Regard all religious faiths with reverence and ponder their teachings: but do not surrender your own judgement.

THE MAHĀBHĀRATA, Shāntiparva 111.17

To you your religion, to me mine.

THE QUR'ĀN 109.3

In my Father's home are many rooms; if it were not so, I would have told you.

John 14:2

. . . we have established the fact that the fundamental categories of thought, and consequently of science, are of religious origin. . . . [And that] nearly all the great social institutions have been born in religion. . . . If religion has given birth to all that is essential to society, it is because the idea of society is the soul of religion.

. . . there is something eternal in religion which is destined to survive all the particular symbols in which religious thought has successively enveloped itself. . . . [Thus religion] seems destined to transform itself than to disappear.

Émile Durkheim, THE ELEMENTARY FORMS OF THE RELIGIOUS LIFE (1915)

The modern man is in general, even with the best will, unable to give religious ideas a significance for culture and national character which they deserve.

Max Weber, THE PROTESTANT ETHIC AND THE SPIRIT OF CAPITALISM (1930)

The Series

Published work on Indian society has grown enormously in recent years. Such writings are not however always readily available. Suitable books of readings would go a long way in meeting the needs of students, teachers and the general readers, but not many of them exist.

Oxford University Press has therefore decided to bring out a series of readings in sociology and social and cultural anthropology in order to fill this gap. The volumes in this series cover a wide range of themes. Some, such as social stratification, kinship, religion and politics are of crucial significance in defining the distinctiveness of society and culture in India. Others, such as population, socio-economic development and environment highlight contemporary concerns.

The series does not try to provide an exhaustive guide to the literature on the discipline. It does however strive to introduce the subject to the interested reader, capturing nuances of theoretical debate and diversities of approach in each area of study.

Contents

Preface to the Enlarged Paperback Edition

The opportunity presented by the production of the paperback edition of *Religion in India* has enabled me to remove a few typographical errors and provide some missing references.

More importantly, perhaps, it has made it possible to make amends for an omission. The limitation of space and the minuscule character of the Parsi community had been the main considerations for the exclusion of Zoroastrianism earlier. On second thoughts, it seemed that this religion also should find a place in the book as four-fifths of the Zoroastrians of the world (numbering about 120,000) live in India. Moreover, they are faced with the unhappy prospect of extinction as a religious community. Their strategies of reorienting to the sacred, therefore, are of a significantly different character compared to the strategies of other religious communities, but they are not lacking in general interest.

Fortunately, I have been able to find a paper already in print, which not only describes some very distinctive Parsi beliefs and rituals pertaining to death, but also attends, even though very briefly, to the problem of corporate extinction. This paper is now included in the book as the Appendix. Incidentally, it touches upon all the five themes of the book—sacred knowledge, sacred space, sacred time, sacred persona, and reorientations to the sacred—and adds to its value as a reader. The list of references and the index also have been accordingly enlarged.

I would like to reiterate here that *Religion in India* is a book of readings, primarily for the teacher and the student. It is not a treatise on Indian religions from the perspectives of theology, religious philosophy, or politics. It consists mainly of fieldwork-based sociological studies of religious belief and practice. Moreover, it treats folklore, or the so-called Little Traditions, no less seriously than scriptural knowledge, or the Great Traditions of Hinduism, Islam, etc. The book does not offer any theses or propositions, beyond what is contained in the readings themselves, nor does it propose any grand conclusions.

1 July 1992 — T. N. Madan

Preface and Acknowledgements

A book of readings serves several readerships but is first of all a pedagogic aid. One of the best ways of getting students started on the study of a specialized field, such as the sociology of religion, is a course of introductory lectures backed by a good book of readings, preparing them for the intensive study of monographs and theoretical works. The preparation of a book of readings presupposes the existence of a considerable body of high quality published work of wide scope. The reader, teacher as well as student, has the advantage of having available between the covers of one volume published materials scattered over a large number of publications many of which may not be readily accessible. There is a disadvantage too in relying on such a book of readings as the editor's preferences and predilections introduce an element of arbitrariness into the process of selection. Ideally, every reader should assemble his or her own best book of readings but, regrettably, this can be done only at the end of the day when lectures have been delivered, examinations passed and degrees won. Our perfect book of readings does not exist: we must do with the second best which some one else has put together.

In 1989 when the Oxford University Press in India embarked upon an ambitious and overdue project of producing books of readings for students of sociology and social/cultural anthropology, which may be of interest to Indianists generally, and to lay readers also, it was but appropriate that religion should have been chosen as the theme of a volume alongside of others on social stratification, kinship, etc. Whether intellectuals welcome or deplore the fact of widespread religiosity in India—they usually do the latter—they may not ignore it if they want to get an adequate understanding of the nature of social reality. I hope I have been able to put together a volume which goes some distance in producing such understanding.

The structure of the book and the considerations that guided the process of selection are stated in the Introduction. Further light has been thrown on the themes and the readings in the prefatory remarks at the beginning of each part. I will not therefore say anything on the same here.

Assembling this book has been a welcome experience, at once educative and enjoyable. It has been somewhat like conducting a seminar, posing questions, suggesting themes, eliciting rich and varied responses—struggling all the time to retain control! It is a particular source of gratification to me to have had the privilege of having met at one time or another all the authors whose work has been included here except Verrier Elwin and P. M. Currie. Indeed most of them have been more than acquaintances and include teachers, pupils and friends. I would like to thank them for what they have taught me. It grieves me deeply that K. S. Mathur, a personal friend, from whose book on Malwa I have included an excerpt, should have died prematurely before his considerable interest in the study of religion could bear more than the first fruit. I also deplore the untimely deaths of L. P. Vidyarthi, (who belonged to the first batch of students I taught at Lucknow University in the early 1950s) and A. R. Sayid (a colleague at Delhi in more recent years).

The enthusiasm which Baburao Baviskar, Ramachandra Guha, Dipankar Gupta and Patricia Uberoi brought to the discussions we had early in 1989 on the making of the readers was infectious. Acting as a trapper of editors on behalf of OUP, I found myself ensnared too! The Press provided (besides tea and pastry!) precious intellectual stimulus and good practical advice. The house-editor nourished the project from uncertain beginnings to what I trust is a worthwhile fruition. It has been altogether a pleasurable experience.

I am indebted to the Institute of Economic Growth in Delhi where I have had, for nearly a quarter of a century, almost complete freedom in the pursuit of my academic interests. The work of selecting and editing the readings was done there during 1989, providing me much appreciated relief from the administrative chores in which I was then engaged. The introductory essay was written early in 1990 at the University of Washington in the beautiful city of Seattle. Warm thanks are due to Biff and Jane Keyes for making the visit possible and for their hospitality to me and my wife. Val Daniel helped in many ways and Paul Brass gave me company: I am grateful to both. I am also grateful to Aradhya Bhardwaj for compiling the index Finally, I would like to thank

Mr H. L. Mehta (Delhi) and Ms Shirley Scotter (Seattle) for assistance with typing, a common skill which I lack. Needless to add, the sage advice of my wife, Uma, throughout the preparation of this book was, as always, an invaluable resource.

Delhi–Seattle
1989–90

T. N. Madan

Introduction

T. N. MADAN

The purpose of this introductory essay is to briefly highlight some aspects of major sociological theories of religion which may be of special interest to Indian readers and Indianists; to outline the core teachings of the different religions of India and to indicate their following; and, to state some of the considerations that have guided the selection of the readings that comprise this volume. Limitations of space preclude a detailed discussion of the theories.

Sociological Interpretations of Religion

Religion, the social phenomenon more than the word, is difficult to define. Aware of this, Max Weber wrote in the very first paragraph of *The Sociology of Religion* that a definition of religion 'can be attempted, if at all, only at the conclusion of the study' (1964:1). Actually, apart from implying the centrality of the notion of the supernatural, identifying a variety of religious ideas, attitudes, actors, and institutions, and examining the relationship of the religious and secular domains, Weber nowhere in this important work, or elsewhere, provides a precise definition of religion. While other major sociologists and social anthropologists may have been more forthcoming with such definitions, they, too, have drawn attention to the problematic character of the task (see, e.g. Nadel 1954 and Evans-Pritchard 1965). Edward Sapir put it succinctly: 'religion is precisely one of those words which belong to the more intuitive portions of our vocabulary' (1949: 346). Many historians of religion have similarly expressed unease with the word religion because of its ambiguity or associations (see Smith 1962 and Cox 1965).

It is not my intention here to join this controversy about definitions. All I need for my present purpose of assembling a book of readings on religion in India is a key idea, and a broad framework derived from it, for an orderly presentation of the selected materials. And my choice is the notion of the 'sacred': *the 'sacred' as a particular class of phenomena, as a kind of knowledge, as a variety of activities in space and time, and as a typology of roles and persons*. It is hoped that the five sets of readings comprising this book will clarify these aspects of the 'sacred' and, besides, indicate the kinds of reorientation to the sacred that occur in modernizing societies. It is, however, important to emphasize here that in making the notion of the sacred the organizing concept of this book, I am not arguing for its exclusiveness in a dualistic framework—the sacred versus the profane or the secular. Such an absolutist dichotomy is not warranted by the relevant ethnographical or historical studies.

Durkheim and Sociological Functionalism

The 'sacred' was identified by Émile Durkheim as the most fundamental religious idea or phenomenon. He wrote: 'A religion is a unified set of beliefs and practices relative to sacred things, that is to say, things set apart and forbidden—beliefs and practices which unite into one single moral community called a church all those who adhere to them' (1965:62). For my purpose what is important in this definition is, first, the notion of 'things set apart' (rather than the narrower idea of things 'forbidden') and, then, the idea of a 'moral community' (whether identified as a church or not), which, in Durkheim's own words, is an 'eminently collective thing' (ibid.:63). Supernatural beings alone, where recognized, may not be seen apart from mankind: persons with supernatural or magical powers (exercised knowingly or unwittingly) may also be seen thus (set apart), just as certain places (temples, mosques, places of pilgrimage) and certain performances or events (births, deaths, marriages, eclipses) may be regarded as being apart, i.e. other than ordinary or routine.

The 'sacred' acquires a sharpness of definition by being contrasted to the 'profane' and the 'secular'. This dichotomy was emphasized by Durkheim in absolutist terms as constituting the very core of religious phenomena. In his own words: 'All known religious beliefs, whether simple or complex, present one common characteristic: they presuppose a classification of things, real and ideal, of which men think, into two classes or opposed groups, generally designated by two distinct terms which are translated well enough by the words *profane* and *sacred*' (ibid.: 52). Durkheim further commented: 'In all the history of human thought there exists no other example of two categories of things so profoundy differentiated or radically opposed to one another' (ibid.: 53). The validity or usefulness of this affirmation, though generally affirmed in a wide variety of ethnographic settings, has been questioned by W.E.H. Stanner (1967) in the context of Australian aboriginal religion. In the setting of the religions of India, too, one would have to exercise great caution in applying this idea, for Indian religious thought is, I think, hierarchical (in Louis Dumont's sense of encompassing of the contrary, see Dumont 1970a), rather than simply dualistic (recognizing binary oppositions). That is, the profane, though the opposite of the sacred, is included in and thus subordinated to it.

Durkheim was persuaded to go beyond the prevailing definitions of religion in terms of gods and spirits by his encounter with the religions of India—particularly Buddhism—in the works of European and English scholars. Noting that, in the opinion of the authorities, Buddhism was an atheistic religion, Durkheim observed that the basic principles or presuppositions—the so-called four 'noble Truths', which are regarded by the faithful as the core of the Buddha's teaching and the foundation of Buddhism—were indeed completely divorced from the idea of the divinity. 'The Buddhist is not interested', Durkheim wrote, 'in knowing whence came the world in which he lives and suffers; he takes it as a given fact, and his whole concern is to escape it. On the other hand, in this work of salvation, he can only count upon himself' (ibid.: 45). Even the Buddha himself, once he had expounded the four 'noble Truths', and outlined the eightfold path to salvation, had 'ceased to be a factor necessary to the religious life' (ibid.: 47). The deification of the Buddha was thus a contingent (if not a spurious) development.

The Jain faith also was atheistic, in fact more strictly so. 'Moreover, if this indifference to the divine is developed to such a point in Buddhism and Jainism', Durkheim concluded, 'it is because its germ existed already in the Brahamanism from which the two were derived. . . . In time, the numerous divinities which the people of India had originally learned to adore, came to merge themselves into a sort of principle deity, impersonal and abstract, the essence of all that exists. This supreme reality, which no longer has anything of a divine personality about it, is contained within man himself, or rather, man is but one with it, for nothing exists apart from it' (ibid.: 48).

Durkheim's dissatisfaction with the available conceptions of 'primitive' religion, notably animism and naturism, arose from his rejection of the worthiness of questions about the truth status and historical origins of religion. Besides, he contended that facts of everyday experience, such as dreams from which, E. B. Tylor had said, primitive men derived the notion of soul (see Tylor 1913), or the phenomena of nature ('fire, water, rain and storm') from which, Max Mueller had asserted, Vedic Indians arrived at their notion of supernatural powers as revelations of the deity (see Mueller 1889), could not 'give us the idea of something whose characteristic is to be outside the world of common experience' (ibid.: 106).

Searching for a better, more scientific explanation, Durkheim turned to the Australian aborigines for insights. He fell in agreement with the prevailing scholarly opinion that aboriginal totemism was the simplest, 'the elementary', form of the religious life. 'If we succeed in discovering the origin of [totemic] beliefs', Durkheim argued, 'we shall very probably discover at the same time the causes leading to the rise of the religious sentiment in humanity' (ibid.: 195). His quest was for sociological causes not historical origins, and he found them in the human need for social life. Religion was a collective phenomenon and it arose from social interaction. For Durkheim, social facts were truly explained only sociologically, not by reductionist propositions.

Presenting a detailed discussion of totemic gatherings among the Australian aborigines, Durkheim located the roots of religious beliefs and practices in social interaction:' if collective life awakens religious thought on reaching a certain degree of intensity, it is because it brings about a state of effervescence which changes the conditions of psychic activity. . . . A man . . . feels himself transformed and consequently he transforms the environment which surrounds him. In order to account for the very particular impressions which he receives, he attributes to the things with which he is in most direct contact properties which they have not, exceptional powers and virtues which the objects of everyday experience do not possess. In a word, above the real world where his profane life passes he has placed another which, in one sense, does not exist except in thought, but to which he attributes a higher sort of dignity than to the first. Thus, from a double point of view it is an ideal world' (ibid.: 469–70).

From this insight Durkheim derived the conclusion that 'the collective and anonymous force of the clan' (ibid.: 253), and that 'the god of the clan, the totemic principle, can therefore be nothing else than the clan itself' (ibid.: 236). Generalizing from the Australian case—the elementary form of the religious life—Durkheim came to consider society as the source and sustainer of religious sentiments and structures and, therefore, god to its members, creating among them 'the sensation of a perpetual dependence' (ibid.: 237).

Durkheim's interpretation of religion, marked by what Stanner called an all-consuming sociological fixation, derives religion from the very nature of social life, and not from a particular primeval event or any psychological propensities of mankind. It is interwoven at its very source with other aspects of the social life, excluding, paradoxically, economic activity (see ibid.: 466, fn. 4). Such interweaving (to persist with the metaphor) is more comprehensive in simpler than in complex secularizing societies. While every religion bears the imprint of the structure of social milieu in which it had its birth, it is by no means totally constrained by its source but acquires a dynamic life of its own, often achieving unanticipated elaborations. These and other ideas, comprising Durkheim's sociological theory of religion, acclaimed as a major intellectual achievement, have been widely influential.

The role of religion in sustaining social solidarity was the central focus of A. R. Radcliffe-Brown's sociological analysis of ritual. Deeply influenced by W. Robertson Smith's emphasis upon institutions and practices in the study of ancient religions, upon rituals rather than beliefs (see Smith 1927), he followed Durkheim closely but rather narrowly. For him, and for others of the influential British school of sociological functionalism (of which he along with Bronislaw Malinowski is considered the founder), the significant question to ask about religion anywhere and anytime was, in what ways and measures it contributes to the maintenance of social solidarity. As he put it: 'An orderly social life amongst human beings depends upon the presence in the minds of members of society of certain sentiments, which control the behaviour of the individual in relation to others. Rites can therefore be shown to have specific social functions when . . . they have for their effect to regulate, maintain and transmit from one generation to another sentiments on which the constitution of society depends' (1952: 157). In his detailed ethnography of the Andaman Islanders, Radcliffe-Brown (1964) had already, even before he came to explicitly formulate his theoretical position, presented a functional analysis of a wide variety of cosmological beliefs, rites and ceremonies through which the Andamanese cope with environmental forces, biological processes, and social pressures. Nature, life and society were shown to constitute a personally meaningful and socially integrated totality.

Radcliffe-Brown may not have been a very original thinker but he was an influential teacher. One of his renowned pupils is M. N. Srinivas, the focus of whose celebrated book on the Coorgs (1952) is on the social integrative role of *mangala*, the rituals relating to marriage, birth, death, etc. As a setting for the analysis of these life cycle rites and ceremonies, he discusses the ritual idiom of Coorg society in terms of the key notions of ritual purity and auspiciousness.

While Srinivas depends heavily upon Radcliffe-Brown's ideas, E. E. Evans-Pritchard denies them any merit (see Evans-Pritchard 1965). His early monograph on the Zande (1937) had been concerned with showing, among other things, how belief in witches, which he maintained could not exist in the sense the Zande said they did, might be explained (for example, by reference to unfortunate happenings). This was straightforward functionalism. In his later classic work, *Nuer Religion* (1956)—which interestingly did not extend the earlier sceptical attitude to Nuer theism—he devoted attention to the problem of 'meaning' but refrained from an explicitly phenomenological analysis. In fact, he maintained till the very end of his life that, for the social anthropologist, 'religion is what religion does' (1965:120). The shift from 'function' to 'meaning' in Evans-Pritchard's work should not, therefore, be emphasized too much. He also remained true to Durkheim's teaching when he presented an interpretation of Nuer religious thought and ritual in terms of the social order. At the same time, however, he characterized religion as an 'interior state' to understand which he recommended recourse to 'intuitive apprehension' (1956: 314–15). His approach was more eclectic than he may have been willing to admit and his unqualified rejection of Radcliffe-Brown is, therefore, indefensible.

In any case, Evans-Pritchard has been less influential in the study of religion in India than Srinivas. David Pocock's excellent study of religious belief and practice in a Gujarat village (1973), written at Oxford, is consistently concerned with the problem of subjective meaning and offers an alternative to the narrowly functionalist approach. In fact, since the publication of Evans-Pritchard's book on Nuer religion, sociological and social anthropological studies of religion have moved more confidently in the direction of phenomenology—a development anticipated in the monumental work of Max Weber.

Weber and Phenomenology

The first principle of Weber's sociology of religion may be said to be his assertion that interpretations of social reality ('social action') generally must begin with 'interpretive understanding' and lead to 'causal explanation'. Accordingly, an understanding of 'religious behavior . . . can only be achieved from the viewpoint of the subjective experiences, ideas, and purposes of the individuals concerned—in short, from the viewpoint of the religious behaviour's "meaning"' (1964:1). Lest such an approach should be misconstrued as a retreat from truly sociological concerns, it may be pointed out that Weber studied preliterate as well as the so-called world religions—viz. Hinduism, Buddhism, Jainism, Judaism, Christianity, and Islam—with a view to exploring, among other things, the relations between religious beliefs and practices on the one hand, and the secular domain of politics, economics, sexuality, wit, etc. on the other.

In contrast to Durkheim, who (as stated above) did not consider economic activity to be expressly attached to religion, Weber paid particularly close attention to the relation between it and the religious milieu. Acknowledging that no economic ethic had ever been solely determined by religion (1958a: 268), he nevertheless argued for a causal relationship between the Protestant ethic and the rise of rational capitalism in Western Europe (see Weber 1930) His judgement was that it was 'only in the modern Western world that rational capitalistic enterprises with fixed capital, free labour, the rational specialization and combination of functions, bound together in a market economy are to be found' and that 'economic grounds' alone do not provide a satisfactory explanation of the phenomenon (Weber 1947: 279). He identified the combined influence of the ideas of 'predestination' and 'calling'—the notion that one's fate and one's work are both predetermined by God—as the crucial element in the teaching of Calvin. To cope with the 'religious anxiety' which the idea of predestination generated, the Calvinist put his faith in the hope that 'God helps those who help themselves. Thus [he] himself creates his own salvation, or . . . the conviction of it' (1930: 115). A worldly asceticism (restraint on immediate gratification) had the unintended consequence of accumulation of capital and expanded investment nurturing capitalism. It was thus that the Christian ascetics 'strode in the market place of life' (ibid.: 154).

Going beyond Europe, where capitalism was an aspect of the process of rationalization, which had been facilitated by theological debates within Christianity, Weber set out to discover the economic ethics associated with the other world religions. A basic premise of this investigation in respect of India was the sweeping assertion that 'Indian religiosity is the cradle of those religious ethics which have abnegated the world, theoretically, practically, and to the greatest extent' (1958a: 323). He made a crucial distinction between 'mysticism', or the attitude of abandoning worldly involvements, and 'rationally active asceticism', which is this-worldly and seeks to master the world.

Weber argued that man's worldly conduct is governed by 'material and ideal interests', yet, often enough, 'the "world images" that have been created by "ideas" have, like switchmen, determined the tracks along which action has been pushed by the dynamic of interest' (1958a: 280). The ideas that he regarded as 'self evident presuppositions' (1958b: 173), and indeed 'the truly "dogmatic" doctrines of all Hinduism', were 'the *samsara* belief in the transmigration of souls and the related *karman* doctrine of compensation' (ibid.: 118). These ideas are joined to caste, 'the fundamental institution of Hinduism' without which 'there is no Hindu' (ibid.: 29). Out of this combination of ideas and institutions the peculiar 'iron cage' (to use a Weberian phrase) of the Hindus is constructed. Weber wrote: '*Karma* doctrine transformed the world into a strictly rational ethically-determined cosmos; it represents the most consistent theodicy ever produced in history. The devout Hindu was accursed to remain in a structure which made sense only in this intellectual context; its consequences burdened his conduct' (ibid.: 121).

Hindu culture and society, Weber believed, were immune to change, and India was incapable of the kind of socioeconomic historical developments that took place in Europe. 'A ritual law in which every change of occupation, every change in work technique, may result in ritual degradation is certainly not capable of giving birth to economic and technical revolutions from within itself, or of even facilitating the first germination of capitalism in its midst'. Further: 'It was impossible to shatter traditionalism, based on caste ritualism anchored in *karma* doctrine, by rationalizing the economy' (ibid.: 112, 113).

The encirclement of the Hindu was thus complete: his culture and society were incapable of generating rational capitalism; the economy rationalized somehow would be unable to change his cultural beliefs and social institutions. The world thus remained for the Hindus (as it did for the followers of other 'popular religions of Asia'), in Weber's final judgement, 'a great enchanted garden' from which 'no path led... to a rational, methodical control of life' (1964: 270). While many scholars have concurred with this magisterial verdict (see e.g. Mishra 1962), or produced parallel arguments (see Saran 1963), others have written strong rebuttals of it (see notably, Singer 1966 and 1972).

Weber's sociology of religion had an immense scope, including such diverse themes as the social basis of varieties of theism, the role of prophets in society, different roads to salvation, and the sociological preconditions of the emergence of universal love. It was produced under the shadow of the secularization of Europe in the nineteenth century (see Chadwick 1975). Although it is doubtful if Weber was deeply influenced by Nietzsche, he could not have been immune to the influence, and Nietzsche had proclaimed the death of god and the consequent loneliness of man (see Nietzsche 1961).

The central concerns of Weber's sociology of religion, therefore, included the related questions of the future of religion and the nature of human existence in modern society. He saw no future for religion but only its replacement by progressive rationalization and the decline of mystery, magic and ritual (to describe which he used Friedrich Schiller's by now celebrated phrase 'disenchantment of the world') (1958a: 155). As for the nature of human existence in modern society, he saw it overcome by a scientific-technological and manipulative world-view and a consumerist lifestyle, deprived of its legitimacy in terms of ultimate values and thus rendered meaningless. He saw modern man trapped in an 'iron cage' of his own making (see Weber 1930: 181) and the future he foresaw was 'not summer's bloom . . . but the polar night of icy darkness and hardness' (1958a: 128). While Durkheim and Weber were both convinced about the decline of institutionalized religion—of Judaism and Christianity—the latter did not share the former's optimism about the future of a secularized world nor his expectation that the religious idea would survive as social morality.

The religious fate of mankind, in Weber's formulation, is constructed consciously by human beings themselves through the world images they fashion and the social institutions they construct. His sociology of religion thus provides an alternative perspective to Durkheim's (which emphasizes the 'exteriority' and 'coerciveness' of 'social facts' which are also, however, 'collective representations'). It has had an enormous influence on contemporary work in the field. Peter Berger, an influential social theorist, for example, looks upon religion as that special human activity through which a comprehensive, meaningful, sacred cosmos is constructed (see Berger 1973). Another influential scholar, the cultural anthropologist Clifford Geertz, also has based his notion of religion as a cultural system—as a system of symbols—in part on the ideas of Weber.

Both Berger and Geertz emphasize the importance of interpretive understanding. Religion for Berger is ultimately the means to bestow 'legitimacy' on social life and to help it to resist the onslaught of chaos. For Geertz, religion makes human life meaningful in the midst of moral perplexities and social conflict. He writes: 'Religious concepts spread beyond their specifically metaphysical contexts to provide a framework of general ideas in terms of which a wide range of experience—intellectual, emotional, moral—can be given meaningful form' (1975: 123).

Studies of religion in India, too, are paying increasing attention to the problem of meaning, focusing attention on religious experience (for example in the study of pilgrimages) and experimenting with the phenomenological approach (see e.g., Gold 1988). Such a concern for reflexivity is, however, scoffed at as a retreat into 'mystification' by scholars who pursue their sociological studies of religion from a Marxian perspective.

Marx and Dialectical Materialism

Among the founding fathers of sociology Karl Marx occupies a unique place in relation to the study of religion, as he was primarily concerned with the abolition of religion and with constructing the socioeconomic conditions under which this task may be accomplished. Arguing that 'man makes religion', and using the metaphor of 'a reversed world', in which it may seem that religion makes man, Marx observed: 'Religion is the general theory of that world, its encyclopaedic compendium, its logic in a popular form, its spiritualistic *point d'honneur*, its enthusiasm, its moral sanction, its solemn complement, its universal ground for consolation and justification. It is the fantastic realization of the human essence because the human essence has no true reality. The struggle against religion is therefore mediately the fight against the other world, of which religion is the spiritual aroma.' Then follow the well-known and oft-quoted lines: 'Religious distress is at the same time the expression of real distress and a protest against real distress. Religion is the sigh of the oppressed creature, the heart of a heartless world, just as it is the spirit of a spiritless situation. It is the opium of the people.' And finally, exhortation: 'The abolition of religion as the illusory happiness of the people is required for their real happiness. The demand to give up the illusions about its condition is the demand to give up a condition which needs illusions. The criticism of religion is therefore in embryo the criticism of the vale of woe, the halo of which is religion.... Religion is only the illusory sun, which revolves round man as long as he does not revolve around himself' (Marx and Engels 1959: 262–3).

It is necessary to look at this passage in Marx's 'Critique of Hegel's Philosophy of Right' carefully because truncated quotation is often used by partisan writers to emphasize either 'the opium of the people' judgement, or to soften that judgement by pointing out the uses of the religiosity of the oppressed. Marx's argument was more sophisticated than either simplification, and the spirit of the passage is indubitably and without qualification hostile to religion. The abolition of religion is required both philosophically and politically, for religion only encourages 'cowardice, self-contempt, abasement, submission, and humbleness', and thus prevents revolt against oppression. Why the exploiters themselves needed religion in their own inner lives is a question to which Marx provided no satisfactory answer.

The criticism of religion may well be, as Marx wrote, 'the premise of all criticism' (ibid.: 262), but it should be noted that Marx wanted to get beyond such criticism towards a reconstruction of human society: he wanted to move from atheism to humanism and, finally, to socialism. The objective was to end both false consciousness and alienation. This comes out clearly in the *Economic and Philosophic Manuscripts*: 'Just as in religion the spontaneous activity of the human imagination, of the human brain and the human heart, operates independently of the individual—that is, operates on him as an alien, divine or diabolical activity—in the same way the worker's activity is not his spontaneous activity. It belongs to another; it is the loss of his self' (Marx 1959: 69).

It is well known that there was a significant change in Marx's philosophical ideas in the mid-1840s (soon after he had written the above named texts of 1844). The later Marxian position on religion is linked to a rethinking about matter and materialism. Thus Marx wrote in his 'Theses on Feuerbach' (1845): 'Feuerbach resolves the religious essence into the human essence. But the human essence is no abstraction inherent in the single individual. In its reality it is the ensemble of the social relations. . . . Feuerbach, consequently, does not see that the "religious sentiment" is itself a social product, and that the abstract individual whom he analyzes belongs in reality to a particular form of society.' From this Marx concludes: 'Social life is essentially practical. All mysteries which mislead theory to mysticism find their rational solution in human practice and in the comprehension of this practice'. (Marx and Engels 1959: 244–5).

Dialectical materialism is thus absolutely opposed to religion as the real, the true, and the rational are opposed to the fantastic, the erroneous and the superstitious, as action is opposed to inaction. It is not therefore at all surprising that there are no sharply focused Marxian studies of the religions of India, though there are broad generalizations about Indian history and religions (see Kosambi 1962 and Bhattacharya 1969), or Marxist critiques (often narrowly constructed) of what their protagonists regard as an illegitimate disguise of the conflict of class interests—nurtured by colonialism—under the fuzzy notion of 'communalism' (see Bipan Chandra 1984). Marx himself did not set a particularly good example for serious discussion in his superficial characterizations of Hinduism, for instance, in his *New York Daily Tribune* article of 1853 on British rule in India. European dualistic categories of thought gave rise to his puzzlement which he expressed in purple passages about 'the religion of Hindustan'—'at once a religion of sensualist exuberance, and a religion of self-torturing asceticism' (Marx and Engels 1959: 475). Nor did he answer adequately (though he believed this could be done easily) the critical question which he himself posed (in a letter to Engels), viz. why the history of the East appears as a history of religions (ibid.: 454).

Sociological interpretations of religion derive in main from Durkheim and Weber and, negatively, from Marx. Malinowski's functionalist analysis leaned heavily on psychological states of mind and traced religious beliefs and practices to individual experiences, fears and hopes. It is not therefore surprising that the focus of his study of religion among the Trobriand Islanders should have been on life-cycle rituals and should have linked religion closely to magic as practical activity (see Malinowski 1974). He and Radcliffe-Brown looked at religion from opposite but not opposed points of views; their perspectives were, in fact, mutually complementary. It may also be noted here that Malinowski's psychological explanations were not particularly influenced by Sigmund Freud or Carl

Jung. He owed more to David Hume and William James, to the notions of natural religion and pragmatism. The insights of Freud and Jung have, however, contributed significantly to a psychological anthropology of religion (see e.g. Obeyesekere 1981 and 1984). The limitation of space precludes a discussion of the same; the character of the present volume also does not require it as none of the selected readings belongs to this genre.

Lévi-Strauss and Structuralism

A major contemporary theoretical development in the study of religion derives from the structuralist movement in anthropology initiated by Claude Lévi-Strauss. In Indianist studies Louis Dumont has been its original and most distinguished exponent. Lévi-Strauss's concerns have been very broad and have subsumed the study of the 'sacred' under forms of thought, modes of classification, mythologies, etc. In fact, he has been suspicious that the 'obsessive' interest of anthropologists in 'religious matters' has misled them to identify 'totemism' as a form of religion instead of a mode of classification (see Lévi-Strauss 1963 and 1966). Lévi-Strauss has proposed that sacred objects owe their significance, not to narrow considerations of utility, nor to their social or moral character, but to their availability as concrete manifestations or embodiments of abstract ideas. The 'primitives' do not *think* differently from the 'civilized' but they *symbolize* differently. Religious systems, comprising myths and rites, are symbolic systems of signs, of communication, which establish through analogical reasoning continuities between nature and culture and between cosmic order and social life.

Dumont also has attended to the study of religion at both the empirical and theoretical levels. His *magnum opus* on India, *Homo Hierarchicus* (1967, 1970a), identifies religious values—more precisely the notion of 'pure and impure'—as the very foundation of the caste system. He had earlier presented a detailed ethnography of the religious aspects of the culture of the Kallar, a south Indian subcaste (1986). Besides, he has written seminal and thematically wide-ranging essays on the structural definition of a Hindu deity, renunciation in Indian religions, and religion and politics (see Dumont 1970b). At a more abstract level he looks at religion in the context of value (see Dumont 1986a). The influence which Lévi-Strauss and Dumont have had on others who have written on religion has been immense.

Particularly influential has been the key idea that 'structures' are not empirically given systems but models of 'ensembles' of relations constructed by the analyst around a 'single true principle' (as Dumont has it), a fundamental 'binary opposition', expressed through a series of 'transformations'. The notion of 'binary opposition' itself is a complex (generative) idea (or relationship), emerging in Dumont's work as 'hierarchy' or 'the encompassing of the contrary' (see Dumont 1970a). Social phenomena, or cultural facts, are seen by both scholars to appear above 'the threshold of consciousness' as 'manifest' expressions of fundamental 'latent' structures. The task of structural analysis is to explicate this relationship and to show that societies differ not in terms of fundamental constituent elements but in the way these elements are interrelated in various patterns.

Among the many authors who have published structural analyses of religion in India, mention may be made illustratively of the work of Ákos Östör (1980, Veena Das (1977), and J. P. S. Uberoi (pp. 320 ff.). As will be seen in the extracts from their work included in this book, all three authors present interpretations of ritual in terms of certain fundamental categories of thought (such as time, space, purity, power and auspiciousness) and in relation to the structure of social relations.

To conclude, it is appropriate to mention, first of all, the widespread influence of the teaching of Robert Redfield and Milton Singer on a whole generation of scholars who have made contributions to the study of several aspects of society in India including, notably, religion. Village level or 'contextual' studies of religious belief and practice have been carried out in terms of a dynamic interface of the 'great' literary (Sanskritic) tradition of Hinduism and local or 'little' oral traditions (see Marriott 1955). A 'common cultural consciousness' is said to have arisen out of this interface, facilitated by 'certain processes and factors that also play an important role in other primary civilizations: i.e. sacred books and sacred objects as a fixed point of worship, a special class of literati (Brahmans) who have the authority to recite and interpret the sacred scriptures, professional storytellers, a sacred geography of sacred centres—temples, pilgrimage places, and shrines—and leading personalities who by their identification with the Great Tradition and with the masses mediate the one to the other' (Singer 1972: 67–8; also see Vidyarthi 1961).

In the studies produced or influenced by Chicago anthropologists, as also in the work of the structuralists and, more recently, of Stanley Tambiah (1985), considerable attention is given to the content and channels of cultural communication: the semeiotic significance of signs and symbols and of religion generally has been explored and ritual action conceptualized as 'performative action' (see Tambiah 1981). The work of Victor Turner (1967, 1969), too, has exerted much influence on those who have engaged in the analysis of symbolic forms and the symbolic analysis of ritual.

From their very inception sociological and social anthropological studies of society in India have accorded a central place to religion. The founding fathers of sociology here, Radhakamal Mukerjee and G. S. Ghurye, wrote on selected aspects of Hinduism on the basis of textual materials. While anthropologists generally covered religion in their comprehensive ethnography, some (notably Sarat Chandra Roy and Verrier Elwin) wrote focused monographs on the subject. Modern, theoretically well-grounded, work was inaugurated by M. N. Srinivas in his book on the Coorgs (1952), but the 1950s and the 60s witnessed some slackening of interest. This has, however, revived vigorously in more recent times which have seen the publication of some of the best work in the field. Extracts from the same comprise most of the scholarly materials collected in this volume.

Religions of India

India is the home of many religions and long time host to some. Followers of all world religions are present among her peoples. Hinduism, a direct descendent of Brahmanism, the Vedic religion of more than 3,000 years ago, is the oldest of the country's religions and has the largest number of followers. Some of the tribal religions may be older though, being the inheritors of prehistoric cultures. The Vedic religion of the immigrant Aryans carried the imprint of its Indo-European origin and was also influenced to a certain extent by the proto-historic Indus Valley Civilization. Jainism and Buddhism took birth around the same time, 2,500 years ago, in north India. Both religions began as sectarian heresies. The founder of Jainism, Vardhamana Mahavira, is believed to have carried to its fruition an already existing tradition of dissent which originated much before his time early in the sixth century BC. The founder of Buddhism, Siddhartha Gautama, was a more innovative and radical dissenter and is said to have attained 'enlightenment' in *c.* 528 BC.

The Thomas Christians of South India have a credible tradition according to which Christianity was brought to India by the Apostle Thomas within living memory of Jesus Christ. Documentary evidence of the presence of Christians in India, however, goes back only to the sixth century. Islam followed two centuries later. Among other arrivals were Zoroastrians (fleeing persecution in Iran at the hands of Muslims in the eighth century) and Jews. The youngest of India's religious traditions is Sikhism, the faith first taught by Guru Nanak at the beginning of the sixteenth century. Many other faiths have arisen and fallen. Among these are two notable experiments in religious unitarianism attempted by the Muslim Mughal emperor Akbar in the late fifteenth century and by the Hindu Bengali savant Ram Mohun Roy in the early nineteenth century. Akbar called his new faith 'the religion of God' (Din-i-Ilahi) and Roy named his congregation 'the Society of God' (Brahmo Sabha).

According to the 1981 census, there were about 550 million Hindus in India constituting 82.64 per cent of the total population of 684 million. About 76 million (11.35 per cent) were Muslims. Christians (16 million) accounted for 2.43 per cent; Sikhs (13 million), 1.96 per cent; Buddhists (5 million), 0.71 per cent and Jains (3 million), 0.48 per cent. Zoroastrians (72,000), Jews (about 18,000) and others, together account for 0.42 per cent. Such 'tribal' communities as are still outside the fold of Hinduism or Christianity are included among the 'others'.

A distinctive feature of the overall religious ethos of India is that religion here influences all aspects of society. Only the Christians would adhere to a doctrinal separation of the religious and the secular domains. The point is not that the other religious traditions do not make this distinction, but rather that the secular domain is regarded as encompassed by the religious—even when considered opposed to it—and not independent of it. The relationship is hierarchical in the sense in which Louis Dumont uses the term (see Dumont 1970a and Madan 1989). Actually, a correct reading of the Christian tradition would include Christianity too in this ethos rather than exclude it. Bankimchandra Chatterji, one of the tallest Indians of the nineteenth century, put it thus: 'with other peoples, religion is only a part of life; there are things religious and things lay and secular. To the Hindu, his whole life was religion. . . . All life to him was religion and religion never received a name from him, because it never had for him an existence apart from all that had received a name' (quoted in Chaudhuri 1979: 11–12).

Now, all world views, whether religious or secular, have their metaphysical foundations, which are the basis and an integral component of social activity everywhere. The root paradigm of all the major indigenous religions of India is that of dharma, which is what Bankimchandra Chatterji had in mind.

A concept of multiple connotations, dharma, as Hindus perceive it, includes cosmological, ethical, social and legal principles that provide the basis for the notion of an ordered universe. In the social context, dharma refers to the rules of social intercourse laid down for every category of persons in terms of social status (*varna*), stage of life (*ashrama*), and inborn qualities (*guna*). In other words, for every person there is an appropriate mode of conduct (*svadharma*) defined by his or her caste, gender, age, and temperament. Such context-sensitive prescriptions are, however, subject to the dictates of general morality (*sadharana dharma*) which are binding on everybody. All activity is goal oriented and dharma as the first goal (*purushartha*) is the basis for the rational pursuit of economic and political goals (*artha*) as well as pleasure (*kama*). An alternative to *dharma-artha-kama* is *moksha* (freedom from rebirth, reward and retribution or *samsara*) and the way to it lies in *sannyasa* or the renunciation of all social activity. The sources of dharma, according to tradition, are four: the original knowledge (*shruti*), remembered teaching (*smriti*), the conduct of good people (*sadachar*), and moral reason or conscience (*atmatushti*).

Jain, Buddhist and Sikh notions of dharma, though different in detail, are fundamentally similar. Thus, for Jains, non-violence (*ahimsa*) is the core of dharma as the immortal and immaterial *jiva* resides in all sentient beings including microscopic forms of life. For Buddhists, dharma (*dhamma* in Pali) as the Buddha's teaching, is more important than the teacher himself. As such it consists of four 'Noble Truths': human existence is marked by suffering, *dukha* (*dukka* in Pali); suffering arises from ignorance and desire; suffering can be ended through freedom or *nirvana* (*nibbana* in Pali); and the way to *nirvana* lies through the 'Eightfold Path' of meditation, morality and wisdom. For the Sikhs, dharma (*dharam* in Punjabi) is the 'moral order' based on 'divine commandment' (*hukam*). For the followers of these religions, dharma is the moral foundation of the good life.

If dharma is the abstract principle of the social order and the consensus about the good life, *karma* is praxis or the individual actor's endeavour to live according to dharma. In Indian religious traditions, human actions have inescapable consequences. While an emphasis on the doctrinal character of karma has been emphasized by Western scholars, within indigenous discourses the stress is on pragmatics, on karma as action. This is particularly true of the Buddhist tradition according to which the individual is the architect of his own destiny, of his suffering or freedom. The moral endeavour of the Jain seeker is to protect himself from the consequences of karma born of passion and to lighten the burden of previous karma. In Hinduism, karma has come to be identified with sacrificial and life-cycle rituals and with religious devotion including pilgrimage. Pilgrimage knows no religious barriers. While Jains are the pilgrims *par excellence*, ever on the move, Buddhists, Hindus, Muslims and Sikhs also consider pilgrimage highly meritorious religious activity.

To the ways of action or karma, rooted in Vedic ritual, and of intelligence (*jnana*), propounded in the Upanishads, Hinduism added a third religious quest, viz. the love of God (*bhakti*). It is sociologically noteworthy that the devotional movement flowered among non-Brahman castes in South India (towards the close of the eighth century) who had been outside the pale of Sanskritic rituals and metaphysics. The rise of devotional religion also expressed a longing for theism after centuries of Jain and Buddhist ascendency. It also represented a moral weariness about, and a social revolt against, the dharmas of caste and gender. Besides, it provided a bond with devotional Islam to give birth to a medieval synthesis.

Islam first came to India with newly converted Arab traders toward the end of the seventh century, followed by the first Muslim invasion in Sind in AD 711. The invasions continued for the next one thousand years. With the conquerors, came the *ulama* (doctors of Muslim law) and the mystic Sufis. While the *ulama* emphasized submission to the orthodox way of life (*sharia*), the Sufi promoted the spiritual quest (*tariqa*) of realizing God through love and the intermediacy of holy men. The *tariqa* is not an alternative to the *sharia*, though in some Sufi brotherhoods it came dangerously close to being so.

Sharia, then, is the basis of social and personal life among the Muslims of India (as it is all over the world). According to it, the unity of God and finality of the Prophet are the foundation of Islam. Besides these two cardinal principles, the denial of which is apostasy, Indian Muslims adhere in principle, though not always in practice, to the obligations of daily and periodical prayers (*namaz*), charity (*zakat*), fasting during the month of Ramazan (*roza*), and pilgrimage to Mecca (*haj*). Shia Muslims, who form about one-tenth of the Muslim population of South Asia, place an additionally especial emphasis on the observance of Muharram. Alongside of the so-called 'pillars' of Islam, Indian Muslims particularly in rural areas, observe many social customs, which are the result of their Hindu environment rather than in accord with orthodoxy.

The coming of Islam to India was a revolutionary event as it broke the ancient bond between India and her indigenous religious traditions. Both religious syncretism and religious conflict followed. The synthesis had high philosophical as well as popular expressions, and flowered as the egalitarian, devotional, Sant tradition, which was called the 'religion of man' by Rabindranath Tagore. In fact, Nanak, the founding Guru of Sikhism, belonged to the Sant tradition and his teaching was characterized, above all, by an emphasis upon 'internal' piety and devotion, and a rejection of caste, ritual, magic and miracles. He wanted to go beyond what he considered the limitations of both Hinduism and Islam.

Apart from the followers of the major religions, there are many religious minorities in India, such as Zoroastrians or Parsis, and three groups (Bene Israeli, Cochin and Baghdadi) of Jews. More noteworthy than these small and vanishing communities are such of the tribal peoples as still follow their own religions (below two million in number), resisting absorption into Hinduism or conversion to Christianity. Found mainly in the eastern, central and southern parts of the country, they were long identified as 'animists' by civil administrators. Ethnographical literature records a wide variety of religious beliefs including, besides animism (as defined by Tylor), totemism (see Ferreira 1965) and pan-theism. At the beginning of the century W.H.R. Rivers had characterized tribal religions as faiths not yet built into Hinduism. Most tribal religions have indeed disappeared thus, but nowadays revitalization movements have emerged among some of the converted peoples, notably in northeast India (such as the Khasi and the Naga). Their prospect is, however, uncertain

Uncertainties, in fact, attend the religious life of all the peoples of India. The slow but steady processes of secularization are in evidence everywhere: religious values (such as 'purity' and 'pollution') are being diluted or displaced by secular values, and religious practices (such as life-cycle rituals) are being abridged or abandoned. People are increasingly placing more faith in 'modern' medicine and putting 'magical' nostrums behind them. At the same time, a heightened religiosity is also in evidence everywhere. New religious cults and movements have arisen within living memory, and, currently, militant religious fundamentalism has found support even among people with a so-called modern education. The readings collected together in this volume will, it is hoped, illumine some of the traditional religious beliefs and practices of the peoples of India and also draw attention to the contemporary scene.

The Readings

As stated at the beginning of this introductory essay, the present book of readings has been assembled around the idea of the 'sacred' in five thematic parts, viz.: sacred knowledge, sacred space, sacred time, sacred persona, and changing orientations to the sacred. This is by no means an exhaustive inventory of themes but they do constitute the core of the sociology of religion. One omission, though, is the institutional or social organizational aspect of religion which is represented here only indirectly in the essays on sacred specialists. Lack of space and the dearth of suitable material are the main reasons for this editorial decision. Each of the five chosen themes and the readings explicating it are introduced at the beginning of each part of the book. I will not therefore elaborate them here. It might however be of interest to describe briefly some of the considerations that have guided the process of selection and the editing of the readings.

(1) The first object has been to cover all the major religious traditions of India. Thus, of the twenty-six readings collected here, fourteen are on aspects of Hinduism including one reading each on a Hinduizing community, viz. the Coorgs, and the so-called 'Untouchables'. There are three readings on Islam in India and two on tribal religions. There should have been more, but a lack of suitable materials has been the constraint, particularly in respect of sociological studies of Islam and Indian Muslims. So far as tribal religions are concerned, there is considerable published material but it tends to be descriptive and lacking in theoretical concerns. There is one reading each on Buddhism (it is about a temple in Sri Lanka), Jainism, Sikhism, and Christianity. Finally, secularism, communalism, religious fundamentalism and religious violence are also considered (one reading on each).

(2) It will be noted that, apart from the excerpts from the books

by Veena Das, Fazlur Rahman, and Satish Saberwal, and the essay by J.P.S. Uberoi, all the work represented here is the product of fieldwork and is rich in observed data. This is true of the work of not only the anthropologists, but also of the students of comparative religion, viz. John Cort, Diana Eck, and Mark Juergensmeyer. Apart from these three scholars and Fazlur Rahman, all the authors except P. M. Currie, who is a civil servant, are anthropologists, although A. R. Sayid would have described himself as a sociologist. Several authors—notably Eck—have drawn upon both fieldwork and textual sources. An excessive emphasis upon the useful distinction between the so-called book-view and field-view, or the textual and contextual, approaches is inimical to a deeper understanding of socio-cultural phenomena in India and should be discouraged.

(3) While theoretically grounded writings have been preferred to those that are simply descriptive, no particular theoretical perspective has been favoured. The effort has rather been to present a plurality of such perspectives. Thus, structural-functionalism (Srinivas), structuralism (Dumont), cultural analysis (Ostor), phenomenology (Cort), and hermeneutics (Rahman), as well as a focus on meaning (Pocock), and the social organization of religious tradition (Vidyarthi), are all represented. It is not however suggested that the work of each author falls exclusively within one particular theoretical framework. This is true of only some of the readings. I will not attempt to place labels on the different excerpts, beyond what has been suggested above, as doing so would be misleading. Also, I should point out that the inclusion of an article, or a chapter from a book, in this volume does not imply that I share the author's theoretical stance or agree with its conclusions. I have been more interested in representing the state of art in the sociology of religion than in promoting particular perspectives.

(4) Most of the readings comprising the volume are of relatively recent composition and represent the current perspectives and styles in the sociological and social anthropological study of religion. Only two of the excerpts are from books published in the 1950s, the earliest of these being M. N. Srinivas's monograph on the Coorgs of South India (1952). As stated earlier in this introductory essay, the publication of this book marked the beginning of a theoretically informed period of the study of religion in India. It may be pointed out that, although Verrier Elwin's book on the Saora, from which an excerpt has been included here, was published in 1955, it predates Srinivas's work in its theoretical orientation and

style. Two other readings by K. S. Mathur and L. P. Vidyarthi have been excerpted from books published in the 1960s. The remaining twenty-two readings represent the work of the 1970s (five) and the 1980s (seventeen). The volume thus bears witness to the current surge of interest in the field.

(5) The making of the sociology of India has been a co-operative endeavour involving scholars from many countries. Of the twenty-six authors of this book, nine hail (or originally hailed) from India, eight from the United States, six from England and one each from France, Pakistan and Sri Lanka. Limitations of space have precluded the inclusion of the work of several outstanding scholars in the field of Indian studies of the sociology and social anthropology of religion. I am particularly sorry for my inability to find room here for the writings of Agehananda Bharati, Arjun Appadurai, Jonathan Parry, Baidyanath Saraswati, and Milton Singer from which I have learned a great deal.

(6) The concern of this volume with the sociology and social anthropology of religion has resulted in the exclusion of all but a couple of readings from the work of indologists and historians of religion. This does not, however, mean that such work is of no relevance to the concerns of the fieldworker. On the contrary, the writings of scholars such as Madeleine Biardeau, Mircea Eliade, J. C. Heesterman, Padmanabha Jaini, Wendy Doniger O'Flaherty, and Romila Thapar are well known and influential among anthropologists engaged in the study of religion in India.

(7) Finally, I have made an effort to select readings of approximately the same length, each requiring not more than an hour to read. Excision and editing have been minimal to retain as much of the ethnography and the flavour of the orignial texts as possible. Wherever footnotes and bibliographical references seemed dispensable, they have been excluded without indicating that this has been done. Abridgements of the text, or the rare editorial clarifications, are, however, clearly shown by using three stops to indicate deletions and square brackets to accommodate additions.

Introductions are limited purpose exercises. I do, however, hope that this introductory essay will help the reader to appreciate the readings collected here. I also trust that they will arouse in him or her an interest in the sociology of religion and capture something of the cultural richness of an ancient land.

I

Sacred Knowledge

The crucial importance of the notion of the 'sacred' in the sociology of religion has been discussed in the Introduction. The first set of five readings in this volume deals with sacred knowledge. Sacred knowledge means, first of all, knowledge that may be considered sacred in itself—by virtue of its source, form and content. In other words, it is essentially and uncontestably sacred for the believers. For theists, there is no better example of sacred knowledge than the 'word of God', brought to mankind by his chosen 'messengers', conveying his 'divine commandments' for human 'obedience', so that social order and moral justice shall prevail. Muslims everywhere and at all times have regarded the Quran, presented in this book in Fazlur Rahman's succinct summary, as knowledge of this very special kind. For the sociologist, sacred knowledge is of interest not for its own sake, as it might be to the theologian, but inasmuch as it illumines our understanding of the everyday life of people, consisting of their activities no less than their beliefs.

Sociological studies of religion, like the theological, deal with themes that various believers consider sacred but they do so in their own manner or style of which there are many. Louis Dumont's structural definition of Aiyanar, a prominent folk deity of South India (in the second essay included here), presents a fine-grain analysis of the homology between the divine and social orders. The supernatural is shown to exist in relation to the social and not as an independent realm. Aiyanar's social significance lies in his being the god, or 'Lord', *par excellence*, for he embodies in himself the fundamental opposition between sacerdotal purity and temporal power, which is also, according to Dumont, the underlying principle of the Hindu caste system.

Whether belonging to a 'great' or a 'little' tradition, gods and goddesses are important elements of human life everywhere in India. David Pocock's account of the dangers that fill day and night, taken from his account of religious belief and practice in a Gujarat village, draws our attention not only to ghosts and malevolent spirits, but also to those fellow human beings who, wittingly or unwittingly, become the medium for the operation of supernatural 'forces', such as the evil eye. When greed and envy bestow on one's gaze the power to damage or destroy, one becomes even like a vengeful god or malevolent spirit, and the community accumulates a well articulated folklore about it and similar matters, identifying sources of misfortunes, warning of reward and retribution, prescribing remedial measures, and interpreting mysteries. This too is sacred knowledge.

The notion of the evil eye already brings into our ken the place of abstract or metaphysical ideas in the domain of the sacred. Among the indigenous religious traditions of India, the most important and best known of such ideas are, as already stated in the Introduction, the concepts of dharma and karma. These have been much written about from both the indological and the ethnographic points of view. The ethnographic account by K. S. Mathur included here is valuable as it testifies to the awareness of such ideas among common people with subtle nuances distinguishing one caste from another. Such awareness may lack in elaboration or refinement of expression but is in basic agreement with what the classical texts say on the subject.

Dharma and karma are two among many fundamental ideas in the religious traditions of India. The concepts of purity and its opposite pollution, have long been recognized as being fundamental to Hindu social organization. In more recent times scholars such as M. N.

Srinivas and Louis Dumont have presented these notions as deserving of close consideration, for without doing so a proper understanding of the caste system—and indeed the Hindu society—is not possible. More recently 'purity' has come to be studied in relation to 'auspiciousness'. The sociological literature on purity and impurity is not only voluminous but also complex. Pauline Kolenda's discussion, with which the first section of the book closes, has the merit of presenting several viewpoints including those of M. N. Srinivas, Louis Dumont, McKim Marriott, and her own.

The Qur'ān

FAZLUR RAHMAN

What is the Qur'ān?

The Qur'ān is divided into Chapters or Sūras, 114 in number and very unequal in length. The early Meccan Sūras are among the shortest; as time goes on, they become longer. The verses in early Sūras are charged with an extraordinarily deep and powerful 'psychological moment'; they have the character of brief but violent volcanic eruptions. A voice is crying from the very depths of life and impinging forcefully on the Prophet's mind in order to make itself explicit at the level of consciousness. This tone gradually gives way, especially in the Medina period, to a more fluent and easy style as the legal content increases for the detailed organization and direction of the nascent community-state. This is certainly not to say either that the voice had been stilled or even that its intensive quality had changed: a Medinese verse declares 'If We had sent down this Qur'ān on a mountain, you would have seen it humbly submit [to the Command] and split asunder out of fear of God' (LIX, 21). But the task itself had changed. From the thud and impulse of purely moral and religious exhortation, the Qur'ān had passed to the construction of an actual social fabric.

For the Qur'ān itself, and consequently for the Muslims, the Qur'ān is the Word of God (Kalām Allāh). Muhammad, too, was unshakeably convinced that he was the recipient of the Message from God, the totally Other (we shall presently try to discover more precisely the sense of that total otherness), so much so that he rejected, on the strength of this consciousness, some of the most fundamental historical claims of the Judaeo-Christian tradition about Abraham and other Prophets. This 'Other' through some

Excerpted from Fazlur Rahman, *Islam*, Second Edition, The University of Chicago Press, Chicago 1979, pp.30–40.

channel 'dictated' the Qur'ān with an absolute authority. The voice from the depths of life spoke distinctly, unmistakably and imperiously. Not only does the word *qur'ān*, meaning 'recitation', clearly indicate this, but the text of the Qur'ān itself states in several places that the Qur'ān is *verbally revealed* and not merely in its 'meaning' and ideas. The Qur'ānic term for 'Revelation' is *wahy* which is fairly close in its meaning to 'inspiration', provided this latter is not supposed to exclude the verbal mode necessarily (by 'Word', of course, we do not mean sound). The Qur'ān says, 'God speaks to no human [i.e. through sound-words] except through *wahy* [i.e. through idea-word inspiration] or from behind the veil, or He may send a messenger [an angel] who speaks through *wahy*. . . . Even thus have We inspired you with a spirit of Our Command. . . .' (XLII, 51–2).

When, however, during the second and third centuries of Islam, acute differences of opinion (controversies partly influenced by Christian doctrines) arose among the Muslims about the nature of Revelation, the emerging Muslim 'orthodoxy', which was at the time in the crucial stage of formulating its precise content, emphasized the *externality* of the Prophet's Revelation in order to safeguard its 'otherness', objectivity and verbal character. The Qur'ān itself certainly maintained the 'otherness', the 'objectivity' and the verbal character of the Revelation, but had equally certainly rejected its externality *vis-à-vis* the Prophet. It declares, 'The Trusted Spirit has brought it down upon your heart that you may be a warner' (XXVI, 194), and again, 'Say: He who is an enemy of Gabriel [let him be], for it is he who has brought it down upon your heart' (II, 97). But orthodoxy (indeed, all medieval thought) lacked the necessary intellectual tools to combine in its formulation of the dogma the otherness and verbal character of the Revelation on the one hand, and its intimate connection with the work and the religious personality of the Prophet on the other, i.e. it lacked the intellectual capacity to say both that the Qur'ān is entirely the Word of God and, in an ordinary sense, also entirely the word of Muhammad. The Qur'ān obviously holds both, for if it insists that it has come to the 'heart' of the Prophet, how can it be external to him? This, of course, does not necessarily imply that the Prophet did not perceive also a projected figure, as tradition has it, but it is remarkable that the Qur'ān itself makes no mention of any figure in this connection: it is only in connection with certain special experiences (commonly connected with the Prophet's Ascension) that the Qur'ān speaks of the Prophet having seen a figure or a spirit, or some other object 'at the farthest end' or 'on the horizon', although here also . . . the experience is described as a spiritual one. But orthodoxy, through the Ḥadith or the 'tradition' from the Prophet, partly suitably interpreted and partly coined, and through the science of theology based largely on the Ḥadith, made the Revelation of the Prophet entirely through the ear and external to him and regarded the angel or the spirit 'that comes to the heart' an entirely external agent. The modern Western picture of the Prophetic Revelation rests largely on this orthodox formulation rather than on the Qur'ān, as does, of course, the belief of the common Muslim.

[This] is not the place to elaborate a theory of the Qur'ānic Revelation in detail. Yet, if we are to deal with facts of Islamic history, the factual statements of the Qur'ān about itself call for some treatment. In the following brief outline an attempt is made to do justice both to historical and Islamic demands. [It should be] explicitly stated . . . that the basic *élan* of the Qur'ān is moral, whence flows its emphasis on monotheism as well as on social justice. The moral law is immutable: it is God's 'Command', Man cannot make or unmake the Moral Law: he must submit himself to it, this submission to it being called *islām* and its implementation in life being called *'ibāda* or 'service to God'. It is because of the Qur'ān's paramount emphasis on the Moral Law that the Qur'ānic God has seemed to many people to be primarily the God of justice. But the Moral Law and spiritual values, in order to be implemented, must be known. Now, in their power of cognitive perception men obviously differ to an indefinite degree. Further, moral and religious perception is also very different from a *purely* intellectual perception, for an intrinsic quality of the former is that along with perception it brings an extraordinary sense of 'gravity' and leaves the subject significantly transformed. Perception, also moral perception, then has degrees. The variation is not only between different individuals, but the inner life of a given individual varies at different times from this point of view. We are not here talking of an intrinsic moral and intellectual development and evolution, where variation is most obvious. But even in a good, mature person whose average intellectual and moral character and calibre are, in a sense, fixed, these variations occur.

Now a Prophet is a person whose average, overall character, the sum total of his actual conduct, is far superior to those of humanity in general. He is a man who is *ab initio* impatient with men and even with most of their ideals, and wishes to re-create history. Muslim orthodoxy, therefore, drew the logically correct conclusion that Prophets must be regarded as immune from serious errors (the doctrine of *'iṣma*). Muḥammad was such a person, in fact the only such person really known to history. That is why his overall behaviour is regarded by the Muslims as Sunna or the 'perfect model'. But, with all this, there were moments when he, as it were, 'transcends himself' and his moral cognitive perception becomes so acute and so keen that his consciousness becomes identical with the moral law itself. 'Thus did we inspire you with a Spirit of Our Command: You did not know what the Book was. But We have made it a light' (XLII, 52). But the Moral Law and religious values are God's Command, and although they are not identical with God entirely, they are part of Him. The Qur'ān is, therefore, purely divine. Further, even with regard to ordinary consciousness, it is a mistaken notion that ideas and feelings float about in it and can be mechanically 'clothed' in words. There exists, indeed, an organic relationship between feelings, ideas and words. In inspiration, even in poetic inspiration, this relationship is so complete that feeling-idea-word is a total complex with a life of its own. When Muḥammad's moral intuitive perception rose to the highest point and became identified with the Moral Law itself (indeed, in these moments his own conduct at points came under Qur'ānic criticism . . . as is evident from the pages of the Qur'ān), the Word was given with the inspiration itself. The Qur'ān is thus pure Divine Word, but, of course, it is equally intimately related to the inmost personality of the Prophet Muḥammad whose relationship to it cannot be mechanically conceived like that of a record. The Divine Word flowed through the Prophet's heart.

But if Muḥammad, in his Qur'ānic moments, became one with the Moral Law, he may not be absolutely identified either with God or even with a part of Him. The Qur'ān categorically forbids this, Muḥammad insistently avoided this and all Muslims worthy of the name have condemned as the gravest error associating (*shirk*) a creature with God. The reason is that no man may say, 'I am the Moral Law'. Man's duty is to carefully formulate this Law and to submit to it with all his physical, mental and spiritual faculties. Besides this, Islam knows of no way of assigning any meaning to the sentence, 'So-and-so is Divine'.

The Qur'ānic Teaching

In the foregoing we have repeatedly emphasized that the basic *élan* of the Qur'ān is moral and we have pointed to the ideas of social and economic justice that immediately followed from it in the Qur'ān. This is absolutely true so far as man and his destiny are concerned. As the Qur'ān gradually works out its world-view more fully, the moral order for men comes to assume a central point of divine interest in a full picture of a cosmic order which is not only charged with a high religious sensitivity but exhibits an amazing degree of coherence and consistency. A concept of God, the absolute author of the universe, is developed where the attributes of creativity, order, and mercy are not merely conjoined or added to one another but interpenetrate completely. To Him belong creativity and 'ordering' or 'commanding' (VII, 54). 'My mercy encompasses everything' (VII, 156). Indeed, the 'Merciful' (Raḥmān) is the only adjectival name of God that is very frequently used in the Qur'ān as a substantive name of God besides Allāh. It is of course true, as modern research has revealed, that Raḥmān was used as name for the Deity in South Arabia before Islam, but this fact of historical transportation from the South is obviously irrelevant from our point of view. If we leave out man, for the time being, i.e. his specific spiritual-moral constitution, and consider the rest of the entire created universe, the interpretation of these three ultimate attributes is that God creates everything, and that in the very act of this creation order or 'command' is ingrained in things whereby they cohere and fall into a pattern, and rather than 'go astray' from the ordained path, evolve into a cosmos; that finally, all this is nothing but the sheer mercy of God for, after all, existence is not the absolute desert of anything, and in the place of existence there could just as well be pure, empty nothingness.

Indeed, the most intense impression that the Qur'ān as a whole leaves upn a reader is not of a watchful, frowning and punishing God, as the Christians have generally made it out to be, nor of a chief judge as the Muslim legalists have tended to think, but of a unitary and purposive will creative of order in the universe: the qualities of power or majesty, of watchfulness or justice and of wisdom attributed to God in the Qur'ān with unmistakable emphasis are, in fact, immediate inferences from the creative orderliness of the cosmos. Of all the Qur'ānic terms, perhaps the most basic, comprehensive and revelatory at once of divine nature of the universe is the term *amr* which we have translated above as order, orderliness or command. To everything that is created is *ipso facto* communicated its *amr* which is its own law of being but which is also a law whereby it is integrated into a system. This *amr*, i.e. order or command of God, is ceaseless. The term used to indicate the communication of *amr* to all things, including man, is *wahy*, which we have translated in the previous section as 'inspiration'. With reference to inorganic things it should be translated as 'ingraining'. This is because with reference to man, who constitutes a special case, it is not just *amr* that is sent down from high, but a 'spirit-from-*amr*' (*rūh min al-amr*), as the Qur'ān repeatedly tells us.

With reference to man (and possibly also to the *jinn*, an invisible order of creation, parallel to man but said to be created of a fiery substance, a kind of duplicate of man which is, in general, more prone to evil, and from whom the devil is also said to have sprung), both the nature and the content of *amr* are transformed, because *amr* really becomes here the moral command: it is not that which actually is an order but that which actually is a disorder wherein an order is to be brought about. The actual moral disorder is the result of a deep-seated moral fact to remedy which God and man must collaborate. This fact is that coeval with man is the devil (*shayṭān*) who beguiles him unceasingly.

The Qur'ān portrays the moral dualism in man's character which gives rise to the moral struggle, and the potentialities man and man alone possesses, by two strikingly effective stories. According to one, when God intended to create man as his viceregent, the angels protested to Him saying that man would be prone to evil, 'corrupt the earth and shed blood', while they were utterly obedient to the Divine Will, whereupon God replied, 'I have knowledge of that which you do not know' (II, 30). The other story tells us that when God offered 'The Trust' to the heavens and the Earth, the entire Creation refused to accept it, until man came forward and bore it, adding with a sympathetic rebuke, 'Man is so ignorant and foolhardy!' (XXXIII, 72). There can be hardly a more penetrating and effective characterization of the human situation and man's frail and faltering nature, yet his innate boldness and the will to transcend the actual towards the ideal consititutes his uniqueness and greatness. This fact of the devil creates an entirely new dimension in the case of man. God 'has ingrained in it (i.e. the human soul) a discernment of good and evil' (XCI, 8); but so artful and powerful is the devil's seduction that men normally fail even to decipher properly this eternal inscription of God on the human heart, while some who can decipher it fail to be moved and impelled by it sufficiently strongly. At times of such crisis God finds and selects some human to whom he sends the angel 'the spirit of the Command' that is 'with Him'. The Command that is with Him is so sure, so definite in what it affirms and denies that it is, indeed, the 'Invisible Book' written on a 'Preserved Tablet', the 'Mother of (all) Books' (LVI, 78; LXXXV, 21–2; XIII, 39). Men charged with these fateful messages to humanity are the Prophets. The Qur'ān 'sent' to Muḥammad is the Book that reveals the Command: Muḥammad is the final Prophet and the Qur'ān the last Book that has been so revealed.

With this background, therefore, the Qur'ān emerges as a document that from the first to the last seeks to emphasize all those moral tensions that are necessary for creative human action. Indeed, at bottom the centre of the Qur'ān's interest is man and his betterment. For this it is essential that men operate within the framework of certain tensions which, indeed, have been created by God in him. First and foremost, man may not jump to the suicidal conclusion that he can make and unmake moral law according to his 'heart's desire' from the obvious fact that this law is there *for him*. Hence the absolute supremacy and the majesty of God are more strikingly emphasized by the Qur'ān. On the other hand among all creation, man has been given the most immense potentialities and is endowed with the 'Trust' which entire creation shrank back in fear from accepting. Again, the idea of justice flows directly from that of the supremacy of the Moral Law, an idea equally emphasized by the Qur'ān. But with the same insistence the Qur'ān condemns hopelessness and lack of trust in the mercy of God, which it declares to be a cardinal infidelity. The same is true of the whole range of moral tensions, including human power and weakness, knowledge and ignorance, sufferance and retaliation, etc. While the potentialities of man are immense, equally immense, therefore, are the penalties which man must face as a result of his failure.

In pursuance of this picture, belief in one God stands at the apex of the Muslim system of belief derived from the Qur'ān. From this belief is held to follow belief in angels (spirits of the Command) as transmitters of Divine message to man, in the Prophets, the human repositories of the Divine revelation (the last in the series being Muḥammad), in the genuineness of the message of the Prophets, the 'Book', and in the Day of Reckoning.

The Qur'ān emphasizes prayer because 'it prevents from evil' and helps man to conquer difficulties, ésspecially when combined with 'patience'. The *five* daily prayers are not all mentioned in the Qur'ān, but must be taken to represent the later usage of the Prophet himself, since it would be historically impossible to support the view that the Muslims themselves added two new prayers to the three mentioned in the Qur'ān. In the Qur'ān itself the two morning and the evening prayers are mentioned, and later on at Medina the 'middle' prayer at noon was added. But it appears that during the later part of the Prophet's life the prayer 'from the declension of the sun unto the thick darkness of the night' (XVII, 78) was split into two and similarly the noon prayer and thus the number five was reached.

The fact, however, that the prayers were fundamentally three is evidenced by the fact that the Prophet is reported to have combined these four prayers into two, even without there being any reason. It was in the post-Prophetic period that the number of prayers was inexorably fixed without any alternative at five, and the fact of the fundamental three prayers was submerged under the rising tide of the Hadīth which was put into circulation to support the idea that prayers were five.

One month's fast, considerably strenuous total abstention from eating and drinking from dawn till sunset, is prescribed by the Qur'ān (II, 183 ff.). Those who may be sick (or experiencing difficulties) on a journey may postpone the fast until a more favourable time. The Qur'ān is believed to have been first revealed in the month of Ramaḍān.

So long as the small Muslim Community remained in Mecca, almsgiving, even though very recurrently emphasized, remained a voluntary donation towards the welfare of the poorer section of the Community. In Medina, however, the *zakāt*, or welfare tax, was duly ordained for the welfare of the Community and tax-collectors were appointed. So strong is the emphasis of the Qur'ān on this point that even prayer is seldom mentioned without being accompanied by *zakāt*. The ban on usury, the moral condemnation of which also started in Mecca, came in a series of pronouncements—one threatening war from god and His Prophet against those who practised usury—on the ground that it rendered the debt 'severalfold' of the original capital and was opposed to fair commerce (*bay'*).

Pilgrimage to Mecca . . . was made obligatory for every Muslim once in a lifetime for 'Those who can afford it', i.e. who can not only pay their way to Mecca and back but can also provide for their families during their absence'. The institution of pilgrimage has been a very potent vehicle of furthering Islamic brotherhood and a pan-Islamic sentiment among Muslims of diverse races and cultures.

The Qur'ān calls upon believers to undertake *jihād*, which is to surrender 'your properties and yourselves in the path of Allāh'; the purpose of which in turn is to 'establish prayer, give *zakāt*, command good and forbid evil'—i.e. to establish the Islamic socio-moral order. So long as the Muslims were a small, persecuted minority in Mecca, *jihād* as a positive organized thrust of the Islamic movement was unthinkable. In Medina, however, the situation changed and henceforth there is hardly anything, with the possible exception of prayer and *zakāt*, that receives greater emphasis than *jihād*. Among the later Muslim legal schools, however, it is only the fanatic Khārijites who have declared *jihād* to be one of the 'pillars of the Faith'. Other schools have played it down for the obvious reason that the expansion of Islam had already occurred much too swiftly in proportion to the internal consolidation of the Community in the Faith. Every virile and expansive ideology has, at a stage, to ask itself the question as to what are its terms of co-existence, if any, with other systems, and how far it may employ methods of direct expansion. In our own age, Communism, in its Russian and Chinese versions, is faced with the same problems and choices. The most unacceptable on historical grounds, however, is the stand of those modern Muslim apologists who have tried to explain the *jihād* of the early Community in purely defensive terms.

The Qur'ānic Legislation

The Qur'ān is primarily a book of religious and moral principles and exhortations, and is not a legal document. But it does embody some important legal enunciations issued during the community-state building process at Medina. Some of the economic enactments we have noted in the previous section. The ban on consumption of alcohol affords an interesting example of the Qur'ānic method of legislation and throws light on the attitude of the Qur'ān to the nature and function of legislation itself. The use of alcohol was apparently unreservedly permitted in the early years. Then offering prayers while under the influence of alcohol was prohibited. Later it is said, 'They ask you about alcohol and gambling. Say: in these there is great harm and also profits for people but their harm far outweighs their profits' (II, 219). Finally a total ban was proclaimed (V, 90–1) on the ground that both alcohol and gambling 'are works of the devil. . . . The devil wants to sow enmity and rancour among you'. This shows the slow, *experimental* legal tackling of problems *as they arise*.

But the most important legal enactments and general reform pronouncements of the Qur'ān have been on the subjects of woman and slavery. The Qur'ān immensely improved the status of the woman in serveral directions but the most basic is the fact that the woman was given a fully-pledged personality. The spouses are declared to be each other's 'garments': the woman has been granted the same rights over man as man has over his wife, except that man, being the earning partner, is a degree higher. Unlimited polygamy was strictly regulated and the number of wives was limited to four, with the rider that if a husband feared that he could not do justice among several wives, he must marry only one wife. To all this was added a general principle that 'you shall never be able to do justice among wives no matter how desirous you are (to do so)' (IV, 3, 128). The overall logical consequence of these pronouncements is a banning of polygamy under normal circumstances. Yet as an already existing institution polygamy was accepted on a legal plane, with the obvious guiding lines that when gradually social circumstances became more favourable, monogamy might be introduced. This is because no reformer who means to be effective can neglect the real situation and simply issue visionary statements. But the later Muslims did not watch the guiding lines of the Qur'ān and, in fact, thwarted its intentions.

The case of the Qur'ānic treatment of the institution of slavery runs parallel to that of the family. As an immediate solution, the Qur'ān accepts the institution of slavery on the legal plane. No alternative was possible since slavery was ingrained in the structure of society, and its overnight wholesale liquidation would have created problems which it would have been absolutely impossible to solve, and only a dreamer could have issued such a visionary statement. But at the same time every legal and moral effort was made to free the slaves and to create a *milieu* where slavery ought to disappear. 'Liberating the neck' (*fakk raqaba*) is not only praised as a virtue but is declared, along with feeding the poor and orphans, to be that 'uphill path' which is absolutely essential for man to tread (XC, 10–16). Indeed, the Qur'ān had categorically told the Muslims that if a slave wants to purchase his or her freedom by paying off in instalments a sum that may be decided upon according to the situation of the slave, then the owner of the slave must allow such a contract for freedom and may not reject it: 'And those of your slaves who wish to enter into freedom-purchasing contracts, accept their proposals if you think they are any good and give to them of the wealth that God has given you. And do not compel your slave-girls to resort to a foul life when they want to be chaste, seeking thereby petty gains of life; but if they act under sheer compulsion, God is forgiving and merciful' (XXIV, 33). Here again we are confronted by a situation where the clear logic of the Qur'ānic attitude was not worked out in actual history by Muslims. The words of the Qur'ān 'if you think they are any good' when properly understood, only mean that if a slave cannot show any earning capacity, then he cannot be expected to stand on his own feet even if freed and therefore it may be better for him to enjoy at least the protection of his master.

These examples, therefore, make it abundantly clear that whereas the spirit of the Qur'ānic legislation exhibits an obvious direction towards the progressive embodiment of the fundamental human values of freedom and responsibility in fresh legislation, nevertheless the actual legislation of the Qur'ān had partly to accept the then existing society as a term of reference. This clearly means that the actual legislation of the Qur'ān cannot have been meant to be literally eternal by the Qur'ān itself. This fact has no reference to the doctrine of the eternity of the Qur'ān or to the allied doctrine of the verbal revelation of the Qur'ān. Very soon, however, the Muslim lawyers and dogmaticians began to confuse the issue and the strictly legal injunctions of the Qur'ān were thought to apply to any society, no matter what its conditions, what its structure and what its inner dynamics. One clear proof that, as time passed, Muslim legists became more and more literalists is reflected in the fact that sometime during the 8th century the Muslim legal doctrine began to draw a very sharp distinction between the clear wording (*naṣṣ*), the text and what was deducible therefrom. There is a good deal of evidence to believe that in the very early period the Muslims interpreted the Qur'ān pretty freely. But after a period of juristic development during the late 7th and throughout the 8th century (the prominent features of which . . . were the rise of the Tradition and the development of technical, analogical reasoning), the lawyers neatly tied themselves and the Community down to the 'text' of the Holy Book until the content of Muslim law and theology became buried under the weight of literalism

Throughout the centuries, Muslims have not only written innumerable commentaries on the Qur'ān from different points of view and with different, indeed, conflicting tendencies, but have evolved a science of Qur'ānic exegesis (*'ilm al-tafsīr*), with its auxiliary branches of learning, including Arabic grammar, lexicography, the Prophetic tradition, the circumstantial background of the verses of the Qur'ān, etc. Indeed, it is claimed by Muslim scholars with a good deal of justice that all the sciences in Islam which are not absolutely secular owe their origin to the Qur'ān. The Qur'ān has also exerted an incalculable influence on the growth of Arabic literature and literary style, and continues up to this day. The doctrine of the 'inimitability' (*i'jāz*) of the Qur'ān, not only in content but even in literary form, is common to almost all Muslim schools, and has attained a cardinal status and found expression in various treatises specially devoted to this topic. Muslim orthodoxy had strenuously resisted any attempt to produce a translation of the Book in any language without the Arabic text. This has contributed not a little to the unity of Muslims who, throughout the world, recite the Qur'ān in their prayers five times a day in Arabic. Only recently in Kemalist Turkey the Qur'ān was translated and produced in Turkish without the original Arabic, although the Arabic text continued to be used in prayers. But even in Turkey, there has been a return to the Arabic text even for ordinary reading. For the purpose of understanding the text, accompanying translations in local languages are allowed.

A Folk Deity of Tamil Nad: Aiyanar, the Lord

LOUIS DUMONT

For the European observer, the God Aiyanar[1] presents a problem. His ill-defined personality seems to contradict the prominent position he enjoys in Tamil villages. It is not that nothing is known of him, but there seems to be so little consistency among his characteristics that his nature cannot be grasped. In order to solve this problem and, without making arbitrary assumptions, to define the incoherent picture which emerges from the literature, I propose in this paper to study the god less in himself than in the relation he maintains in the village pantheon. I shall draw upon data collected at first hand in some localities of Madura District (Kokkulam, in Tirumangalam Taluk) and Ramnad District (Kamuthi, Mudukkulattur Taluk). Although the method is generally applicable, and the basic relations involved prevail very widely, the conclusions do not bear automatically for other areas. The neighbouring Tinnevelly District would probably require some adaptation. As to the deities of Kerala or Mysore who are sometimes considered as homologous to Aiyanar, they are left out altogether.

The Problem

Three main authors have studied the god in detail at first hand or discussed him at length. The description of Ziegenbalg, a Danish

Excerpted from Louis Dumont, 'A Structural Definition of a Folk Deity of Tamil Nad: Aiyanar, the Lord', in *Religion, Politics and History in India*, École Pratique des Hautes Études, Mouton, Paris & The Hague, 1970, pp. 20–32.

[1] It is the main name in the area. In written Tamil *aiyaNār*, locally often *aiyēN*, *aiyeNār*, even *aiya*(*r*); *sāstā* (not *sāttaN*) is the main name in Tinnevelly, and sometimes in Ramnad.

missionary in Tranquebar (Tanjore District) belongs to the first half of the eighteenth century. It was used later by Oppert, Professor of Sanskrit at Madras, who completed it with Sanskrit mantras, but added arbitrary speculations of his own. Finally, Bishop Whitehead, in a little book containing some excellent descriptions of village cults, discussed the god from a theoretical point of view in connection with the districts of Tanjore and Trichinopoly. A brief summary of these three authors will reveal the problem (see Zeigenbalg 1869: 133–5; Oppert 1893; 450, 454, 504–10; Whitehead 1921).

We are told that the god has his temple in almost all the villages (which is true), and that he is their principal and sole male divinity (which seems less true, but allowance has perhaps to be made for regional differences). But who is this universally found god, and whence comes his pre-eminence? To these questions our authors give two different answers. Oppert is quite arbitrary: for him the god is autochthonous or Dravidian, an eater of blood offerings, chief among the demons, a masculine counterpart of the Mother Goddess as represented by the village goddesses. Whitehead takes an opposite view: for him, Aiyanar is a Brahmanic god, or a strongly Brahmanized one, to whom such sacrifices are not offered and who is opposed in this matter to the village goddesses, whom alone he considers to be Dravidian. Thus the cult of Aiyanar in the Tamil country would be an index of greater Brahmanization, as compared to the Telugu country.[2] Such divergent opinions may be due in part to insufficient observation or to local variations, which are possible, as we shall see. But they result first of all from hasty interpretations rooted in the idea, which has done so much harm, that Indian culture is merely a juxtaposition of Aryan and so-called Dravidian or other elements. In order to avoid this pitfall, we shall attempt to get a more reliable view of the data by insisting upon the god's double relation, on the one hand with the 'demons' and with the goddesses on the other.

If Aiyanar's essence is doubtful, what in fact are his main characteristics? In oral tradition, he was born from Shiva who was seduced by the feminine form Vishnu had assumed in order to free him from a threatening Asura. Oppert gives a good version of the episode though the commentary is of poorer quality: there is no justification for speaking of 'incest' (in popular tradition and elsewhere, Vishnu

[2] Whitehead, *op. cit.*, pp. 17–18, 33, 89. This view is nearer to the truth. The assumption that the goddesses have nothing to do with Brahmanism, and that their nature is different from that of Aiyanar is arbitrary.

and Shiva are brothers-in-law), nor for supposing that the Brahmans invented this 'disgusting' story in order to degrade Aiyanar. We shall find that it has quite another function.

Aiyanar may be represented either as a warrior, on foot or riding a white elephant or a horse, or as seated between his two wives, carrying a sceptre or whip and wearing a meditation band.[3] The Seven Mothers (or Seven Virgins) are sometimes mentioned as present in his temple. Outside are found horses usually in terracotta. These are offered to the god and his suite for his mainly nocturnal rounds. The escort is composed either of the god's generals or vassals, or of demons. The troop riding in mid-air in the night recalls the well-known theme of the Wild Hunt, but here it is a matter of watching the village land, of which Aiyanar is first of all the guardian. The god also has occasionally to do with the rain, and in any case his temple is usually situated on the bank of the reservoir in which rainwater is gathered for irrigation purposes. There may be a daily cult, and there is a yearly festival, when blood sacrifice is offered, either to the god himself or to his attendants.

Most of the authors take Aiyanar to be 'the king of the demons'. One *District Gazetteer* gives a much better formula of Aiyanar's relation with the demons: 'He is their master although he is not one of them'.[4]

Aiyanar and the Village Goddess

If the association of Aiyanar and the village goddess does not appear in the preceding summary, this is because it appears only in their local functions: the goddess is also concerned with the protection or prosperity of the village. To make this clear, we should first of all remove the misunderstandings arising from the use of such terms as 'village god', 'mother goddess' or 'mother goddess of the village'. The term 'village god' is ambiguous because it can have the broader meaning of the gods who have their temples in the village (which has a social implication, opposing as it does the popular gods to the official gods of the Brahmanic temples), or more strictly it can signify the gods of the local cummunity. There is a difference between the two, for in the village, gods and temples are found which interest

[3] A cloth girdle circling round the back and supporting the knees of a seated person, Skrt. *yogapaṭṭa* (Ziegenbalg: *vāgupaṭṭai*; Jouveau-Dubreuil: 'bāhupaddai').

[4] See Pate 1917. The description of religion is excellent, but, as we said at the beginning, this district is slightly different from ours.

only a part of the inhabitants. There are lineage temples in a village with one and the same caste, and there are temples belonging to sundry castes in a multicaste village.[5] The question deciding the issue is: 'Who participates in the collection which covers the expenses of the festival?' If each household in the village takes part, strangers excluded, then and only then are we dealing with a village cult in the strict sociological sense. In general the female deities which our authors call 'village goddesses' are of this nature: there is one, or several of them, in each village, in whose cult the whole community collaborates and from whom it derives benefit. But if, going a step further, we are told to regard these goddesses as identical with the village like eponymous goddesses, or if we are invited to qualify them, in what appears to be an analogous manner, as 'mother goddesses', then we should be on our guard. In reading Whitehead's work, which for the greater part is devoted to them, we might get the impression that each of these goddesses is necessarily peculiar to one village. On the contrary, in each region they are relatively few in number, each one generally honoured in several places and some of them from one end of the country to the other.[6] Moreover their essential function is the protection of the village against epidemics, and one of the most widely spread is *māriyammaN* or *māriyammei*, the smallpox goddess. A linguistic fact has played a part in the identification of these goddesses as 'mothers'. Their name is generally a compound, the second part of which, as in the preceding example, is very like *ammā(ṭ)* which in kinship terminology designates, among others, the mother. But *ammā(ṭ)* in its widest sense refers also, in the language of politeness, to all women and girls. For instance, this is the case with divinized virgins (*kaNNi*). Rather than translate *māriyammaN* as 'Death-Mother',[7] we shall call her Smallpox Lady. While it is true that the village places itself under the protection of such a Lady, it does not follow that it honours her as a (or its) Mother.[8]

[5] There are also gods reserved for the private devotion of individuals, like certain images of Pilleiyar (Ganesha).

[6] They can therefore not be called 'local', except in the extremely limited sense that their geographical spread is less than that of the great brahmanical deities. Whitehead has examples of borrowing from one locality to another (p. 23). *Contra*, see Elmore 1925, *passim*.

[7] This is an etymological rendering from Sanskrit *māri*, death. But the meaning is neither present nor implied for Tamil villagers, for whom *māri* means only smallpox.

[8] This is said only about the fundamental nature of the goddess. It does not mean that all maternal shades of meaning are absent. For more details see my *A South Indian Subcaste*, 1986, pp. 431 ff. see p.33

It is advisable to interpret Aiyanar in the same manner. Certainly *aiyaN*, *aiya*(*r*) (Sanskrit *ārya*) is 'father', but it is also an equivalent of 'Sir' and, as we shall see, is a name for the Brahmans. If *aiyaNār* is opposed to *ammaN* (locally also *aiyēN-ammaN*) it is as the Lord or Master to the Lady and not exactly as the father to the mother (locally *aiya-amma*).[9] This is confirmed by observation: there is no question here of these deities being coupled together as husband and wife, as is so frequently the case. Their temples are distinct and one deity is not represented in the other's temple: Aiyanar's wives are altogether different. If the two deities are complementary in sex and name, this is in connection with their relation to the village, with the role they both play in its prosperity. Even their priests are different. While the goddess' priest is usually a *paṇḍāram* (garland-maker), a vegetarian, a sort of imitation of a Brahman, the priest of Aiyanar is generally the potter who makes images and horses, a meat-eater and the authentic priest of meat-eaters (Madura and Ramnad Districts).

A concrete example will show how Aiyanar and the Goddess are actually brought together in ritual. In Kokkulam and in the neighbouring localities the festival of *vaḍakku vāsal selli ammaN*, the Lady of the North Gate, is celebrated in the month of *puraṭṭāsi* (September-October) in rough synchronism with the great Hindu festival of the Goddess (*navarāttri*, the Nine 'Nights'). The ceremonies are spread over several days and the cult of Aiyanar takes place on the day after that of the Lady. The one removes the disease (that is the reason for the orientation of her temple towards the north, and her name), the other with his temple on the bank of the tank seems to be concerned with the prosperity of the fields. It is difficult in these localities to get at a more precise value or function; the date of the cult of Aiyanar is probably different in those places where he acts explicitly as rain-maker.

Two facts that I think are new allow us to insist upon Aiyanar in his male aspect, identical in that with Shiva, as is indicated in the myth of his birth. Like his father he is identified with the *linga* on one side and with the bull on the other.

At Kokkulam I collected a version of the Aiyanar birth story which on the whole is close to that reported by Oppert. The story is very

[9] The terms for goddess and for mother or lady are so close to each other that the dictionaries are likely to give a wrong impression of identity. I believe that, within a given group at a given time, the two can always be distinguished by different endings. The same holds true on the male side.

widespread. In this account, Shiva's semen is, with the co-operation of the Black God, deposited on the bank of the reservoir to protect it. There, it assumes the form of the *linga*. If the latter has disappeared in our time, this is said to be because the cult it requires is too complicated. But it still exists and one could find it if one were to dig in the earth beneath the present anthropomorphic image of the god. This idea is also found elsewhere.

The bull is well known as Shiva's vehicle, honoured as Nandi in Shivaite temples. The villagers identify the two; thus in Kokkulam (in the settlement called Tengalapatti) a bull, attached to a lineage temple and exclusively used for stud services, lives practically at liberty and on occasion charges the carts on the road; the villagers referring to these bursts of temper smilingly call their author *sivaN*. One kind of bull race, witnessed in a neighbouring village, is known from the literature. It is rather a profane and sportive occasion. . . . But apart from this *jalli-kaṭṭu*, I found, under the name *erudu kaṭṭu* (tying the bull), a different sort of race. In Kokkulam as well as in Kamuthi, where I observed one, the race is dedicated to Aiyanar and takes place near his temple the day after the erection of the terracotta horses. A huge rope made by the Untouchables is tied at one end round the bull's neck, while the other end is allowed to trail far behind him so that it hampers his movements. The young men try to master the bull by seizing the rope. In this manner, one after the other and in hierarchical order, the bulls of the local notables are brought into the game. At the end, the rope is left looped up in a tree near the temple. In both associations, with the *linga* and with the bull, Aiyanar appears as a double of Shiva. However, we can note one difference: just as the *linga* is said to be buried, the sexual aspect of Aiyanar is latent and applied rather than affirmed and celebrated, just as the couple the god forms with the goddess exists only in relation to the village.

That a couple should appear in this way, on a functional level, says much in favour of the reality and depth of the notion. Still, when confronted with explicit couples, like Shiva and his consort, in Hinduism, some writers have been at pains to 'explain' them as a sort of accidental reunion of two deities of opposite sex. If, on the contrary, one admits that the couple is itself a religious entity, then one can take an overall view of some tribal religions and well-known Hindu figures, as well as of our Tamil village deities. Among the Maria Gonds of Bastar the male god of the clan is associated in each village with a different goddess, the mother of the village, so that there is a couple of gods in each village, the male element being the same in all villages of the same clan (see Grigson 1938: 196–7). In orthodox Hinduism the same Shiva has different wives in different towns, as Kamakshi in Conjeeveram, Minakshi in Madura. (It is true that the god changes his name in each place, but he is everywhere the same while his wife on the other hand is conceived of each time as a distinct incarnation of Parvati.) Half-way between these two cases, in our Tamil village, we can observe the local functions divided between a god and a goddess. Aiyanar is the same everywhere (although he can always be distinguished by a different name). The goddess is neither different in each village, nor is she everywhere the same. She is not the goddess of the village except in a functional sense. Beneath the differences in personalities and functions, the couple is present from one end of the chain to the other, and the diversity in the forms which the couple assumes only bears witness to the reality of the category, whether overt or implied.

Aiyanar Associated with the 'Black God'

This second association is still more important than the first. In order to understand it, we shall temporarily leave Aiyanar and sum up the structure of the lineage pantheons. The descriptions of the lineage temples belonging to the Pramalai Kallar in Kokkulam will be our source. These people, or rather some specialists among them, have more definite ideas on the subject than others, and one can verify the principles they express in many less theologically minded groups. It is in lineage temples, where the priests are Kallar, that the pantheon is most numerous and best articulated. (For details, see Dumont 1986: 395 ff.). These temples comprise at least, twenty-one gods, all present at the time of the annual cult at least, whether or not they are otherwise identifiable by representations or even plain stones. These gods are classed into two categories: the pure (*suttam*) gods who do not eat meat, and the meat-eating gods who are impure (*asuttam*) for this reason. This opposition bears some relation to a distinction often made in the literature between gods of Brahmanic origin and inspiration, borrowed from the large official temples, and local and popular gods, often called 'demons' by the authors. But such formulas are not rigorous; we must stick to the only clear distinction applied by the worshippers themselves, which bears on diet. It has a social implication which will be emphasized later.

The opposition between vegetarian and meat-eating gods is very strongly marked; it is expressed in a dichotomy bearing on space, on the priesthood and on the cult implements. The temple is turned to the east and the chapel sheltering the principal god is situated almost on the east-west axis; the vegetarian gods are to the north (Brahmanism, as they say, came from the north), and the meat-eating gods to the south. Next, in view of the two different kinds of food to be served, it is best to have two kitchens, two priests (a 'great' priest and a 'little' priest), otherwise serious complications are to be expected, and also two sets of implements as well as two boxes to keep them in and shelter the divine in its latent form in the interval between two festivals. The opposition is marked also in legends such as that in which with extreme violence the main local god opposes the attempt of a Brahmanic trinity to establish itself in his neighbourhood, but is finally forced to give in. More dramatic perhaps is the legend which depicts the confusion of a man in whom are incarnate at the same time a vegetarian and a meat-eating god—both, however, present in an entirely regular and even necessary manner—until an arbitrator ascribes to them respectively the right and the left sides of the man's body. We might take this as a symbol of the necessity of the co-existence of the two opposing principles: the body of the possessed man is divided like the temple itself, the divine is a whole constituted precisely by this fundamental opposition.

This structure of the divine needs to be considered in relation to the social order. It is clear that the relation between the vegetarian and the meat-eating deities is of the same order as that between vegetarian and meat-eating men. The criterion of diet is one of the main criteria in the hierarchical ordering of castes in South India. The two kinds of gods of which the temple is composed are in the relation of superior caste (the Brahman caste for example) to inferior caste (that of the meat-eating devotees in our case). Moreover, the distinction is a particular form of the opposition of purity and impurity, the principle of the caste system. Finally, the temple reflects the society in a simplified form, it symbolizes it. This is probably the reason for what might at first sight appear a strange syncretism, but is in fact much more.

Hence, important consequences follow. Not only are pure and impure gods as closely interdependent as pure and impure castes, but we can also say something about the degree and nature of the belief bearing on the two kinds of gods and on the rites addressed to them. The people are meat-eaters, and in their lineage temples, where they themselves officiate, the essential rite is blood-sacrifice. There is no doubt that they identify themselves only with the impure gods who occupy a position in the pantheon homologous to their position in society. These, it would seem, are *their* gods, and they believe in them more, and more immediately. Why therefore are they not content with them, and why in addition do they install pure gods that, by their own confession, they serve badly and frequently annoy? Gods of whom it cannot be said that they feel them as intrinsically more powerful? One might speak here of imitation or, following Hocart, of 'snobbery'. It is true that among those groups the cult of the pure gods shows the mark of pharisaism, that belief in them is relatively conventional and that in the last analysis the pure god is not present in the temple by virtue of his intrinsic superiority, but as *the god of the superior castes*. It would appear as if the caste joins to its own gods those of the castes that dominate it. Here we have to substitute a psychology of imitation and addition for a psychology of conversion.

This again is not enough, for the inferior meat-eating gods themselves only exist at this stage by the sanction or guarantee of the superior gods. Only the presence of the latter maintains the reality of the former. The same legend which praises the omnipotence of a Black God and widens its domain beyond all measure, also recognizes that he was originally the servant of a great Brahmanic god. As regards the nature of this Black God, the village theologian engages in a complicated but revealing discussion. On the one hand, the Black God is identical with one of those evil demons, *pēy*, who have only an ephemeral existence and are not the object of any cult; on the other, he rules by virtue of a sort of proxy of the great (vegetarian) gods, and one is even told that he takes on his black, demonic appearance only in order to deceive the demons whom he fights. (This is clearly the position of the castes of intermediary status: they have no being, they do not exist for themselves but are opposed in turn to the Brahmans like non-being to being and to the Untouchables as being to non-being, solidary in the first place with all those who are below them and in the second with all who are above.) One can see that the illogicality of a dichotomy in the divine does not entirely escape the indigenous mind, which sees it as a contradiction between affectivity (identification with the Black God) and speculation (the pure god is supreme). This contradiction reflects the social position of the meat-eater: he must not only recognize the superiority of the vegetarian but even admit that he derives his own reality from him.

This is important from a theoretical point of view: we can say that in a very particular way a characteristic does not exist here except in its relation to its opposite. In the caste society, nothing is true by nature and everything by situation, there are no essences but only relations. To say caste is to say structure. This is the origin of the familiar impossibility of universal judgements in India: as long as one considers particular objects—instead of relations—no consistency, no principle can be found.

We are now able to return to Aiyanar. The opposition described is met with again, under an exemplary form, in the relation of Aiyanar as a pure, vegetarian god, to a meat-eating god locally called the Black God, *ka Ruppu-sāmi* or *kaRuppaN*. In fact, these names can be seen as referring to categories rather than to individual gods; each concrete Aiyanar or Karuppu has his own particular name. This pair constitutes the simplest and most concentrated illustration of the divine as we have defined it. This is clearly expressed in the Karuppu temples, where most often the central shrine is double, one part sheltering Karuppu and the other Aiyanar. In this context, Aiyanar appears as condensing Brahmanism in his person; in him Shivaism and Vishnuism are not distinguished but, on the contrary, blended as they were at his birth. If he is a duplicate of Shiva, it is an enlarged duplicate, for it transcends the distinction of the two great gods of Hinduism. Also, in the story of his birth the interdependence of castes is very pronounced; the two great gods are embarrassed by the semen of one of them, and 'just as important people sometimes have need of a sweeper,' in the same way they call for Karuppan and extricate themselves from the affair with his assistance.

Aiyanar and Karuppan are as master and servant, and while being opposed they participate the one in the other. Thus, at the time of the festival when terracotta horses are offered, at least a pair must be given: one for Aiyanar, to whose nature alone the gift is befitting, as we shall see presently, but another also for Karuppan who accompanies him (this corresponds to the legitimation of the lower gods already mentioned). Conversely, the blood-sacrifice which is properly offered only to Karuppan can, if it is offered in Aiyanar's temple, appear to apply to him also. Here is the contradiction which we promised to solve at the outset. There are in fact two ways of seeing the main god of a temple. He can be regarded either in himself or as embracing all the deities which surround him, vegetarian and meat-eating deities together. In the first case, a curtain is drawn before Aiyanar at the time of blood-sacrifice to isolate him from it:

in the second case, it would seem to the observer, and indeed ordinary villagers themselves might say, that the sacrifice is offered to him. More generally, we can suppose that the pantheon tends to become homogeneous, the superior gods adopting the characteristics of the lower and *vice versa*. Thus, in the village the great gods become incarnate like the others in a possessed dancer. This tendency is held in check only in circumstances where the distinction is felt to be pertinent, as is the case here for the distinction in diet.

Aiyanar, then, commands the inferior gods, not because he is one of them, but precisely because he is different from them—such is hierarchy in the caste society. But at this point again interesting complications arise. If, in the theory of caste, the first rank belongs to the Brahman, we can say that in actual fact the hierarchy is bicephalous, except that the second head, the king, is not recognized when confronted with the first. Aiyar is the commonest name for the Brahman, and Aiyanar as his name indicates is above all a Brahman. He is vegetarian, he sometimes wears the sacred thread and more often the meditation band, and no doubt in the first place it is as such that he rules over the inferior gods. But the royal component is also present. He is, we were told, 'the king of the demons', he holds a sceptre (or perhaps a whip), he has for his mount a white elephant or a horse (this is definitely a royal feature in South India), he is a warrior and his suite, sometimes said to be composed of 'demons'—i.e. in our language inferior gods—is also represented as a body of feudatory horse men (*pāleiyakkārar*, 'poligar'). Also, as we shall see, he has two wives. To sum up, we can say that what characterizes Aiyanar is the union of these two series of features; in him the Brahman and the warrior king are blended. He is the Lord *par excellence*, first by his sacerdotal purity, but also by his temporal power.

Conclusion

The double association of the god, with the goddess on the one hand and with Karuppan on the other, is reflected in the calendar in some places as for instance in Kokkulam. The cult of Aiyanar occurs twice a year. While in the September festival it follows that of the goddess, in May-June, on the contrary, Aiyanar is associated with the Black God, and the festival in its full development comprises, on the first day, the erection of the clay horses mainly in the temple of the Black God, on the second day, the bull race in front of

Aiyanar's temple. (Actually this entails great expense and does not take place each year). This clear expression of Aiyanar's double association is not general, it is due here to the circumstance that the temples in Kokkulam have a dual value, as local temples (September) and as lineage temples, or more precisely as temples common to the seven local lineages (May).

It may well be imagined that the two fundamental oppositions which have helped us to define the nature of the God play in a variety of ways. In fact, one may wonder whether the whole of South Indian society, at least according to the idea which the people themselves have of it, is not constructed on these two principles. In the present case it may be that their combination is also responsible for the fact that Aiyanar has two wives. This cannot be positively demonstrated, but it would be in accordance with a frequent pattern. According to Ziegenbalg, only one of Aiyanar's two consorts[10] bears the Shivaite mark on her brow. The triad would then combine the sexual couple with the lack of sectarian differentiation of the god which has been noted above. But this kind of triad is also found in the case of other gods. It is permissible to see in it a condensed picture of polygamy as consecrated by custom. In this case one of the two wives is normally of her husband's rank, the other of inferior rank, this combination being a royal, rather than a Brahmanic trait. The hypothesis seems verified when we learn that one of the wives has a clear complexion (high caste) and the other a dark complexion, as for Murugan-Subrahmanya between *deyvayāNei* (Skrt. *devasenā*) and *valli*, for Vishnu between Lakshmi and Bhumidevi (in agreement with the royal aspect of Vishnu). More remotely one thinks of Krishna and Rukmini on the one hand, of Krishna and Radha on the other. Only, in the case of Aiyanar, we know nothing of the wives but their names, nothing, in particular, about their complexion.

To sum up, Aiyanar is the Lord: the Lord as complement of the Lady, the Lord as high caste god ruling low caste gods. High caste he is on two counts: as a 'pure' god transcending sectarian limitations, and as a king ruling his subordinates. He concentrates in himself the religion and the state at the level of the village, while at the same time keeping the value of a god attached to a particular place.

[10] The two wives are mostly known as *pūraṇei* and *puḍkalei* (Skrt. *pūrṇā, puṣkalā*), also *madanā* and *varnaṇi*.

The Evil Eye

DAVID F. POCOCK

Momad[1] put on my raincoat and a large 1930s style trilby hat, known as a double-crowned Terai, and, looking to my eyes rather sinister, pranced up the lane to the village of Sundarana in the Kaira District of Gujarat. Ten minutes later he was back, crestfallen and carrying the coat over his arm. 'What happened?' I asked. 'Oh it's Surajben' he said, 'she told me to take it off'. 'But why?' I asked. 'Well', he said, 'people would think I looked too beautiful'. I had scarcely been in the village a month at this time. Why on earth Momad should be thought beautiful in a hat and coat several sizes too large, and badly travel-stained, I could not imagine. 'But why, Momad?' I persisted 'Why shouldn't you look beautiful?' 'People', he said, 'would think that these are fine things'. 'But so what if they do?' 'Well', he replied, 'some people believe I would fall ill—it is *najar*'.

The word *najar*, which in this context I translate as the evil eye, is also in common use with less dramatic meanings such as a 'look', as in 'have a look', or 'sight', as in 'short-sighted'. Before I discuss its malevolent significance any further let me give a more detailed example. This concerns the same Surajben, the wife of Momad's patron in the village, Kishor, and whom Momad, although a Muslim, addressed affectionately as *māsi*—mother's sister.

Some months after the incident of the raincoat Surajben gave birth to her fifth son, Bhailal. Very soon afterwards the baby came out in a rash, which made it fretful and wretched.

Excerpted from David F. Pocock, 'The Evil Eye—Envy and Greed', in *Mind, Body and Wealth: A Study of Belief and Practice in an Indian Village*, Basil Blackwell, Oxford, 1973, pp. 25–40.

[1] The name is a corruption of Mohammad. Momad is one of a small group of Muslims in the village known as Vora. This name is a corruption of Bohora, the name of a large Shia Muslim sect.

Surajben took him to the dispensary in Petlad and followed the doctor's instructions about bathing, powdering and the like. Momad and I went for a walk the evening after she returned from Petlad. 'You remember we were talking about *najar*?' he said. 'Yes, of course'. 'Well, Surajben thinks that Bhailal has been struck by it'. 'Oh really—what's she going to do about it?' I asked. 'She's done it already', said Momad. He told me that Surajben had put some chillies and a scrap of the child's hair into a small brass bowl. On to these she had put a hot coal and inverted the bowl on a flat metal eating dish. Over this she had poured liquid buffalo dung. The bowl could not then be lifted and this had proved to her that the child was suffering from *najar*. Apparently a less elaborate test would have been to wave chillies round the child's head and throw them in the fire. If the gas from the chillies had escaped there would have been no *najar*, and another cause for the sickness would have had to be found. 'So the baby is suffering from *najar*?' I said, 'what does she do now?' 'We shall have to wait and see', said Momad.

Within two days things were a little clearer. Surajben's husband's second cousin, Chiman, had no children. It seems that he had visited Surajben shortly after the child was born and made some comment about the way it could already move its eyes and notice things. Surajben had decided that this was the source of *najar*. You do not accuse people to their faces in such matters and, indeed, it is usually assumed that the guilty party is unaware of the damage done. Surajben therefore embarked on the following course of treatment: she made a point of visiting more frequently with her husband's kinsman and of inviting him to her house as well. As often as possible she would give him the child to hold; he, frankly fond of children, was always happy to hold it. Surajben was very pleased with the results. She had put a black thread round the baby's neck, as most mothers do by way of added precaution, but by giving the child a daily dose, so to speak, of Chiman's *najar*, its power diminished. The baby was allegedly always very ill after each treatment, but progressively less and less so, until finally the rash disappeared entirely.

When I saw Bhailal three years later, he was a very healthy and remarkably well-built little boy. Like all mothers who fear the envy of others, Surajben had deprived him of the formal appearances of care. Apart from the black thread with its little brass amulet he wore nothing, and his bleached brown hair grew to his shoulders. Surajben said that he was five years old, and therefore it was five years since I had visited them. I did not argue; Bhailal certainly looked a healthy five-year-old.

Najar, the evil eye, is the eye of envy, and it is an inevitable feature of a world in which men set store by looks, or health, or goods, or any pleasant thing. Even if, as is likely, one sets no store by one's mere subsistence, the very deprivations of others give grounds for fear. Since there is no one who cannot find someone whose plight is in some way worse than his own, so there is no one who is completely immune to envy and so to *najar*. Let me describe some typical *najar* situations. Doors should always be closed while eating out of doors. For example in the fields, if someone passes, one should offer him food. If food is offered, and can be accepted on caste grounds, some, be it only a little, should be eaten to demonstrate good will. A man in the village once suffered a fever because when he was drinking tea outside his house a stranger, to whom he offered some, had refused it. The fever was only cured after he had given a coconut to the goddess. The stranger in this case was presumed to be deliberately malevolent—*melo manas* (literally, a dirty man). A woman was once feeding her child and looked at it with great affection. Her mother-in-law, fearing for the child, suddenly directed the young woman's attention to the stone flour-mill, which immediately broke in half. Here there is no question of envy, but of permanent evil eye unconsciously exercised. Envy enters only when we realize that it was the mother-in-law who spread the story through the village! A man bought a new hookah of the portable kind and was walking back from the town with it. A passer-by asked him where he had brought it, and it broke at once. A woman had a child and another asked to see it. It died. Whenever you feel that someone is looking at you, immediately pretend to take great interest in some worthless object, and so direct his attention towards that.

Although *najar* can run freely wherever there are human values, it is to a certain extent limited by a kind of realism. My battered hat and stained raincoat together with other marvels such as my typewriter were not dangerous to me, as far as I could understand, any more than a landlord who lived in a village nearby had anything to fear from his silk shirt. *Najar* seems to be apprehended more from those with whom one is, in most other respects, equal, or has reason to expect to be. In a society governed by hierarchical principles in which status is given by birth, some seem to be naturally in a more favoured position than oneself, and one would not regard their superiority as a deprivation. This seems quite reasonable to me. We also do not really envy, that is truly covet, something which is not within our reach. What affect us more closely are the things which seem to just elude our grasp—the things which are only just better than the things we have, and with which, therefore, we can compare them.

The range of *najar* is limited, therefore, by the nature of caste society, which accords a status to each group, and by the weakness of human imagination, which reduces the number of material desires to the scale of existing material goods. But clearly there are other human goods which are neither accorded by caste nor beyond the range of any human being to conceive, such as health, beauty, popularity and the like; to this extent all men are vulnerable to all men.

On the face of it this seems an absurd situation: it means that no one can enjoy the very simplest and common joys of life because of a constant anxiety that he is exciting the envy of someone else. Actually something like this can happen.

I was in another village, in the house of a relatively wealthy man who had been very good to me. I will call him Swāmidās because he was a devoted servant—*das*—of Swāmi Narāyan, the deified founder of a Gujarat sect. We were sitting outside his front door one evening, looking out on the small courtyard into which the door of a poorer kinsman's house also opened. After a pause in our conversation he suddenly voiced his train of thought and said, 'I *would* like to buy that house, but it's difficult.' 'But what on earth do you want it for, Swāmidās?' I asked. 'Well, you know, my children play out here, they play with the children from that house and it makes difficulties.' I remained silent. 'You see', said Swāmidās, 'sometimes I give my boys something nice—like an apple from Bombay, and the other children see it and of course they would like an apple too.'

Swāmidās was dreaming out aloud because there was no real likelihood that his kinsmen would sell their ancestral home. I do not think that, even if it had been possible, he would have forbidden his children to play with their cousins. He was far too generous a man to make his children secretive about the little luxuries he gave them. He was also far too sensible to allow himself to be forced into dispensing apples from Bombay to all the children in the neighbourhood. I never heard Swāmidās make a similar remark, and certainly he regarded beliefs about *najar* as ignorant superstitions. Nevertheless, he was expressing a real anxiety about his own affluence which was not large enough to cancel out the poverty of his children's playmates.

The sequel to the story about Surajben and her baby throws more light on the situation. Let me say something about her first. She herself was a tall, very fair woman, in her forties, but prematurely aged. She was, I think, rather conscious of her position as the wife of one of the most influential men in the village and a little over-concerned to stress her sensitivity in caste matters. I remember that she once told me how she had eaten at a railway station in a room where a Vaghari was present. The sight so upset her, she insisted, that she had been sick all the way home. The Vaghari are very low-caste herdsmen in Gujarat and the word has connotations of extreme filthiness. Surajben had five children, all boys. Her husband, Kishor, was a partner and manager of a small irrigation works owned by Swāmidās and some others who lived in a nearby village. The family had a financial security unknown to the bulk of the villagers. They ate rice every day and used wheat where the majority used millet. In short this was a family blessed in every way.

I had often spoken with Surajben about the beliefs and practices in which women were said to be the peculiar authorities. Amongst other things we had spoken of *najar* and she had explained a great deal to me. *Najar* was usually unconsciously exercised and sprang from desire. If one was content and did not feel desire one's eyes could not hurt others. But there were some who had a kind of permanent core of envy in them amounting to hatred, and such people could be recognized from their eyes which were unusually big and burning. If I observed Choto, for example, I would see what she meant. Choto had walked into the house one day when she was frying *bhajiān*, fritters; he had only glanced at the pan, but the whole batch was spoiled.

Choto was, in fact, a distant relative of her husband. They were both members of the same descent group and they were linked at the seventh inclusive generation. There is a saying in Gujarat to the effect that a distant cousin is a near relative when he is rich, but a poor brother is soon forgotten. The section of the lineage to which Choto belonged was extremely poor. Their area of the village was a crowded, dirty shanty town: Choto lived with his grandfather, his still unmarried sister, his mother, the uncle whom she had married after his father's death and the baby born of this marriage—all in a 'house' of two rooms, both of which would have fitted twice into Surajben's kitchen/dining-room.[2]

Choto's father and uncle had divided the property in the lifetime of the former; Choto now had a fragment of unirrigated land on which he grew chillies and a few other spices. His uncle/stepfather maintained the mother and baby himself on his own share—Choto could scarcely support his grandfather, his sister and himself from his land; he relied mainly upon his employment at the irrigation works. He was paid in cash and also in kind in that he had an occasional meal at Surajben's.

Here by any human understanding was a delicate situation. However, whereas Momad accepted patronage and, except in a few asides, showed no resentment, Choto burned. Momad was a Muslim and was treated as a member of a lower, but not polluting, caste. He was used to eating Surajben's food aside from the rest of the family, and to washing up his own utensils afterwards. Choto was of the same caste as Surajben, a Patidar, and as such could eat with the family. As a kinsman he had a right to be regarded as an equal. But he was to all intents and purposes a house servant as well as an employee of the husband.

Choto's father had been a rake and had died young, it was said, from drinking illicit liquor. Choto enjoyed something of his father's reputation. At night he told outrageous stories of his love affairs to the group of us who slept down by the irrigation works. These stories, like his ghost stories, were so enjoyably rich in exaggerated detail that no one ever challenged their veracity. He did have impressive eyes, large and glowing under thick eyebrows; he was not unaware of what Surajben said of their power.

On my second visit I got to know Choto quite well. Momad had gone to teach in a primary school some miles away. My Gujarati had much improved and Choto spoke no English. He was in touch with a side of village life very different from that represented by Surajben and her immediate family, and I was made fully aware of their disapproval of this new friendship. With Choto I enjoyed the

[2] The re-marriage of the widow by a younger brother of the deceased is an economical custom much condemned by people of good family and pretension. Choto's family was looked down upon by those who had relinquished this custom within living memory. Choto's sister, although past the age at which village girls are usually married, still shamefacedly wears the blouse and skirt of a maiden.

underworld of the village; whereas in Surajben's family I had learned how things should appear, with Choto I discovered a lot about how things are.

I employed Choto as my *sāthi*, my companion, and shortly afterwards he began to wear a black thread around his neck with a brass amulet attached. I never discovered whether this was to guard him against the envy of his new employment, or whether he spoke the truth when he said that it was because he had been ill. We spoke of *najar* one day and I mentioned the one case that I knew in some detail, that of Surajben's baby, Bhailal, and the suspicion that rested on Chiman.

Choto didn't let me finish my story. Chiman, so much older, was a friend of his. They went drinking together in the fields at night and Chiman knew how to cook the partridges that Choto occasionally killed.[3] 'That's stupid', he said, 'why should Chiman look at Surajben's baby? His own brother's got several sons and they've none of them ever been sick. If Chiman were like that, that is where *najar* would have struck'. 'I am sorry.' I said, 'I thought you knew, and anyhow I just took it for granted that Surajben knew what she was at.' 'Surajben', he almost spat the name out, 'she thinks of nothing but *najar*. I couldn't count the number of times she's called me out in the night to make some offering to the goddess—*mātāji*, she's just mean that's all. Do you know I once dropped in when she was frying *bhajiān* and when she heard me coming she shoved the pan under a bed to hide it'? The implication was clear: had Choto found Surajben preparing *bhajiān* she would have been obliged to offer him some. I remembered Surajben's own account some three years earlier of what I assume was the same incident. 'It's the same with that whole damn family', said Choto, 'their life is such, *najar* is bound to strike'.

Choto's view of things is complicated. He certainly believed in *najar*, but had grounds to defend Chiman, his friend, from the accusation. *Najar* was not then the kind of innocent weakness I had supposed. There was an implication of a moral defect, short of conscious malice. Moreover it was attracted not by mere envy but by meanness and a refusal to share good things. That was Choto's opinion and this came close to making sense of *najar* to me. *Najar*

[3] The Patidar are in principle vegetarian, but meat-eating is not unthinkable. The fact to note is that a man might eat meat, or drink alcohol, out in the fields; he would not dream of bringing such things home to pollute the house. Similarly, a man might have sexual intercourse with an Untouchable woman, but he would not take food or water at her hands.

situations came into being not simply when people had enjoyable qualities or goods, but when people having these things took pride in them, and enjoyed them, in some sense, as though they had deprived others of them. Thus a good-looking man would only be likely to accuse others of *najar* if he were himself vain.

Ghosts

I mentioned earlier Choto's horrendous ghost stories and how they were met by a 'willing suspension of disbelief'. The villagers enjoy frightening themselves with ghost stories: the taste seems universal. The young also indulge in elaborate practical jokes. There's a man in Sundarana [a village in the Kaira District of Gujarat] now in his sixties, a Bareia by caste, who told me how, years ago, Kishor, Surajben's husband, and some others rigged up an oil lamp and an old *dhoti* in a thorn bush near his home in such a manner that it popped up moaning every time he tried to enter the lane. He stayed out in the fields petrified and cold all night. This had happened when they were in their late teens, at a time of life when inter-caste friendships were still possible, and a certain laxity over the rules of caste was tolerated so long as it was concealed. If marriage does not naturally induce responsibility in these matters, the marital status imposes it.

The old man who told me the story, together with Choto and his audience, believed nevertheless in ghosts at an altogether more disturbing level. The old man told me once, after a night of storytelling in which he had fully participated, that Choto was a shocking liar of course, but all the same it was not good to tell such stories because they could bring about the very horrors that they described. There were certain parts of the village, outside the residential area, where no man in his right mind would ever walk alone. Collective representations are often contagious and affect even the outsider. I certainly could not avoid a sense of uneasy tension when I had occasion to walk in the vicinity of such places at night.

The general word for ghost is *bhut* and the word connotes a terrifying ugliness, but not necessarily malevolence. Many ghosts are feminine and may still be called *bhut*, but *bhutaḍi*, a diminutive form, designates a female spirit. The word *bhut* is interesting; it derives from the Sanskrit notion of existence and the continuity of being and can have this meaning still in Gujarati literature. *Bhutkal* means past time, *kal* meaning time or period, or, in grammar, the past tense. *Bhutmātra* is the totality of being; *bhutdāya*, compassion for all beings, and so on. The use of the word *bhut* to mean horrendous ghosts is a special development.

Among the *bhut* there are special kinds. There is the *zan* (from the Arabic *djin*); this is the spirit of man versed in the evil arts *meli vidhya* (literally, dirty science); there is also the *bakrākshas*—the ghost of a Brahman. But apart from the word *bhut* itself the very commonest is *chudel*. The *chudel* is the spirit of a woman. Unlike all other *bhut* her appearance is seductively beautiful. A man might meet such a woman in the fields and could only know his peril from the fact that her feet pointed backwards. In a country where the women wear the *sāri* down to their feet this deformity might well go unnoticed, but even so, the stories have it, the *chudel* is so utterly beautiful that men have been knowingly seduced and as a result of sleeping with her, reduced to impotence for the rest of their lives.

Ghosts are most usually feared when they inhabit the fields. The few who enter houses are more manageable and sometimes even benign. The phenomena reported are rather like those attributed to poltergeists among ourselves; they throw pots, cloths and furniture without harming human beings. There is, for example, a Muslim house in Sundarana which was infested in this way about a hundred years ago. The *bhut* began its activities by hurling down bricks from the wall. It is said that a Patidar neighbour, who was called in to witness this, observed, characteristically, that there would be a good deal more sense in the situation if the spirit were to throw down gold, whereupon, on that one occasion, a shower of gold descended. This spirit is still said to be active occasionally.

Some house ghosts go as far as to possess their victims in such a way that they destroy their own property. The only help is to buy a charm, preferably of iron. In general it is believed that iron makes any ghost burst into flames and disappear. This does not always work. There was a man in Sundarana who had a house built by the local carpenter but did not pay his bill. The carpenter died and possessed the house owner so that the man went mad and destroyed his own house. No iron charm would work and so it was concluded that the carpenter had been a secret adept in the evil art and had become a *zan*. If a possessing spirit can be persuaded to speak through its victim and express its grievance, and if this grievance can be met, then it will usually go away in peace.

Grievance is common to all these manifestations of the dead even though some are nameless and the grievance is not known. It is simply assumed that they are consumed by some unidentifiable regret. Most often, however, the regret relates to the known obligations of others which have not been fulfilled, such as the carpenter's unpaid bill. More generally the grievance may derive from unfulfilled desire. There was a field in Sundarana haunted by the *bhut* of a man who had owned an adjoining field. He had maintained, throughout his life, an acrimonious border dispute with his neighbour, which he had finally lost. The *chudel* is said to be the spirit of a woman who died childless; her revenge is appropriate just as her regret can never be assuaged. It is interesting that, in a society in which women are usually blamed for a sterile marriage, impotence strikes the man who copulates with this spirit. There is a kind of justice in the folklore.

It is not difficult to understand that this belief in an unfulfilled desire relates closely to the belief in *najar*. Just as I will fear the envious evil eye only if I am aware of my own greed, and vanity is only a form of greed, so will I only fear the activity of ghosts if I have a guilty conscience. Many villagers said that to be unafraid was the best protection of all, and this is what the old man was getting at when he said that ghost stories were dangerous. Fear generates the profounder guilt to which a general belief relates, just as specific guilt relates to the belief in a specific ghost. I never heard that spirits were restless because of some ritual inadequacy in the funeral ceremonies. With the exception of the *chudel* all cases related to unpaid debts, land disputes, or vows unaccomplished, that is to say, things which the living might remedy with the family or kin of the deceased.

Some ghosts only require feeding from time to time, usually by a peepul tree. This food is taken at night by someone who does not look behind him, either coming or going. Such ghosts, together with those who regularly inhabit houses and those who possess people, come close to incorporation in the permanent pantheon of the village. There was one such permanent ghost site in Sundarana where food was left regularly and a lamp given occasionally. Some spoke of the ghost there as a *mātā*, kind of goddess [see Pocock 1973: 41–80] and also as the spirit of the great-grand-mother of a man in the village. We shall see that a development from ghost to goddess is not impossible. All that is needed is more trouble associated with the spot, and a greater attention consequently paid to it, for others to start venerating the place. This is not hypothetical. Elsewhere in Gujarat, particularly Saurashtra, the spirits of women who have committed suttee, and even those who have proved themselves otherwise to be true *sati*—chaste and virtuous models of wifely behaviour—are deified under the general term *mātā*, although their immediate descendants continue to distinguish them as *sati*.

The reader who has some knowledge of Indian beliefs might well ask at this point: 'What about reincarnation, transmigration or re-birth? If Hindus have such beliefs how can they at the same time believe in ghosts?' To this I could add that the villagers also have beliefs about heaven and hell, more particularly the latter. One afternoon a young man was sitting by me as I was resting in a darkened room. He was very kindly ridding the room of flies by snatching them out of the air as he sat. I congratulated him on his practised ease. 'It's nothing', he said, and then with a slightly worried look, 'but I sometimes worry about all that walking, walking, walking'. It was altogether too hot to press the matter at that time; it later emerged that he was speaking of hell, a hell in which man is obliged to walk on and on for ever and alone. On the other hand the belief in re-birth according to the law of *karma* was occasionally expressed, and there was even a little ritual about it connected with funeral ceremonies. The night after a cremation the women would spread flour on the floor, cover it with a sieve and leave a lighted lamp on top of the sieve to burn all night. In the morning they said that they could discern in the flour the footprint of the creature into which the departed soul had entered. This was not a universal or in any way mandatory practice, and indeed it was dismissed by some men as a foolish superstition. A far more regular institution was the throwing out of food, curds and water, most often on the anniversary of a death. It was believed that if the crows took this food it would in some way benefit the departed soul. I never saw the crows pay any attention to these offerings nor did I ever see anyone wait to see whether they would.

The villagers of Sundarana, like the majority of peoples known to social anthropologists, were very vague about the after-life. I suspect that much of the information collected from different parts of the world on such matters is more often synthesized on the spot, in response to Western query, rather than the integrated theory that is sometimes presented in the works of anthropologists. When Indian peasants, or philosophers for that matter, are confronted with the ancient 'contradiction' between a belief in individual survival in hell or as a ghost on the one hand, or on the other, the belief in re-birth, they can very easily sythesize the two beliefs: death is followed by a period of punishment or reward which varies in length according to merit, but ultimately the law of *karma* requires a re-birth unless the soul has been freed for ever from the operation of that law.

I do not think it very sensible to give in to a desire to solve contradictions in this way, and I find support for this view from village conversation. For the social anthropologist it is not only a question of *what* is said, but *who* says it and to *whom* and *where*. Thinking over remarks about the after-life in this way it seems clear to me that there is a rather simple formula underlying this 'contradiction' in beliefs. Re-birth is primarily for other people. Just as few Westerners accept fully the finiteness of their own existence, so that death tends to be thought of as something that happens to others, so the Gujarati peasants when they speak of themselves as individuals conceive of a hell or some sort of heaven. It is when they speak of others, when they are looking for some wider theory to explain the grief, sorrow and misfortune of others, that they have recourse to the theory of re-birth. Certainly they do not deny salvation to others, equally they apply the re-birth theory to their own occasional griefs but primarily the emphases are distributed as I have described.

There is another aspect of the matter. It seems clear in some contexts that actually these two beliefs are not at the same level. The belief in some kind of eternal salvation relates to the future whereas the belief in re-birth relates to the past. Some sin in a previous life 'explains' why a man is born as an Untouchable, or why some woman has had the great misfortune to survive her husband, and is obliged to live out the inauspicious life of a widow.

Let me conclude with a summary note on *najar* and beliefs about ghosts. Both are clearly related to human obligations and the failure to meet them. Joyce Cary in *The Horse's Mouth*, talking of the secretive way in which tramps in a London doss-house cook their food, speaks of the 'evil eye which is the eye of envy'. Certainly, at one level, the belief in *najar* tells us something about the greed and avarice which can only be found in their purest form where people live on the bread-line, have never lived anywhere else, and do not expect anything more. It also tells of the acute value placed upon, for us, the ephemeral goods of youth, good looks and vitality in a population where the average expectation of life is only thirty years, where women are soon prematurely senile, and young men show signs of muscle wastage at twenty-five.

At the level of the sociological, *najar* tell us of status and equality. *Najar* is not to be feared between equals, such as brothers, nor between people whose status is clearly different and defined. It is most to be feared when those who should be equal are not so in fact. From this point of view natural good looks, which might be the gift of all, may be envied by any. At the social level, however, *najar* bites deepest within the caste, especially in a large caste such as the Patidar, where, in one lineage, a man may live in contentment while his kinsman spends his life near to starvation. When some do accumulate wealth, the fear of *najar* defines the ways in which wealth may be enjoyed, that is with modesty, it requires all men to be generous according to their means.

The evil eye can be turned away, and its ill effects can be cured. The belief in ghosts speaks more of irremediable ills past, and of unavoidable evil in life itself. The wilful over-looker who is the embodiment of pure unmotivated malice, the practitioner of the black science and the barren woman—for these there are no remedies. Among the ghosts are also those who have been cheated of their dues just as, in a sense, the barren woman is cheated. Such beliefs underlie the value of a good death which leaves neither material nor moral debt or loan behind it.

Hindu Values of Life: Karma and Dharma

K. S. MATHUR

[This essay] deals with three of the most important and widely-believed concepts of Hinduism. These are: (i) *punarjanama* or *avāgamana*, i.e. the theory of transmigration of souls, (ii) *karma* or the doctrine of deserts, and (iii) *dharma* or the Hindu scheme of values. These three concepts are linked in a chain of reasoning and are known as such to Hindus all over the country. Through the popular media of *kathā* (narratives), *bhajan* (devotional songs), and *vārtā* (talks or lectures), these doctrines are taken to the people by the wandering Brahmins, ascetics, bards and devotional singers. It is, therefore, not surprising, that even illiterate villagers in remote villages are acquainted with the popular doctrines of Hinduism. . . .

The Theory of Transmigration of Souls

According to Hindu belief, this life by itself alone would have no meaning; it has meaning only as a link in a chain of births extending from the past into the future. An old Brahmin of Potlod [pseudonym of a village near Indore in Madhya Pradesh] expressed it thus:

> A worldly existence is a stage of transition from past existence towards future worldly lives. Life is a process. It does not start with a child's birth; it does not end with a person's death. Birth and death are merely landmarks in one of a series of phases of worldly existence. When a child is born or a person dies, there is merely a shift in his position. It is like an actor acting on the stage, then going behind the curtains and changing, and then reappearing on the stage in a new garb. But he is the same man. Lord Krishna said in the Gitaji that just as a man discards old clothes and wears new ones, the soul discards worn and torn physical bodies and assumes new forms.

Excerpted from K. S. Mathur, 'Hindu Values of Life', in *Caste and Ritual in a Malwa Village*, Asia Publishing House, Bombay, 1964, pp. 78–95.

This belief in the continuity of life despite births and deaths, creation and destruction is at the base of the Hindu social and metaphysical thought. It is expressed in such popular sayings as 'He who has come will go, and he who has gone will come again', or 'This universe is a circular passage; we keep on moving but we move in circles; this is an endless process'.

An important corollary to the theory of transmigration is the belief in the immortality of the soul. The soul is called *jīva* (life-substance) or *ātmā* (one's spirit), and is considered to be a part of God who is called *Paramātmā* (the Supreme Spirit). The soul, we are told, is immortal and eternal; it cannot be cut by sharp-edged weapons nor burnt by fire nor drenched by water; it does not experience any pain or pleasure.

The people of Potlod [in the mid-1950s] do not claim to know at what moment the soul enters the physical body or when exactly it leaves. It is invisible, but Pannalal Darji [of Tailor caste] thinks that the *jīva* enters the body while it is still in the making; it animates the foetus in the womb and makes it grow; without the *jīva*, nothing would grow; the *jīva* or *ātmā* leaves the body—its 'terrestrial abode'—at death or decay, to fly away and leave the plant, animal or man dead; it then enters some other physical body, and so the cycle of births and deaths goes on.

Kala Bai, an old Rajput woman, added:

> The *jīva* is the instrument for animation, and devoid of it, the dead or decayed body quickly disintegrates into the five elements out of which it is said to have been created; earth, water, fire, heaven, and wind. But death does not affect the *jīva*; for it, death is merely like the shedding of old and rotten garments and the donning of a new garb.

Each individual soul, the people believe, has to go through a large number of worldly existences or 'incarnations'. Said Ambalal Lohar [of Blacksmith caste]:

> According to the holy *Purānas*, each *jīva* has to pass through 8,400,000 different births and deaths. But all these need not necessarily be human. As a matter of fact, the *Purānas* say that, it is rare for a *jīva* to be born into a human body. Most of the eight million and four hundred thousand lives are lived in the form of insects, such as flies, mosquitoes, and other lowly forms of life. Unending, this cycle of births and deaths goes on, until either the full quota of lives for a soul is exhausted (which comes only at the end of creation) or the *jīva* acquires such *punya* (spiritual merit) that it merges with the Supreme Soul—the Paramatma or God Almighty. But such a merger of an individual *ātmā* with *Paramātmā* comes only once in a millennium or so; it is a very rare phenomenon.

The Law of *Karma*

The transmigration of souls is governed by a cosmic law, known as *karma*. It is the law of the universe controlling births and deaths. In terms of the law of *karma* alone it is possible to understand why some souls are born as animals, others as insects or birds, and others as human beings. It accounts for the divergence in the physical forms the same soul might take in its different worldly lives. As Rama Singh Chohan [Rajput] said:

> *Karma* alone can explain why some persons in this world are happy, successful, physically well built, and, in general, occupy a high position in life, while others are born deformed or become disabled, poor, wretched, and miserable in their low station in life.

The word *karma* is from the Sanskrit root *kri*, meaning 'to do'. Literally, then, the word *karma* means 'that which is done', or 'action'. The doctrine has for its basis the very popular notion that all action has its reaction, and that the type of reaction is causally connected to the type of action. Shivji Ram, a Khati young man, told me:

> Nothing is more plain and easily understandable to us agriculturists than the phenomenon that we reap what we sow. Similarly, if we are told that a good deed is rewarded and a bad action punished, it is really quite simple and logical. After all, that is justice, and God is just. Therefore, the doctrine of *karma* which means the inevitable working out of action in new life has wide and popular appeal.

Considered together, the two concepts of transmigration of soul and *karma* are taken to mean, as Shiv Charan Dube, an old Brahmin... said, that the form and destiny of one worldly existence is determined by the behaviour of the individual *jīva* in its previous worldly existences or incarnations. The idea is that a man's body, character, capacities, temperament, his birth and station in life, his wealth, and the whole of his experience in life, of pleasure or of pain and misery, taken together form the just recompense for his deeds, good and bad, of earlier existences. Every act necessarily works itself out in retribution in a subsequent rebirth. The expiation works itself out not only in a man's passive experience but also in most of his actions. And then, these new actions form new *karma*, which must necessarily be expiated in another life. And thus, the cycle of *karma* and reincarnation goes on, almost never ending.

Some complication in the popular mind is created by the problem: is the destiny of an individual soul predetermined in all its aspects and activities, or is it at all possible for an individual to participate, even to a limited extent, in the working of the forces of natural law? In other words, does the individual possess any power to shape his own destiny, or is he simply a passive tool in the hands of the powerful forces of fate?

The people of Potlod are divided in their views on this matter. Some feel that *karma* is a cruel and cold divine law and men are not able to influence its working. 'Every action in the present life is controlled by past karma', they say. 'How then is it possible for a man to act independently? All this talk about a man doing as he pleases does not make sense.' Cases are quoted of persons who have been doing good *karma* all their lives and who yet find themselves in perpetual trouble and misery, whereas people who have never bothered about good *karma* flourish and succeed in the world. It is significant to note that such an opinion is commonly held by poor and illiterate folk.

Some people hold a different view in this matter of individual liberty to act. Most of such people in Potlod are well-read in the Hindu scriptures, and one or two have read a few English books on the philosophy of *karma*. Ramanand Dube [Brahmin] quoted Lord Krishna as saying in the Gita that man had the right of doing *karma* (*karmanyevaadhikāraste*) which will determine his soul's future worldly existence and the . . . station therein. Ajodhya Prasad Thakur [Kshattriya] quoted S. Radhakrishnan:

> The cards in the game of life are given to us. We do not select them. They are traced to our past *karma*, but we can call as we please, lead what suit we will, and as we play, we win or lose. And there is (individual) freedom—freedom of action.

All my informants, however, agree on one point, viz. that good *karma* leads to *punya* or spiritual merit, and bad *karma* results in the accumulation of *pāp*, or sin. In popular belief, the *karma* and its reaction for every individual is controlled by an elaborate system of what may be called divine accountancy.

The people say that in the court of Yama—the Lord of Death—there is a clerk whose name is Chitragupta. (The name means 'Invisible Writer'.) He is said to record in his books all the actions performed by every individual in the universe. Nothing is hidden from him. He even records a man's thoughts. For each good thought or *karma*, the individual gets a 'merit entry', and for each wicked thought or deed, he is given a 'demerit entry'. When a person dies, his soul is taken to the court of Yama, and Chitragupta is asked to read the record of his thoughts and actions in his worldly life, and to balance the account. If his acts of merit outweigh his sins, he is sent to heaven and is later reborn in the world in a better form of life; however, should the 'demerit' side prove to outweigh the 'merit' side of the ledger, the soul is condemned to hell-fire and is later reborn in a baser form and station of worldly life.

Baba Haridas Vairagi, quoting from the Upanishads, said:

> As the *jīva* moves out of the body, life is extinguished; a man's knowledge and actions and his consciousness of former births and deeds is extinguished. His *jīva*, or *ātma*, is influenced by his conduct and behaviour, that is, his *karma*. He whose deeds have been good becomes good; he who has done evil deeds becomes evil himself. By holy deeds, he becomes holy; by sinful ones, sinful. It is for this reason that they say that a person consists merely of desires; as his desire is so his will; as his will so his deeds, so will be his evolution.

Dharma

This leads us to our third and most complex concept, that of *dharma*. All that is *dharma* is good and right, and conversely, all that is not *dharma* (or *a-dharma*) is bad, wicked and wrong. In the popular mind, *dharma* is a synonym for 'righteousness, goodness, virtue' and is an attribute of 'all that is true, all that is austere and pure, and all that has divine beauty and virtue' (*satyam, shivam, sundaram*).

Perhaps the nearest English equivalent to the word *dharma* is 'good and righteous conduct'. According to the *karma* theory only *dharma*, i.e. good thoughts, knowledge, conduct and behaviour lead to the acquisition of spiritual merit and its worldly rewards, prosperity, well-being and virtue.

Sources of Dharma

The sources for the derivation and statement of the principles of *dharma* are many. There is a vast store of spiritual wisdom, divine knowledge and logical analysis in the sacred literature of the Hindus. This is mostly in Sanskrit,the liturgic language of the Hindus, and consists of the Vedas, Brahmanas, Upanishadas, Epics (the Ramayana and the Mahabharata), Samhita, Aranyakas, Sutras and Smritis, the Nitis, the Puranas, and the Dharmashastras. To the ordinary villagers most of these are neither available, nor intelligible. Even the village Brahmin who can read and understand bits of

Sanskrit does not have the knowledge, nor the time to cultivate such knowledge for the understanding of the higher philosophy of *dharma* contained in these books.

Ideally, it is prescribed that the Brahmin should read, understand, and analyse the Vedas and other religious literature and interpret [these] to the other castes. According to the theory of the divine creation of the four *varna*, contained in the *Purusha Sukta* in the hymns of the *Rig-veda*, the job of the Brahmin *varna* was to read and write, teach and preach, offer and officiate at sacrifices. The Brahmins were obliged by this tradition to undergo a life of study, meditation, and penetration into the mysteries of God and *dharma*; in exchange for a life of study and benefit to the community, the Brahmins were supported by the rest of the community—by the grant of freehold and rent-free lands, alms and regular gifts. The Brahmins still swear by the theory of divine creation of the *varna* system and wish to perpetuate the privileges accruing to them. The special grants still continue . . . but the Brahmins have given up their former pursuit of higher philosophy and divine knowledge. The present-day rural Brahmin is so busily occupied as to have hardly any time for devotion, the study of religious literature, or the pursuit of meditation and spiritual wisdom.

Among the people of Potlod, I found recognition of three sources for the statement and interpretation of *dharma*. The first of these consisted of myths and legends (*kathā*), which have largely been borrowed—in toto or in a modified version—from the Puranas and the Epics. There is, for example, the myth of Savitri-Satyavan, very popular among the women, which narrates the story of a righteous woman who revived her dead husband and acquired from the god of Death three boons, the first for long life and prosperity for her husband, the second for a son and heir for her father, and the third for the lost throne of her father-in-law. Then there is the myth of King Nala and his queen Damyanti who lost . . . everything in a game of dice, but regained . . . [it] through righteous action in which they persisted even in the face of severe odds. Then there is also the myth of Jaratkaru, an unmarried sage who was told by his suffering ancestors to marry and beget a son so that they could be assured of continued oblations. And there are the numerous legends connected with the exploits of Rama in his conquest over the *rakshasa* [demon] King Ravana, including the story of how Rama killed a Shudra ascetic for which deed he was given the title of 'Defender of the Social Order' (*Maryada-Purushottama*). There are stories (from the Mahabharata) of the five Pandava brothers and their queen Draupadi who suffered innumerable privations in spite of their righteous conduct, but who defeated the forces of *a-dharma* (un-righteousness) in the Great Battle of Bharata by perseverance and righteous *karma*. There are the very popular legends about Hanuman, who, because of his service to Rama, and because of his practising great physical austerities, was made immortal and the 'highest of the lesser gods' (Mahabir). He is one of those deities whose worship is very popular with villagers of all castes. He is worshipped by the offering of a coconut on most festival days and in times of distress and trouble. Widely known also is the myth of Ganesha, or Ganapati, who was given the singular honour of being worshipped first on all ceremonial occasions in recognition of his wisdom and devotion to his father, Lord Shiva.

All these stories, myths and legends have their moral. And the moral [is] emphasized when the particular myth is narrated on specific ritual occasions—the birthday of a god . . ., the anniversary of some one or other of his or her valiant deeds . . ., or a religious rite the existence of which depends upon the moral of the myth concerned. For example . . . when Monday coincides with the fortnightly New Moon Day, women of Brahmin and certain other 'clean' castes keep a fast for the whole day, and in the evening break the fast after worshipping the Moon (Chandra) and Death (Yama) gods. The specific aim of this rite and fast is the effort by the fasting women, through physical austerities and worship, to prolong the lives of their husbands. Many of these myths are celebrated in songs (called *bhajan*) which are sung during the performance of rites, and also on other occasions.

Of all the sacred books popular in the village community, perhaps the most important is the *Rāma Charit Mānas*, the Sacred Lake of the Works of Rama, a modified version of the [Sanskrit epic] Rāmāyana. It is in Hindi, written in verse by a seventeenth century poet-saint, Tulsi Das. The book is divided in eight cantos, and portrays Rama as an ideal man, in his familial, social, and kingly relations, and . . . as an incarnation of the god Vishnu. The way he lived and acted is regarded as a model of righteous conduct and behaviour; everything he did was in order to live according to *dharma*, and to uphold *dharma*. The Ramayana by Tulsi Das has become extremely sacred to, and popular with, the common people [in north India]. It is read by almost everybody who can read Hindi, and for those who cannot, it is read by professional priest-minstrels. Both reading the book and listening to it are regarded as acts of *dharma*.

A second book, quite popular with the educated villagers, but rather less known to others, is the *Bhagavadgītā*, popularly known as Gītā or rather Gītājī (to give it ritual honour by suffixing '*jī*'). The Gita is in Sanskrit verse and is divided into eighteen chapters. The book contains the message delivered to Pandava Arjuna by Lord Krishna on the eve of the Great Battle of Bharata [described in the epic Mahābhārata]. The very theme of the book is the doctrine of *karma*, *dharma*, and rebirth, and the ways suggested by Lord Krishna for the emancipation of the human soul from the cycle of rebirth and *karma*.

Both these sources for the statement and interpretation of *dharma*, viz. the Purana myths and the two sacred books (Ramayana and Gita), are more popular with the Brahmin and other 'clean' castes (of the Kshattriya and Vaisya *varna*). With the Shudra *varna* and untouchable castes, these are both less known and less popular.

The third source of *dharma*, however, is one which is universally accepted by all castes, the final and supreme authority in all practical matters. The nature of *dharma*, the people say, is extremely complex, more so for ignorant, unread, and untutored minds. The principles of *dharma* are unfathomably deep, and so, for all practical purposes, the average common man should generally follow the path trodden by his ancestors and predecessors, in accordance with the best available traditions of the class or caste to which he happens to belong. Tradition is thus the best and most important source of *dharma*, one which takes precedence over all the other sources, literary or mythical.

Traditions vary from region to region, and from caste to caste. Naturally, then, the tradition that a person draws upon is the tradition of his particular caste. Even the myths from the epics and Puranas uphold a man's right to adhere to his caste tradition, howsoever degrading it might appear on the surface. A story quite well known in the village community and often narrated by elders is that of the hunter and the Brahmin.

A Brahmin, vain of his knowledge and superior *varna*, was told by his teacher to go and learn from a hunter-butcher the secret of *dharma*. The Brahmin was surprised: how was it possible for the hunter-butcher, who killed animals and sold their flesh, and who did not know a word of the sacred literature, to practise *dharma*, and to preach *dharma* to a man of the Brahmin *varna*. The hunter told the Brahmin that though he was a hunter-butcher by caste and trade, a man of a low and 'unclean' caste, he scrupulously observed his duties: he followed the trade of his caste, even though that involved butchering innocent animals for food, lived truly and honestly as a member of his caste group, gave alms according to his mite, and worshipped his caste deities regarding them as manifestations of the highest God. He strictly adhered to his caste traditions, and that was the reason why in practice he pursued *dharma* and did good *karma*. Being born in a particular caste—high or low in the hierarchy—is not in a man's hands; this is determined by his destiny, which in turn is formed by his *karma* in his last worldly existence. But having been born into a particular caste and station of life, it is incumbent upon a person to live righteously in accordance with the traditions of his caste, for that, and that alone, is his *dharma*. To abandon the duties related to one's caste and profession is considered to be both shameful and sinful; to hold to the *karma* suited to one's caste is certainly in keeping with the principles of *dharma*. Because *karma* carried out in this manner, and this alone, does not pollute the individual soul, even though the *karma* (particular to one's caste) happens to be unclean or polluting. The physical uncleanliness and pollution that arise from such *karma* are considered to be mere atonement for past *karma*. Only if the atonement is properly and fully carried out is it possible for the soul to attain a higher form and station in life in the next worldly existence. If, on the other hand, a person shirks from carrying out duties fitted to his caste and station in life, he will be deemed to have acted in an un-righteous way, and he will have to suffer for it in future worldly existence.

The Principles of Dharma

The principles of *dharma* may be classified into three broad categories.

Certain codes of moral conduct are of universal application in Hindu India. Everywhere, respect has to be shown to elders. Respect towards elders is demonstrated in several ways. The most common of these is the general Hindu way of greeting elders. When a person meets an older kinsman, be it at his house or in the village lane, he salutes the latter by bending the upper part of his body and touching the elder's feet with his hands, at the same time uttering *pailagi Ba* ('I touch your feet, Sir'). To unrelated elderly persons of the village, one shows respect by simply uttering the salutation without the accompanying gesture. Women are expected to show respect for their elders by covering their faces with a veil in the presence of the latter and avoiding them in everyday life. On ceremonial occasions, she is expected to salute her elders—of both sexes—by touching their feet with both hands, and then placing her hands on her forehead.

Younger men are always expected to greet elders first, in the prescribed fashion. Similarly in their speech and behaviour with elderly people, young persons have to observe certain rules of social etiquette. For example, they have to avoid laughing aloud, expressing opinions unless they are asked for, and making jokes. In talking with elderly people, even unrelated, one has to avoid addressing them by name,but by a suitable kinship term, such as *Ba* (Sir), *Ma* (mother), *Dada* (brother), or *Bai* (sister).

Moral rules of behaviour, said Ram Chandra Khati, require a person to be kind towards those younger than himself, respectful towards elders and friendly with equals. He should be obedient and patient in his dealings and decent in his manners. To help a person in need is a social virtue and a man who is willing to help even his enemy is respected by everybody. Lastly, he should be a believer and should honour and respect gods as if they were his elders. He should visit temples and observe appropriate fasts and feasts required by his social traditions.

All these moral principles, which constitute the first category of rules of *dharma*, may be considered positive rules or injunctions which should be followed in order to have a normal and healthy life in the community. For the individual, these serve as avenues by which he gains *punya* or spiritual merit for his soul; he who conforms to these rules of behaviour, so to say, gets a 'merit entry' in his *karma* register, the fruits of which he expects to reap in latter lives.

In the present worldly life, he is regarded as a virtuous or holy man and commands the respect of everybody in the community. On the other hand, non-conformity to these rules results in a person's moral degradation and disregard in the community, and is believed to get him a 'demerit' entry in his *karma* register. In the second category of the principles of *dharma* are included all those rules of behaviour and rites the aim of which is the acquisition of extra merit and moral advancement for the individual who practises them. In this category of rules of *dharma* are included, in the words of Girdhari Mali [of Gardener caste] of Potlod, such phenomena as alms-giving to Brahmins, mendicants, temples and the needy, construction of temples, cowsheds and bathing places at rivers, wells and tanks, and special devotion to the gods, Brahmins and cows—the three beings most sacred to all Hindus. Ratan Lal Bania [of Trader caste] said that for all those who desire to earn extra *punya*, there are several traditional paths to follow; such persons may pursue divine knowledge through the reading of scriptures, and meditation and self-concentration; they may perform special worship (*pūjā*) and sacrifices (*yajna*) in the name of the gods; they may visit famous religious centres in their region and in far-off parts of the country and bathe in the waters of the seven sacred rivers to wash off their *pāp*, and earn *punya*. These are all considered to be pious acts, and he who performs them not only amasses spiritual merit for the next existence, but also gains prestige as a righteous man in this world.

These rules and rites are optional. Like the injunctions of the first category, the correct observance of these special rules and rites is believed to lead to the acquisition of additional spiritual merit for the devotee's soul. The difference between these rules and the rules of the first category lies in the consequences that are believed to result from the non-observance of the sacred rules. Whereas non-conformity to the positive injunctions of the first category leads to sin and ritual blemish and the consequences attendant thereon, the non-performance of the rites and actions of the second category does not lead to any degradation of the person concerned, in this or in any after-lives.

The third category of the principles of *dharma* consists of rules that are considered absolutely essential for a person to follow. These are in the nature of negative rules or prohibitions and are concerned with what a person must not do. [The] prohibitions are based on popular notions about purity and pollution. These notions are believed by the people to have a ritual sanction, they are deeply rooted in mystical beliefs and supernaturalism, and have, therefore, been termed 'ritual rules' as distinct from 'moral rules'. The distinction, as we shall presently see, is in the sanctions and in the consequences that result from non-conformity to the two types of rules.

The everyday social actions of a person are governed by these ritual prohibitions. These rules, for example, prescribe whom one may marry and decree whom one shall not marry; they guide the commensal and dietary behaviour patterns of people, and they also prescribe the rightful ways in which people may earn their living. . . .

Correct observance of these prohibitory ritual rules . . . the people believe, acquires a 'merit entry' for the person in his *karma* register; thus he is able to avoid, as Panna Lal Darji said, ritual blemish, the fire of hell, and a bad form and station in future worldly lives. Non-observance of these rules gives the transgressor a 'demerit entry' with all the consequences that follow. So far these prohibitions are similar to moral injunctions.

The most important function of the rules of ritual prohibition, however, lies in another field. These rules are based on certain mystical notions about purity and pollution. Transgression or violation of these rules is believed to pollute the person. This means that should a person commit ritually prohibited acts, he becomes ritually impure; and this results in the loss of his normal group status; and his expulsion (temporary or permanent) from his caste.

The process of readmission to his caste of an expelled member is controlled by religious and social traditions. It consists of three different acts: admission of his guilt by the expelled man, his penance and penalization by the caste community, and finally his reacceptance by the symbolic act of co-dining.

The purpose of penance is to wipe the ritual taint off the person. To the fear of the ritual taint is added the more concrete fear of the ritual pollution that a person is believed to contract in transgressing any ritual prohibition; the very performance of the act degrades him from his normal ritual status. He becomes not only polluted but also polluting, and as such a potential danger to the entire community. The social function of penance is, thus, to remove the ritual pollution and restore the person to his normal (group) ritual status. In this sense, it is a purificatory rite, and its performance by the violator of the taboo is insisted upon by the social groups to which the individual belongs, viz. his family and caste and the village community. . . .

From the viewpoint of their observance, the principles of *dharma* are grouped by the people under the following heads:

(i) *sarva sādharan dharma*, or general rules of *dharma* meant to be observed by all Hindus in the community;
(ii) *jati dharma*, or caste *dharma*, based on individual caste traditions;
(iii) *kula dharma*, or rules of *dharma* common to a *kula* or patrilineage;

(iv) *vishesh dharma*, or special rules; and
(v) *āpad dharma*, or rules of *dharma* meant to be observed in times of distress.

Every Hindu is a member of his village community, which is itself part of the regional (Malwa) community and of the all-India Hindu community. This aspect of a person's religious behaviour is conditioned by the principles of what is known as *sādharan dharma* (*dharma* for all, or common *dharma*). Principles of all-India Hinduism, and local and regional religious cults constitute this common *dharma*. It thus involves participation in the worship of the gods (some of whom are purely local godlings, whereas others are gods of the all-India Hindu pantheon), observance of certain rites and festivals common to all the people, and abiding by tenets common to all Hindus, such as the sanctity of the cow and certain other animals and plants, and superiority of the Brahmin and holy men.

Jati dharma is by far the most important set of rules. A person is born into a caste, and it is considered to be meritorious for him if he dies an honourable and truthful member of the caste, that is to say, if the person obeys all rules of caste carefully, so as to avoid conflict with his caste and its elders, and thus escapes the severe penalty of excommunication. It is considered to be the most singular discredit and dishonour for a person to be expelled from his caste; for this means that he has not been observing the rules of his caste, and thus not conforming to the *jati dharma* that was prescribed for him by destiny, a person's birth in a particular caste having been dictated by his destiny and his *karma* in his last worldly existence. Not observing the rules and duties of one's own caste means a 'demerit entry' in after-life, and a stock of bad *karma* for the next worldly existence. In terms of this life, it gives rise to a state of ritual pollution which continues to taint the offender till it is atoned for by means of ritual purificatory observances. Only then does the community re-accept the person and restore him to his normal group ritual status.

Each *kula*, or patrilineage, has its own ritual cult. They have their daily observances, elaborate, as in the case of the Brahmin, Vairagi or Gosain households, or just nominal, as among the other castes of Potlod. There are a number of other domestic rituals connected with changes in the form and membership of the household and lineage, viz. birth, adoption, marriage and death. To keep the unity and solidarity of the household and family intact, ideal interaction patterns between different types of relations in the family and lineage are invested with mystical and moral force. All these ritual concepts and observances constitute a person's *kula dharma*, or that aspect of his *dharma* which is dictated by the tradition of the family and lineage in which he happens to have been born.

There are special rules . . . framed with a view to exempt certain persons and age-groups from the pursuit of the common rules of *dharma*. Children, insane . . . disabled . . . and very old persons are not expected to understand and observe all the rules of *dharma*. These are, therefore, absolved from the obligation of conforming to the action-pattern set by . . . *dharma*. The king or local chief and the master of scriptures is not always bound by the more general rules of righteous conduct. For each such special social role, there is a distinct set of rules, prescribed by traditions and sanctioned by religion.

All the rules of *dharma* are suspended when a person goes out of his 'cultural context'. Thus, for example, when a villager goes to cities or travels over long distances in trains and buses, he is not so punctilious as when in his village. He has to eat at public food-shops and hotels; he may have to sit next to an 'untouchable'; in government offices and law courts, he has to deal with people whose caste and ritual status he does not always know. I know of a large number of cases from Potlod—and my personal knowledge from elsewhere substantiates this point—of otherwise orthodox and religious minded persons behaving, in these circumstances, in a manner which is definitely contrary to the accepted general rules of *dharma*.

In Hindu scriptural traditions, a person is permitted to overlook the rules of *dharma* if he is in great trouble. Cases are cited where famous sages and learned men ate impure food for the sake of saving their lives. Similarly, rules of common *dharma* do not bind a *sanyasi*, that is, one who has [renounced] the worldly life. Rules of *dharma* are believed to apply to only those who live as regular members of conventional society.

For the Hindu villager, his village constitutes the conventional type of society, in which he lives for a major part of his life. The rules of righteous conduct with which he is familiar refer to and obtain in that conventional social situation. The town or city, with its industries and offices, and mechanized life, is a different type of social entity; the pattern of life is different; the social and cultural situation is largely changed. The general and popular view is that the actions of a person in a socio-cultural context which is not his own are not to be considered his normal social actions, and that, therefore, he is not to be judged on the basis of the former. What he does in the city is no business of his caste community in the village, so long as his actions do not infringe the solidarity of the social groups to which he belongs.

The word *dharma* is from the Sanskrit root *dhr*, meaning 'to hold'. The etymological meaning of the word, thus, is 'that which holds a thing and maintains it in being'. For example, fire glows, radiates heat and light; it burns to ashes most objects which come into contact with its flames, and thus it 'holds' itself as fire; without these qualities, it would not be fire. This, then, say the learned, is the *dharma* of fire. Similarly all the rules of conduct and behaviour which help a person maintain his social and ritual position, in this worldly life and in forthcoming lives, together constitute his *dharma*.

In the social sense, *dharma*—or *dharam* as it is popularly known to the people of Potlod village—is composed of all those elements, moral rules and ethical codes, beliefs, concepts and theories, rites and observances, that are designed to hold together the social system. The social function of *dharma* is to hold together, maintain, and perpetuate a given social order. It is thus that all such phenomena, as for example, superstitions, myths, magical and liturgic formulae, norms of etiquette and conduct, social injunctions and prohibitions, and legal codes which aim at strengthening the current social order and counteract disruptive tendencies—both from within and without the system—constitute *dharma*. The *dharma* of a social group is the law of its existence; it is the way the social group maintains itself as an integrated group. According to the Hindu view of life, it is only righteous action—righteous in a given context—that can serve this purpose of perpetuating a social order. And thus *dharma* comes to be equated with and mean all 'righteous belief and action', that is, a proper way of living and behaving in society.

Dharma is the Hindu scheme of values. The Hindu belief is that *dharma* is the law of the universe, and society the manifestation of the divine law. Most village Hindus believe that if the tenets of *dharma* are not properly adhered to, the prescribed rites not performed in the right way, and the taboos or ritual avoidances not observed, in short, if the *dharma* is allowed to decay, there is bound to be chaos and disorder, and society will come to an end.

Purity and Pollution

PAULINE KOLENDA

The principle of purity-impurity pervades and partly explains the hierarchy of castes [in India]. Gods, people, social groups (*jatis* and minimal patrilineages), animals, and things may be ranked in a hierarchy of degrees of purity and impurity. Each member of each of these categories possesses, as an individual *attribute*, some capacity to pollute others. Each, however, may become more polluted, either temporarily or permanently, through *transactions* with *more* polluted beings, things, or happenings. Indeed, such transactions *display* the relative rankings of beings and items in a hierarchy of degrees of purity-impurity. This principle may be understood through the underlying Hindu imagery relating to living and dead organisms. . . .

Priestly-Purity Necessary for Transactions with the Gods

A central point in Hindu ritual is that it is necessary to make offerings to the gods in order for human affairs to continue without undue disaster. The intermediary between the general society and the gods is the priest, typically a Brahman. The Brahman priest must be pure in order to communicate with the gods, and satisfactory communication with the supernatural powers is necessary for the good of the king and of the society. This idea goes back to the ancient Aryan idea of *rita* (order), the belief that the sacrificial offerings made by Brahmans were a necessary part of the natural order. If such offerings were not made, or if they were not made correctly, then nature would go awry—rain would not fall, epidemics might

Excerpted from Pauline Kolenda, 'The Caste System Analyzed: The Ideology of Purity and Pollution', in *Caste in Contemporary India: Beyond Organic Solidarity*, Benjamin/Cummings Publishing Co., Menlo. Park, Inc., CA 1978, pp. 62–85.

prevail, and so on (Basham 1954: 113, 236–7). It was, thus, vital for the Brahmans to be pure. As A. M. Hocart saw clearly with respect to caste-ordered ritual in Ceylon, the function of lower castes was to absorb pollution for the higher castes (Hocart 1950). In India, too, the lower castes absorb pollution for the Brahman and for the other 'twice-born' (Gould 1958; Dumont 1970: 55).

...M.N. Srinivas (1952: 101–2) and Edward Harper (1964: 152–5) have specified three conditions of pollution and purity for Mysore villagers—a state of normal purity, a state of impurity, and a state of ritual purity. In the latter condition, one might transact with divinities, namely gods and ancestors. Means of purification include taking a bath and wearing pure clothes. There are many agents causing states of impurity. Contact with lower-caste persons is only one such agent. Others include contact with death, birth, menstruation, sexual intercourse, defecation, urination, bodily dirt, and eating.

Stevenson's 'Hindu Pollution Concept'

H. N. C. Stevenson (1954) delineated the underlying principle of pollution. Basically, any waste product from a human, animal, or divine body is impure. With death, the entire body becomes waste. A Brahman priest, in preparation for his religious service, purifies himself from the pollution of his own body, as well as from any pollution acquired by contact with polluted persons or places. Thus a Brahman officiant in a temple today remains continent, fasts, bathes, and wears a clean waist cloth before appearing before the god in the temple. His purity can be only temporary, because he will soon have to defile himself by eating, defecating, and so on. If a member of his family or patrilineage should die, or if a wife of one of the male members has a child, the priest cannot appear in the temple for many days. He is assumed to be polluted by the birth or death pollution pervading his family or patrilineage (it pervades male relatives and their wives in a patriline up to second cousin).

Dietary and Marital Customs

Besides pollution from a caste's traditional occupation, its dietary and marital customs are relevant to its ritual rank. Absorbed into Hinduism from Buddhism and Jainism was a belief in nonviolence; and, consequently, a belief that a vegetarian diet characterizes the purer castes. There are, furthermore, degrees of non-vegetarianism. It is especially defiling to eat the meat of the sacred cow. The next worst is eating pork, then mutton, then chicken, then fish, then eggs. Consistent with this, Brahmans are usually vegetarian; middle castes may eat chicken or mutton; and Untouchables may eat these plus pork or beef, as well.

To be pure, a high caste woman should have only a single sexual partner throughout her life. Those castes which allow a woman to marry only once are considered to be higher than those which allow widow remarriage, or which allow women to divorce and remarry. When a Brahman *jati* is said to have *no divorce,* what is meant is that a woman is not allowed to have a second husband. Men, whether Brahmans or of other castes, are allowed to have more than one wife. Even as his first wife is virginal, so a Brahman's second or subsequent wives are virginal upon marriage. Of course, in many middle and lower castes, widow remarriage is allowed. Sometimes women are allowed to divorce and remarry, but this is one of the customs which keeps them in a low rank in the caste hierarchy.

Pollution Inherited by Caste

The priest's impurity is also temporary; by various cleansing actions, he can become pure again. For lower castes, impurity is permanent. Lower caste members suffer a kind of inherited defilement. The Barber deals with bodily wastes—hair and nail clippings; he washes the male corpses, and his wife washes the female corpses of his higher caste *jajmans* (clients). The Washerman washes dirty clothing, stained by bodily excretions. The Sweeper removes human filth; he eats from pots spoiled by birth and death pollution pervading a *jajman's* house; he wears clothing in which a *jajman* died; he eats left-over food that has touched the mouths of others, or meat from dead animals. So degrees of defilement relate to the ranks in a caste hierarchy. The Barber is less defiled than the Washerman, who, in turn, is less defiled than the Sweeper, and so on.

The idea of pollution-contagion is universal in Hindu India. Anything touched by a polluted person spreads the pollution to others who touch it. This notion is expressed in rules about giving food and water, and touching persons and their belongings. An orthodox Brahman will not take boiled food or water from anyone of lower caste rank. He may take food coated by purifying milk or *ghi* (clarified butter), products of the sacred cow, from professional confectioners, and from some other persons of somewhat lower caste rank. Since fire purifies, he may take from almost anyone raw ingredients which will be purified in the process of cooking.

Dumont's Purity-Impurity Principle

Louis Dumont's book, *Homo Hierarchicus*, is a major theoretical work on the caste system. The underlying principle of this hierarchy is purity-impurity. Following Stevenson, Dumont defines impurity as 'the erruption of the biological into social life'. Hindus are temporarily impure when in contact with twelve polluting secretions of the body (Dumont 1970: 61, 49). Castes are separate, but interdependent hereditary groups of occupational specialists. It is the principle of purity-impurity which operates to keep the segments separate from one another. Each *jati* closes its boundaries to lower *jatis*, refusing them the privilege of intermarriage and other contacts defined as polluting to the higher *jati*. Each *jati*, in turn, is excluded by the *jatis* ranking above it in a local caste hierarchy. Thus, differences in degree of pollution create closed segments, as each segment tries to preserve its own degree of purity from contamination by lower castes. It is, in turn, excluded as a contaminator by castes above (Dumont 1970: 59–60, 197).

Biological Substantialism: The Dividual-Particle Theory of Pollution

Dumont, Stevenson, Srinivas and Harper's method of analysis involves the specification of the principles relating to agents and states of impurity and purity. It is not clear in their analyses whether the principles they specify are clearly articulated by native informants or not. Since the three states of purity and impurity mentioned by Harper and Srinivas have names in the Mysorean informants' languages, we may be fairly sure that these stages are recognized by the informants themselves. This is not so clear for Stevenson's principles of internal and external, temporary and permanent pollution. It is also not clear whether native informants could articulate Dumont's point that a principle of purity-impurity results in boundedness, the closure of *jati* units; or whether the point made by Hocart and Gould that lower castes 'absorb the pollution' of upper castes is articulated or recognized by their Hindu informants.

The issue of the natives' understandings, or cognitive view of their own societies was not ascendant in anthropology at the time these scholars were writing in the 1950s and 1960s. Most scholars did not address that issue. In the 1970s, however, the issue of 'emic' versus 'etic' conceptualizations has been in the forefront of social-cultural anthropology. . . .

McKim Marriott, an anthropologist, and Ronald B. Inden, a historian well-versed in Bengali and Sanskrit, have tried to characterize the 'emic' view—the natives' 'model' of the Hindu caste system (1973, 1977). Their 'ethnosociology of the caste system' takes major account of what others, such as Stevenson, have considered as the 'Hindu pollution concept' but treats this concept as part of what Hindus believe about physics, biology, and sociology. Specifically, their view takes up the human bodily contribution to social processes. It can answer such questions as: What is it that actually defiles water for a higher-caste person when it comes from the hands of an Untouchable? What is it about the semen of a higher-caste man that does not pollute a lower-caste female sexual partner?

The Indian anthropologist, Sarat Chandra Roy, suggested some decades ago that lower caste persons may once have been thought to have possessed some invisible power such as the powers of *mana* and *tabu* believed in by Oceanic peoples (Roy 1934, 1937, 1938). Radcliffe-Brown (1952: 139). . . followed by M.N. Srinivas (1952) suggested that ritual power was projected into objects by the attribution of holiness or uncleanliness in people themselves. Thus the sacredness of objects was a projection of a people's reverent attitude. Marriott and Inden would object to these as 'etic' explanations of the human contribution to pollution processes (although they do not actually use the terms 'emic' and 'etic'); these theories come out of anthropology's store of ideas, not out of the minds of native Hindus. Their own explanation aims to be 'emic'; it is an attempt to state the sociology of the natives themselves, a Hindu 'ethnosociology'.

Marriott and Inden draw their understanding not only from the ethnography of everyday avoidances and exchanges, but from Hindu writings, including the Vedas, which concern sacrificial worship, from Brahmanas, Upanishads, from classical books of moral and medical sciences, and from late medieval moral code books of certain castes in Bengal. . . . These writings are sometimes seen by outsiders as 'prescriptive'—as giving principles for behaviour—but Marriott and Inden see in them more than that.

They see them as records of the cognitive concepts, the ways of thinking of reflective, educated Hindus. Hindu native models today may be derived from such writings. By using such sources, Marriott and Inden claim to have found some ways in which Hindus themselves understand caste processes.

What they find is this: Unlike Westerners who think in terms of a duality of separable body and spirit, or body and mind, Hindus think monistically. Hindus believe that a person inherits a *unitary coded substance*. The code 'programmed' into the person's substance or body relates to his or her *varna*, *jati*, sex, and personality.

With respect to *varnadharma*, the code for members of each of the four *varnas* (priests, warrior-rulers, herdsmen-agriculturalists, servants), Marriott and Inden explain the sacrificial superman found in the Ṛig Veda. He is a 'Code Man' from which the 'genera' (*varnas*) of human beings were derived. Each genus (*varna*) is believed to have received its particular code from a different part of the body of the 'Code Man'.

Similarly, one's *jatidharma*, the duty of one's *jati*, is encoded into one's bodily substance, as are the duties for one's sex and personality. Such a code does not determine exact behaviour, however, but represents 'internal formulae for uplifting conduct', prescriptions for what one knows one should do as *naturally* appropriate for one's own kind of person.

There are features of the coded-substance that explain the process of pollution. First of all, this coded-substance is made up of coded-particles (in Sanskrit, *piṇḍas* and other terms). These particles—bits of hair, sweat, saliva, etc.—may be shared or exchanged with others, and it is such particles that mix into food, water, and other things transferred in interpersonal transactions. Thus, one gives off coded-particles and gains coded-particles from others. One should try to gain suitable or better coded-particles (those coming from gods or higher castes), not worse coded particles (those coming from lower castes or defiled persons) than one's own. One may get better particles through 'right eating, right marriage, and other right exchanges and actions' (Marriott and Inden 1977: 233). One may rid oneself of inferior particles through disposal as in excretion, or other processes 'often aided by persons of suitably lower genera'. As understood by Hocart and Gould, lower caste persons absorb pollution, here specified as inferior coded-particles, from higher caste persons.

A second important feature of a coded-substance is that its parts or particles can be loosened to separate and combine with other kinds of coded-substance. . . .

This theory of coded-substances which are inherited, and which break up into coded-particles, especially through the catalyst of heat, to recombine with other kinds of particles, offers a theory of pollution-contagion. Presumably some of the coded-particles of the lower caste person's coded-substance is actually transferred to the higher caste person, through food, water, touch, or contact with the lower caste person's bodily products. Such a theory may strike a Western reader as strange. It is a theory, however, which is to be found in the revered writings of Hindus themselves, and thus represents the native point of view, according to Marriott and Inden.

Marriott and Inden say that the instability of the coded-substance of the person, its ready break-up into particles, shows that the Hindu view of the person is of a one that is 'dividual', a one which divides up into separable portions. Such a 'dividual' image contrasts with the Western image of the person as an 'individual', these authors say. They also assert that the monistic Hindu view which does not separate substance from code—i.e., body from morality—marks it as very different from Westerners' typically dualistic mode of thinking. Because of the instability of a person's coded-substance, the Hindu person must strive to maintain his appropriate coded-substance and possibly better it, not just avoid pollution, Marriott and Inden claim. '. . . the players have at stake also the preservation and transformation of their own natures' (Marriott 1976: 112).

The *Gun*, A Theory of Pollution

Marriott and Inden's student, Marvin Davis (1976), has gone on to explain the nature of 'coded-substance' from the viewpoint of Hindus of West Bengal. Davis learned of this folk-theory largely from interviewing Bengali Hindus, but the theory is drawn from Hindu holy books, including the Bhagavad Gita . . . . Since these works are known widely in India, we may expect to find this theory held in other areas besides West Bengal. Davis's 'emic' explanation, the Hindus' own cognitive model, enlarges the simpler 'etic' models which represent the outsider's views in Stevenson's and Dumont's analyses. Davis's 'emic' explanation connects with philosophical Hinduism as Stevenson's and Dumont's do not. It is not primarily a theory of pollution, but it does incidentally explain pollution and purity.

Here is an outline of this folk model:

All beings and things in the Hindu cosmos are made out of one substance, a female substance called *prakriti*. This basic material becomes differentiated into three substances by the joining of the female *prakrti* with male matter, *purusa*. Thus, a female natural *substance* joins with a male cultural principle, or *code*. So it is that *prakriti* and *purusa* make up what Marriott and Inden have called coded-substance.

The three basic materials (*guns* or *gunas*) formed by the union of *prakrti* and *purusa* are *sattvagun*, *rajogun*, and *tamogun*. *Sattvagun*, a white substance, 'generates goodness and joy and inspires all noble virtues and actions'. *Rajogun*, red, 'produces egoism, selfishness, violence, jealousy, and ambition'. *Tamogun*, black, 'engenders stupidity, laziness, fear, and all sorts of base behaviour' (Davis 1976: 9). Differing beings and phenomena have differing proportions of the three coded-substances.

The hierarchy of beings is composed of Brahma, the creator, at the top, followed by the gods, then humans, then demons, animals, plants, and minerals at the bottom. In Brahma, the three *guns* are present and in balance. In other beings, one or the other *gun* predominates. The gods are largely *sattvagun*. Among men, the four *varnas* differ. The Brahmans are largely *sattvagun*. The Kshatriyas are largely *rajogun*, and the Shudras and Untouchables are largely *tamogun*. Demons and animals are largely *rajogun*, while plants and minerals are largely *tamogun*.

This native theory is close to Stevenson's Hindu pollution concept and Dumont's principle of purity-impurity, since *sattva* may be translated as purity, and *tamogun* as impurity. *Sattvagun* and *tamogun*, however, imply considerably more than just purity and impurity. How does *rajogun* come in? It is a 'material mode that activates the other two *gun*' (Davis 1976: 9).

Foods are related to the three *guns*. 'Cool foods' (milk, clarified butter, most fruits, and vegetables) make *sattvagun*. 'Hot foods' (meat, eggs, onions, mangoes) make *rajogun*. Spoiled or stale foods make *tamogun*, as do beef and alcohol. Food from the gods, *prasad*, is fraught with *sattva*; so it is beneficial to eat food which has been placed before, and hence tasted of, by the gods. The left-over food of the gods then makes *sattvagun*. The left-over food of humans makes *tamogun*, except when left-over food of very high caste persons is eaten by very low-caste persons, when, presumably, it also makes *sattvagun* (Davis 1976: 21).

What Stevenson called 'permanent pollution' may be understood in this theory as admixtures of the *guns* in a *jati*, with *tamogun* in sizeable proportion. The differing proportion of the *guns* in different *jatis* relates to caste diet, work and life-styles, marriage patterns, and inter-caste transactions. Different castes have different diets. Vegetarian castes would be more *sattvagun*; non-vegetarian, more *rajogun*. Those which drink alcohol and eat beef, and left-over and spoiled food would be more *tamogun*. The work of Brahmans makes *sattvagun*; that of scavengers, tanners, prostitutes, work connected with the animal impulses of humans, makes *tamogun*. Occupations that maintain life in the ordinary world such as agriculturalists, herders, artisans, and traders make *rajogun* in their adherents.

According to this theory, Davis agrees with Marriott and Inden that persons and *jatis* do not have fixed coded-substances. Both persons and *jatis* may strive to improve their coded-substances, their admixtures of *guns*, by eating *sattvik* foods and doing *sattvik* work such as religious ritual, meditation, and learning. Similarly, they should try through marriage to maintain or improve the coded-substance of person and *jati*.

Davis relates the Bengali Hindus' theory of human conception. Food changes into digested food, which changes into blood, which changes into flesh, which changes into fat, which changes into marrow from which are derived semen in the male, and uterine blood in the female (Davis 1976: 19). In the conception of a child, the semen of the male and the uterine blood of the female unite. Intra-caste endogamy can be understood as a practice ensuring that these uniting components in conception will transmit to a child blood of equal *gun*-composition from both parents. . . .

Particles of inferior coded-substance, *rajogun* or *tamogun*, may be transferred with boiled food, raw uncooked food (from the hands of Untouchables), or with drinking water. It is less easily transferred through food cooked in the cooling *ghi* which seems to make food fried in *ghi* (clarified butter) productive of *sattvagun*. So a higher caste individual might take food cooked in *ghi* from the hands of a lower caste person, from whom he would not accept boiled rice or drinking water. Since heat tends to purify food, the higher caste person might take raw uncooked food from all but the lowly Untouchable.

The actions which improve one's coded-substance can, through concerted change in habits, raise the coded-substance of the whole caste. . . .

RANKING CASTES BY RULES OF POLLUTION-CONTAGION

The castes in village Khalapur [in north-eastern Uttar Pradesh] may be ranked by the criterion of pollution-contagion. In 1955, eighteen villagers of nine different castes were asked about the ritual interactions they would permit themselves to have with twenty-one other castes. Could the person of the other caste touch one's children? Could he or she touch the informant? Would one take dry food from a person of the other caste? Would one take *pakka* food (cooked in *ghi*) from a person of the other caste? Would one take *kachcha* (boiled) food from a person of the other caste? Could such a person smoke the bowl of one's pipe? Would he or she touch one's water vessel? One's cot? Could the person of the other caste come into one's cooking area?

It was found that these ritual gestures, ones which would involve pollution-contagion, were regularly ordered by the Khalapur respondents by degrees of seriousness of the pollution transmitted. Most serious was the transfer of boiled food, or touching a water vessel, coming into a cooking area, or touching one's earthenware vessel. Least serious was the transfer of dry food, or touching one's children. Food cooked in water is considered to be more easily contaminated than is food protected by being cooked in *ghi* (clarified butter, product of the sacred cow). Water is also readily contaminated. The cooking area must be kept pure, because all food is prepared there. Porous earthenware vessels used for boiling food are more easily polluted than brass vessels which are used for frying or baking, the [impurity] of which can be cleaned by ashes (see figures 1–4). Respondents would allow more castes to perform the less polluting actions with respect to themselves than would allow the more polluting actions.

The number of other castes allowed to perform each action varied according to the respondent's own rank. A Brahman respondent would allow very few other castes to perform the more seriously polluting actions, while a lower caste person, such as a Potter, would allow [a larger number of] other castes to perform the more seriously polluting actions. Furthermore, all respondents tended to allow actions involving pollution to other castes in much the same order. If a Brahman would take *kachcha* food from a person

Figure 1

Ritual Purity Continuum of Six Items

Score 0	1	2	3	4	5	6
	13 touch children	1 touch you	7 smoke bowl of pipe	4 touch brass utensils	8 accept fried (*pakka*) food	9 accept boiled (*kachcha*) food
	10 dry food	2 cot				12 water vessel 3 cooking area 5 earthenware vessels

(Mahar 1959: 139)

Figure 2

Scoring from Six Items of the Purity Pollution Continuum

Score	Items					
0	—					
1	13					
2	13	1				
3	13	1	7			
4	13	1	7	4		
5	13	1	7	4	8	
6	13	1	7	4	8	9

(Mahar 1959: 139)

from any other caste, it would be from a Rajput or Merchant. A Potter woman, of lower caste rank than the Brahman, would take *kachcha* food from a Rajput and Merchant, and also from the Goldsmith and Carpenter.

From the responses of eighteen persons of nine different castes, a ranking of fifteen castes emerged with the Brahman at the top followed by representatives of the Kshatriya and Vaisya *varnas* locally, the Rajputs and Merchants, with the Untouchable Shoe-

Figure 3

Scale-Picture of Responses Indicating Ritual Distance For Manbhi, Brahman Caste, Female, 40

	Can touch our children	Can accept dry, uncooked food	Can touch me	Can sit on our cot	Can smoke bowl of pipe	Can take water from his hand	Can touch our brass vessels	Can accept fried (Pakka) food from him	Can smoke our pipe	Can accept boiled (Kachcha) food from his hand	Can touch our water vessel	Can touch our earthenware vessels	Can come on our cooking area	
Items:**	13	10	1	2	7	11	4	8	6	9	12	3	5	Score
CASTES:														
Rajput	x	x	x	x	x	x	x	x	x	x				10
Merchant	x	x	x	x	x	x	x	x	x	x				10
Water-carrier	x	x	x	x	x	x	x	x	x	[0]	x			10–11
Goldsmith	x	x	x	x	x	x	x	x	x					9
Genealogist	x	x	x	x	x	x	x	x	x					9
Barber	x	x	x	x	x	x	x	x						8
Gosain	x	x	x	x	x	x								6
Shepherd	x	x	x	x	x	x								6
Carpenter	x	x	x	x	x	x								6
Potter	x	x	x	x	[0]	x								5–6
Washerman	x	x	x	x	x									5
Grainparcher	x	x	x	x	x									5
K. P. Weaver	x	[0]	x	x										3–4
Jogi	x	[0]	x	x										3–4
Mus. Rajput	x	x	x											3
Oilpresser	x	x												2
Mirasi	x	0	[x]											1–2–3
Ch. Weaver														0
Shoemaker														0
Chamar														0
Sweeper														0

No. Deviant Responses: 5
Total Responses: 273

(Mahar 1959: 133)

Figure 4

Scorings of Castes Derived from Manbhi's Scale-Picture (Figure 3)

Score	
10	Rajput, Merchant, Water-carrier
8	Genealogist, Goldsmith, Barber
6	Gosain, Shepherd, Carpenter, Potter
5	Washerman, Grainparcher
4	Jogi, Kabir Panthi Weaver
3	Muslim Rajput
2	Oilpresser, Mirasi
0	Chamar Weaver, Shoemaker, Chamar Sweeper

(Mahar 1959: 137)

makers, Chamars, and Sweepers at the bottom. The ranking of fifteen castes for Khalapur [was as follows] [see Mahar 1959]:

1 Brahman
2 Rajput
3 Merchant
4 Goldsmith
5 Genealogist
6 Barber
7 Water-carrier
8 Grainparcher
9 Shepherd
10 Muslim Rajput
11 Oilpresser
12 Beggar
13 Shoemaker
14 Chamar
15 Sweeper

A number of subsequent studies affirmed the relationship between pollution-contagion and caste ranking (see Mayer 1960, Marriott 1968, Beck 1972). What has become increasingly clear, however, is that pollution-contagion is not the only basis for caste ranking in locality. H. N. C. Stevenson referred to *secular* criteria of stratification, especially economic and political power of various kinds. This stratification may well be reflected in what might appear to be a hierarchy based on the Hindu Pollution Concept (Stevenson 1954: 63).

Louis Dumont who emphasized the purity-impurity principle as the basis of hierarchy in the caste system was, nevertheless, troubled by the high ranking (usually just below the highest ranking Brahmans) of the Kshatriya-style dominant castes whose life-style was often quite impure. They usually ate meat and drank liquor, and as warriors indulged in violence, at least in the past, as did the Rajputs of Khalapur. Their diet and occupation might be considerably less pure than those of castes ranked below them such as the Vaishya Merchants. As in Khalapur, the Merchants are strict vegetarians, and follow a peaceful non-violent occupation of shop-keeping or trading.

To solve this inconsistency in ranking castes by purity-impurity alone, Dumont turned to the writings of the ancient Hindus concerning the four *varnas*. Here he found a clear subordination of the king (Kshatriya) to the priest (Brahman). The religious principle, the principle of purity, was given highest priority, as indicated by the highest rank being given to the Brahman priest. However, for the king to perform his duty, which was to rule, he had to have high status; otherwise the king's dignity, his usefulness, would be denied (Dumont 1970a: 77). So the king and, analogously, the local Kshatriya-style dominant castes, receive rank just below the Brahman priest, even though they may be more impure (or more *rajogun* than *sattvagun*) than the Vaishya who are in rank below them.

While Dumont rather lamely explains the high rank of the dominant caste or kings by introducing the requirement that they be respected by their subjects—they must be dignified—he does not take up the problem of ranking lower castes which do not seem to have anything to do with removing pollution from the higher castes. How is the rank of certain artisans determined? Why in Khalapur does the Goldsmith have higher rank than the Grain-parcher? Neither seems to function as a remover of pollution for higher castes. The greater skill of the Goldsmith and the preciousness of gold perhaps accounts for his higher rank.

McKim Marriott has suggested that other principles besides purity and pollution [operate] as criteria in ranking castes. The giver of food is always ranked higher than the receiver. To reverse this statement, the served is ranked higher than the servant who is paid in food.

Marriott notes that the work of many castes in Kishan Garhi, Uttar Pradesh does not involve the removal of pollution. The work of Carpenters, Gardeners, Jogi devotees, Watermen, Cottoncarders is: . . . explicitly intended to exalt the master and his caste, not by avoiding or subtracting negative qualities, but by adding proof of his honour, religious merit, liberality, or power (Marriott 1968: 144–5).

Servants are usually paid in the currency of foods and grain, so food transactions reflect the social relationship of served and servant. Marriott suggests that the food most readily accepted in intercaste transactions are also the most expensive and preferred foods. *Kachcha* food (boiled food) is considered to be inferior and less preferred because it lacks the very much preferred *ghi* (clarified butter). *Pakka* food, made with *ghi*, is superior food . . . 'the only kind of meal which can be offered in feasts to gods, to guests of high affinal status, to those who provide honorific services, and generally to persons of other castes . . . Ghee (clarified butter) is the costliest of the fats known locally' (Marriott 1968: 144).

Left-over food and feces can be understood not only as polluted substances, so that those having to remove them are polluted, untouchable, but also as materials of 'small monetary and nutritional worth'. Their removal indicates the 'extremity of domination' of the servant by the served (Marriott 1968: 144).

Raw foods which are readily accepted by high castes from lower castes often include highly preferred, costly foods such as wheat flour, sugar, *ghi*, and fruit. Unground grain may be preferred, because it can be used readily as a currency in a variety of subsequent transactions (Marriott 1968: 143).

Marriott concludes that the heart of the system of caste rank is serving and being served, not purity-impurity. The end result is the maintenance of a certain kingly style of life which the dominant caste particularly tries to enjoy, and which other castes may also emulate. In Kishan Garhi, in fact, an action may be defined as polluting in some contexts, but not polluting in others. The key is the maintenance of the subordination of the servant to the served. . . .

Marriott has gone on to claim that Indian society is highly transactional (Marriott 1976). With respect to caste, the giver is of superior rank than the receiver, and the served is superior to the server. This exchange of service for gifts of food and other goods seems to be at the heart of the caste system, and is, of course, at the heart of the *jajmani* system. A serving caste's capacity to pollute is presumably adjusted to the degree of servitude. . . .

Castes can be ranked by the balance between the inter-caste

transactional contexts in which a caste is a *giver* and those in which a caste is a *receiver* of foods and other gifts. While other castes may exchange services and products with one another, the largest giver is the landed dominant caste or castes who control the most important food, grain.

Do we then, by Marriott's analysis, end up with a kind of economic model of the caste system? Is purity-impurity an incidental, even epiphenomenal concept? Does a caste's capacity to pollute match the degree of its servitude? This is what Marriott seems to be saying. Yet we still have the problem of why the Potter has a lower-ranking servitude than does the Carpenter, or why the Shoemaker ranks below the Laundryman. To explain such rankings, we must either use the economist's arguments about supply and demand, the sociologist's arguments about difficult-to-acquire skills being more highly valued and ranked, or the Hindu pollution concept which suggests that skills connected with more polluted substances are ranked lower than those connected with less polluted substances. By the Hindu pollution concept, the Shoemaker dealing with highly polluted leather, a product of a dead animal, is more polluted than the Washerman who deals with filth of living humans.

How does Marriott reconcile the coded-substance, the *jatidharma* of various transactors, with his emphasis on servitude? Coded-particles are transferred in inter-caste transactions, his ethnosociology says. Marriott, like Dumont and Stevenson, seems left with the problem of the relationship between the coded-particles of *jatidharma*, so much like purity and pollution, and power relationship of a politico-economic sort epitomized in the dominant caste. Is there any real inconsistency? The serving-and-being-served is the *form* of the relationship. The removal of pollution and avoidance of pollution by the avoidance of certain transactions (the lower caste transmitting polluted food or water to the higher caste) is part of the *content* of such consistently hierarchical relations. That other services may be involved, such as assuring the higher caste patron of various honours, may be accepted as part of the content of the relationship, as well.

The importance of purity relates to the need for the Brahman to be pure in his transactions with the gods. The importance of honour and the submission of the subordinate relates to the need for the king or ruler—in the village, the dominant caste—to carry out his apical role, his kingly style of life.

Purity-Impurity as Social Integrator

The absence during much of Indian history of a single integrated political unit was balanced by the universality of certain cultural institutions. The principle of purity-impurity is especially important in the absence, as well, of an ecclesiastical organization enforcing both hierarchy and caste boundaries.

Despite the lack of an established religious organization, the presence of Brahmans in a region seems to correlate with much more rigorous prohibitions against lower castes. Thus, in South India where Brahmans were not only powerful spiritually but also materially, such prohibitions were very strong. The system is considerably weaker in Ceylon and in the foothills of the Himalayas where there are few Brahmans. Similarly, untouchability is weaker in the Panjab and in Uttar Pradesh, areas strongly influenced for several hundred years by Muslim rule (Dumont 1970: 58).

Among Christians and Muslims living in India and among Hindus in some overseas communities, caste exists *without* an ideology of purity and pollution—suggesting that this concept is not essential for the existence of caste systems among Indians (Dumont 1970: 46). Dumont, who sees the principle of pollution and purity as central in the Hindu caste system, explains these anomalies thus. He hypothesizes that the Hindu setting influences Muslim and Christian communities decisively, since each of these non-Hindu religions failed to offer any alternative social structure to displace the already existing pre-conversion caste system (Dumont 1970: 210–11).

Further Readings

Ahmed, Akbar S.,

1988 *Discovering Islam: Making Sense of Muslim History and Society.* Routledge and Kegan Paul, London.

Drawing upon textual materials, fieldwork in Pakistan, and travel in several countries, Ahmed attempts an answer to the question as to what it means to be a Muslim today. Without losing touch with the theological foundations of Islam and its worldwide historical vicissitudes, Ahmed succeeds in bringing out the significance of cultural settings and historical specifities for the definition of Islamic identity.

Babb, Lawrence A.

1975 *The Divine Hierarchy: Popular Hinduism in Central India,* Columbia University Press, New York.

Based on intensive fieldwork, this ethnographically rich book presents an account of the beliefs and rituals that consitute Hinduism in the lives of villagers in central India.

Carman, John B. and Frederique A. Marglin, eds.,

1985 *Purity and Auspiciousness in Indian Society,* E.J. Brill, Leiden.

This set of papers by anthropologists and indologists illumines the related key concepts of purity and auspiciousness from Hindu, Buddhist and Jain perspectives.

Keyes, Charles F. and E. Valentine Daniel, eds.,

1983 *Karma: An Anthropological Inquiry,* University of California Press, Berkeley and Los Angeles.

O'Flaherty, Wendy Doniger, ed.,

1980 *Karma and Rebirth in Classical Indian Traditions,* University of California Press, Berkeley and Los Angeles.

These two indispensable volumes bring together the work of indologists, philosophers, and anthropologists on the central notion of *karma* in the cultural traditions of India.

Madan, T.N., ed.,
1989 (1982) *Way of Life: King, Householder, Renouncer*, Motilal Banarsidass, Delhi.
Contributed by anthropologists, indologists and philosophers, the essays in this book discuss Hindu and Buddhist conceptions of the good life.

McLeod, W. H.,
1976 *Guru Nanak and the Sikh Religion*, Oxford University Press, Delhi.
A well-researched and balanced account of the basic teachings of the first guru of the Sikhs and subsequent developments.

Singer, Milton, ed.,
1966 *Krishna: Myths, Riteṣ and Attitudes*, University of Chicago Press, Chicago.
This set of essays by anthropologists and indologists discusses a number of aspects of Hindu Vaishnavism focussing on the worship of Krishna and covering metaphysics, ritual performances and personal devotion.

II

Sacred Space

A believer's relationship with and experience of the sacred is generally realized in a place-time framework. In classical Hindu thought, the virtuous person or moral agent (*patra*, literally 'vessel'), that is one who lives according to *dharma*, is comprehensible only in social (*varna-ashrama*) and spatio-temporal (*desh-kal*) settings. A liberated person would of course be one who has transcended these limitations. The manner in which religious traditions define and classify space and time as sacred, opposed to secular or profane, varies but the notion is widespread.

In the Islamic tradition the earth, and indeed the whole universe, is God's creation and there is no such thing as profane ground. Even so, the mosque is designated as the ideal sacred place for collective prayers and the *ka'bah* in the centre of the mosque at Mecca is the holiest ground, indeed the destination of the pious pilgrim (*haji*). For the Hindu, too, the earth and all that stands on it bears divine signature: in fact she is a divinity herself. And yet there are special holy places, like the *tirtha* where rivers, themselves sacred, meet.

What Mecca is to the Muslim, Prayag—the confluence of the Ganga, the Yamuna and the unseen Sarasvati—is to the Hindu, and Bodh Gáya—where Gautama found enlightenment—is to the Buddhist. Sacred places or centres, the believers expect, will reveal to them man's place in the cosmos and transcend the merely physical and social worlds. This is why sacred places are never 'chosen' but 'discovered' by man. As sociologists, we are however committed to the view that not only society but even the sacred is socially constructed—and this includes sacred space and sacred time.

The first reading in this part deals with one of the best known and most fascinating examples of sacred space known to us in ethnographic literature, namely the buffalo dairy among the Toda of Nilgiri Hills in South India. Here we read Anthony Walker's account of a place that is man-made and yet sacred—we read, in fact, of the sacred represented by gods and goddesses that live in the mountains and yet are everywhere, of animals who are both less and more than human beings and both useful and sacred, of herdsmen who are priests and who combine economic and ritual activities. The basic principle of social life is rich and yet simple, conceiving of an all-embracing sacredness which admits of encompassed contraries and of degrees of purity.

The Toda dairy is a unique institution. Heralivala Seneviratne's essay presents a more familiar example of sacred space, namely a temple—the Temple of the Tooth at Kandy in Sri Lanka—which he defines as a spatial expression of a particular mode of worship. We encounter in this article a variety of forms, architectural as well as ritual, and multiple layers of significance, both individual and collective, private and public. We meet the lay devotee, the monk and the sacred king. We discover equivalences and transformations which link the temple-palace, the cardinal square, the mundane city and the divine macrocosm in one complex whole. We are shown that sacred places are not only enclosed but they also unfold, as it were, and the sacred-secular, or religious-political, dichotomy is of limited interpretative value in Buddhism and, indeed, in all of India's religious traditions.

Hardwar, at the foothills of the mountains, is one of India's holy towns, located on the banks of the Ganga, sending down its holy waters into the plains and receiving homage from the pilgrims who come here to wash off sins and earn ritual merit. Even the last traces of demerit that cling to the half-burnt bones and ashes of a dead Hindu are finally washed off here by sinking them in the river. Ann

Grodzins Gold's sensitive portrayal of such a pilgrimage to so holy a place is the theme of the fourth reading.

A buffalo dairy for work and worship, a temple for devotion, ritual, and authority, a sacred river at a particular turn of its flowing journey ultimately lead us to the sacred mega-city, Kashi. In Diana Eck's account of it, we discover the rich complexity of the notion of sacred space, multi-dimensional and multi-layered. Kashi includes in itself all the other sacred places of India; it is where man and god dwell together, where birth and death merge; it is therefore the embodiment of wisdom for the Hindu—indeed it is Brahman, the Supreme Reality.

The first four readings describe particular sacred places. In the last, by Veena Das, we move from the concrete to the abstract to explore Hindu concepts of space. Based on a manual for domestic ritual performances, the essay seeks to analyse spatial logic, in terms of such notions as the left-right dichotomy and the cardinal points, and in relation to certain specific rites such as those related to birth, death and the feeding of ancestors. The ethnographic and theoretical materials illumine one another.

The Toda Dairy

ANTHONY R. WALKER

Toda ritual life revolves, for the most part, around the operations of their sacred dairies, wherein specially ordained dairymen-priests process the milk of buffaloes of appropriate ritual grade. . . . By way of preview I should like to quote Emeneau's (1938: 111–12) succinct description of Toda religious practices, and at the same time point out how we differ in emphasis. He wrote:

> The religion of the Todas is a highly ritualized buffalo-cult. Every important operation connected with the buffaloes is conducted according to rule, milking and converting the milk successively into butter and ghee, giving salt to the buffaloes, taking them on migration to fresh pastures, burning over the pastures, giving a buffalo a name when it has calved for the first time, introducing new utensils into the dairy and preparing new coagulant for the milk, rebuilding and rethatching the dairy, consecrating dairymen, and even drinking buttermilk from the dairy. All the rules apply to the sacred buffaloes; ordinary ones are treated with much less ceremony. Infractions of the rules involve pollution, and most of the precautions surrounding the cult seem designed to prevent pollution of the milk by contact with profane persons or utensils. The milk, as the primary product, is most liable to pollution and the successive operations finally result in ghee, which possesses so little sanctity that it can be sold to outsiders.

Where Emeneau gives priority to the buffaloes I prefer to begin with the dairy, which by all evidence appears to be the prime source of sanctity. It will also become clear . . . that a distinction merely between 'sacred' (temple) and 'ordinary' (domestic) buffaloes is too simple, and even misleading.

In addition to the corpus of beliefs and practices associated with the sacred dairies, Toda religion also encompasses a belief in certain traditional anthropomorphic divinities. Although care and

Excerpted from Anthony R. Walker 'Dairies, Dairymen and Dairy Herds', in *The Toda of South India: A New Look*, Hindustan Publishing Corporation, Delhi, 1986, pp. 119–28.

concern for these gods and goddesses plays a relatively small part in Toda religious life, some of them are intimately associated with the dairies, and so we may usefully begin by looking at these supernatural beings.

Deities

Toda have a traditional pantheon of gods and goddesses who are sometimes mentioned in formal prayers and their attributes and activities recalled in legends (cf. Rivers 1906:443–57). These Toda divinities are called by the general name *töwtiṭ*,* meaning 'gods (*töw*) of the mountains (*tiṭ*)', because most of them are believed to reside on particular Nilgiri peaks, although the river gods are also included in the . . . category. These *töwtiṭ* are associated in a particularly important way with the sacred dairies, since several of them are said to have created the *ïtwïḍmoḏ* (Rivers's *etudmad*) or 'principal settlements', and to have instituted the dairy operations there.

Of all these traditional anthropomorphic deities, the goddess Tö·kiṣy is clearly the most important to the Toda. To her is attributed the division of the sacred buffaloes and dairies between the subcastes and clans. Indeed she is believed to be the creator and supporter of the greater part of the social and ritual institutions of the Toda people, even of the Toda themselves. . . .

Tö·kiṣy is particularly associated with the hamlet of No·ṣ, for it was here that she is said to have divided the buffaloes into their various grades of sanctity, so giving No·ṣ for all time the status of preeminent Toda settlement; but she is also believed to be all-pervasive and omnipresent. Like Rivers (1906: 186) before me, I was told that Tö·kiṣy lives in England and America, just as she lives in the Nilgiris.

But neither Tö·kiṣy nor any of the other *töwtiṭ* constitute so immediate a divine presence as the *töwno·ṛ*, 'gods (*töw*) of the sacred places (*no·ṛ*)'. These are the gods of the dairy-complexes or, more correctly, the gods which are the dairy-complexes. In other words the Toda view their dairies, together with all the contents of the buildings and the associated pens, calfsheds, pasturage and water supply, not merely as sacred but as divine, partaking in the divinity of the *töwno·ṛ*. Conceived for the most part as a diffused force, *töwno·ṛ*. occasionally are thought of in anthropomorphic terms.

* *This word appears as töwəiṭ in the original.* Editor.

Thus Toda sometimes talk or sing of a *töwno·ṛ* 'becoming angry' or 'attending the council of the gods'.

Not all Toda dairies fall into the *töwno·ṛ*, or divine, category. Those that do, include the dairies isolated from the domestic settlement, and those located within the hamlets designated as *ïtwïḍmoḏ* (*ïtwïḍ* important, principal'). As previously mentioned, these principal hamlets are said to have been created by the *töwtiṭ* or 'gods of the mountain'. There are other, less important hamlets which Toda call *maxmoḏ* (*max* 'inferior'), whose dairies are not regarded as *töwno·ṛ*. In contrast to the divinely-created principal hamlets, these subsidiary settlements are said to be of human origin, established from time to time when the herds of principal hamlets became too large to be tended there. The dairies of the *maxmoḏ*, therefore, are ritually inferior to those of the *ïtwïḍmoḏ*, and dairymen-priests are not inducted directly into them. A man who is to serve in a subsidiary hamlet's dairy must first be ordained for, and serve a short time in, a *töwno·ṛ* dairy belonging to the same clan.

The Dairy-Complexes

In outward appearance the Toda dairy buildings, with two extant exceptions, resemble the traditional barrel-vaulted dwelling huts of this people (Figures 1 and 2). The exceptions are buildings with a circular base and conical roof. . . . The front and rear walls of some barrel-vaulted dairies are now made of stone rather than the traditional wood. Some front walls have carvings of buffaloes, sun, moon and even the five Pāṇḍava brothers of Mahābhārata fame on them,[1] the work not of the Toda themselves but of hired stonecarvers. Inside, the majority of dairies are divided into two rooms, front and back (Figure 1), although certain types have just a single room. A few dairies have three rooms (Figure 2); such a building is found only in a hamlet which doubles as a funeral place for males. Usually the funeral places are separated from the hamlets, but where a hamlet is also used as a funeral place, one of its dairies must have three rooms, because at one point in the obsequies the male corpse has to be laid inside the temple, and yet the sacred dairy vessels must be preserved from the contamination of death. Both require-

[1] Recent Toda attempts to identify with the Hindu mainstream have included associating themselves with the Pāṇḍava brothers who, as may be recalled, were all married to the same wife, Draupadī. Thus the Pāṇḍavas offer the Toda a convenient Hindu 'mythical charter' for their own traditional practice of adelphic polyandry.

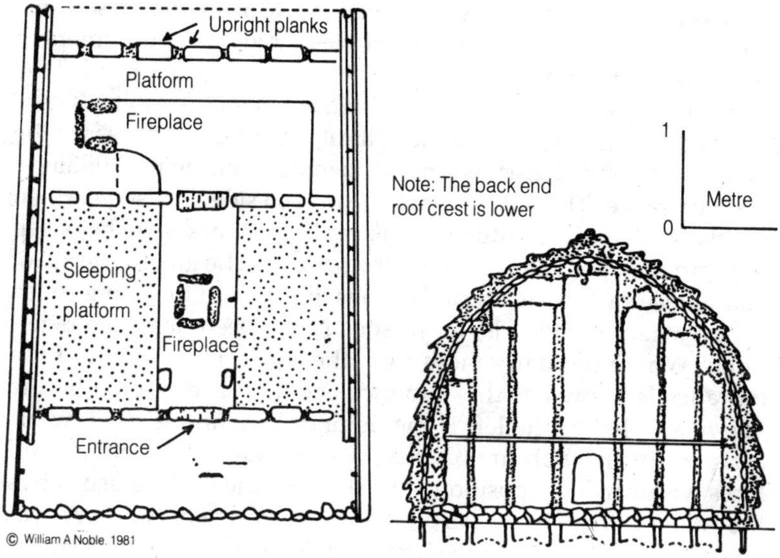

Figure 1. A Töwfiɫy Poɫy.

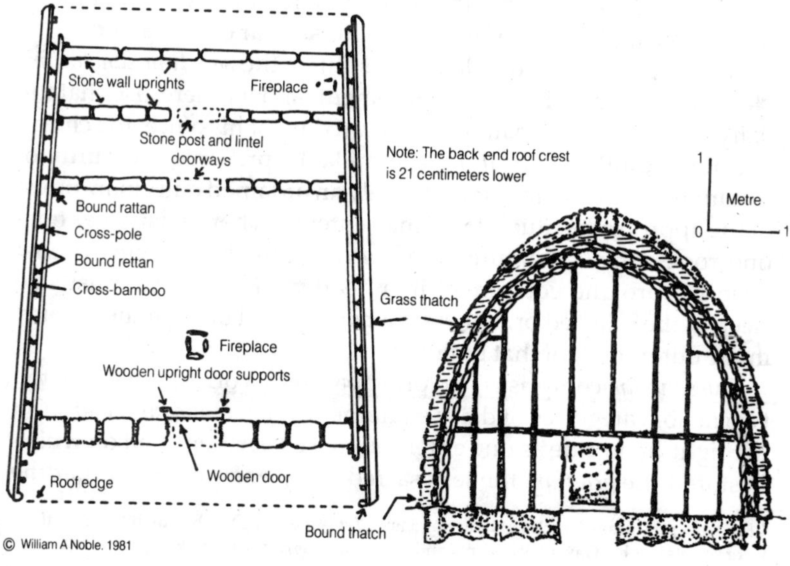

Figure 2. The No s to r foɫy and funerary dairy.

ments are fulfilled by having a middle room which serves to separate the corpse, in the outer room, from the sacred dairy equipment in the innermost room.

In a two-roomed dairy, the partition between the rooms is constructed like the front and back walls of the building. Access to the inner room is through a low narrow opening similar to the building's main entrance. The outer room has, on each side, a raised earthen couch like that of the ordinary dwelling hut; on these couches sleep the dairyman and his assistant, if he has one. The great majority of dairies face eastwards, the auspicious direction of the rising sun; a very few face westwards, for reasons I have been unable to determine. Where the dairy faces east, the couch to the right of the entrance is known as the 'superior bed' and is occupied by the dairyman; that to the left is the 'inferior bed' and is used by his assistant, usually an unordained boy or youth. Where the dairy faces westward, the position of the two couches is reversed. Thus the 'superior bed' is always on the northern side of the dairy, but again Toda informants have been unable to tell me why. Between the two couches is a fireplace, used not for cooking but merely for warmth. Certain equipment not associated with the dairy ritual is kept in this outer room: a bamboo water vessel for the dairyman's ablutions, an axe for chopping firewood and a basket for bringing rice or other foodgrains into the dairy. Firewood is stacked in the outer room and the dairyman keeps his secular clothing here.

The inner room of the dairy constitutes the *sanctum sanctorum*. Here is kept the sacred dairy equipment, and it is here also that the dairyman performs the most important duty of his office: the churning of milk into butter and buttermilk. To preserve the purity of this inner room and its contents, only an ordained dairyman-priest of the appropriate ritual status may enter it. Where a dairy has only one room, this constitutes the *sanctum* and the dairyman must keep his profane equipment in a nearby calfshed. He must also sleep in the calfshed or, if there is a two-roomed dairy in the hamlet, in the outer room of that building.

The *sanctum* comprises two principal areas, corresponding to the two major categories of dairy equipment: *er̲taṭfar̲ and po·taṭ far*.[2] On the right-hand side as one enters is a raised earthen shelf on which is stored the *er̲tatfar̲*, the less sacred dairy equipment, and at the

[2] *Far̲*, from *par̲*, means 'articles of house or dairy'. *Taṭ* is the name for the bulbous red earthenware vessels in which raw milk is stored and churned. *Po·* is from *po·s̲* 'milk'; hence *po·taṭ* is 'milk pot.' The etymology of *er̲* (in *er̲taṭ*) is unknown.

back of the *sanctum* is another such shelf, or ledge, on which the *po·taṭfar̠* is kept. The *er̠taṭfar̠* comprises principally the earthenware and bamboo vessels (no metal ones are allowed in the dairy) used to store and to carry away the products of the dairy: butter, buttermilk and ghee. The *er̠taṭ-po·lmačok,* for example, is the bamboo cylinder (like a *pïn* but shorter) in which buttermilk is taken out of the dairy. *Er̠taṭ* earthenware vessels are also used for the dairyman's cooking purposes. The dairy lamp is included in this category, as are the firesticks with which the dairyman produces fire by friction. Because some of the *er̠taṭ* equipment comes into contact with the impure world outside the dairy, the whole category is considered much less sacred than the *po·taṭfar̠*: vessels and other utensils used for milking and for storing and churning the milk.

The *po·taṭ* itself is a large, bulbous earthenware pot in which the milk is churned; the equipment which takes its name from this pot includes the bamboo milking vessel (*po·taṭpïn*), a cane used to keep the calves at bay during milking, a small earthen pot for the wet butter which is added to the milk during churning, the rattan churning stick with its accompanying rope and rattan rings, rattan straps used for carrying the earthenware vessels when they must be transferred to another dairy, and rattan base rings which support the bulbous pots. All these objects of the *po·tat̠* category must be preserved in a state of high ritual purity, most particularly those which come into contact with the milk itself. The total separation of the *poṭatfar̠* from the impure secular world requires that the products of the churning must always be transferred to vessels of the *er̠taṭ* category before they are removed from the dairy. And even within the *sanctum* itself, the two categories of equipment are always kept apart, to prevent the defilement of the more sacred by the less sacred one.

On the left side of the inner room is the fireplace where the dairyman cooks his food. This fire, unlike that of the outer room, is usually kept burning throughout the period that the dairy is in use. Should it go out, the dairyman must light it with fire produced by friction. Ordinary matches or lighters, defiled by their association with the impure world outside the dairy, are not allowed within the dairy building at all. The fire in the outer room is lit with a firebrand from the inner room.

Certain of the more sacred dairies traditionally possess ritual objects which, although classed as *po·taṭfar̠*, are held to be much more sacred than all other dairy appurtenances. These are called *moṇy* (Rivers's *mani*) and are attached to the back wall of the *sanctum*. Most ethnographers of Toda society have described these sacred objects as 'bells', albeit 'without tongues', as Rivers (1906: 424) reports. So far as I have been able to determine, only a very few of the extant *moṇy* even resemble bells. Some are pieces of iron of no recognizable shape or utility; others are silver or gold rings, and at least one was reported to me as being a smallish metal vase, some two-thirds gold and one-third silver. Since access to Toda dairies is forbidden to all but ordained Toda dairymen-priests, and the *moṇy* are always covered with ferns (believed to protect them from defilement) whenever they must be taken out of the dairy, I have never had the opportunity to examine one closely.

The fact that these *moṇy*, whether bell-shaped or not, are hung (encased in rattan strips) around the necks of sacred buffaloes to be sacrificed at a funeral and that one used to be hung around a buffalo's neck as the highest grade of Toda dairy (now defunct) when the temple herd was being moved, suggests that they might well have their origin in cattle-bells. Perhaps other objects that were considered sacred came in time to be identified with the cattle-bells and were then given the same name, *moṇy*, which certainly means 'bell' in many of the Dravidian languages.

Another dairy vessel, an earthenware pot of the type called *mu·* (similar to the *taṭ* but smaller), is unique in that it is not kept inside the dairy building at all. This *mu·* is buried in the ground at some distance from the dairy, either at the entrance to the buffalo pen or in a *shola* not far from the dairy area of the hamlet. The purity of the dairy, as we shall see, is particularly linked with this buried pot, and any time the dairy is defiled by contact with impure persons or objects, part of the purificatory ritual involves digging up this *mu·* and replacing it with a new one.

The Routine of the Dairy

The principal objectives of the Toda sacred dairy operations are for the dairyman-priest, a man ritually more pure than ordinary men, to milk the temple buffaloes in his charge and to process their milk in the dairy, producing butter, buttermilk and ghee. The milk drawn for a dairy is sacred. Of the milk products, on the other hand, buttermilk and butter have much less sanctity and ghee none at all. Thus it is possible to interpret the entire Toda dairying ritual as a procedure for diluting the extreme sanctity of the milk in order that its final product, ghee, may be consumed by all.

Temple buffaloes are for the most part owned by individual families. Only certain very sacred herds, as we shall see, are or were owned by a patriclan as a whole. When several families in a single hamlet own temple animals, they may jointly hire a dairyman-priest to look after all of them. In this case the owners share both the expenses (dairyman's food and wages) and the profits (from ghee sales) according to the number of buffaloes they give into the dairyman's care. Alternatively, if the number of temple buffaloes is very large, each owning family may have one of its members act as dairyman-priest for its own animals. In such a case, one dairy may have two or even three resident priests.

The daily routine at the dairy begins soon after dawn when the dairyman leaves the outer room of the dairy, or wherever else he has spent the night, and salutes the rising sun. To do this, he first removes his shawl from his right shoulder—a ritual sign of respect—and then raises his open right hand vertically to his forehead, at the same time uttering the single word *so my*, 'lord'.[3] After this, he goes to the buffalo pen and releases the animals. An unordained man or boy may also perform this task, for although only a priest may milk the temple buffaloes, it is permissible for an ordinary male (but never a female) to touch them.

Leaving the buffaloes to graze in the vicinity of the hamlet, the dairyman returns to his dairy to process the milk which he drew on the previous evening. With his churning stick he breaks up the milk, by now coagulated, which has been stored overnight in the earthenware *po·taṭ*. Then he pours off some of the milk into another earthenware pot called *aḍymu·*, leaving one or two litres in the *po·taṭ*. To the milk in this first vessel the dairyman adds a little butter from a previous churning, together with some water, and proceeds to churn the mixture until it separates into butter and buttermilk. He pours the buttermilk into an earthenware vessel of *eṟtaṭ* grade, called *parfy*, leaving only the butter in the *po· tuṭ*. Then he adds more milk from the *aḍymu·* and repeats the operation, continuing in this fashion until he has exhausted his milk supply. Finally he removes the butter and stores it in its special earthenware vessel, another *mu·*.

His churning work completed, the dairyman prepares his milking equipment, putting a little buttermilk coagulant, *pep*, into his bamboo

[3] Borrowed from Tamil, and ultimately derived from the Sanskrit ***savamin***, master, lord.

milking vessel, the *po·taṭpïn*, and dabbing some butter inside the rim. *Pep*, which hastens coagulation, is also ritually important; the butter is to anoint the teats of the buffaloes, easing the milking task. He picks up the short rattan cane with which he will control the calves and is ready to leave the dairy. Stepping outside, the dairyman turns and salutes the dairy by raising his milking vessel and cane in his right hand to his forhead. Then he goes to the buffaloes in his care and milks them, usually not far away. Each time his milking vessel is full he returns to the dairy to empty it into the *po·taṭ*.

When the milking is finished, the dairyman comes out of his dairy and hails the dwelling area of the hamlet, calling out that he is now ready to distribute buttermilk from his recent churning. An ordinary man or youth comes to the dairy and receives the buttermilk in an *e̱rtaṭ* grade *po·lmačok*. This he carries to a prescribed spot, which may or may not be marked with stones, at the boundary between the sacred and secular areas of the hamlet. The women come to this boundary point and he pours the buttermilk into their vessels, which may be of any kind, for them to take away to their households for consumption.

Now the dairyman prepares and eats his morning meal, which he cooks in the inner rooms of the dairy and eats in the outer one. His fare comprises rice, frequently cooked in buttermilk but sometimes in milk, eaten with a slab of butter or ghee; his drink is either water or buttermilk.

If he has enough butter from his churning, the dairyman may now make ghee, using the fire in the inner room of the dairy for this purpose. The ghee, if there is much of it, is likely to be sent out for sale in the Nilgiri bazaars.

So ends the morning's dairy work; the dairyman leaves the dairy, closing the door behind him. He may now accompany the buffaloes to pasture or else busy himself in the vicinity of the hamlet, collecting water and cutting firewood. Frequently, my own observations suggest, he spends a good part of the day snoozing in the shade or chatting with men who come to see him. He may visit the domestic area of the hamlet and even enter the dwellings, provided that he avoids contact with any part of the structure other than the sleeping platform and floor, and provided also that the three primary symbols of womanhood—pestle, winnowing basket and broom have first been removed from the house.

Around 4 p.m. the more highly ritualized afternoon dairying

procedures begin. The dairyman bows down at the entrance to the dairy, touches his forehead to the threshold and enters the building. Next he bows at the threshold of the inner room, enters, and touches first a vessel of the less sacred *er̠taṭfar̠* and then one of the more sacred *po·taṭfar̠*. He fans up the fire or, if necessary, rekindles it by using his firesticks, and then lights the dairy lamp. Lighting the lamp is an especially important ritual act, during which the dairyman recites the prayer of his particular dairy. Discounting the brief utterance *so·my* in the morning, this is the first formal invocation of the day. The prayer begins with a recitation of the *kwas̠m* (sacred names) of the hamlet, the dairy, the buffaloes, the cattle pen and nearby natural phenomena like hills, streams, swamps, etc. (cf. Emeneau 1974: 24–5), and ends with a series of requests for boons. Several examples of this latter part of the dairyman's prayer were recorded by Emeneau (1974: 16), one of which he translates as follows (I have altered his format slightly):

> May butter become sufficient for rubbing on the priest's garment! May butter become sufficient for rubbing on the priest's front lock of hair! May that which gives milk give milk! May that which grows grow! May the barren women bear children! May the barren buffaloes bear calves!
>
> May the god of the dairy subdue disease! May the god of the dairy subdue illness!
>
> May the god give us living children! May the god give us living calves! May the god subdue forest dogs! May the god subdue jungle dogs! May the god subdue creepers that catch on the leg! May the god subdue thunder that strikes on the head!
>
> May the god subdue the messenger of death! May the god subdue the Tamilians!

After the lamp has been lit and the prayer recited, the dairyman churns the morning's milk, stores the butter and buttermilk properly, and then milks the buffaloes. Once this task is finished, he pens the animals for the night and, facing the entrance to the pen, recites the same prayer that he used when lighting the dairy lamp. His dairy work concluded, the dairyman prepares and eats his evening meal, after which he may retire to bed.

The foregoing basic description of the dairy, and of the daily routine associated with it, holds good for all Toda dairies.... Both dairies and buffalo herds are graded into a complex hierarchy according to relative sanctity; the higher they are, the more elaborate is the ritual associated with the daily tasks of the dairyman, and the higher must be the purity in which the dairy, its appurtenances, and the dairyman himself are maintained. This in turn requires increasingly stringent precautions against defilement of the dairy complex, including more elaborate ceremonies to purify the man who is to become the priest and more severe rules of conduct for the dairyman's daily life.

The Meaning of Space in the Temple of the Tooth in Kandy

HERALIVALA L. SENEVIRATNE

In the first part of this paper, I describe the space of the Temple of the Tooth, known as the Palace of the Tooth Relic, in Kandy, Sri Lanka. In the second part, I attempt to contextualize the Temple within the broader sacred building complex of the city, suggesting that elements of cosmo-magical symbolism,[1] common in South and Southeast Asia, underlie this complex.

There are two varieties of religious buildings in Buddhist Sri Lanka, *vihāra* and *dēvāla*. *Vihāra*, which we can designate by the term 'temple', are Buddhist temples which house images of the Buddha and his disciples. *Dēvāla* are 'shrines of the gods', containing images of the gods derived primarily from the Hindu pantheon, but incorporated into Buddhist worship. We may use the term 'shrine' to refer to them. Although the Temple of the Tooth houses a representation of the Buddha, namely the Tooth relic of the Buddha known as Daladā, and is therefore a *vihāra*, it must be classed in terms of architecture and space, in the *dēvāla* (i.e., 'shrine of the gods') category rather than the *vihāra* (the 'Buddhist temple') category. The reason for this is that in the state-sponsored cult at the Temple of the Tooth, the Tooth Relic is treated as a divinized representation of the Buddha: although the Relic certainly has a Buddha-aspect, it also has a clearly defined divine aspect, which is the primary focus of its cultic worship at the Temple of the Tooth.

Excerpted from Heralivala L. Seneviratne, 'An Exploration of the Meaning of Space in the Temple of the Tooth in Kandy', *Puruṣārtha* 8, Ecole des Hautes Etudes en Sciences Sociales, Paris, 1985, pp 177–95.

[1] Cosmo-magical symbolism is explained in note 6.

Worship of the Buddha in divinized form goes back to the early history of Sri Lanka. In India too with the rise of Buddhism the Buddha was accepted by some kings as the primary object of cultic worship for gaining prosperity and well-being for the kingdom, though with the decline of Buddhism these rulers returned to the worship of Hindu gods. The state cult in early Hindu and Buddhist kingdoms was built around the idea that the king must, through mystical means, establish access to the heavenly world and enable the uninterrupted participation of the human kingdom in the eternal bounties characteristic of that world. It was therefore neccessary, if the Buddha were to be the primary object of worship in this cult, that he be worshipped in a super-human form.

The main distinction between the *vihāra* and the *dēvāla* is that the former is a relatively 'open' place and the latter a relatively 'closed' or inaccessible place. This is in keeping with the fact that the Buddha, a historical human person who expounded a philosophy, led a life of daily involvement with society to whose members he actively explained it; whereas the gods are powerful non-human beings, access to whose benevolence is only possible through the observance of meticulous rules designed to keep them secluded from the impurity of human beings. Figure 1 illustrates the two structures.

The *vihāra* consists of a rectangular image house surrounded by a veranda. The roof is of two slopes, the outer one sheltering the veranda (Coomaraswamy 1908: 118). A *dēvāla* consists of a series of rooms in a row, connected with each other. The first is a spacious rectangular area called the 'long house' (*diggē*), next an ante-room followed by the sanctum which houses the images of the gods. The sanctum is known as the 'palace' (*māligāva*). The sacred area of a *vihāra* is usually accessible from three directions, the fourth being the direction where the images are located. The *dēvāla*, in contrast,

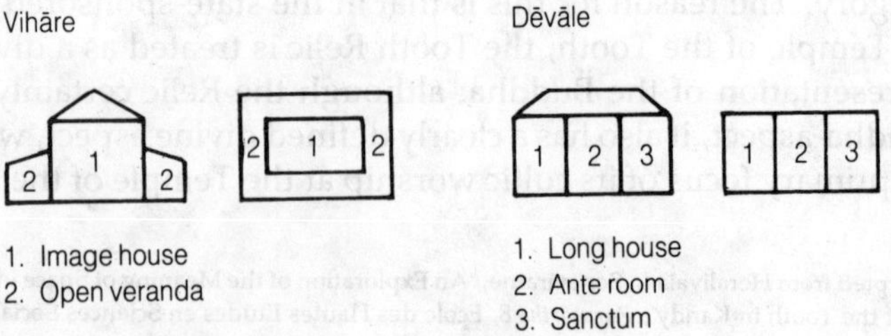

Figure 1. Vihāra and Dēvāla

has only one door which opens into the ante-room. A worshipper would first enter the long house, then the ante-room and only then reach the sanctuary, where he is forbidden to enter, and curtains shroud even his view of the divine images. The idea of the long house itself is significant for it expresses the distance that exists between man and god.

The central space of the Temple of the Tooth is laid out as an elaboration of the space in a *dēvāla*, with a long house, ante-room and other spatial devices which make it a 'closed' place. (During the official worship the central area is literally closed to the public, although it is accessible at other times, expressing the dual, i.e., Buddha-like and god-like, aspects of the Tooth Relic as worshipped in the state cult.)

In strictly Buddhist worship, an individual freely visits a *vihāra* and worships the images and other representations of the Buddha directly by chanting Pali stanzas and making offerings such as flowers and incense. The benefit of this worship is the acquisition of 'merit' (Sinhalese, *pin*; Pali, *puñña*) whose primary value lies in the facilitation of good future births. In contrast, the primary form of worship of the gods consists of a worshipper approaching the deity through the mediation of a priest. The purpose of such worship is the achievement of an immediate benefit, such as health or success in an enterprise. In the Temple of the Tooth both kinds of worship take place, because of the Tooth Relic's dual nature of possessing a Buddha aspect and a divine aspect.

The difference between propitiation of a god at a *dēvāla* and the state-sponsored worship at the Temple of the Tooth, both of which seek mundane benefits, is that, whereas the former is a private act seeking benefit for private individuals, the latter is a public act where the benefits sought are for the society as a whole. The desired benefits, as noted before, are prosperity, well-being, protection and so forth, with specific mention of timely rainfall, a climatological phenomenon indispensable for an agrarian society. These expectations were summed up three times every day in the concluding chant of the rituals of the dawn, day and evening:

> May the rains fall in time which is the cause of a bountiful crop. May the world be happy and the king be righteous.
>
> May the gods and naga of great supernatural power, of sky and earth, share this merit and ever protect the world and the teaching (of the Buddha).

The first stanza envisages harmonious and smooth working of the existing natural order of things and righteous rule of the king to result from the performance of ritual. Whereas the second, with the idea of merit from worship to be transferred to the gods who, pleased with the merit they receive, protect the world, recalls more strictly Buddhist worship productive of ultra-mundane benefits, but shares the focus of the first stanza in placing importance on the mundane benefit of protection. In both stanzas, the benefits sought are public and not private. The ritual therefore cannot be privately organized: it is a cult of the state whose sponsor is the king.

It is the nature of this worship that determines the organization of space of the Temple of the Tooth: the Temple is but a spatial expression of the form of worship. While certain spatial features express the private worship of the Tooth Relic in its Buddha aspect, the dominant pattern of space allocation expresses the worship of the Relic as a divinized form of the Buddha.

The official worship at the Temple of the Tooth is an elaborate one and I shall confine myself to a description of the spaces involving this worship, namely the dawn, day and evening ritual performances. That is, we will concentrate on the central space which is the essence of the Temple. Other spaces are either peripheral, such as rooms for the different categories of ritual performers, store rooms, offices and so forth, or elaborations, which need not concern us in an understanding of the central space.[2]

The main entrance to the Temple faces west. Through steps and a tunnel a person entering the Temple reaches a hall of about two thousand square feet, almost empty except for the pillars that support the upper storey. This hall, which is also accessible from the north and south, is called *hēvisi maṇḍape*, Drumming Pavilion. In this area drums and musical instruments are played during ritual performances.

The area to the west of the Drumming Pavilion is elevated except for the entrance tunnel that divides the area. On the north side elevation is a *stupa* and in the south, an image house known as *palla māle*, the Image House of the Lower Floor. Thus, the two floors of the Temple denote not simply two elevations, but two places of worship, reminiscent of a general classificatory pattern among the Sinhalese between 'upper' and 'lower' categories. The Image House

[2] The authoritative work on the Temple of the Tooth is Hocart's minor classic (1931), minor only because of its slim size of about 40 text pages. . . .

of the Lower Floor (indicated in Figure 2 as 'Lower Floor Shrine') is important because a ritual performance identical to that of the Upper Floor, performed for the Tooth Relic, is performed there simultaneously with the former. Steps on the west side of the south elevation lead to an octogonal structure known as the *pattirippuva*,

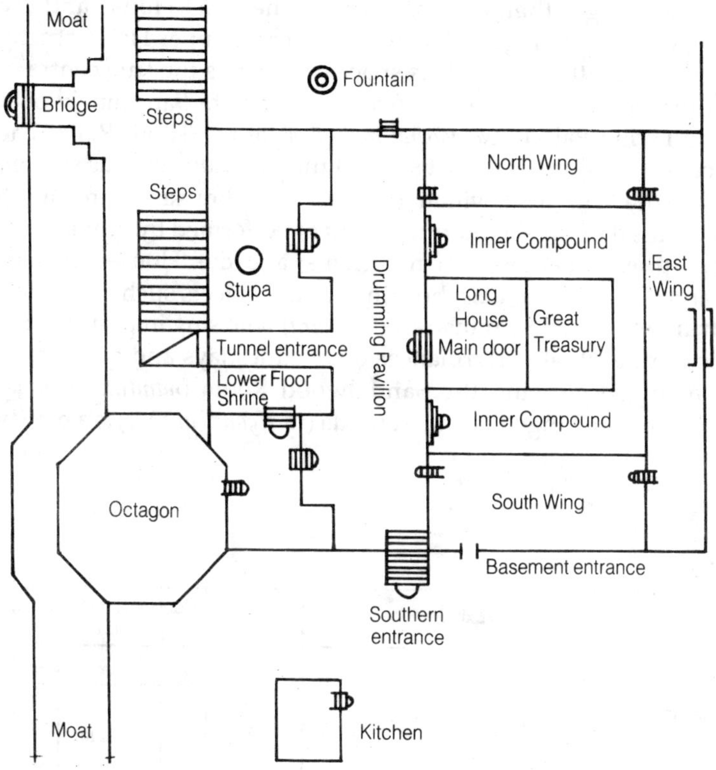

Figure 2. The lower floor of the Temple of the Tooth

which has no intrinsic relation to the central ritual, but is meaningful in terms of the relation between kingship and ritual to which we shall refer later, for the octogon is an illustration of the fusion of temple and palace.

To the east of the Drumming Pavilion, and surrounded peripherally by the north, east and south wings of the Temple and an interior courtyard ('Inner Compound' in Figure 2), is the physically and ritually central space of the Temple.

Its lower floor consists of two rooms, the 'Long Houses' (*diggē*) and the Great Treasury (*maha aramudala*), the first reminiscent of a *dēvāla*, as noted before.[3] The space above these constitute the Upper Floor of the Temple. This floor is accessible from the Long House through a very narrow staircase ('Stairway' of Figure 3), and through large stairways from the north and south sides ('Entrance Stairway' and 'Exit Stairway' of Figure 3). Although the upper storey of the Temple is larger than the space above the Long House and the Great Treasury as Figure 3 shows, the term 'Upper Floor' strictly refers to the latter space. This space constitutes the true centre of the ritual because on its far end (east) is located the Sanctum, known as the Living Palace (*väḍasiṭina māligāva*) of the Tooth Relic. The spaces on the north and east sides of the Sanctum serve as storage spaces, the 'Clothes Pavilion' (*halu maṇḍape*) housing some of the objects used in the sacred ritual (*tēvāva*) performed by monks, acting as priests, behind drawn curtains; and the 'Housewatcher's Veranda' (*gepalun barăňde*) housing certain objects such as musical instruments, used by minstrels (*kavikāra*) who sing in praise of the Relic during ritual performances on Wednesdays and quarters of the moon, occupying the Sandalwood Room (*haňdun kūḍama*) (Figure 3). The Pingo Placing Veranda (*kattiyana barăňde*) is a pantry

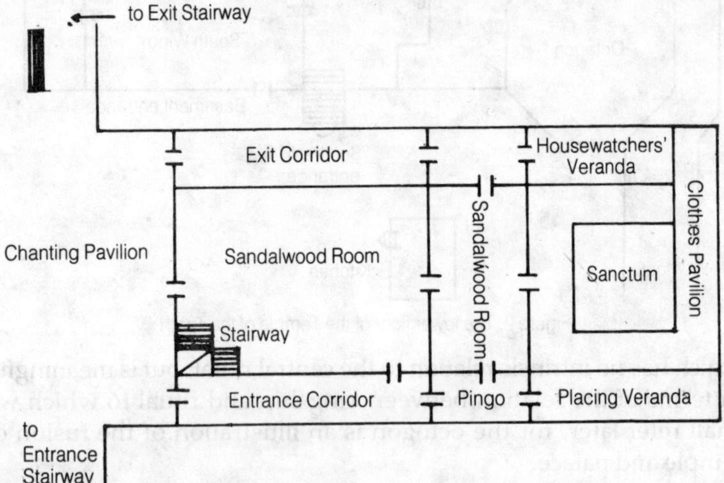

Figure 3. The upper floor of the Temple of the Tooth

[3] These are also characteristic rooms in the king's palace because in the Kandyan state rituals, Buddha, gods and king were treated similarly, suggesting the sacral nature of kingship.

and storage room for the gold and silver vessels used in the elaborate food offering which forms part of the daily ritual performances.[4] The Sanctum, as already mentioned, houses the Daladā, the Sacred Tooth Relic. During the official ritual performances, no one but the officiating monks and a sole lay assistant (*vaṭṭerurāla*) of high caste are allowed in the Sanctum, and even when it is open for public worship, a monk stands at its threshold and accepts offerings on behalf of devotees. Those who wish to cross the threshold are not barred from doing so, but the fact that not all of them do it cannot be fully explained in terms of the over-crowding which requires worshippers to maintain a smooth flow of traffic.[5] It can be understood as a spilling over into the open phase of ritual, a characteristic feature of the closed phase where worshippers are not allowed to go into the Sanctum. The open phase, as suggested before, is an expression of the Buddha aspect of the Tooth Relic and the closed phase, the divine aspect. The fact that an officiating monk stands at the threshold of the Sanctum even in the open phase and accepts offerings from worshippers, which is an act of mediation, expresses the relatively 'closed' nature of even the 'open' phase, and thereby the pronounced affinity of the Temple to a *dēvāla*.

Thus the space of the Temple of the Tooth illustrates the fusion of two modes of worship, first, the official worship sponsored by the state and performed by functionaries remunerated for their services. This mode, structured on the pattern of Hindu worship known as *pūjā*, expresses the divine aspect of the Tooth Relic. The second mode is the free worship of the Buddha as the Enlightened One by individual worshippers suffused with religious emotion, which does not form an indispensable part of the first mode. In the first mode the benefits expected, as mentioned before, are prosperity, well-being, and protection for the kingdom as a whole, and the benefits are mundane. In the second mode, the expected benefit is merit (*pin, puñña*), which is understood as an enhancement of an individual worshipper's moral worth, capable of facilitating happy future births. Though the space in the Temple illustrates both modes of worship, the first mode occupies primary importance because of the state-sponsored and nationally significant nature of the cult.

[4] These performances are described in detail in Seneviratne 1978: 38–64.

[5] The line of worshippers starts at Entrance Stairway and past Entrance Corridor, Pingo Placing Veranda and Sandalwood Room, reaches the threshold of the Sanctum and moves along Exit Corridor to Exit Stairway (see fig. 3).

The primacy of this mode relates the Temple space to that of the broader sacred complex of Kandy located immediately outside the Temple. We now turn to an exploration of the meaning of this relation.

Our understanding of the Temple and its rituals can be broadened by placing the Temple and its ritual in the context of a large complex of ideas which underlie the organization of polity and sacral kingship in South and Southeast Asia. This complex of ideas, referred to as 'cosmo-magical symbolism'[6] (Wheatley 1967: 9), though clearly expressed in numerous Sanskrit texts, monumental remains, lithic records and present-day popular belief, have been for long ignored by scholars. In recent times, however, several studies have emerged that bring out in some detail these ideas and emphasize their indispensability in understanding South and Southeast Asian society.[7] These ideas are varied in their detail, but in essence express the fact that the great temples of South and Southeast Asia must be understood not in narrowly pared-down religious terms that appeal to certain types of modern religious individualism, but in terms of a broad range of mystical ideas about man's attempt to enhance prosperity and well-being in harmonious relation with his fellow social beings and the natural and supernatural worlds, through the mediation of sacral kingship. In this view, the temple exists, not in isolation, but in integral relation with space exterior to it. Temple space occupies the centre of the city which is a microcosmic, mundane representation of the divine cosmos. The temple space periodically expands its boundaries to suffuse the city with its intensity, much as the cosmos exists by expanding and contracting.

Cosmic expansion and contraction is expressed in the Sanskrit texts as the awakening and returning to sleep of Puruṣa, the Cosmic Man. Purāṇic literature describes how, at the beginning of a cosmic cycle (*kalpa*), Puruṣa in the form of a great god awakens and gener-

[6] This term is used by Wheatley 1967 : 9. It refers to the idea that the city is a 'centre', an *axis mundi* that united heaven and earth (Eliade 1959 : 12). The ancient city of the orient was built as an imitation of the divine cosmos, 'as a repetition of the paradigmatic work of the gods' (Eliade 1961: 31). Colossal expenditures were incurred in some South and Southeast Asian societies 'to render their city a worthy likeness of Indra's capital on Mount Meru' (Wheatley *op. cit.*, 10).

[7] Some examples are Hocart 1927, 1936, Heine-Gelderne 1942, Dumont 1962, Wheatley 1967, 1971, Tambiah 1976, Heesterman 1957, Gonda 1966, Inden 1976. I am indebted to these and other works in my attempt to suggest that Kandy must be understood as a sacred city expressing cosmo-magical symbolism.

ates from his body the cosmic phenomena—sun, moon, lunar mansions, signs of the zodiac, continents, countries and so forth. He further generates from his body a logically complete social order consisting of the four castes (*varṇa*). At the end of the cycle, these units return to the body of the Cosmic Man who sleeps till the beginning of the next *kalpa*.

In the human world the analogy of the Cosmic Man was the king. just as Puruṣa symbolized the unity, potency and power of the cosmos, the king represented these for the kingdom. As the kingdom was a microcosm of the cosmos and all units of the cosmos belonged to a single quality and order of things, a disturbance in one unit would cause disturbance in the others. For example, celestial events such as the movements of the planets and eclipses were considered to influence the affairs of the human world. Human beings could avert dangers and intensify well-being by directing the course of the aberrant events through appropriate ritual behaviour. The person pre-eminently capable of effecting such direction was the king. The person and behaviour of the king was therefore considered to be intimately associated with the health, prosperity and well-being of the kingdom.

The king was the mediator between the human and divine worlds. In this role the king was charged with the task of facilitating the worship at the centre of the kingdom which alone kept the kingdom in health and prosperity, averting natural and other disasters. Further, the king's good behaviour and his adherence to *dharma*, the law of righteousness, was conceived as magically producing good results, in addition to the benefits that must empirically result from righteousness. Thus, if the king were righteous the planets would behave normally, the rains fall in time and the crops and animals multiply; but if he were cruel, the planets would behave abnormally, the rains fail and wither the crops away, causing famine, pestilence and war and thereby, the destruction of the social order.

As the kingdom and the larger mundane world were considered microcosmic replicas of the cosmos, the kings, even petty rulers were styled emperors of the world and of the universe. The kingdom was magically demarcated by forts erected at four points situated in the four directions. The capital, protected by fortifications, was conceived to be located at the centre of the kingdom and was the territory of effective contact between the king and the kingdom. As the city symbolized the kingdom the king could circumambulate the kingdom by ritually circumambulating the city.

The capital, as was the kingdom, was conceived as a square divided into smaller squares. Of these the central square consisted of the 'house', i.e., temple, of the king's deity, a microcosm of Puruṣa, who mediated between the king and the divine cosmos, just as the king did between the kingdom and the deity. The temple, as the abode of the divine microcosm on earth, faced the east, just as the macrocosmic Puruṣa did, when he generated the universe at the beginning of the cosmic cycle. The king, as the human, and therefore subsidiary microcosm of Purusa in the mundane world, appropriately occupied a house, i.e., the palace, located to the west of the temple. Equally appropriately, the king's audience hall, where the king enacts the role of the microcosmic human Puruṣa, i.e., kingly rule, was placed to the east of his private quarters. Thus, the audience hall, the locus of the king's public personality and mystical aspect, was located between the temple and his private chambers. In terms of these ideas the temple/palace does not stand in isolation but is the central space of the city and the kingdom. It is the locus of the *axis mundi* that united the city with the divine macrocosm.

Actual cities of South and southeast Asia were built in varying degrees of approximation to this ideal city, conceived as microcosmic of the divine cosmos. The builders of such cities as Ankor-Wat and Madurai, to give two well-known examples, followed the model closely though in different ways, whereas numerous other cities in South and Southeast Asia only faintly resemble the model.

Kandy, the capital of the last kingdom of Śri Lanka subdued by the British in 1815, was one of those cities which did not have any close resemblance to the model of the divine city. But there is no doubt that the idea lay beneath the visible structures of the city that survive up to the present day. From the earliest period of Aryan colonization of the island about the 5th century B.C., there is evidence to suppose that cosmo-magical symbolism guided the building of cities even though the details of the model were not followed. The most dramatic example from Śri Lanka is the rock fortress of Sigiriya whose 5th century builder Kāśyapa, it has been suggested, built his capital in imitation of the divine fortress of Kuvēra, the god of wealth (Paranavitana 1950). This indicates that a given king could select his own deity as the mediator between his kingdom on the one hand and the divine macrocosm on the other. Evidence from India illustrates this, for kings are sometimes known by the particular deity with whom they had a special affinity; for example, *paramamahēśvara* (supreme worshipper of Śiva), *paramabhagavata* (supreme worshipper of Viṣṇu), and *paramāditya-bhakta* (supremely devoted to the Sun).

The Indian evidence also illustrates that this supreme deity of a king's special affinity could be a divinized form of the Buddha, for we find the title *parama-saugata*, 'supreme worshipper of the Buddha'. It is this particular form of the Buddha that became the predominant divinity associated with kingship and the polity in Śri Lanka. Soon after the arrival of Buddhism on the island in the 3rd century B.C., a divinized form of the Buddha seems to have replaced or subordinated the existing deities as the resident of the city's central temple, the palace/temple complex, just as in some Indian counterparts, with the disappearance of Buddhism, Buddhist icons were replaced by images of Hindu gods. The Buddha, in divinized form, was repesented in the early cities of Śri Lanka by the Bowl Relic of the Buddha, brought to the island in the reign of King Devanampiya Tissa (247–207 B.C.). *Mahāvaṁsa*, the ancient chronicle of Śri Lanka, expresses in clear terms how the Relic was located in the conceptual centre of the city, the palace itself: '[. . .] the bowl that the Sambuddha had used the king kept in his beautiful palace and worshipped continually with manifold offerings' (XX, 13; Geiger 1960: 137). The Tooth Relic of the Buddha which arrived in Sri Lanka during the reign of Kirti Sri Meghavarna (362-409 A.D.) joined the Bowl Relic as representations of the divinized form of the Buddha. These two relics jointly held this status until about the 12th century, when the Tooth Relic became the supreme icon of worship in the state cult of Śri Lanka, as expressed in the king's act of offering kingship to the Relic (Rahula 1956: 75).

The centrality of Buddhism and divinized Buddhist icons in kingship in Śri Lanka, and their occupancy of the conceptually-central structure of the capital, i.e., the palace/temple complex, suggest the notion of a capital microcosmic of the divine city. Instead of a deity, it is the divinized form of the Buddha that is the true sovereign and mediator for the well-being of the kingdom. In so far as four major gods derived from Hinduism were subsidiarily worshipped in the cult of the state, the magical centre of the city extended to encompass the shrines of these deities located in the vicinity of the temple/palace complex. Space at the Temple of the Tooth in the Kandyan kingdom must, in this sense, be considered to extend beyond the physical boundaries of the temple/palace building itself. However, the preeminent part of the state cult was the worship of the Tooth Relic, which placed within a Buddhist framework the cosmo-magical symbolism whose origins were pre-Buddhist.[8]

The Kandyan kingdom as a whole was, geographically, a centre oriented polity, expressive of the *maṇḍala* model or the 'Galactic Polity' (Tambiah 1976: 102–31) to which many South and Southeast Asian polities seem to conform. Figure 4 (a) and (b) illustrate the real and schematized versions of the Kandyan kingdom respectively.

The kingdom consisted of two circles, first an outer circle of 12 provinces known as *disā*, and second an inner circle of 9 smaller provinces known as *raṭa*. At the core, as a third circle was the capital, the city of Senkadagala, the present-day Kandy, and within it was located the sacred complex in Kandy consisting of the Temple of the Tooth and the shrines of the four major deities. The king's palace being a part of the Temple of the Tooth was included in this complex. It is in relation to this complex as a whole that we can properly understand the space at the Temple of the Tooth. Again, though not physically, the Temple was conceptually the centre of the complex. This fact was clearly brought out by the periodic liberation of the conceptual structure from the constraints of stone and masonry which took place during the pageants. For pageants are but moving temples with no walls and ramparts to hinder the free expression of their inner relations. In the pageants primacy is clearly focused on the Temple of the Tooth.

Though not elaborated in one to one terms to conform to the microcosmic model of the divine macrocosm, there can be no doubt that the general pattern of cosmo-magical symbolism forms the essential base of the city of Kandy. Physical evidence of this has asserted itself in some structures. For example, the man-made lake in Kandy is called Kiri Muhuda, a Sinhalese rendering of the divine *Kṣīra Sāgara*, Ocean of Milk. Beautification could possibly explain the deliberateness, but not the name, of the lake. Some streets of Kandy have names such as *Vaikunṭha Vīdiya* (Street of Viṣṇu) and *Deva Vīdiya* (Street of the Gods). The parapet that adorns the Temple of the Tooth and surrounds most of the lake, and so pictorially indispensable to the modern-day tourist post cards, is known as

[8] Not surprisingly in Śri Lanka, other aspects of the state ritual were also given a Buddhist touch. For example, in the ritual of royal consecration which was based on the Sanskritic pattern, the clay for pots containing regalia was selected from Buddhist sites. In an analogous instance, the clay for the *mṛt snāna* ceremony of the Hindu *abhiṣeka* (consecration), with which the new king was ritually daubed, was selected from sites of an anthropomorphized earth. This recalls the generation of the universe by Puruṣa, associating the king's body with the earth, just as Puruṣa's body is associated with the universe, thereby repeating the macrocosm-microcosm theme.

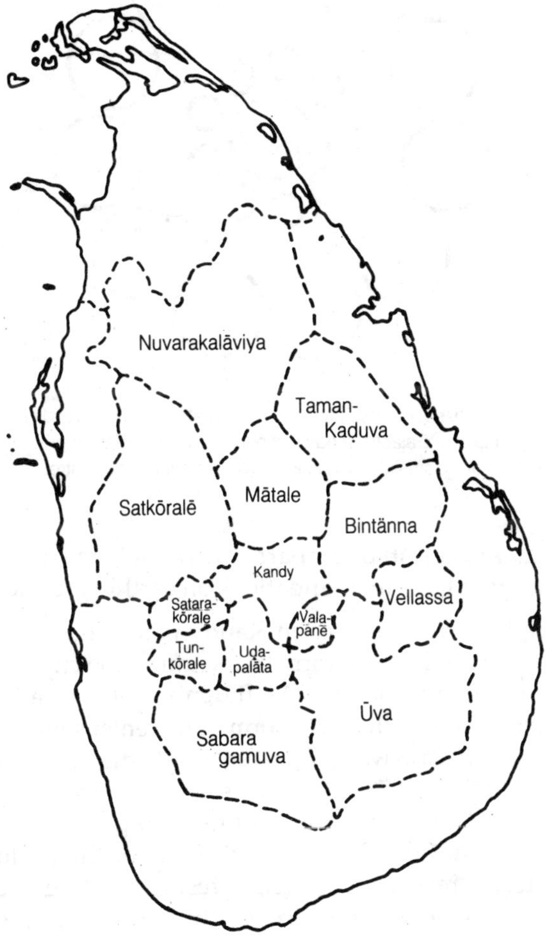

Figure 4 (a). Kandyan kingdom: a centre-oriented polity. The named divisions show the 12 larger provinces (*disā*). The 9 smaller provinces (*rata*) are shown in the dotted area surrounding Kandy, the capital.

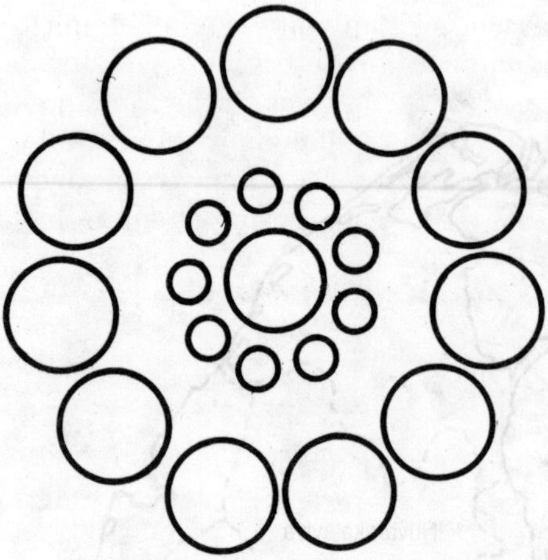

Figure 4 (b). Schematized representation of the centre-oriented Kandyan polity as a *mandala* or 'Galactic' model: an outer circle of the larger provinces, an inner circle of the smaller provinces, with the capital at the centre.

the *ahas pavura*, 'celestial rampart', with obvious suggestions of fortifications that have no foundations on earthly ground.

The temple/palace building in Kandy is the counterpart of the cardinal square in the ideal form of the mundane city which replicates the divine macrocosm. As Inden's study of authoritative Sanskrit texts describes that ideal form, 'The center square or "heart" of the site (*vāstu-hṛdaya*) was to be given over to the temple or "house" of the king's deity' (1978: 33). This is exactly what we find at the Temple of the Tooth : the centre of the complex is the Sanctum where the Daladā, the Sacred Tooth Relic of the Buddha in its divinized form, resides. The king's residence, 'the subordinate centre of the kingdom as microcosm' (Inden loc. cit.), was to the north of the temple, a further departure in detail, for in terms of the directional symbolism we are concerned with here, it should be to the west, but since it is not located east of the temple, it does not violate the essence of the symbolism.

It is often remarked that since about the twelfth century, kingship in Śri Lanka had been inextricably bound with the 'possession' or 'custody of the Tooth Relic. These terms are misleading since they suggest ownership, as if the Relic were an item of property. The real meaning is quite different. The Tooth Relic is, as far as state ritual was concerned, an animate symbol, a microcosm of the Buddha in his divinized form, the cultic worship of which was necessary for maintaining the relation the human world has with the divine cosmos, which facilitated prosperity and well-being for the kingdom. In this form the Tooth Relic is the sovereign overlord of the kingdom, the human king being the subordinate medium of relation between the kingdom and the cosmos. As mediator between the kingdom and the divine cosmos with the help of the divinized form of the Buddha as expressed in the Tooth Relic, the king was both human and divine. As Inden states referring to the Hindu king (op. cit., p. 29), the Buddhist king was neither a transcendental being like the kings of early Egypt, nor was he simply a human agent of the divine, like the kings of medieval Europe. He was divinity, priest and worshipper on the one hand and active ruler and warrior on the other. The terms 'possession' or 'custody' of the Tooth Relic by the king obscure his subordinate partnership in dominion over the kingdom and relating it to the divine cosmos. Far from being the 'owner' or 'custodian' of the Tooth Relic, the king was the Relic's inferior.

The king performs the dual function of sacrificing to the Tooth Relic, and protecting the kingdom from external and internal disorder by the magical powers of his body that he receives by the ritual of consecration. The king's physical prowess is often expressed in Hindu-Buddhist ideology as the power of his two hands (Gonda 1969 : 5). Thus kings are called *dīrgab'āhu*, 'long armed' or *mahābāhu* 'great-armed' and the like. In Śri Lanka some of the commonest names for kings are Parakramabāhu, 'valour-armed', Jayabāhu, 'success-armed', Vijayabāhu, 'victory-armed', and Gajabāhu, 'elephant-armed' and so forth; and the parricidal and incestuous father of Vijaya, the first king of Śri Lanka, was Siṁhabāhu, 'lion-armed'.

The physical and moral sustenance of the kingdom required that the king play his role as chief sacrificer so that the kingdom be meaningfully related to the cosmos; and as guardian of temporal authority, engage himself in maintaining the integration of the polity. In the Kandyan Kingdom this meant the performance of certain daily and cyclical rituals.[9] The daily rituals based, as men-

[9] Daily rituals are described in detail in Hocart 1931, and both types, daily and cyclical, are described in Seneviratne 1978.

tioned before, on the Hindu mode of worship known as *pūja*, consisted of attending to the bodily needs of the Tooth Relic, in its form as divinized Buddha, by washing, dressing, fanning and offering food, perfume, colour, light and sound. The cyclical rituals periodically reiterated the vital connection the kingdom has with the divine cosmos. These rituals also represented an overflowing of temple space into the city. The duration of the Perahära pageant, held in the lunar month of Äsaḷa (June-July), represented a period of time in which the city was charged with an intensity of ritual value symbolically expressed in the erection of poles, known as *kap*, which exemplified the mediating *axis mundi*. As the *kap* poles were erected in the centre of the city, the pageant's circumambulation of them also meant symbolic possession of the city and, by extension, the kingdom, by the dominant icons of the pageant.

From the point of view of the kingdom as a whole, the duration of the Äsaḷa pageant also saw an inward flow: the chiefs of the provinces expressed their religious and political loyalty to the centre by participating, as traditionally required, in the annual pageant. The kingdom's conceptual periphery thus moved centripetally to meet and be encompassed by the centrifugally moving space of the temple/palace complex, rendering inseparable religious belief, political loyalty and geographical concept.

Sinking Flowers at Hardwar

ANN GRODZINS GOLD

Two possible sequences of Ganges [Gaṅgā] pilgrimage both from participatory experience are known to the residents of the village of Ghatiyali in Rajasthan.

Ladu Ram, like all those who make the flower pilgrimage within twelve days after a death, had all critical rites executed with dispatch in Hardwar following the death of his father. If, however, flowers are saved beyond those days (or if silver flowers are later fashioned), they may be taken on a longer journey and treated to more elaborate ritual attentions in a number of crossing places. I observed this lengthened version of the flower pilgrimage during a thirty-day bus journey to Puri and back. A good number of the pilgrims left wearing around their necks pouches with flowers. Although the tour was not focused wholly on attentions to the dead, these pilgrims had the opportunity to perform rites on behalf of their deceased kin and ancestors at several important sites along the way. Most notably they had their heads shaved in Prayag, deposited the flowers and offered flour balls in Gaya, and on the way home secured pots of Ganges water from Hardwar. They had their names inscribed as bringers of flowers in the priests' record books at all three places and several others as well.

This routine is not fixed. I know of several cases, for example, when bones were placed in the confluence at Prayag. However, certain aspects of the sequence are adhered to quite firmly. When the bus owner attempted to change the order of events on our trip by making Hardwar an early stop on the way east, his pilgrim passengers would not agree to this. They insisted, first, that they must

Excerpted from Ann Grodzins Gold, 'Sinking Flowers at Hardwar', in *Fruitful Journeys: The Ways of Rajasthani Pilgrims*, Oxford University Press, Delhi, 1988, pp. 202–13.

obtain pots of Ganges water from Hardwar only, and second, that they didn't want to worry about maintaining the purity of these pots over the course of the whole month-long pilgrimage. Therefore, the Hardwar stop would have to be made on the return journey.

Inexplicably, although Banaras was a major place for *darshan* and bathing by all our pilgrims, it was not—despite its fabulous reputation as giver of release—a key spot for the flower bearers. Only one, subtle act was performed there: the invitation to Bhairuji, Banaras-dweller. While bathing in Banaras, each pilgrim with flowers inwardly invited Bhairuji to attend his Celebration of Ganga, whenever it would be held back in his home village. Bhairu-from-Banaras, however, will possess the water carriers during Celebration of Gaṅga even after a pilgrimage like Ladu Ram's which touches only Hardwar. The invitation must be given on the banks of the Ganges, but not necessarily in Banaras itself.

Round Trip to Hardwar

The events preceding Ladu Ram's Hardwar pilgrimage relate to the events which immediately followed the death of his father and included the cremation. He left Ghatiyali on the morning of the fourth day . . . having gathered the bone and ash remains, or flowers, from the cremation ground on the third. Shortly after performing Path Mother's [also a shrine in the village] worship, Ladu Ram boarded the 11:30 a.m. bus to Devali. My research assistant and I accompanied him.

As we travelled we discussed the various special requirements of this journey. Ladu Ram was carrying his father's old walking stick; he contrasted its worthlessness in monetary terms with the necessity to worship it and carry it respectfully all this way. The walking stick still bore multicoloured string (*lacchā*) tied on it by the pandit at Path Mother's shrine. In Hardwar Ladu Ram would put the walking stick in the Ganges along with his father's remains, he told me, and purchase two others: one to take home and one to give to a beggar in Pushkar. He said that 'old people' (like his father) used canes and that he would give such a stick to another old man for the sake of the soul of his dead father. If he gave a cloth, a cane, or anything else to the poor here on earth, that thing would become available to his father's spirit. From the charities of the son, Ladu Ram, 'peace' (*shānti*) and 'happiness' (*sukh*) would also come to Mangilal's spirit. Waxing still more enthusiastic on the fruits of his pilgrimage, and especially of giving to the poor in crossing places, Ladu Ram concluded, still speaking of his father's soul, 'He may get release, he will get everything.'

Another important item that Ladu Ram was taking to Hardwar was a tiny slip of paper bearing a hand-written invitation to 'God' (vaguely, *bhagvān*) to attend the funeral feast. On most festive occasions Ganeshji, the deity of auspicious beginnings, receives the first invitation. But Ganesh is neither worshipped nor invited during a period of death pollution. By 'God' Ladu Ram meant Vishnu, and he told me that he would deliver this slip in Hardwar through the priest who conducted the rituals there.

Ladu Ram was not wearing shoes, but he did put on thick warm socks. He explained, after my question, that going shoeless had to do, not with any renunciation or asceticism, but with 'nonviolence' (*ahimsā*). When you wear shoes, he said, you cannot avoid treading on and crushing to death small living creatures and thus committing 'sin' (*pāp*). Ladu Ram added that he was going shoeless for the sake of *dharma* and that during this particular time, following his father's death, it was especially necessary for him to act in accordance with moral duty. At the Kota train station, where we had a fairly long wait, he squirmed a little and joked nervously about how crazy he must appear to other people, carrying the old walking stick and wearing a good watch but no shoes. He said, 'If I were wearing the flowers on the outside' (displaying the pouch momentarily), 'then everyone would understand at once'. Nevertheless, he immediately tucked it away again beneath his shirt and sweater. Despite being out of sight, the flowers, embodying Mangilal's spirit, were a presence travelling with us. Ladu Ram, as anyone wearing flowers must do, invited the deceased's spirit to participate whenever he took food, drank, or urinated.

On the long, slow train-ride from Kota to Hardwar, Ladu Ram spoke at length about his family, his education, and his childhood. He seemed glad of the chance to unburden himself. He was the only surviving offspring of his parents, several siblings having died. His elder brother had passed away when Ladu Ram was very young, and, he told me now, since that time he had felt very heavily the importance of serving his parents. While still a child he was not able to do very much, but as he grew older and more capable he sought to fulfil his childhood resolutions. It was for these reasons that he was now undertaking this arduous journey. It was winter, and chilly, and there was much talk throughout the trip recalling the comforts of home and contrasting them with the journey's discomforts. The theme of hardship and peril on the 'road of dharma' (*dharmarāstā*) was often evoked.[1]

Arriving at Hardwar station around 3.30 p.m. we encountered the traditional multivocal confusion of a pilgrim centre terminal: *paṇḍās* ('pilgrims' priests') seeking clients, cart-drivers seeking fares. There were no touts present for our *paṇḍā's* house, but we knew, through advice from experienced co-villagers, that we should ask for the 'gourdman'—so called because of the logo on his sign, an ascetic's dry gourd water-carrier. This gourdman dealt with most castes of pilgrims from our areas of Rajasthan. We thus contracted with a cart-driver to be delivered to the gourdman's rest house (*dharmashālā*), where the signboard indeed announced that he catered to Jaipur, Ajmer, Kekari, and Sawar. As we were residents of Ajmer district and Kekari subdistrict, and Sawar was our closest market town, we were well assured that we had come to the right place.

The gourdman's rest house was a place where Rajasthanis, particularly illiterate, non-Hindi speakers, might feel at home. The priests all understood the Rajasthani vernaculars and sprinkled their Uttar Pradesh Hindi with bits of them. Since much of their livelihood depends on periodic tours of Rajasthani villages to collect grain pledges made by former pilgrims, they are quite familiar with the geography, customs, and social structure of the area. At the rest house, moreover, one inevitably met people from close to home, if not actual acquaintances. We were joined on our first evening by a potter from Kota and dined with him, but there was not enough common ground to continue the companionship. The next day, however, Ladu Ram ran into a fellow schoolmaster from Sawar who had actually taught for several years, and been much respected, in Ghatiyali. This man, literate and witty, was good company, and we toured Rishikesh with him and travelled home together as far as Ajmer.

[1] Most villagers believe that pilgrimage imperils one's health. My research assistant found the unaccustomed cold of Uttar Pradesh unendurable and announced on the first day that if he had to stay in such a climate for a week we would have the job of depositing his flowers in the Ganges too. When I returned from this first Hardwar journey, several people made a point of telling me how tired and weak I looked. One of them later explained, when I complained that it was not pleasant to hear this, that such comments were appropriate and standard greetings for a returning pilgrim. After the long bus pilgrimage, on which I had indeed lost weight and sleep, I could hardly move through the village streets without hearing several comments on my lamentably depleted condition.

Ladu Ram, who had hoped to complete the ritual work that day, was gradually calmed and persuaded by the *paṇḍā* that his business must wait until morning. The *paṇḍā's* conciliating talk went something like this: 'As you desire; if you say in the night, then we will have to do it in the night, but I must tell you it is done in the morning, early in the day. But if you tell us to do it at midnight, then we will do it at midnight.' After several rounds of protest and smooth rebuttal, Ladu Ram's final objections subsided, and the *paṇḍā*, assuring him that it was after all a good thing to spend one night in a crossing place, turned to the first formal matter.

This was to locate Ladu Ram's family in the bulky looseleaf 'record books' (*pothi*) kept by Hardwar pilgrims' priests. These books were organized according to districts within Rajasthan and after that by village, caste, subcaste, and *gotra*. After several false tries, the *paṇḍā* began reading out names that did belong to Ladu Ram's relations, noting the move by one branch to another village, and the most recent entry of a pilgrimage seventeen years ago. Ladu Ram was pleased to hear this recitation, and we all agreed that hearing the names gave us full trust in the *paṇḍā*.

Having read out the records, the *paṇḍā* proceeded to bring them up to date, inscribing in his book all the information he could extract from Ladu Ram about marriages, births, and deaths in the extended family. He also inscribed my research assistant's name and my own as companions to the chief pilgrim, a customary practice.

The *dharmashālā* was a busy place; other *paṇḍās*, all members of one lineage, were engaged in the same activity of reading and writing names with other groups of pilgrims. This steady flow of business, they assured me, was quite normal. Seeing no other woman among the groups of pilgrims at the gourdman's rest house, I asked the reason for this,having read and heard that it was not only proper but enjoined to perform pilgrimage *joṛe* ('paired') with one's spouse. The reply I received from my fellow pilgrims, with which the *paṇḍās* concurred, was that it was indeed absolutely necessary to have your wife with you on 'journeys to crossing places' (*tīrthayātrā*). If you left her behind, it was sinful and your pilgrimage would surely be fruitless and useless. However, the task of sinking flowers was not that kind of *tīrthayātrā*. It was not made for the sake of wandering, seeing the gods, or bathing. Rather, our purpose, like those of our fellow guests at the rest house, was to make flour-ball offerings to the spirits of the dead. A pilgrimage made in haste for this single purpose did not require the presence of women, who in fact could only slow you down. I learned later that this definitive response was contextualized in our particular situation at that time. Flour-ball offerings may well be made by paired couples. However, the currently fashionable practice of placing bones in the Ganges within the twelve days following a death rarely allows for the company of women, simply because there is too much business to be attended to at home.

Having completed all the preliminaries and become resigned to passing the night, we were advised by the *paṇḍās* to go to Hardwar's famed bathing *ghāṭ*, Har kī Paiṛī ('the Lord's Stairs') and enjoy the *darshan* of twilight *āratī*—an offering of lights and prayers to the great river. After that we might come back and eat a good dinner. Our first sight of Mother Ganges at nightfall, with pilgrims' leaf-cup offerings of flowers and burning oil wicks twinkling as they floated downstream, aroused some deeper emotion in all of us. The dominant atmosphere at the *ghāṭ*, however, was of a pleasurable promenade; the crowd seemed composed mostly of bourgeois pilgrims—women in nylon saris and men in Western clothes. A scratchy cinematic rendition of *āratī* music blasted out over loudspeakers, and we soon retraced our steps to follow the *paṇḍā's* second piece of advice and take our meal. After dinner, all suffering from the cold, we wanted nothing but to wrap up in blankets and go to sleep in our bare room.

In the complaining spirit of the moment I asked, 'Why do you have to bring the flowers here anyway, when it's so much trouble?' Ladu Ram replied at this time with reference to the descent-of-Ganges story which he and Vajendra, my assistant, were able to produce orally. Immersion of bones in the Ganges, they concluded, was done to give peace to the soul, as well as 'deliverance' (*uddhār*, a close synonym to *moksha*). Here in Hardwar Ladu Ram thus gave a mythic and soteriological reason for his journey, whereas on the train he had stressed service to his parents.

The next day began with tea and shaving, which was executed deftly by several barbers attending to clusters of pilgrims huddled about warming fires. Ladu Ram waited his turn, was duly tonsured, and we all headed for the river once more, accompanied by a guide from the rest house. On the way we stopped to purchase two indispensable things: pots in which to collect and carry home Ganges water, and brightly coloured flowers to be used in the worship at the river. Ladu Ram spent thirty-five rupees on a fine brass waterpot with a screw-on lid. At the *ghāṭ* we went to the gourdman's designated area. There under a big umbrella sat another *paṇḍā* connected with our rest house, a vendor of *pūjā* supplies. Ladu Ram paid two and one-half rupees for 'flour-ball ingredients'.

Two distinct but consecutive rituals were now performed. The first was sometimes referred to as 'worship of the Ganges' (*Gangā kā pūjan*) and sometimes as 'worship of the bones' (*asthi pūjan*; note the use of the Sanskrit word *asthi* for 'bone' here rather than the euphemistic *phūl*).[2] This rite preceded the placing of the bones in the river and a Ganges bath. The entire action at the *ghāṭ* was sometimes subsumed under the name of the second rite—'flour-ball act' (*piṇḍa kriya*)—in which, of course, the chief accomplishment was making 'flour-ball offerings' (*piṇḍadān*) to the spirit of the deceased.

Having removed his father's bones from the red pouch, Ladu Ram sat facing the *paṇḍā*, holding them in his hands. On top of them, according to the *paṇḍā's* instructions, he put a coconut and on top of that a red flower. Ganges water was poured over all of this. On the ground in front of Ladu Ram a number of coins were laid out along with three leaf cups containing red and yellow flowers. The text of the ritual which I recorded and had transcribed is partly in a very simplified Sanskrit and partly in Hindi. The *paṇḍā* had Ladu Ram repeat after him phrases identifying himself and the time and place and stating his purpose as having brought his father's bones. Still repeating, Ladu Ram asked that his father receive a 'dwelling in heaven', a 'dwelling in Vaikunth' (Vaikunth being a particular named heaven), and a 'true passage' (*sat gati*),[3] and that all his sins be destroyed.

The *paṇḍā* then arrived at what, for him, was the highlight of the occasion: 'From Laduji's hands, for father Mangilal's satisfaction, gift of grain, gift of cow, gift of clothing, gift of utensils, feast for Brahmans', building up to a 'gratuity' (*dakshiṇā*) for the *paṇḍājī* 'given joyfully, with a happy mind, for father's satisfaction'. At this crucial moment he ordered us to turn off the tape recorder and

[2] For the duration of this ritual I will call the bones 'bones' because real flowers figure in the action; not only I but my companions as well were several times confused as to what was meant when the *paṇḍā* instructed Ladu Ram to do something with 'flowers'.

[3] *Gati* indicates a good outcome after death, but not necessarily an exit from *samsāra*. Its literal meaning, 'the action of going from one place to another', simply implies a change of state, which might be from ghost to ancestor, as well as from bound to liberated. Although some scholars of devotional Hindi literature translate *gati* as 'salvation', I will use the more literal 'passage', which may be understood in context either as passage from one existence to another or out of creation altogether.

repeated once more the list of desirable gifts. Ladu Ram volunteered one-half maund (20 kilograms) of wheat to be collected in the village along with one loincloth. The *paṇḍā* waxed eloquent on the many services he was performing and demanded a cash gratuity, to be paid now. Ladu Ram settled, after some haggling, on twenty-five and a quarter rupees and, after yet more badgering, one 'Brahman *bhojan*'—that is, the cost of one good meal for a *paṇḍā*.

Returning to the ritual format, Ladu Ram obediently repeating 'with a happy mind', pledged these things. He then very rapidly placed the bones in the river and slid his father's walking stick in after them. He was instructed to bathe and to rinse his mouth. After bathing and dressing in dry clothes, Ladu Ram was seated once more facing the *paṇḍā* for the flour-ball offerings. Before him was a *pūjā* tray on which, arranged in a circle, were red powder, turmeric, puffed rice, and grains of wheat and rice. In the centre was incense. On top of the rice a red thread was placed representing 'cloth' and next to the incense was a white curled thread, the *janeū* ('sacred thread') worn by twice-born males. On a separate leaf were five *piṇḍas*—balls made of wheat flour and water—one for each day since Mangilal's death.[4]

The *paṇḍā* greeted the gods in Sanskrit, and Ladu Ram repeated once more the date, place, his name, and prayer for his father's reaching heaven and receiving release. Water was poured onto Ladu Ram's head, and he drank three times and washed his hands. The *paṇḍā* picked up one *piṇḍa* and rolled it between his palms, then put it into Ladu Ram's hand and placed a flower on top of it. A pitcher of water was poured over the *piṇḍa* now, and the *janeū* was placed on it. Something of every item from the *pūjā* tray was also put on top of the *piṇḍa*, as well as another red flower. Ladu Ram lit incense. During all these actions the *paṇḍā* continued to recite verses, including prayers evoking worldly well-being and reminiscent of the stated goals of regional shrine pilgrimage: 'Keep happiness and peace in the house, increase wealth, increase progeny, live with love.'

Ladu Ram was instructed to speak the name of Ram 108 times. Then all the major crossing places, including Mathura, Kashi, Puri, and Dwarka, were invoked as givers of release. Father Mangilal's

[4] While in the flour-ball offerings of the twelfth day the *piṇḍas* represent the new *pret* and the three preceding generations of ancestors, here they are part of the series of daily *piṇḍa* offerings prescribed to build up the body of the *pret* part by part during the days immediately following death.

release and true passage were again called for. Mother Ganges was asked to 'destroy all sins from birth to birth', and again to 'increase riches, grain, and progeny, to give peace to father's soul, to make father's deliverance, to make father's release, and to make our pilgrimage fruitful'. Finally, 'Victory to Ganges Mother!' was softly [chanted].

Ladu Ram's brass waterpot, which had temporarily vanished, was brought out by another *paṇḍā*, already filled with Ganges water, sealed with wax, and marked with auspicious red powder. It was worshipped. Ladu Ram, as instructed by the *paṇḍā*, then held the first flour ball to his forehead and to each shoulder, from left to right. Finally he placed it, and the others as well, in the river. The *paṇḍā* told him to make three 'water offerings' from his hands and to sprinkle himself with Ganges water and take three sips. Then he announced soothingly that our programme was finished. We all received forehead marks from the priest under the umbrella and paid him a small amount of money.

It was at this point that we met up with the Ghatiyali schoolteacher and decided, after much debate, to do some sightseeing with him. Ladu Ram would probably have preferred to go straight home, as he was in much anxiety over the coming twelfth-day feast and all the arrangements required for its success. At the same time, however, there was a sense that it wasn't right to come all this way and not at least visit Rishikesh and Lakshman Jhula, the two most famed attractions in the area. As these sights were associated by all in our village with the Hardwar pilgrimage, people would be sure to ask us if we had viewed them; it might even be inauspicious to neglect key *darshans*. Our tour was rapid and perfunctory, but the Gita Temple and the magnificent mountain scenery did distract Ladu Ram's mind briefly from his home worries.

After this side trip, Ladu Ram completed his Hardwar business by purchasing two new walking sticks and a coloured straw basket in which to carry home his sealed pot of Ganges water. We were also 'given' (at one and one-quarter rupees per person) white-sugar-candy *prasād* and yellow straw garlands at the gourdman's rest house. As our dilapidated and springless bus pulled out of the Hardwar depot, Vijendra in a low voice let out the traditional cry uttered when pilgrims leave a crossing place, proclaiming the triumph of its chief deity: 'Speak! Ganges Mother's victory!'

After about twenty-four hours of discomfort unmitigated by conversation, as we were all too cold and tired to engage in it and the buses too noisy in any case, Ladu Ram reached Pushkar. Pushkar is called by Rajasthanis of our area the 'last crossing place' because for them it is mandatory to stop there on the way home from any Ganges pilgrimage. Hurrying from the bus stand toward the lake shore, Ladu Ram told me that, rather than seek a family or caste *paṇḍā* here, he could just as well do his business at 'any old *ghāṭ-vāṭ*', and his sole aim was to do it quickly. We proceeded, therefore, to the nearest *ghāṭ* where willing *paṇḍās* immediately performed worship of Pushkar and worship of the pot of Ganges water on Ladu Ram's behalf. In the course of these rites Ladu Ram bathed in Pushkar Lake and then bathed his sealed pot of Ganges water with Pushkar water. The reason he gave for this was that Pushkar was the 'guru of all crossing places' and the 'navel of the universe'. Pushkar water thus could only improve the purity of Ganges water. However, the seal was not broken on the Ganges-water pot.

Ladu Ram went from the lake to have *darshan* at his 'lineage seer' temple, a temple dedicated to Gautam Rishi, the chief ancestor of all Brahmans of his subcaste. On the way from this temple back to the bus stand for our return to Ajmer, he gave away the spare walking stick, but only on the second try, as one beggar refused to accept it (whether because of its inauspiciousness or its uselessness I was not able to determine).

Our pilgrimage was effectively complete now, but we had missed the last bus that would give us a connection to Ghatiyali and had to pass the night in Ajmer. Here a minor contretemps occurred which casts some light on the ambiguous status of the pilgrim who journeys within the twelve days after death, during the time of death pollution. We had been welcomed at the home of my research assistant Vajendra's wife's elder sister and her husband, who fed us well and offered us a place to sleep. Our relaxation there, however, was suddenly interrupted by some excited conversation which I was not able to follow entirely. Collecting our belongings and rushing out of the door, we were conducted by the husband to a nearby Jain rest house and obtained a room and quilts there.

After the dust settled I learned that we had unwittingly committed a very grave mistake in going to Vajendra's relations' house in the midst of this pilgrimage with flowers. We had rendered their home 'bad' (*kharab*) or 'impure' (*ashuddh*). According to Ladu Ram, he and Vajendra had not been aware of this contagion and neither had our hosts. The furor had arisen only when an old neighbour woman, who paid strict attention to such matters, snooped out the reason for our presence there. Vajendra's wife's sister's husband was then forced in embarrassed fashion to hustle us on our way. The rest of our return was uneventful. Ladu Ram stored the pot of Ganges water in his home shrine; on the twelfth day after his father's death, following the worship of Path Mother [who is considered the Ganga herself], he would festively welcome Ganges Mother and Bhairuji Banaras-dweller to his house as honoured guests. . . .*

* *[The narrative proceeds to describe the Ghatiyalis' experience of a second, more elaborate and prolonged, mode of carrying 'flowers' to a crossing of rivers for immersion. This takes them to Prayag in Uttar Pradesh and further east to Gaya in Bihar (see the readings by Eck and Vidyarthi in this volume)].* Editor

Kāshī: City of All India

DIANA L. ECK

'All the *tīrths* on earth are here in Kāshī', said an elderly widow from Jhansi, now living in Kāshī in her old age. 'If you stay in Kāshī you never need to go anywhere else on pilgrimage.' The notion she expressed, as we walked by the Ganges late one afternoon, is an ancient one, voiced over and over in the Sanskrit Purānas and given geographical expression in the temples and *tīrthas* [places of pilgrimage] of Banāras. The whole world is here in this one place.

Just as the gods are all present in Kāshī, so are all the sacred places present here. There is no need to go elsewhere. . . .

Spatial transposition is a fascinating fact of India's spiritual geography. Kāshī, of course, is present in a thousand places in India, each with its own temple of Kāshī Vishvanātha, some even boasting a Panchakroshī Road. Kāshī is the paradigm of the sacred place, to which other places subscribe in their claims to sanctity. At the same time, Kāshī includes all the other *tīrthas* within it. According to Purānic commentators, these *tīrthas* exist only partially and in gross form in their separate places, but in their fullness and in subtle form, they exist in Kāshī. Kāshī is dense with *tīrthas*.

The presence of all *tīrthas* in Kāshī is more than a matter of literary eulogy, for many *tīrthas* and groups of *tīrthas* are part of Kāshī's sacred geography. The various temples, wells, pools, parks, and streams of the city symbolically embody the whole of India. When we ask the question, 'What kind of *place* is Kāshī?' one of the answers we find is that Kāshī is a place that gathers together the whole of India. Kāshī is a cosmopolis—a city that is a world.

Excerpted from Diana L. Eck, 'City of India', in *Banaras: City of Light*, Alfred A. Knopf, New York, 1982, pp. 283–303.

The Seven Cities

The 'Seven Cities' (*saptapurī*) are known all over India. In the north, there is Ayodhyā, the capital of Lord Rāma; Mathurā, the birthplace of Krishna; Hardvār, the gate of the Ganges; and Kāshī, the city of Shiva. In Central India is Ujjain, sacred to Shiva. In the West is Dvārakā, the capital of Krishna. And in the South is Kānchī, sacred to both Vishnu and Shiva. All seven are said to bestow *moksha* [liberation from the round of birth and death] at the time of death.

Still, as a contemporary Hindu guide to the *tīrthas* puts it: 'Among these seven, Kāshī is held to be supreme.' In Kāshī, those who think about such questions maintain that the other six cities bestow *moksha* only indirectly, by first bringing the good fortune of rebirth in Kāshī. Only Kāshī leads directly to *moksha*, with no stops on the way. The story of Shiva Sharma, the brahmin from Mathurā, bears this out. According to the *Kāshī Khanda*,* Shiva Sharma, when he saw the first grey hair upon his head, renounced home and family for a life of pilgrimage and simplicity—an age-old tradition. He went on a pilgrimage to all the seven cities, intending finally to live out his days in Kāshī. As fate would have it, however, he died in Hardvār. Shiva Sharma was fetched by a heavenly chariot, which took him through the various realms of heavens to Vaikuntha, the highest heaven. After enjoying his stay in heaven, Shiva Sharma was reborn in Kāshī, and only at the end of that lifetime did he obtain the liberation of *moksha*. 'Other places of liberation cause one to reach Kāshī', it is said; 'And having reached Kāshī one will be liberated, and not elsewhere, not even by a million *tīrthas!*'

The other six cities are said to be located in Kāshī, as well as in their native places. . . .

Shiva also explains the various locations of the cities of liberation in Kāshī as well as the seasons for visiting each of them. The living religious tradition and the 'text' of the sacred geography of Banāras bear him out. First there is Ayodhyā, the capital city of the Sun Dynasty of Lord Rāma. From here Rāma went forth into exile, along with his brother, Lakshmana, and his wife, Sītā. After years of struggle, Rāma finally returned to Ayodhyā, the episode enacted in the famous Bharat Milāp fair in Kāshī. South and west of Dashāshvamedha are parts of the city called Rāma Pura and Lak-

* Kāshi Khanda *and* Kāshi Rahasya *are the two traditional texts (see References at the end of the book) on which Diana Eck has drawn heavily in this description of Kāshi. Page references for quotations, not included here, may be seen in the book, pp. 393–5.* Editor.

shmana Pura, for the famous brothers. It is Rāma Kund which is said to be Ayodhyā—a large, clay-banked pond just north of Luxa Road. This place is also famous as Rāmeshvaram, the southern *tīrtha* at the tip of India, where Rāma established a Shiva *linga* [emblem] when he returned from Lankā after rescuing Sītā. Rāma Kund, with the small Rāmeshvaram Temple on its bank, is a quiet pond today, more attractive to water buffaloes than to bathers. The scriptures prescribe a visit here in the hot season, Jyeshtha and Āshādha.

Mathurā, as we have seen before, is located at Bakariā Kund in Kāshī. In the height of its glory, the atmosphere there must have been as eclectic as that of the other Mathurā to the west, with Buddhist, Vaishnava, and Sūrya traditions intermingling with the tradition of the cowherd hero-god Krishna. According to the text, Mathurā should be visited in the spring months of Chaitra and Vaishākha, but in Kāshī no Hindu visits Mathurā at all today, for its ruins have been turned into mosques.

Hardvār is located at the base of the Himālayan foothills where the Ganges enters the plains of north India. It is one of the several places in India where the Kumbha Melā and the Half-Kumbha Melā bathing fairs take place every six years. In Kāshī, Hardvār is at Asi Ghāt. While there is no particular shrine at Asi Ghāt to indicate the presence of Hardvār there, the Hindu guidebooks affirm it to be so. And the religiously literate people of the Asi neighbourhood, such as the brahmin women who bathe here daily before dawn, even through the cold winter months, know that this is Hardvār. Every year in the winter month of Māgha especially large crowds bathe at Asi, as at Hardvār in the north. And when the day of the Half-Kumbha Melā comes around—a time when tens of thousands of pilgrims flock to Hardvār—Asi Ghāt is suddenly inundated with bathers too. And the low wooden *chaukīs* where riverside vendors and priests sit are stacked high with *kumbhas,* the fat clay water pots, representing the famous *kumbha* of old which held the nectar of immortality. This nectar, churned up from the ocean at the beginning of time, is said to have splashed the earth in four places as it was whisked away to heaven by the gods: Prayāga, Hardvār, Nāsik, and Ujjain, the four sites of the Kumbha Melā pilgrimage. One such pilgrimage took place during the first fortnight of Vaishākha in 1974, and the Kāshī *panchānga* prescribed: 'In Kāshī, bathe at the confluence of the Asi and the Ganges.'

Kānchī in the Tamil South has its abode in Kāshī in the Panchagangā Ghāt area, 'at the side of the Bindu Mādhava Temple'. Like the other cities of liberation, Kānchī is established in Kāshī in a locale, not in a particular temple. Kānchī in Tamilnādu has two parts, Shiva Kānchī and Vishnu Kānchī. In addition, it is the 'bench' of the goddess Kāmākshī, one of the most important goddesses in South India. Like Kāshī, the whole complex of Kānchī has a trans-sectarian significance. In one Purānic *māhātmya*, Kāshī and Kānchī are said to be Shiva's two eyes. The season for pilgrimage to Kāshī's Kānchī is the fall, especially the month of Kārttika.

Ujjain, in Madhya Pradesh, is a very old city, sometimes known by the name of Avantikā, 'The Victorious'. It is famous for its *linga* of light called Mahākāla Shiva. In Kāshī, Ujjain extends from the area around the Kāleshvara Temple, dedicated to Shiva as 'Lord of Death', to the temple of Krittivāsa a short distance away. Since the temple of Krittivāsa is now a mosque, the focus of Ujjain is in the shrines of Kāleshvara, Old Kāleshvara, and Great Kāleshvara in the temple complex now dominated by the 'Death-Conquering' Shiva, Mrityunjaya. The winter months of Mārgashīrsha and Pausha are prescribed for a pilgrimage to this part of Kāshī.

Finally, Dvārakā, the capital city of Krishna in his later princely life, is located in the far west of India on the coast of the Saurāshtra peninsula of Gujarāt. In Kāshī, Dvārakā is situated in the area called Shankhoddhāra in the southwestern outskirts of the city. Here one can glimpse something of the ancient Forest of Bliss. [*Ānandavan* is one of the many traditional names of Kāshī. *Forest of Bliss* is also the title Robert Gardner chose for his outstanding ethnographic film on Banaras.] The temple and its adjoining *ashram* sit on the banks of a large pond, which is the centre of a quiet and semi-rural neighbourhood. Above the door of the temple is painted 'Shrī Dvārakādhīsha Shankudhāra', and the Vaishnavas who live here and teach Sanskrit to young resident boy-students are in the tradition of Rāmānanda, the fifteenth-century devotional leader of Banāras. Although the temple itself is not ancient, the site contains some very old remains, the most notable being the Pāla period Vishnu, at least nine hundred years old, standing in a separate shrine within the walls of the temple compound.

The name Shankhoddhāra means the 'Salvation of Shankha'. But who is Shankha? In this context, Shankha is said to be the name of a demon, slain and also saved by Krishna. There is, indeed, a shrine and story to this effect in Gujarāt's Dvārakā. In Kāshī, however, Shankha is a very old name attached to one of the great *nāgas* [serpent deity] who owns and guards the treasures of the earth. We know him from Buddhist texts, which tell of four great *nāgas* of India, who were said to hold up the four quarters of the earth. Shankha was the *nāga* of Banāras, and there is evidence that Shankha had a significant cultus in Banāras even in the time of the Buddha. Might we imagine that this deity was saved by one of the great gods in the fashion of so many of these autochthonous deities of the life cult—incorporated into the entourage of an ascendant deity? The rainy season months, associated with the *nāga*, are prescribed for pilgrimage to Shankhoddhāra, and traditionally there have been *melās* at this site in the months of Shrāvana and Bhādrapada.

These six cities of liberation are all said to be located within Kāshī, the seventh. Each has its own *māhātmya* [eulogistic text], of course, but none of the other cities makes Kāshī's sovereign claim to include and comprehend the rest. The positioning of the cities of liberation in Kāshī must have occurred after the time the *Kāshī Khanda* was complete in the fourteenth century, for this illustrious group is not mentioned there. When the rounds of pilgrimage to the seven are described in pilgrim manuals of the past two centuries, they take their lead from the *Kāshī Rahasya*. The circuit of the cities of liberation is not a common pilgrimage in Kāshī. In most of the cities there are no shrines to visit; they are simply parts of the geography of Kāshī. The important thing is that these others are here and everyone knows they are here. They contribute their lustre to the power of Kāshī, whether anyone visits them or not.

The Four Abodes

Kāshī also contains the four *dhāmas*, the 'abodes' of the gods at the four directional compass points of India. Kāshī is not one of the *dhāmas*, although it is sometimes said to be at the centre of the quadrant of the others. These four *dhāmas*, all ancient shrines in their own right, were given further emphasis in the ninth century when, according to tradition, the great philosopher Shankara travelled around India, organizing the Dashanāmī orders of *sannyāsins* and establishing monastic centres at these places. Some say he established a centre in Kāshī as well. In any case, it seems certain that Shankara visited Kāshī and perhaps spent several years here in the course of his travels.

The term *dhāma* is very ancient and has a variety of meanings that cluster around 'dwelling place' and 'light'. A *dhāma* is the location of divine power in a place, or as one scholar has put it, a 'refraction' and 'embodiment' of the Divine. It is the dwelling place that is imbued with the light, the refulgence of the holy. In this sense, Kāshī, the place of divine light, is the *dhāma par excellence*.

The northern refraction of the divine light is called Badrīnāth, a Vaishnava site located high in the Himālayas, set between mountains named for the sage-gods Nara and Nārāyana, along the banks of one of the mountain rivers that comes to form the Ganges. Open only during the summer months, Badrīnāth is one of the most popular of Himālayan pilgrimage places and a favourite retreat for ascetics. When the snows close the shrine a woollen cloth is wrapped around the deity, and the monks and ascetics move down the mountain to Joshimath for the winter. In Kāshī, Badrīnāth is placed at Nara-Nārāyana *tīrtha*, in the northern sector of the city between Gāya and Trilochana Ghāts. There is also an image of Badrīnāth within the compound of the Kedāra Temple.

In the far South, at the tip of India in Tamilnādu, is the *dhāma* of Rāmeshvaram. Here it was that Lord Rāma, with the help of the monkey armies, built the great bridge to the island of Lankā where the wicked Rāvana held Sītā in captivity. When he had slain Rāvana, Rāma returned to Rāmeshvaram and established a *linga* there as a penance for killing Rāvana, who was a brahmin as well as a demon and whose death incurred for Rāma the terrible sin of killing a brahmin. The *linga* Rāma established came to be considered one of the great *lingas* of light, so holy that it destroys the worst sins by merely beholding it. In Banāras, Rāmeshvaram is present by name and reputation in three different places: the temple at Rāma Kund in central Kāshī, the village of Rāmeshvara on the Panchakroshī Road, and the shrine of Rāmeshvara at Mān Mandir Ghāt.

As for the refractions of the Divine in the west and the east of India, we have already taken note of Dvārakā, the western *dhāma* in Gujarāt. In the east, on the coast of the Bay of Bengal in Orissa, is Purī, where the great Krishnaite temple of Jagannāth is situated. The temple of Jagannāth is one of the largest in India, its sanctum with its various subsidiary pavilions and kitchens covering an entire city block. It houses the blockish, wide-eyed, brightly coloured images of Krishna Jagannāth, with his brother, Balarāma, and sister, Subhadrā, images that show the ancient roots of these deities in the folk traditions of Orissa. One of India's most vibrant *melās* [fair] takes place in Purī, beginning on the second day of the waxing fortnight of Āshādha, just as the monsoon rains are about to begin. The images of the Jagannāth deities are taken out on their own pilgrimage (*yātrā*) on giant chariots (*ratha*) some forty-five feet high. The *melā* is called the Ratha Yātrā, the 'Chariot Pilgrimage', and it attracts tens of thousands of people to Purī each year. In Kāshī, the site of Purī is now near Asi Ghāt, in a large pastoral temple compound. Here, too, the sandalwood images of the deities are taken out for the *darshana* [viewing of the idol] of everyone during the time of the Ratha Yātrā festival. For three days, they remain in their chariots at 'Ratha Yātrā' crossing, before being taken back to their temple.

The pilgrimage to the four *dhāmas* of India is quite popular, especially in these days of bus pilgrimage tours. In Kāshī, the presence of the four *dhāmas* is widely known and is an impressive fact of the city's sacred geography. A pilgrimage to the four *dhāmas* is described in the pilgrim manuals, but perhaps more significant is that these refractions of the divine light enhance the many-faceted light of Kāshī.

The Twelve *Lingas* of Light

Hindus love the story of the argument of Brahmā and Vishnu and the sudden appearance of a blinding shaft of light between them, a light so brilliant and so fathomless that both gods were humbled by it. It is not surprising that many places of pilgrimage in India have appropriated the story of the appearance of the fiery *linga* as their own. It applies, in a sense, to every place that people have experienced as a place of hierophany, where the Divine has broken through the earthly. In these places, they say, the *linga* was not established by human hands, but is 'self-born'. In the beginning, it was a *linga* of light. It is not clear just how, out of all the places that have claimed to be *lingas* of light, a group of twelve came to be recognized. There are many more than twelve, but this group has the imprimatur of the wider Hindu tradition.

All twelve of India's *lingas* of light are located in the sacred geography of Kāshī, and their presence here adds to Kāshī the dignity and weight of some of India's mightiest *tīrthas*. Among them is Someshvara, or Somnāth, the 'Moon's Lord', located on the sea-coast in the western peninsula of Gujarāt. It is also called Prabhāsa, 'Place of Splendour', and indeed until its devastation by Mahmud of Ghazni in the eleventh century, it was one of India's most splendid temples. Today the temple is being restored. In Kāshī, Someshvara is located just north of Dashāshvamedha on the heights of Mān Mandir Ghāt. Also present in Kāshī is Mahākāla, the 'Great Lord of Death', whose *linga* of light is located in Ujjain, one of the cities of liberation. Here Mahākāla is found in the compound of the 'Old Lord of Death', Vriddhakāleshvara. From eastern Bihār comes the very popular and powerful Vaidyanāth, the 'Lord of Physicians', with many miracles to his credit. In Kāshī, Vaidyanāth is located in the Kamacchā area and is the most important *linga* in that part of the city. The *linga* of light called Bhīma Shankar is claimed by two locations, one in Mahārāshtra and the other near Gauhātī in Āssām. In Kāshī, its location is undisputed: in the famous temple of Kāshī Karavat in Kachaurī Lane, one of the busiest lanes in the city, and the *linga* is located some twenty feet below the ground, where it is honoured daily by priests who approach it by a tunnel entrance. From the street-level temple, Bhīma Shankar may be seen from above. Among the other *lingas* of light in Kāshī are two great *lingas* we have already discussed: Kedāra from the high Himālayas, and Omkāra located on an island in the Narmadā River in Madhya Pradesh.

Finally, of course, the Vishveshvara *linga* is in Kāshī, at the very centre of the city. In its true sense, however, the *linga* of light here is the entire sacred zone of Kāshī, of which the Vishveshvara *linga* is a symbol. Kāshī includes all the other luminous *lingas*, for it is not only the place where a single hierophany of light took place, it is that hierophany of light. As we shall discuss later, Kāshī itself is said to be a vast *linga* of light, a light extending five *kroshas* to fill the entire sacred zone.

Other *Tīrthas* in Kāshī

Prayāga is one of India's most famous *tīrthas*. The name means 'The Sacrifice', and it reminds us of the way in which pilgrimage to a sacred place came to be considered the primary substitute for the Vedic sacrificial rites. Known as the 'King of *Tīrthas*', Prayāga is located at the confluence of the Yamunā and the Ganges Rivers, about fifty miles as the crow flies from Banāras. (Today it bears the Muslim name Allahabad, City of Allah.) According to the Hindū tradition the mysterious, sacred underground river, the Sarasvatī, is also said to emerge there, at the confluence called the Trivenī, 'Where Three Rivers Meet'. Bathing at this confluence, it is said, is always auspicious. Sins from countless lives begin to 'tremble like a tree struck by a great wind' when one prepares to go to Prayāga. Especially during the month of Māgha people come to Prayāga to bathe, and every twelve years they come by hundreds of thousands to India's greatest *melā*, the Kumbha Melā.

Prayāga is also located in Kāshī, and in two places. The first is Prayāga Ghāt, on the riverfront adjacent to Dashāshvamedha. . . .

The second place in Kāshī said to be Prayāga is Panchagangā Ghāt. There are several temples of Mādhava or Vishnu in the original Prayāga, two of the most important being the Bindu Mādhava and the Venī Mādhava Temples. Likewise here at Prayāga-in-Kāshī there is a temple site of Bindu Mādhava atop the great flight of steps of Panchagangā, and many people, conflating the two temples of Prayāga, call this 'Benī Mādhava'. In addition, it is said that in the month of Māgha all the places of pilgrimage in India become pilgrims themselves and make a journey to Prayāga to bathe, to deposit the load of sins they have accumulated during the year, and to become pure again. In the *Kāshī Khanda*, however, Vishnu says that the *tīrthas* of Kāshī do not need to go to Prayāga for this purpose, but are purified in Kāshī, going first to the 'Five Rivers' of the Panchagangā. Moreover, they say that Prayāga itself comes to Kāshī bearing its great burden of sins, accumulated from all the other *tīrthas*, and washes them off at Panchagangā Ghāt during the autumn month of Kārttika.

Along with Prayāga, other *tīrthas* of considerable fame live in Kāshī. There is Kurukshetra, the holy 'Field of *Dharma*', where the war of the Mahābhārata was fought, located at a great *kund* in southern Vārānasī. There is Kāmākhyā Devī, whose famous 'image' in Āssām—but a depression in stone—is one of the pre-eminent 'benches' of the Goddess in India. In Kāshī, she resides in a small temple and lends her name to an entire section of the city, 'Kamacchā'. And there is Pashupatināth of Nepāl, located in the new Nepāli Temple and also in the narrow lanes between Chauk and the Ganges; the Himālayan Lake Mānasarovara, located on Nārada Ghāt; the Narmadā River, present in Revā or Revarī Tālāb; and the Godāvarī River, flowing through 'Godauliā'.

Some of the *tīrthas* that have come to Kāshī are among the most sacred sites in the city; others are neglected or covered over now by buildings, streets, or parks. Some, like the Godāvarī, have been incorporated by name into the common topography of the city. The important thing about the location of these many *tīrthas* in Kāshī is not that by being in one place they may be visited more conveniently, but rather, by being in this one place, they need not be visited at all. We have noted that there are pilgrimage rounds, established by the tradition, to visit the cities of liberation and the *lingas* of light, but these are not common pilgrimages, and one doubts they ever were. Here all these *tīrthas* contribute to the glory of Kāshī. Coming to Kāshī, pilgrims come to that one place where, according to tradition, all these sacred places arise, where they all dwell, and where they all, finally, dissolve at the end of time.

It is said that once Lord Brahmā took a balancing pan, the most common equipment in any Indian marketplace, and weighed Kāshī on one side against the heavens and all their gods on the other. Kāshī, being heavier, came down to rest on earth, while the heavens rose up to fill the sky. The weight of Kāshī is the cumulative weight of the city of all India. We have seen that the *tīrtha*, in general, has a cumulative nature. Better than a single river is the place where two rivers meet, as at Asi Sangam; or three, as at Prayāga; or five, as at Panchagangā. The place is the sum of its constituents—the gods and the *tīrthas* that abide there, the rivers that flow there. Kāshī is the place where all gods and *tīrthas* abide, where all sacred waters flow. There is no other place in India that is host to the myriad sacred powers that have gathered in Kāshī. It is no wonder that Kāshī outweighed the heavens. . . .

The Eight Directions

In any *mandala* . . . the directions are extremely important, for they guard and frame the sacred universe at its borders. There may be four directional guardians; or eight, counting the intermediate directions; or ten, including a guardian above and below. While Kāshī has a host of other guardian deities, these directions have an additional significance. They represent all space, for all space is included within the embrace of the compass points.

In the vision of Banāras as presented by the *Kāshī Khanda*, this city is said to be the place where the directions originate. It is the centre, and all the directions have their starting point here. We have met the notion of Kāshī as the centre and origin of the universe before. The *linga* of light, of course, is a fiery *axis mundi*, arising from the netherworlds, piercing the earth at Kāshī, and rising up through the highest heavens. And in the story of Manikarnikā, we are told that Shiva and Pārvatī created Kāshī, in the beginning, to be the very ground under their feet. It follows then that everything else begins in Kāshī, including the directions that mark the bounds of space.

The stories of the directional guardians occur in the *Kāshī Khanda* in the context of the larger story of Shiva Sharma, the Mathurā brahmin who made the pilgrimage to the cities of liberation, but died in Hardvār rather than in Kāshī. Remember that Shiva Sharma was taken in a chariot to the highest heaven, where he enjoyed himself for many years before being reborn in Kāshī. On the way, however, the good brahmin passed through all the different heavenly realms, including the kingdoms presided over by the various directional guardians. Shiva Sharma's accommodating charioteers told him the stories of each of these directional guardians, all with a common plot. Long ago a certain great devotee practised austerities in Kāshī for an impressively long time and was rewarded by Shiva by being appointed the regent of one of the directions.

Who are these directional regents? Some of them are well known to us from the ancient Vedic pantheon. There is Indra, for example, the Vedic war god, who now guards the east. There is Agni, the Vedic fire, who is in charge of the southeast. Yama, the God of Death, guards the south; and Nirriti, a much-feared black-goddess of death and decay, guards the southwest. In the west is Varuna, who rules the waters and who had a very high position as the guardian of the moral order in Vedic times. In the northwest is Vāyu, associated with the wind. In the north is Kubera, the wealthiest of the great *yakshas* of ancient India, with his capital at Alakā in the Himālayas. Finally, in the northeast is Īshāna, one of the forms of Rudra-Shiva. Of these regents, Indra, Agni, and Varuna were among the greatest of Vedic deities. The Hindu tradition never forgets such deities, but as the imaginative myth-making process continued, these deities found their places not in the centre, but in the far reaches of the Hindu *mandala*.

The positioning of the directional guardians around a sacred space is clearly evident in Hindu temple construction. The temple *is* a cosmos, and its sanctum is often surrounded by these cosmic guardians. The Rājarānī Temple at Bhuvaneshvara in Orissa and the sanctum of the Lakshmana Temple at Khajurāho are good examples of this conceptualization in the temple architecture of north India. The various directional deities are represented in their respective corners of the temple-cosmos, carved with iconographical detail.

The cosmos of Kāshī is not as clearly visible or organized as that of a temple, but its elements are schematically the same. The directional guardians have their posts in the various parts of the city, although in rather a random fashion. They abide in the very places where each of them, in the beginning, established and worshipped a Shiva *linga*. While it is not a perfectly circular and well-appointed *mandala*, the presence of these directional regents here serves its symbolic purpose: to locate all of space within the sacred borders of Kāshī.

One may easily find the temples of these directional lords in Kāshī . . . and there is a bona fide 'Pilgrimage to the Eight Directional Guardians' prescribed in the pilgrimage manual, the *Kāshī Yātrā Prakāsha*, but again there is little evidence that this is an important modern pilgrimage route. The very presence of these eight lords tells the pilgrims what they want to know: one need not travel the globe in search of the sacred, for one has come to Kāshī.

Above the Earth, on Shiva's Trident

The whole of the cosmos embraced within the eight directions is said to be gathered together within the five *kroshas* of the city of Kāshī. Moreover, Kāshī not only gathers up and condenses everything that is auspicious and blessed in this world into a single place, Kāshī also transcends this world. Kāshī is India's great 'crossing place'. Here the threshold of the finite is crossed over. Kāshī is as a bridge, beginning on this shore and linking us to the far shore.

Where is Kāshī? According to the *Kāshī Khanda*, this city is in the world, but not limited by it. It is in the middle of the universe, but not in the midst of the universe. Pārvatī, in her admiration for the city, exclaims to Shiva at one point in the *Kāshī Khanda*, 'Even though it sits upon the earth, Kāshī is not an earthly city.' Similarly, in the *Kāshī Rahasya* it is said that the city is not made of earth. Therefore, when everything else in the universe is submerged in the waters of destruction at the end of time's cycle, Kāshī alone does not sink. . . .

Where is Kāshī? In another common image, Kāshī's true location is described as high above the earth on Shiva's trident. When the waters of the *pralaya* [dissolution of an age] swell to engulf the whole of creation, they do not touch Kāshī. Kāshī is exempt from the *pralaya*.

It is often said that Kāshī is simply not attached to the earth. In colloquial Hindi, the city is said to be 'separate from the three worlds'. In the scriptural traditions of the Purānas, it is called by the lofty term *lokottara*, 'above the earth', or 'transcendent'.... Those who are of keen vision, such as *yogis*, are the only ones who truly can 'see' Kāshī.

What does it mean to say that Kāshī rests on top of Shiva's trident? It is, after all, an earthly city in the sense that people build houses, buy and sell goods, elect city officials, and use the Vārānasī pin code numbers on their postal addresses, as do the residents of any other city in India. Everyone knows that it sits on Shiva's trident, but people have quite different understandings of what that means. 'It is a geographical thing', said one. 'If you go to the far side of the Ganges, you will see that Kāshī sits on three hills, like the three points of Shiva's trident.' 'It means that Shiva protects Kāshī', said another, a priest. 'The trident is Shiva's weapon,and with it he protects his devotees. To say that Kāshī is on top of his trident means that Shiva protects all the people who live in Kāshī and gives them liberation.' 'It just means that Kāshī is different', said a medical doctor. 'This is a way of saying that we who live here have a life and culture that are very different from others, and that this place is different from other places.' A businessman put it this way: 'The three points of Shiva's trident are the three worlds: the netherworld below, this world of birth and death where we live, and the world of heaven above. Kāshī is above all these, and separate from them.' The wife of a *pūjārī* explained, 'Lord Shiva said that Kāshī cannot be destroyed. Even when the whole world vanishes, Kāshī will not vanish. This is what it means.' Finally, the philosophical *sannyāsin* Karpātrī said, 'Kāshī has a subtle form that is separate from this earth. That subtle Kāshī sits on Shiva's trident.'

In all these interpretations, one hears the same overtone: Kāshī is set apart from the rest of the world. It is different, separate, unique. Even the most casual visitor would agree. As the creator Brahmā said, according to the *Kāshī Khanda:* 'Many times have I, who spread out the creation, created the world. But Kāshī is of another sort, created by Shiva himself.'

Kāshī *Linga* of Light

In the *Kāshī Rahasya*, the time is recalled when the earth has sunk into the waters of the flood, as it does at the end of each cycle of ages. The great sages, from their vantage point in the heaven of the sages, look out and see that the earth has sunk, and they call upon Vishnu to assume his boar incarnation, to dive into the water and raise the earth up again. Scanning the waters, the sages see something astounding: a great shaft of light, rising and fanning out over the waters like an umbrella. 'What is this light which shines above the waters of destruction', they ask, 'and why does it not sink when everything else is submerged in the ocean?' Vishnu tells them, 'This is the supreme light, famous in the scriptures as Kāshī.'

In telling the sages about Kāshī, Vishnu contrasts Kāshī with everything else on earth. Everything else is created, but Kāshī is not. Everything else is, in the end, too dense and heavy to float in the ocean of the *pralaya*, and so it sinks. Kāshī, however, is made of luminous wisdom and does not sink. When the earth sinks, Kāshī floats above the waters of destruction. And when Vishnu retrieves the earth from the bottom of the sea, he brings it up and places it as *terra firma* beneath Kāshī. But Kāshī is not attached to the earth as other places are.

The City of Light transcends the cycles of time and the eternal evolution and dissolution of space. This is the light that Brahmā and Vishnu saw. They tried to discover its source and its top, but they could not. It was called a *linga* of light—the 'partless' (*nishkala*) form of the Supreme Shiva, Sadā Shiva, an unfathomable brilliance, transcending the three worlds. 'The *linga* Vishnu and Brahmā saw, that very *linga* is known in the world and in the Vedas as Kāshī.'

The word '*linga*' ordinarily refers to the image of the Supreme Shiva, either established by human hands or self-manifest, as the focal point of worship in a temple. The word 'Kāshī' ordinarily refers to a city, sacred as it is. Here, however, we have an extraordinary statement: the city is a *linga*. The whole of the sacred zone of Kāshī, encompassed by the Panchakroshī Road, is an enormous *linga* of light, the focal point of worship in the sanctum of the entire universe: 'This great place, Avimukta, bounded by the five *kroshas*, is to be known as the one *linga* of light, called Vishveshvara.' The phrase 'the *linga* whose extent is five *kroshas*' is common, both in the Kāshī *māhātmyas* and in the descriptions of the city offered by the priests of the city today.

The city is the embodiment of the Supreme Shiva. The sages ask, innocently, 'Why does Kāshī have a feminine name if it is a *linga?*' Shiva tells them that 'he' is both Shakti and Shiva, both the manifest and visible energy of life and the unmanifest, invisible spiritual essence. Taking form in the world, active and luminous in the world, is Shakti. Kāshī as Shakti is a goddess, with a *mūrti* or 'image' form. She is also a city, with a *kshetra* or geographical form. And she is the embodiment of *chit*, 'luminous wisdom', which is always feminine.

Sometimes Kāshī is said to be the very body of Shiva. For instance, 'This city is my body—measuring five *kroshas*, with wealth of unfractured magnitude, the very cause of *nirvāna*.' Since the body is a primary symbol of the whole, it is an appropriate image for Kāshī, which is the whole. The rivers Asi and Varanā are the two great arteries of Shiva's mystical body here. In the language of *yogis*, they are called *idā* and *pingalā*, and the third artery, *sushumnā*, where duality is transcended and *moksha* achieved, is identified with Matsyodarī River or with Brahma Nāla. The various *tīrthas* and *lingas* here are said to correspond to the parts of the body of God.

Whether Kāshī is spoken of as Shiva's *linga*, Shiva's *shakti*, or Shiva's body, this is a visible and earthly ford for the crossing to the far shore of liberation.

Embodiment of Wisdom

The most persistent image of Kāshī is light. The language of light is also the language of wisdom—'enlightenment', 'illumination', 'vision'. *Chit*, 'luminous wisdom', is sometimes said to be 'pure consciousness'—the wisdom of the utterly lucid mind. Another word for such wisdom is *jnāna*—the deep knowing, the liberating insight for which all renouncers and *yogis* aspire. Kāshī is also called *jnānasvarūpa*, the 'embodiment of liberating insight'. It is so called because this is the place where Shiva reveals such insight to the dying. . . . In this context, however, as we look at the more mystical interpretations of Kāshī as a place, we ask, 'Where is that "place" that embodies *jnāna* and where *jnāna* is revealed?' It is Kāshī, to be sure, and yet we find that Kāshī is also an interior place; it is one's very soul.

The world *krosha*, meaning a unit of measurement about two miles long, might also be considered a *kosha*, a 'sheath, layer', says the Vishvanātha *mahant* Rām Shankar Tripāthī. Just as a person is composed of these five *koshas*, so is Kāshī. Like the sheaths of the tall field grasses or the layers of an onion, the sheaths or layers of the person become progressively softer and more subtle, from the outer sheath made of food (*anna*), to the inner sheaths made of breath (*prāna*), heart (*manas*), intellect (*vijnāna*), and bliss (*ānanda*). The invisible *ātman* is here, at the centre of these sheaths. The five-*krosha linga* thus describes the inmost self, the place where wisdom is attained.

The sacred city is also an interior landscape. The *Jābāla Upanishad* explores its 'geography':

> 'Who is the eternal unmanifest *ātman* and how can I know it?' asked the seeker Atri.
>
> The sage Yājnavālkya replies, 'That which is the eternal, unmanifest *ātman* is to be worshipped in Avimukta. It is established in Avimukta.'
>
> 'In what is Avimukta established?' asks Atri.
>
> 'It is established between the Varanā and the Nāsī.'
>
> 'What exactly is Varanā and what is Nāsī?'
>
> 'It is Varanā because it "obstructs" all sins committed by the senses. It is called Nāsī because it "destroys" all sins committed by the senses.'
>
> 'Where is its place?'
>
> 'The place where the nose and eyebrows meet—that is the meeting place of heaven and the beyond. This meeting place [*samdhi*] does the knower of Brahman worship at dawn [*samdhyā*]. This Avimukta should be worshipped. This Avimukta is called "wisdom." Whoever knows this, knows.'

The place where Brahman is realized is called Kāshī. It is Light. It is Wisdom. It is what enables one to see and, therefore, to make the crossing: 'Look, dear! Look at Kāshī—a boat set for the crossing, a motionless refuge, set just above the earth, a boat not of wood and nails, but the illuminer of all people, whom she rescues from the sea of being.' Kāshī may be located on the plains of north India, on the bank of Ganges, on the tip of Shiva's trident, or where the nose and the eyebrows meet. Wherever that place is, it is the place where one is able to see into the true nature of things. 'In Kāshī', it is said, 'one sees one's own soul.'

Kāshī as Brahman

Finally, Kāshī is described with the most spiritually reverberating term of Sanskrit philosophy: Brahman. This is the Supreme Reality, that which underlines and transcends all. Within the soul, it is called *ātman*. It is the least tangible and the most real of everything that exists. Here in Kāshī, Brahman is said to take the tangible form of a place: . . . The few philosophical terms used to describe Brahman are also applied to Kāshī: it is *paramātman* (the 'supreme soul'); it is *chidānandamayī* ('made of consciousness and bliss'); it is *nishprapancha* ('without expansions'); and it is *anākhyeya* (the 'unspeakable').

In the *Kāshī Rahasya*, the student Dīpaka asks his teacher about its nature: 'What is Kāshī? Who made it? How does it work wonders? How is this great place, beloved of Shiva and Vishnu, so powerful? And how did that, which is without form, take this great blissful form?' The teacher explains: 'Kāshī is said to be Brahman, of which this turning world is an expansion. Knowers of Brahman call that which is without expansion "Kāshī."' In interpreting this passage, the commentator quotes the *Garuda Purāna* to similar effect: 'Kāshī is said to be Brahman, for here Brahman is revealed.'

Kāshī is Brahman. And Brahman not only illumines the world without, it dwells inside the citadel of the five *kroshas*, the world within. To the great Shankara is attributed a hymn entitled the 'Five Verses on Kāshī':

> The repose of the mind is peace supreme,
> And that is Manikarnikā, the greatest place of pilgrimage.
> The stream of wisdom is the pure, original Ganges.
> I am that Kāshī whose essence is self-knowledge.
>
> Where the magic of the world is made,
> Where the whole world of moving and non-moving things
> seems the dalliance of the mind,
> Is the One Place with the nature of the Supreme Soul—
> Truth, Luminous Wisdom, and Bliss.
> I am that Kāshī whose essence is self-knowledge.
>
> The intellect, Bhavānī, holds sway within the five sheaths
> in the household of each body.
> The witness, Shiva, the omnipresent, is the inner-soul.
> I am that Kāshī whose essence is self-knowledge.
>
> In Kāshī the light shines.
> That light illumines everything.
> Whoever knows that light, truly reaches Kāshī.
>
> The body is the sacred field of Kāshī.
> All-pervading wisdom is the Ganges, Mother of the Three Worlds.

Devotion and faith—these are Gayā.
Devout meditation on the feet of one's own guru—this is Prayāga.
And the highest state of consciousness, the inner-soul,
  the witness of the hearts of all people—
  this is Vishvesha, the Lord of All.
If all this dwells within my body,
What other place of pilgrimage can there be?

'I am Kāshī.' It is this radical interiorization of the *tīrtha* that has led some to conclude that one need not go on a pilgrimage at all. The truly luminous place is to be found only within oneself. And yet pilgrims continue to come to this place, every day on every train and bus. Arriving, they touch the dust of Kāshī to their foreheads, so tangible is the substance of Kāshī's sanctity. They come to walk these particular streets, to bathe in these waters, to see these divine images, to see the city itself. Even those who know Kāshī to be the luminous *ātman* deep within would not consider staying home. Beginning with the tangible substance of Kāshī's dust, they have seen in this city one dimension of meaning after another. They have finally seen Kāshī as Brahman, the light of all. And yet they do not relinquish the dust.

Concepts of Space in Ritual

VEENA DAS

The Grihya Sutras [manuals of domestic rituals] deal with different types of domestic ceremonies. These ceremonies centre around the sacred fire that every householder is expected to establish on setting up his house. There are four types of ceremonies described in the Grihya Sutra of Gobhila,* and there is in addition a miscellaneous universe of discourse. The principles of classification which the text uses to describe the various types of domestic ceremonies will become clear as the analysis proceeds.

The first type of ceremonies relates to the rituals which are to be performed when the domestic fire is first established. The usual prescription for this in the Grihya Sutras is that the sacred fire should be set up either at the end of the period of study or at the time of marriage. Gobhila begins with the setting up of the fire at the conclusion of the period of study. The second type of ritual acts relates to fire sacrifice which a householder should perform at various fixed points of time, e.g. daily fire sacrifices to be performed in the morning and evening, fortnightly fire sacrifices to be performed in the morning and evening, fortnightly fire sacrifices to be performed at the advent of the new moon and full moon, and fire sacrifices to be performed at the time of harvesting. In addition there are some prescribed sacrifices to be performed in the 'dark' months of winter for protection from snakes. But for reasons which will become clear later these sacrifices are described along with regular yearly fire sacrifices to ancestors. The third type of ceremonies are

Excerpted from Veena Das, 'Concepts of Space', in *Structure and Cognition: Aspects of Hindu Caste and Ritual*, Oxford University Press, Delhi, 1977, pp. 93–109.

* *The Grihya Sutra of Gobhila is considered to be the most complete of the extant texts on domestic rituals*. Editor.

those which have to be performed at various rites of transition, e.g. marriage, pregnancy, childbirth, tonsure, initiation,etc.

Rites to be performed for ancestors in the months of winter every year are of a fourth type. These rites are described as separate from rites to be performed on occasions of marriage, childbirth, etc. The rites for ancestors are described along with ceremonies to be performed for protection from snakes and, as we shall show later, there is a structural identity between the two. Textbooks on the history of Sanskrit literature often mention that the 'burial of the dead' (*sic*) is an important theme in the Grihya Sutras. In fact, the rites at cremation are often thought to belong to the same class as the rites to ancestors. However, it may be pointed out here that the only Grihya Sutra which describes the procedure to be followed at cremation is that of Ashvalayana. The other Grihya Sutras . . . do not deal with this subject at all. In contrast to this, descriptions of other rites such as marriage, propitiation of ancestors, full moon and new moon sacrifices are found in all the Grihya Sutras. . . .

In addition to the rites described above, the text also suggests a set of rites for the fulfilment of specific wishes—such as those for discovering hidden treasure, attaining fame, etc. These are clearly not obligatory on the householder.

The Right/Left Opposition

In the case of all the rituals mentioned above, the text lays great emphasis on a clear specification of the use of the right and left sides. In fact the right/left opposition is so important that it runs through the entire text. This is, of course, not a surprising finding. The different characteristics of the right and the left hand, and their importance in different cultures, was recognized by Hertz (1960) as early as 1909. He had argued that the right and left sides can be shown to be associated in a consistent manner with the sacred and the profane (in the sense of negatively sacred) respectively in a large number of cultures.[1] Thus the right hand, according to him, is the hand which is used for worship and for the performance of various pure tasks. The impure tasks, according to him, are usually relegated to the left hand which is also considered to be particularly

[1] There is a departure in Hertz's usage of the term profane from Durkheim's. As is well known, the term profane was closer to the category 'mundane' in Durkheim who did not consider sacred to be equivalent to good.

adept in dealing with demons, magical practices and sorcery. In the Indian context, however, the attention given to the opposition of pure and impure has been so overwhelming that the right/left opposition has been subsumed under this general opposition of pure and impure.

An attempt will be made to show that such an identification of right with pure and left with impure is not correct. In Hindu ritual there are clearly specified contexts in which the left hand is used for offering worship, as for instance, to ancestors which if it were primarily an impure hand it would not be eligible for. An attempt will also be made to show that none of the oppositions which Hertz associated with the right/left opposition such as that of religion and magic, gods and demons, priest and shaman, are sufficient to explain the complexity of the right/left opposition in Hindu ritual. In order to explore the various meanings associated with the right and the left, let us examine the different contexts in which the use of the right or the left is prescribed in [the Gobhila] Grihya Sutra.

Three different types of rules have been formulated about the use of the right or the left in this Grihya Sutra. There are some contexts in which the use of the one side is prescribed and the other proscribed. For instance, oblations to the fire during the wedding ceremony have to be given with the right hand while the oblations to ancestors during the periodic ancestor-worship have to be given with the left hand. Secondly, we find a number of contexts in which the direction of movement is prescribed either from right to left or from left to right. For instance, in the fortnightly rituals performed at the domestic fire to mark the advent of the new moon and full moon the sacrificial food has to be stirred, while cooking, from left to right. In the rituals to ancestors, or in the rituals to be performed for protection from snakes, the food has to be stirred from right to left. Thirdly, there are contexts in which both the right and left are used but precedence is given to one over the other. For instance, in the tonsure ceremony, both the right and left sides of the child's head have to be shaved but the right side has to be shaved first. Similarly, while pounding grain during the new moon and full moon ceremonies the right hand is placed above the left, but in the ancestor-propitiation ceremonies the same action has to be performed by placing the left hand above the right.

Now let us see the different contexts in which the texts give explicit prescriptions for the use of right and left.

RIGHT

1. The sacrificial cord which a householder wears must be suspended over the left shoulder so that it hangs from left to right when performing fire sacrifices relating to (a) daily oblations to be offered on the domestic fire in the morning and the evening, (b) in rites performed at full moon and new moon, (c) in rites associated with marriage, pregnancy, childbirth, tonsure, initiation, etc. and (d) in rites performed at the harvest and first-fruit festivals. When a person is wearing his sacrificial cord in this manner he is known as *yajnopavītin*.

2. During the setting up of the domestic fire for the first time and during the marriage ceremony, the subject of the ritual has to circumambulate the fire so that his right side is towards the fire.

3. In rituals associated with morning and evening oblations, full moon and new moon ceremonies, marriage, pregnancy, childbirth, tonsure, name-giving and initiation, the right side should be used to the exclusion of the left. For instance, the groom and the bride must offer oblations to the fire with their right hands. Similarly, during some rites in the ceremony the groom must touch the right shoulder of the bride with his right hand. To give another instance, as soon as the child is born the father should smear its tongue with barley and pounded rice using the thumb and fourth finger of his right hand.

4. In all the rituals mentioned above the movement of objects or persons is always from left to right. The sacrificial food cooked for these occasions has to be stirred from left to right. In rituals to be performed for the new-born baby or in the name-giving ceremony the child must always be passed from the left side to the right side. Similarly, in rituals to be performed at the end of the period of study under a guru the student always moves from left to right.

5. In all these rituals when both hands have to be used, as for the ritual pounding of paddy, the right hand is placed above the left hand.

6. Though in oblations offered to ancestors, whether in the course of daily fire sacrifice or in the periods prescribed for such purposes during the year, the left predominates over the right, there

are a few [steps] in these ceremonies in which the use of the right is prescribed. For instance, there are three pits which are dug for ancestors in a special enclosure during the annual propitiation ceremony. In the middle pit, oblations[2] are made with the formula, 'Adoration to you, O fathers, for the sake of terror, for the sake of sap', and this oblation has to be offered by turning the palm of the left hand upwards. But in the other two oblations which are made at the first and the third pit, the formulae say, 'Adoration to you, O fathers, for the sake of life and vital breath' and 'Adoration to you, O fathers, for the sake of comfort'. These two oblations have to be made with the palm of the right hand turned upwards.

LEFT

1. In the rites performed for ancestors and for protection from serpents, the subject has to wear his sacrificial cord suspended from the right shoulder towards the left side of the abdomen. When the sacrificial cord is worn in this position the subject is known as *prāchīnāvītin*.

2. The direction of all movements, when the rite is connected with ancestors or snakes, is from right to left. For instance, the ritual implements for these occasions have to be fetched from right to left. While cooking the sacrificial food, the pot ladle has to be stirred from right to left.

3. Liquid oblations to serpents, ancestors, and a few other deities whom we shall mention later have to be poured from right to left. When the annual ancestor-propitiation ceremony is being held the left side predominates over the right in the entire ritual. However, even on other occasions such as daily fire sacrifices, harvest and first-fruit sacrifices, and sacrifices to be performed on the fulfilment of specific wishes, some oblations have to be made to ancestors. On these occasions, though the right predominates over the left generally, the oblations to ancestors have to be poured from the right to the left.

4. Oblations to serpents and ancestors have to be made with the left hand.

5. As mentioned earlier, in the course of the annual propitiation

[2] These are not oblations to the fire. They may be oblations of food, a piece of linen, etc. . . . [T]he sacrificer may either light three fires or one, depending on whether the fire is taken from the *shrauta* fires or the *grihya* fire.

of ancestors, when oblations are made with the formula, 'Adoration to you, O fathers, for the sake of terror, for the sake of sap', the palm of the left hand has to be turned upwards.

6. When both hands have to be used in any rite connected with ancestors or serpents, the left hand should be placed above the right hand.

7. In the course of some rituals, there is a specific rite for driving away demons, 'dispellers of wealth' and other undesirable elements. This is done by throwing a blade of holy grass (*dūrva*) towards the left, using the left hand for the purpose. The ritual formula accompanying this rite is 'The demons, the dispellers of wealth, have been driven away'.

8. One particular context in the use of the left hand which seems exceptional and must, therefore, be mentioned here relates to the tonsure ceremony. As mentioned earlier, the right side dominates over the left in the ritual. However, when the child's head is first symbolically shaved with a ritual razor made of wood, a person touches the child's head with the holy *dūrva* grass, first on the right side, then the back and then the left side, using his left hand for the purpose.

This description shows that the right side has precedence over the left in rituals to mark the passage of time, as in the morning and evening oblations to the domestic fire and the fortnightly oblations to be offered to the fire on the advent of the new-moon and full-moon. Similarly, in all rites of transition except death the use of the right side is prescribed. In contrast, in all rites to ancestors as also in rites for protection from snakes, the use of the left side is prescribed. In the rituals in which the right side dominates, oblations are always made to deities that are conceived as basically benevolent and kind. In the other rituals, the ancestors provide the main focus and when oblations are made to deities in the course of ancestor-propitiation ceremonies, these are usually deities who inspire terror and are explicitly associated with death, such as Rudra.

The opposition between right and left, thus, is clearly associated with 'rites to gods' and 'rites to ancestors'—the former being associated with propitiation of divine beings who are friendly and benevolent, the latter being associated with those supernatural beings who have to be appeased, who inspire terror and have the potential of causing great harm if they are not regularly propitiated. The opposition between the pairs, right/left and gods/ancestors, is further associated with a number of antithetical pairs, such as even/odd, day/night, vegetables/meat and sundry others.

In view of the importance attached to the pure and impure in Indian sociology, the readers' attention should be explicitly drawn to the fact that the opposition between pure and impure is not attached in the text to any of the antithetical pairs in the series that have been mentioned above. In the rites in which the right side dominates, the sacrificial offerings consist of vegetables and grain, the number of Brahmans to be invited is even, and the sacrificial food which is left over is consumed by the householder and his family. In the rites to ancestors and serpents, in which the left side dominates, the sacrificial food consists of grain and meat, the number of Brahmans to be invited is odd (three being the number most often prescribed) and the sacrificial food which is offered to ancestors cannot be (with one exception to be mentioned later) consumed by the householder and his family. Instead, it must be burnt in the fire, thrown in the water, or given away to Brahmans. The rites to gods are said to be dear to the day and the sun, while rites to ancestors and serpents are rites of darkness, dear to the night and have to be performed in the winter months, the 'dark half of the year'.

In fact the text stresses the opposition between the two types of rituals so emphatically that the technical terms used for the sacrifice, the sacrificial food and even the *dūrva* grass, which is strewn on each of these occasions, are different. When offering oblations to ancestors, the sacrificer is known as *'yajnopavītin'*, symbolized by his sacrificial cord hanging from the left shoulder towards the right side. When he is offering oblations to ancestors his cord is suspended from the right shoulder to the left side and he is known as *'prāchīnāvītin'*. The holy *dūrva* grass which is strewn around the domestic fire during these two rites is also of different types. The grass strewn for rites to gods is 'cut from the place where the blades diverge from the stalk' while the grass strewn for rites to ancestors is cut from the root. The sacrificial food offered to the gods is known as *āgya* while the sacrificial food offered to ancestors is known as *piṇḍa* or *bali*. This series of antithetical pairs, taken together, express an opposition between the two sides of the ultramundane, one relating to the good and benevolent, and the other relating to appeasement of beings that can cause terror and discomfort. Nothing expresses it more beautifully than rites performed during ancestor-propitiation when the palm of the right hand is held up when oblations are offered to ancestors for the sake of 'life, vital breath and comfort', but the palm of the left hand is held up when the oblation is made 'for the sake of terror, for the sake of sap'.

Despite the fact that a number of observers have been so impressed by the uniqueness of Hindu religious beliefs (e.g. Dumont 1970), one finds that the opposition of the right and left, the association of the former with life, vital breath and comfort, and the latter with terror and sap, is not unique to Hindus.

In his essay on the right hand, Hertz (1960) drew attention to the fact that the right side is often the side of the sacred and the left that of the profane and impure. . . .

Hertz is correct in stating that left is associated with death and demoniacal beings. But surely death is associated with not only demons but also ancestors, with both the *preta* (ghosts) and the *pitri* (fathers). Ancestors come to share the powers which the demons possess but they also have a direct interest in the continuation of their lines and hence the welfare of their descendants. It is notable that in the formulae accompanying the fire-sacrifices in which the right side dominates and the benevolent deities are worshipped, the dominant theme is that of subjugation to the gods. In the hymns accompanying the rites to ancestors the major theme is the reciprocity between the householder and his ancestors.

During the performance of the ancestor-propitiation ceremony, for instance, the householder looks at his own house and addressing his ancestors says, 'Give us a house, O fathers'. Then he looks at the *pinda* offering that he has made, saying 'May we give you an abode, O fathers'. The same is repeated for food, clothes, etc. and special formulae are recited so that the householder may beget good progeny. One of the verses with which the ancestor-propitiation ends is, 'Go away, O fathers, friends of *soma*, on your hidden, ancient paths. After a month return again to our house which will be rich in offspring, in valiant sons, and consume our offerings.'

Thus, though ancestors have the power to cause great harm, they also have the potential and the interest to bestow wealth and progeny on their descendants. Unlike the demons, then, they do not have to be driven away or simply appeased but they have to be propitiated so that they may grant these boons to their descendants. The association between ancestors, material prosperity and progeny is symbolized in the rituals in a number of ways. In the course of the fire-sacrifice performed in the mornings and the evenings some offerings are made to ancestors. Significantly, one of these offerings has to be placed on the bed of the householder, 'so that Kama, the god of love, is pleased'. One does not need very much imagination to see that ancestors are conceptualized as the appropriate persons to bless the procreative activities of the householder. Similarly another offering is made at the entrance of the house so that 'riches may enter'. . . .

The association of the deities of the left with death, night, magical powers, and terror is not confined to the Grihya Sutras. In the study of Konku society, Beck (1972) relates a number of folk myths which show a similar association. Beck has argued that the right/left division is an important principle behind the organization of caste in South India. She finds that the deities of the left hand castes are usually female and are associated with death, sorcery, serpents, and darkness. They usually recruit followers by resorting to various tricks and succeed in establishing themselves as clan or lineage goddesses. . . .

The Cardinal Points

We shall now take up the meaning of the four cardinal points in the domestic ceremonies described in the Grihya Sutra of Gobhila. In order to avoid unnecessary repetition, we shall not enumerate all the contexts in which the cardinal points are categorized, but the major contexts are given below:

East

1. In the preparation of all rites to gods (e.g. new-moon and full-moon rituals, marriage, pregnancy, etc.) the sacred site is prepared by drawing lines on the ground, as shown in the following diagram. Three of these lines are drawn from west to east.

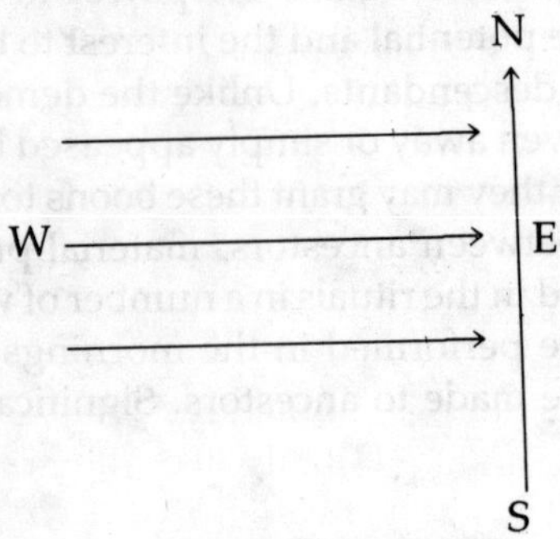

2. Before commencing the fire-sacrifice the householder is directed to strew the ground with the sacred *dūrva* grass. The direction in which the blades of grass should point vary according to the type of ritual being performed. In the case of the morning and evening oblations, and also for the new-moon and full-moon ceremonies, the blades of grass should point towards the east.

3. The sacred fire is placed to the east of the house for the rituals of marriage, pregnancy, rituals of childhood and initiation.

4. In the case of rituals of marriage and pregnancy, the subject (bride or pregnant woman) is required to sit on the western side of the fire buf she must face the east.

5. At the conclusion of the ritual to mark the end of a person's period of study, the subject drives away either in the eastern or northern direction.

6. When a cow has to be sacrificed, its head should be towards the east and feet towards the north if the rite is sacred to the gods. However, care must be taken to see that no blood is spilt towards the east.

7. If one is desirous of fame one should build a house with its door towards the east.

North

1. While preparing the sacred site, one line has to be drawn from the south to the north.

2. The sacrificial food on the occasion of the new-moon and full-moon ceremonies has to be placed on northward pointing grass.

3. During the rituals of marriage, pregnancy, childhood, and initiation, the subject is required to sit on northward pointing grass.

4. During the performance of these rituals, various ritual movements have to be made from south to north. For instance, during the birth ritual the mother passes the child to the father from south to north. Similarly in the marriage ritual when all the oblations have been made the husband stands towards the southern side of the bride and faces the northern side for the rite of holding his bride's hands and reciting some *mantras*.

West

1. The respective subjects in rituals of marriage, pregnancy, childbirth and other childhood rituals sit on the western side of the fire

on northward pointing grass. The subjects themselves should be facing the east.

2. For the performance of the rites to ancestors a special enclosure has to be built on the southern side of the house. The entrance to this enclosure has to be towards the west.

3. During the new-moon and full-moon ceremonies, a winnowing basket, a mortar and a pestle have to be placed on the western side of the sacred fire. The sacrificial food which is offered to the gods on the occasion has also to be placed on the western side.

4. For the ancestor-propitiation ceremony as also for the rites for protection from serpents, a mortar in which paddy is ritually husked is placed to the west. But, as mentioned earlier, the husking of paddy for these rituals is done by placing the left hand above the right.

5. If a cow is being sacrificed in a rite sacred to ancestors, then its head should be towards the south and feet towards the west.

6. The entrance of one's house should not face the west.

SOUTH

1. During the morning and evening oblations the offerings to ancestors are placed on the southern side of the fire. The same is true of the offerings made to ancestors during the ancestor-propitiation ceremony.

2. For the ancestor-propitiation ceremony some *dūrva* grass which has been cut from the roots is strewn round the sacred fire. The blades of grass should point towards the south.

3. During the tonsure ceremony the ritual implements (brass vessel with hot water, a razor made of wood, and the metal razor which the barber is to use later) are placed towards the south of the fire but the hair that is shaved is thrown on a heap of cow-dung which is on the northern side of the fire. After the child's head has been shaved the hair is taken away to be buried or thrown into flowing water in a northerly direction.

4. The cow which is sacrificed during the rites to ancestors has its head towards the south and feet towards the west.

5. During the ancestor-propitiation ceremony the sacrificer draws a line from north to south and recites a formula saying, 'The *asuras* [demons] have been driven away'.

6. A person who is desirous of children, cattle, and fame should build his house so that it faces the southern direction. However,

the Palasha tree which is associated with Yama (god of death) should not be planted towards the southern side as this entails danger of death.

This detailed enumeration of the contexts in which the different cardinal directions are made use of shows that east and north are associated with those rituals in which the right dominates, and south and west with those in which the left dominates. The rule that a cow being sacrificed to the gods should have its face towards the east and feet towards the north while in the case of a cow being sacrificed to ancestors, the face should be towards the south and feet towards the west, makes this association explicitly. The other rules also are consistent on this point. For instance, while preparing the sacred site for rites to gods, lines have to be drawn from west to east, and from south to north. Thus east and north are the directions *towards* which movement takes place in these rituals. The grass which is strewn round the sacred fire for these occasions either points towards the east or towards the north. Within the general category of rituals in which the right side dominates, a symbolic distinction is made between rites to mark the passage of time (e.g. morning, evening, advent of new moon, full moon, etc.) and rites to mark the passage from one status to another (e.g. marriage, pregnancy, childbirth). In the former rituals the grass strewn round the fire points towards the east and in the latter case towards the north. At the conclusion of any of these rites, the subject goes either in the eastern or the northern direction.

West is the direction which is associated with both ancestors and prosperity/fertility. Its association with ancestors is shown by the rule according to which the entrance to the enclosure, in which the ancestor-propitiation ceremony is held, is made towards the west. Significantly, since ancestors enter the world of the living during specified periods when they are propitiated, from the west, ordinary mortals are not allowed to use the same direction for entry. Hence the rule that a house should not have its entrance towards the west. The western direction is also associated with material prosperity and fertility of women. This is the side in which symbols of agricultural prosperity such as winnowing basket, mortar and pestle for husking paddy are placed. Also, at the rituals of marriage, pregnancy, and childbirth, the bride, the pregnant woman and the mother, respectively, sit on the western side of the fire. In view of the earlier analysis of the association of ancestors/other deities of the left with the power to bestow wealth and progeny on their descendants, it is not surprising to find that the direction in which symbols of prosperity and fertility are placed is also the direction from which ancestors enter to receive their share from their descendants. Thus the western side is associated with the benevolent aspect of ancestors and other deities of the left.

The southern direction is associated with death. The injunction that the Palasha tree which is associated with Yama should not be planted on the southern side of the house as this produces danger of death derives from this association. Correspondingly, south is associated with demons and other evil beings. Thus there are rules in which the *dūrva* grass is thrown from the north to the south, or a line is drawn from the north to the south, driving away Asuras, 'dispellers of wealth', demons and other evil beings. In the ancestor-propitiation ceremony the householder first drives away these evil beings and then invites his ancestors to accept his offerings. The sacrificial offerings to ancestors, serpents, and other deities of the left are always placed facing the southern direction. Thus south is the side in which the sacred beings associated with death such as serpents, ancestors, demons, and other left hand deities live. Along with the left side, the south is the cardinal point which figures in all rituals in which the danger emanating from these sacred beings has to be neutralized. It is in this context that one can understand why, during the tonsure ceremony, the barber and the other persons who officiate at the ritual are on the south and *dūrva* grass is pressed on the child's head with the left hand. Since the hair which a child had in the womb is considered to be a particularly apt object with which magical spells can be worked to harm the child, the left hand has to deal with this danger. The hair is thrown on a heap of cow-dung to the north, symbolically assuring the child's welfare and his progress in life. Thus, along with the right side, the east and the north figure in rituals in which the life processes and the good-sacred dominate and the left along with south figure in rituals in which death, magic, sorcery, and generally the bad-sacred dominates. West, as we have already pointed out, represents the harnessing of the left hand deities and ancestors for the welfare of their descendants and devotees.

The analysis of the means by which space is categorized shows that in association with the symbolism of laterality, the cardinal points provide symbols for representing different types of movements—the movement of time, the passage from one social status to another, especially connected with the continuation of the household through proper channelling of the forces of fertility and representation of death as a passage from the status of a living human being to that of an ancestor. This is why so much emphasis is placed in the domestic ceremonies on ritualizing the advent of the new moon and full moon, the events connected with fertility such as marriage and childbirth and, finally, the ritualization of death. In this Hindu ritual does not seem to be different from other systems of ritual.

Further Readings

Bhardwaj, Surinder M.,

1973 *Hindu Places of Pilgrimage in India: A Study in Cultural Geography*, University of California Press, Berkeley.

A cultural geographer's work, the book describes ancient and modern Hindu pilgrimages and ranks different places of pilgrimage in terms of their relative importance. The deities associated with the pilgrimages are identified, and social profiles of the pilgrims and their motives for undertaking the pilgrimage analysed.

Eliade, Mircea,

1974 *Patterns in Comparative Religion*, American Library, New York.

This work by an historian of religion explores various aspects of the notion of the sacred in different religious traditions. It develops the notions of heterogeneity of space and time in terms of the sacred-secular dichotomy.

Morinis, E. Alan,

1984 *Pilgrimage in the Hindu Tradition: A Case Study of Bengal*, Oxford University Press, Delhi.

A methodologically sophisticated and detailed ethnography of the Shaiva, Vaishnava and Shakta pilgrimage traditions of West Bengal. Examines two levels of meaning in pilgrimage—as experienced by the pilgrims and as set out in traditional texts.

Saraswati, Baidyanath,

1975 *Kashi: Myth and Reality of a Classical Cultural Tradition*, Indian Institute of Advanced Study, Simla.

A succinct account of how the people of Kashi look at their cultural tradition and at themselves in relation to it. How and to what extent they respond to the forces of social change and modernize their tradition.

Troll, Christian W., ed.,
1989 *Muslim Shrines in India*, Oxford University Press, Delhi.
Bringing together documentary, interpretive and theological perspectives, the essays comprising this book describe the location, architecture, rituals and worship that characterize Muslim shrines in India. The socio-economic and cultural facets of pilgrimages also are examined.

III

Sacred Time

The mode of thinking that creates the heterogeneity of space also creates the heterogeneity of time. Just as there are temples, churches and mosques, places of pilgrimage and thanksgiving, there are notions of auspicious, inauspicious and neutral time. There are five specified times of the day for the Muslims to say their daily prayers (*namaz* or *salat*) facing the Mecca. In India this means that one faces the west. Easter and Christmas come every year round, reminding Christians of the cosmo-moral significance of certain events which valorize the relationship of god and man. Among the Hindus, the festival of Kumbh not only brings millions of pilgrims to Prayag, Hardwar and other holy places but also reminds the believer that time is cyclical—that what exists must dissolve and reappear. This is the Hindu notion of *samsara* or 'total flux', the phenomenology of time.

Sacred space and sacred time together and inseparably, provide the setting for meaningful performances of the kind broadly called 'ritual'. If sacred places and performances have been presented in two separate parts of this book, this has been done to achieve a sharpness of focus by turn rather than to assert any absolute difference between space and time as categories of experience and understanding. Moreover, as sociologists we must adhere to the basic principle that both concepts are universally cultural constructs.

Writing about the famous festival of the goddess Durga in Bengal, Ákos Östőr from whose book on the subject an excerpt is included in this part observes: 'The goddess partakes of not only the spatial but also of the temporal dimensions of life. She represents the full cycle of time, within the year and in the cosmos. Annually she visits the town, neighbourhoods, households and temples. At that time all actions revolve around her and everyone is involved in her celebration' (p. 33). It is not, however, the organization of the Durga *puja*, beginning with the making of her images in clay, and the day-by-day progression of the ritual, that are presented here from Östör's account, but the more general exegesis of the *puja* in terms of concepts, actions, and objects. For a fuller description of the events and a concluding analysis the reader must turn to the original.

Frédérique Marglin deals with another famous Hindu festival, namely the annual Ratha Jatra, or the chariot journey of Lord Jagannatha at Puri in Orissa, out of the temple, and back into it. The ancient practice of self-immolation under the wheels of the chariot, drawn by devotees and 'servants' of the god (which introduced the word 'Juggernaut' into English), has long been prohibited. Marglin's concern is not with sensational tid-bits but with serious ethnographic analysis of a major ritual performance and its symbolic significance. She emphasizes the character of the Ratha Jatra as a ritual of life, death and renewal and brings out its cosmological, social and political ramifications. The palace-temple relationship in Puri is in significant ways similar to that in Kandy discussed by H. L. Seneviratne. Marglin also identifies for the reader the actual role and true character of the much misunderstood temple dancers called the *devadasis*. As symbols of auspiciousness they represent one of the key values of social life.

In the third reading we turn from periodical, festive, public rituals to a more personal performance. In an essay specially written for this volume, John Cort describes *puja*, or devotional worship, of the images of spiritual teachers (*jina*) in Jain temples. It is presented as an aesthetically pleasing and spiritually uplifting experience. Nothing is unimportant in this act of loving and total dedication: the architecture of the temple, the cleanliness and orderliness of its precincts, the beauty of the image, the aesthetic quality of the offerings, and the inner peace of the worshipper. *Puja* performances are, with variations, characteristic of all the indigenous religious traditions and have influenced the other religious communities also.

Sacred time is not concerned with gods and goddesses, metaphysical ideas, and spiritual beings alone: as auspiciousness (or inauspiciousness) it is a matter of everyday human concern. M. N. Srinivas writes of *mangala* rites on the occasion of the auspicious event of marriage in the life of a Coorg. Apparently, such rites were traditionally performed at the time of every event of social significance involving some alteration of status ('passage'), but with changing times marriage alone survived as the main occasion for the rite. By comparing *mangala* rites with some of the rituals connected with death, Srinivas highlights the notion of 'inversion' in the context of the life-death opposition.

Pilgrimages are a time honoured mode of religious devotion in India and emphasize the notions of both sacred space and sacred time. An account of a Hindu pilgrimage to Hardwar has already been presented. The fifth reading in the present part of the book is an historically grounded account of the annual pilgrimage to Ajmer which attracts numerous Muslims from India and abroad and some Hindus too.

Prophets and other holy persons mediate between the supernatural and human domains and, given their special status, events in their lives may be recalled with reverence and gratitude. The act of remembrance may normally be one of joyous celebration, but it could also be of repentence and mourning. The first ten days of Muharram (or Moharram), the first month of the Islamic calendar, are observed by Shiah Muslims all over the world as sacred time *par excellence*. During these days, and particularly on the tenth day, the faithful mourn the martyrdom of Husain, the second son of the Prophet Muhammad's daughter Fatima and his cousin Ali, at Karbala. A. R. Saiyid's essay is of much interest as it presents an account of the observance of Muharram in a socio-cultural setting which is primarily Hindu. It is also of interest to note how some elements of festivity have entered into the recollection of an event which is essentially sad and sombre.

Cyclical Time: Durgāpūjā in Bengal: Concepts, Actions, Objects

ÁKOS ÖSTÖR

The most common account of *pūjā* given by the people is based on an analogy between the service of a deity and the treatment of a guest. The guest is to be honoured above everyone else. The host invites his guest, goes part of the way to meet him, and welcomes him. . . . When the time comes for him to leave the host bids him farewell and reminds him to come again. The ideal way to treat a guest is the way to treat the gods: guests are like deities, and gods are guests among men.

Deities are part of the world as men know it, but when the special festival of a deity is celebrated the god is regarded as a traveller from a distant land visiting his followers, devotees, and subjects. The gods live in the Himalayas and travel across the land through the sacred rivers. Any geographical landmark may be the abode of a god, just as any lake or river may be a vehicle for a deity. Land and water are linked closely to the idea of divinity. Any hill is related to the Himalayas in some way, and the water of *pukurs* (water tanks) and streams is related to the sacred Ganges. A deity can be in two places at the same time. Like men, the gods are tied to localities, but unlike men they have different manifestations in different places and situations. The deities who come and go at the seasonal festivals are the same as the ones whose *pūjās* go on for the twelve months of the year in permanent temples. The seasonal *pūjās* are more intense, however, concentrating on particular aspects of the deity in question.

In the devotional and line cults the aspects of a certain deity are

Excerpted from Ákos Östör, 'The Exegesis of Puja: Concepts, Actions, and Objects', in *The Play of Gods: Locality, Ideology, Structure and Time in the Festivals of a Bengali Town*, The University of Chicago Press, Chicago, 1980, pp. 50–71.

deliberately separated and celebrated apart from the general meaning of the same deity. The deity who comes to his devotees in the seasonal worship has just as specific a meaning in the particular festival as do the purely regional, local deities. Men choose these aspects themselves, or the deity forces people to note his presence in a particular locality. The intensity of worship itself separates the manifestations of the same deity; the god that dwells in the Himalayas is also the god of the local temple, the object of seasonal worship, and the inhabitant of the local jungle or hill.

When a deity is invited for a celebration out of time and out of place, one of his many functions and meanings is selected for special contemplation. Then the house of the worshipper becomes the dwelling of the god, the Himalaya itself. The house or the temple is transformed into a festive place where a distinguished guest is honoured and entertained. The gates are decorated with mango leaves, a sign of auspiciousness (*maṅgal*) and joy. The gateposts have *maṅgalghaṭs* leaning against them, with banana leaves stuck inside. These are different from the invocation vessels, being ordinary pots, signs of welcome and happiness, marking the passage of a deity and bringing welfare to the inhabitants. They also mark the place of the worship, the approach to the locality of the *pūjā*. The banana tree itself is sacred, being one of the Nine Durgās (*nabapatrikā*).

The *pūjā* itself consists of many parts, each of which is a step in the service of the deity as a guest. Usually this service is performed through the offering of sixteen items, *saladān*. The god is welcomed in the place of the *pūjā*, invoked into the *ghat*, offered a seat, water to wash his feet, a towel to dry him, and oil and turmeric to rub on his body. A goddess is offered red lacquer to paint her feet, collyrium to paint her eyes, a mirror and sacred thread to prepare herself for the public. Then the deity is honoured with beautiful and precious things, all representative of certain attitudes and thoughts found in the human world: light, incense, camphor, flowers, sandalwood, silk garments (unstitched, complete, and uncut), and food, raw and cooked. These are all honorific items, varying in amount and preparation according to the occasion. These steps are to be found in any *pūjā*, big or small. The items are offered in deed and in imagination, through *mantras* and oblations of water.

Just as the deity is prepared for the homage of his subjects, so the worshippers must ready themselves for the encounter with the deities. They bathe and fast, so that both the inner and the outer person may be purified. They wear pure cloth and tie it in the fashion peculiar to rituals. But only a priest can perform the full service of the deity; he is pure by the definition of his office, and the worshipper must use him as an intermediary. But even the priest must go through a series of elaborate purifications in order to perform the *pūjā*. In these purifications all the constituent elements of life are treated separately, and so we can find in the *pūjā* the indigenous ideas of creation and the functioning of living things symbolized in clear, explicit ways. The priest knows the rules of the worship, the actions, the incantations, and the proper pronunciation. There must be a specialist, since the rules are complicated and only a Brāhmaṇ can follow them correctly. There is an element of magic (*kriyā*) [transformative action] in the doings of the priest, especially in the way the image of a deity is invested with life. The priest is not necessary for all acts of worship. Non-Brāhmaṇs can perform the *pūjās* of their *kula* (line) deities and of their personally chosen gods. But images that have been invested with life,the powerful images of major temples, must be worshipped by Brāhmaṇ priests. The annual festivals of all gods, regardless of their investiture with life or their appearance as direct manifestations of a deity, also must be worshipped either by Brāhmaṇs or by particular non-Brāhmaṇ ritual specialists. Only the Brāhmaṇ can offer cooked rice to the gods, and only the specialist can offer cooked food to the deities in the non-Brāhmaṇic rites.

The idea of *pūjā* is built around service, respect, and honour. People refer to *pūjā* as *ṭhākur sebā*, the service of the lords, or *sammān deoyā*, the expression of honour. *Sebā* is an attitude of devotion and, together with *sammān*, constitutes subservience. *Sebā* is also the offering of food, an act that symbolizes honour and respect. *Sebā* in other contexts symbolizes the same range of attitudes: a service given to husband by wife, children to parents, *sissa* to *guru* (disciple to preceptor). But only the offices of priest and king are institutionalized objects of *sebā* on behalf of society.

The Goddess and the Three Qualities

According to the Caṇḍī legend, there are three forms of the goddess, corresponding to the three *guṇas* [essences]: Mahā Kālī, or *tama guṇ*, Mahā Lakṣmī, or *raja guṇ*, and Mahā Sarasvatī, or *sattva guṇ*. These three forms issued from the goddess as her first creation; they also form the basis of the social order and of the people's participation in the *pūjās*. This classification differs from *jāti-bicār* (caste divisions) in that it refers to types and ways of worship (*mat*). There are different approaches to the gods, varying from one *guṇ* to another. The *sāttvik mat* is the way of Vaiṣṇavas; most commonly this means worship without animal sacrifice, a purely devotional attitude in which the worshipper does not demand anything for himself. The *rājasik mat* is worship with pomp and great insistence on power, the ego (*ahaṃkār*), stressing the self, aiming to derive many benefits from the *pūjā*. *Tāmasik mat* is the *pūjā* of the householder who wants all kinds of things from the deities in carrying out his everyday duties: help to continue some kind of existence in the bondage of *sangsār*, the world of daily living that according to the *sāttvik mat* is but a world of illusion. Though the three goddesses correspond to the three ways of worship, each one of them can be worshipped according to the other ways as well. Thus *sāttvik* Kālīpūjā is the worship of the goddess without animal sacrifice, liquor, or Tantrik symbolism, a way that concentrates on the benign aspects of this terrible goddess, who is represented without the garland of skulls and the blood that is associated with *tāmasik* worship.

Mat refers to the Purāṇa or the Upapurāṇa followed in the ritual sequences: the different sacred books about the worship of deities prescribing different objects, *mantras*, and offerings as well as different rules of action.

Sattva, raja, and *tama* are qualities (*guṇas*), types, and styles of life. They correspond to the three major deities Brahmā, Viṣṇu, and Maheśvār. The first is truth, the way of the renouncer; the second is power, the way of the ruler; the third is the way of everyday life, the householder pressed by social burden. *Dharma, artha, kām, mokṣa* are categories of experience, in terms of which one ought to lead one's life. *Dharma* designates duties, *artha* the means of living, *mokṣa* the liberation from contingencies of living, and *kām* the desires of worldly life. *Sattva* is the way to *mokṣa; dharma* is primarily *rājasik*, the responsibility of rule; *kām* and *artha* are the units of everyday life—*tama*. These categories are linked together in a hierarchy—there is *dharma* for the householder: the *dharma* proper to *tama*, just as the *dharma* proper to the action of the king is the *rajasik* way of life. The links are progressive; there is no *mokṣa* in the *tāmasik* way of life. Renunciation, or *sattva*, is the way to liberation. Hence these categories do not define discrete areas of experience: to any action there are several dimensions: *rājasik* and *tāmasik*, and *dharma, kāma,* or *artha* all together or in varying combinations. The complex process is determined by the laws of *karma* (action in terms of these categories) resulting in the ever-recurring cycle of rebirth (*janmāntar*) that is ended only by *mokṣa*.

Dharma, artha, kām and *mokṣa* mean something and do something. They tell people how to act in a given context with a certain aim in mind. They limit the possibilities within a set, and they provide the ways of exploring these limitations. A significant feature is the shared or overlapping characteristics of categories. Kṛṣṇa, a *sāttvik debatā*, and Kālī, a *tāmasik debatā*, may have *rājasik* festivals.

The goddess expresses the created world, and the three qualities define the whole of creation. The goddess herself is *māyā*, or illusion, which again characterizes the created world. She engages in *līlā* (cosmic play) giving rise to birth and death, the process of creation (*srisṭhi*). These terms define the nature and origin of life. *Dharma, artha, kām* and *mokṣa*, the four principles of experience, the rules proper to living things, include both models for and models of living. *Bhakti* (devotion), *mānsik* and *brata* (vows and wishes), *sādhanā* [ascetic practice], *ārādhanā* [prayer], *yoga*, and *kriyā* are aspects of action governed by these principles. These actions are also attitudes proper to the three qualities and their corresponding categories in society. The goddess, the qualities, and the created world (*prakriti*) are different ways of defining the same totality. The goddess is defined in relation to the *puruṣa* (male) principle, expressed through various divinities in different ideologies. The supreme deity Bhagavan is the hierarchically highest expression of this principle.

The ways of knowing this system and the processes within it are also given to us by indigenous accounts. Ultimately everything (goddess, Bhagavan, qualities) issues from *brahman*, the Immense One, the One without gender, quality, or characteristic. Everything is one in *brahman*. The many necessarily participate in the one. This knowledge is *brahmajñān*. It tells of unity and diversity, of elements and units in an abstract scheme that ultimately yield the totality, *brahman*, the truth (*tattva*). The elements constituting the expressions of *brahman*, in terms of *brahman's līlā* with the goddess, creation itself and all the things in the world animate or inanimate are defined in a hierarchical, segmentary way. *Tattva* is fundamental unity, its elements being water, fire, earth, sky, and ether. These are divided into twenty-five *tattvas* (ether, for example, is divisible into the five winds). These elements constitute and work the human body. *Brahman* is also the *parmātmā*, the universal soul, a unity in which participate a multiplicity of parts (*ātmā*). *Ātmā*, as a part of *brahman*, informs everything else in body, mind, and the constitution of the person. Further subdivisions are consciousness (*caitanya*), mind (*mon*), intellect (*buddhī*), ego (*ahaṃkār*). Some ideologies arrange the relations among these terms (and the direction of the processes in which they partake) differently than others do. I am not concerned here with the parallel between these systems and the major schools of Indian philosophy. Rather, I want to draw attention to these relationships and the processes they designate in action.

The work of element, soul, and consciousness is determined by the law of *karma*. The different series (*tattva*, consciousness, or other subdivision of *ātmā*, self, soul) partake of a process that eventually merges all diversity back into *brahman*. Hence a most pervasive feature of the ideological field is a belief in the oneness of the world. Time and time again townsmen wind up their discussions of the work of the gods with the observation that All is One. Whatever god or goddess may be at work, they are all parts (*aṅga*), manifestations, or incarnations of a basic unity. These series (spirit, awareness, object, element), the terms of their relationships, and the laws according to which they act are expressed in the symbolism of *pūjā*.

Pūjās, are part of the processes symbolized. If there are *sāttvik*, *rājasik*, and *tāmasik* ways of doing *pūjā*, the act of performance accomplishes and brings about the state to which the category refers. *Pūjās* for *mokṣa* bring liberation, *pūjās* for *kāma* result in the favourable intercession of a deity. *Rājasik pūjās* bring power, *tāmasik pūjās* help with the problems of everyday life. The same *pūjā* of the same deity can be performed with different combinations of these categories. *Debī* is pursued by people for profit or desire, liberation or devotion, or just for the sake of the act itself, leaving all work in the hands of the goddess. Any cycle, any arrangement of the categories subject to the law of *karma* can be brought to fruition by *pūjā*. Each time a deity is changed, or the direction of the act is changed (from *kām* to *mokṣa* for example), the other units rearrange themselves accordingly. Viṣṇu, though the god of *mokṣa*, may be worshipped for profit; the goddess Kālī, though a *tāmasik* deity, may grant liberation. *Śakti pūjās* of desire, power, and pride may be performed in the way of love and pure devotion (*bhakti*). The referents of symbols overlap, and categories are not mutually exclusive—they define ideal types of action and can be rearranged within the total system.

Sattva, *raja*, and *tama* also define sections of society and ways of living. Kings, though *rājasik*, may lead a *sāttvik* life, non-Brāhmaṇ castes, though *tāmasik*, may perform *rājasik pūjās*. The significance of these terms is not in the concrete groups they define but in the principles they refer to, which can be applied to the interpretation of concrete reality.

Categories such as consciousness (reality and *ātmā*) provide not only a system of meanings but also a way of knowing. Concepts such as *buddhī, mon, ahaṃkār* [egoism] give the processes of cognition, the separation of the true (*tattva*) from the illusionary (*māyā*). Knowing these terms is *brahmajñān*. This designates the total indigenous schema of concepts, categories, and meanings. According to local ideologies, no man can sustain this knowledge and awareness unless he is outside the social universe: a renouncer, guru, or saint. Men can achieve glimpses of this truth, only to withdraw behind the veil of illusion and grope towards the truth by means of symbols and metaphors. Men in the world are incapable of the consistency required by *brahmajñān*. They are aware of the concept, but they realise that their actions are often inconsistent with it. The *tāmasik* principle of everyday life is more immediate, giving special concession to those deceived by *māyā*. Men in particular contexts are bound by lesser principles.

Elements of Ritual

Sacrifice

A sacrifice can be animal or vegetable. In the *sāttvik* way of worship no blood sacrifices may be offered. But in Vishnupur [a town in West Bengal] both kinds of sacrifice are common. Durgāpūjā used to have human sacrifice, but since the kings were converted to the devotional Vaiṣṇava movement in the sixteenth century, there has been no [such] sacrifice. The Mrinmoyī Debī of the town is the *rājā's* goddess; when the kings stopped the human and animal sacrifices, the whole town followed their custom. According to old people, the custom of animal sacrifices was not easily abandoned; people used to offer blood to the goddess secretly, against the express orders of the king. Later the blood sacrifice came back in a major way in the observance of Kālīpūjās. But even today there is no animal sacrifice to the Goddess Durgā anywhere in Vishnupur. Nor are non-vegetarian and 'hot' foods—meat, fish, eggs, onions, garlic, and certain kinds of pulses—offered to the goddess (except for one temple, a sister temple of the goddess in a nearby village, where the distinctive feature of the *pūjā* is the offering of cooked fish).

Vegetables are a common replacement of the banned animal sacrifice. *Kumra bali*, the sacrifice of pumpkin, is the most common substitute. Here the pumpkin is treated as a sacrificial animal: anointed with vermilion, it is dedicated to the goddess. In the king's *pūjā* rice and pulses mixed together constitute the sacrificial animal; the seven small piles of grain made by the priest constitute the sacrifice and stand for the seven *śaktis* [power] of the goddess. The meaning of sacrifice is the casting away of one's sins and faults. By sacrificing their sins, making them into demonic beings through *mantras*, men not only please the gods but recognize what is divine in themselves.

Incantations and Gestures

Mantra is *śakti*; words have power to accomplish what they say in the context of the *pūjā*. The word, *mantra*, is itself sacred, but in the *pūjā* it is also efficacious. The power of *mantra* is associated with *pūjā* and *kriyā*, otherwise words cannot accomplish what they say: word and action together produce an effect in *pūjā*. Power comes from 'vibration'; word is sound, *sabda*, that produces vibration, energy. This energy has results when allowed to unfold in the ritual context. A *mantra* is efficacious even when the object to which it is directed is unware of it; *mantra* has the quality of a spell. Because of its independent energy, it can act independently. There is widespread belief in Vishnupur in the power of certain religious ascetics who can direct a *mantra* at a man for good or evil. People accept the action of the *mantra* when uttered by such an ascetic, even when the man at whom the *mantra* is directed is unaware of it. Hence *mantras* have to be pronounced correctly, because they have inependent power (power inheres within the proper sound). [In fact] the Universal Being, *brahman*, is itself associated with sound. In *pūjās* a *mantra* can replace all objects and offerings. *Mantra* is also the aim with which men offer gifts to the deities, the aim being stated and brought about by the recitation. The recitation of *mantras* has to be done *jathāśakti*, 'with all the power possible'. *Mantras* often name a deity in the particular object in which it is invoked: The goddess who dwells in the *bel* tree, the goddesses in the *nabapatrikā*. In the *mantras* of the *snān* [ritual bath] the different waters and objects through which the bathing of the Debī is performed are named, together with appellations of the goddess as the Beloved of Śankar (Śiva), the Lover of Śiva: 'Let the Lover of Śankar be anointed. . . .' *Mantras* always name a wider series of objects in which the goddess is manifest than is explicit in the ritual itself. There is a vocative element in *mantra*: 'Let the seven waters of the seven rivers be contained in this vessel. . . .'

Mudrās are gestures similar in efficacy and nature to *mantras*. *Mudrā* is a sacred figure shown by the hands of the priest. A thing shown is a thing achieved: gesture is both meaning, event, and result. Several *mudrās* are particular to Durgāpūjā, but a particular set is basic to all *pūjās*. The *mudrā* shows something for a deity and represents something on the worshipper's behalf.

Mudrās act in conjunction with *mantras*: action and idea, *mudrā* adding to the meaning of *mantra*. In itself the *mudrā* also brings about what it represents. First in the sequence is the *ābahan* (invocation) *mudrā*, appropriately formed by two hands cupped together **palms upward. The *sthāpan* (installation) *mudrā* is the reverse of** the above, expressing the entry of a deity, the establishment of the *ghaṭ*. The *Saṅgbodhanī mudrā* (joining and union) is made by the two fists placed side by side, the fingers curled under the thumbs. The *sammukhi mudrā* is formed by the two fists with the thumbs held up. These *mudrās* occur in the initial stages of *pūjā*, when a deity is invited with gestures and words, placed on a seat, and asked to stay and to grant safety for the devotees. The same *mudrās* recur throughout the *pūjā* in the context of offerings for the supporting deities. No matter how often a *mudrā* recurs, regardless of the context, it means the same thing. . . .

Beyond invocations there are sets of more complex *mudrās*. Such are *mudrās* of union and merging, expressing the relation between a male and female deity. These *mudrās* are linked to the concept of *śaktī*, just as *mantras* are, expressing the power and energy that issues from the union of the god and the goddess. The *mudrā* shown at the time of the encounter between Durgā and the male element expresses a union that effects all action, including the actions of the *pūjā*. The *yoni mudrā* symbolizes the possibility and power of action.

Some *mudrās* parallel the categories of *pūjā*: *ārādhanā* is both an attitude and a gesture (palms together). Others are equivalent to the object of offering, as in the shell *mudrā*, and water *mudrā*. Further, there are *mudrās* invoking sacred images: the tortoise *mudrā*, the sacred mother cow *mudrā*.

There are other actions, designated by the term *nyas*. These are not merely yogic exercises of breathing. *Nyas* may be any manner of enumeration, dissection, quantification, and qualification. In performing these actions the ritualist is directed to meditate on the

Goddess Sarasvatī, and the elements of the world are to appear as parts of a system of knowledge, a unity. *Bhutsuddhi*, the purification of the elements, is also a certain kind of *nyas*; the ritualist is directed to meditate on the parts of a unity. He is told that in imagination the world is dissolved through fire and gives place to its constituent elements. Enumerating these and joining them with the units of energy and life in the Tantrik scheme (different coils, *kul-kundalinī*, in the body), the *ātmā* (soul or self) is made to rise to *parmātmā*, the universal soul. The process is to be achieved through concentration and the utterance of sacred syllables that are efficacious in themselves.

Welcome

Bodhan and *āmantran* are the initial welcoming rituals in Durgāpūjā. Connected with the primary invocations, welcome, and respectful reception of the goddess are the rites of *belbaraṇ*, *kalpārambha*, and *saṅkalpa*. They share certain general features, and all welcoming rites include a *saṅkalpa*, the central act of the rite. *Bodhan* is the awakening of the goddess, an invitation to the annual festivities.

Āmantran, an act of greeting performed for deities alone, is related linguistically to the ordinary word for invitation, *nimantran*. These rites together designate *kalpārambha*, the beginning of the period of worship (*kalpa*, age, time, sequence; *ārambha*, beginning). *Belbaraṇ* is also an early act of the Durgāpūjā, the welcome under the *bel* tree (*baraṇ*, welcome). *Baraṇ* always refers to ceremonial occasions, whether these are directed at divinities or men. This rite is performed only at the time of Durgāpūjā; no other deity has a welcome under the *bel* tree. Most generally *baraṇ* is performed on the evening of the sixth day in the bright phase of Āśvin, Ṣaṣṭhīpūjā (*pūjā* of the sixth). This *pūjā* is not yet that of the goddess; it approaches the Debī as manifest in the *belgāch*, Śiva's favourite tree.

Bodhan is not only the initial rite of Durgāpūjā, but also the opening act of the *pūjās* of the seventh, eighth, and ninth lunar days. The tenth day holds the immersion rite; there is no welcome on the last day. In the welcoming rites the goddess is invoked in a series of items: *bel* tree, *ghaṭ*, and *nabapatrikā*. But this is not *śakti pūjā*—up to the seventh day the goddess is worshipped merely through her creation.

The representations of the goddess are regarded as spectators who do not actively participate in the preliminary rites. Offerings are made to *bel* tree and *ghaṭ*, both of which symbolize the goddess.

The many companions and attendants of the goddess and other major deities are also invoked. Once the *ghaṭ* is 'established', the gods can be invoked in it. Offerings may be placed on the *ghaṭ* (flowers and water libations) or touched to the *ghaṭ* or spread around the *ghaṭ* (raw and cooked food), but in each case they reach the gods through the vessel.

Time

The *kalpa, saṅkalpa* is a declaration of intent on the part of the worshipper. The goddess is told who will offer *pūjā* to her and for how many days. Doing *kalpa* on the Kṛṣṇa Nabamī means doing *pūjās* for the next sixteen days till the end of the festival. The *rājā's pūjā* has separate *kalpa* for each of the three Durgās. A *kalpa* on any of these prescribed days carries with it the obligation to do *pūjā* from then on till the day of immersion. *Kalpa* for the major days of the *pūjā*, is done on the evening of the sixth, but it can be done on the seventh, eighth, or ninth, but not on the tenth day. So the Durgāpūjā may extend from two to sixteen days, not more, not less. For one *pūjā* one *kalpa* is enough, but people may offer *kalpa* (and *pūjā*) on any of the prescribed days within the same sequence; in a line *pūjā* the members of different lines may do *kalpa* on different days, in honour of the same deity. The most popular *pūjā* sequence, from the seventh day to the tenth, is the period of Rāma's offerings to the goddess for the boon of killing Rāvan. . . .

Celebration of the Ghāṭ

The morning after *belbaraṇ*, the bathing of the *nabapatrikā* is performed at the *ghāṭ*. The *pūjā* order follows that of the previous night; only after the ***ghaṭasthāpan*** and the initial *pūjā* is the ceremonial bathing of the *nabapatrikā* performed. The eight small jars used in the rite, together with a single larger one with a hole in its bottom, called the 'thousand streams', are the nine necessary items. The eight jars stand for the eight holy waters and rivers, the ninth representing the waters of the holy land, Bharat, India. Each aspect of the goddess is honoured in these ceremonial oblations: water, the most sacred liquid, encompasses land and earth, all of creation.

In the *Mahāsnān*, the goddess is bathed with Ganges water and the earth of seven localities. The goddess is symbolized in different ways in these rites; the manifestations in the Candī legend (the nine Durgās of the Debī Māhātma) are honoured in the bath, the seven *śaktis* in the *bali* (the seven 'powers'), and the *asṭhanāyika* (the Eight Mistresses, the eight subsidiary forms of the goddess) in the *sandhipūjā*. The forms of the goddess are accounted for in their almost infinite variation. In doing these acts the priest must wear a ring made of the sacred *kusa* grass, a sign of Debīpūjā, and a protection from the dangers of *śakti*, which will be present when the goddess is invoked. The final object to be mentioned in the *ghāṭpūjā* is the *dakkhinābarta* shell. It is used as a vessel, and its rareness is a sign of sacredness. It belongs to that class of things in nature which, like the *sālāgrām* stone, are living deities, 'incarnations' of divinity. Both these things had, at one time, living beings in them; according to the indigenous ideology, the cavity in both once housed small organisms. These objects are 'living' in the sense that no ritual is needed to invoke a deity in them; divinity is incarnate in them as they are found in riverbeds and the sea. The motion of water contributes to their sacredness and life.

Elements of Ritual

Objects

In these *pūjās* the goddess may be represented anthropomorphically, but the images are not as yet invested with life; they are just representatives. In the *belbaraṇ*, the *tulsī* tree (sacred to Visnu) is worshipped; it is also an image of the goddess, the consort of Visnu. Its leaves are offered in all *pūjās* except that of Lakshmī, who is her rival. Viṣṇu himself is present through the sacred ṣālāgrām stone. Śiva is there through the trident or the *liṅga*. Viṣṇu and Śiva stand for the *puruṣa* [male] principle here.

Tree symbols are dual; the *tulsī* plant is a symbol of both Viṣṇu and the goddess, the *bel* tree is a symbol of Śiva and the goddess. In the rite, divinity is invoked in the trees, and the trees are then worshipped with the various objects, the *maṅgal pātra*, vermilion, oblations, and flowers. The deities most important in the annual ritual cycle are then invoked in the *ghaṭ*. The *ghatasthāpan* serves to bring the deities to the locality of the ritual. The unseen divinities are thus comprehended through their manifestation in the *ghaṭ*; the ritual and the symbols allow men to concentrate in a direct way on the otherwise abstract idea of divinity. The invocation takes place at night; no one should disturb the arriving deities. Without quiet, the ritual may not work. The goddess is 'called' at night, and in the morning she is received at the *ghāṭ*. She is thought to arrive in a boat, and then the *nabapatrikā* becomes the centre of the ritual. Later the same morning the image of the goddess itself is invested with life, and from then on the goddess in her own form is the centre of attention.

In the *belbaraṇ pūjā* the tree is treated as a goddess. The first action is the recitation of the *saṅkalpa*, following the general purification of the whole environment by the name of Viṣṇu and the water of the Ganges. More purifications follow later, but after the declaration of intent to perform *pūjā* the *ghat* has to be 'established' so that it becomes fit to receive the gods. First to be received by the *ghaṭ* is the Goddess Caṇḍī; actions and objects accomplishing this involve the items described above. The recitations of *mantras* ask the spirits of these items and the gods associated with them to receive the offerings and to come down among men. The sacred thread purifies the items destined for the deities. It is touched to different items: *ghaṭ*, earth, rice, water, branch of mango leaves, fruits, flowers, vermilion, and *svastik* (a sign meaning peace). Everything must be purified: the seat on which the priest sits, the offerings, and the worshippers. Water is sprinkled around, and flowers are offered to accomplish the aim of the recited words.

There are corresponding changes in the state of the priest. The ritualist must perform *aṅganyas* (counting and touching the parts of the body, purifying them), *niyantran* (a breathing exercise that purifies the five 'winds', which constitute life and are symbolic of divinity in men—elements shared by all created things, men and gods), *ekāgrotā* (concentration on the gods that symbolize these elements so that service may be done and the gods appear at the *pūjā* to the welfare and benefit of everyone). The priest must recite the *gāyatrī* (the divine *mantra* that confers twice-born status on the Brāhmaṇ and allows him to approach the gods). *Pranayan* is 'deep' meditation that unifies, in an ideal whole, the diverse elements thus purified, allowing the priest to invoke and bring down all the deities to be worshipped.

The *pūjās* (offerings of flowers and water with the appropriate *mantras*) of Pancadebatā are next. Gaṇeś, Śiva, Durgā, Viṣṇu, and the sun are worshipped one by one. All other deities and spirits (*bhūtas*) are worshipped then, with short *mantras* and a few drops of water on a flower. This part of the *pūjā* is concluded with sacrifice, uncooked rice, and fruit offerings. The *bali* consists of making seven small piles of rice and mustard seeds and reciting the *mantra* that dedicates the offering to the gods. Mustard-seed oil and rice are the two essential requirements of daily life. This sacrifice represents blood sacrifice without bloodshed. The form, *rūp*, of the goddess is given in her *dhyen* (a *mantra* of meditation describing the appearance of the goddess and aiding human imagination). The mark on the *bel* tree is a sign of the goddess; Caṇḍī is asked to manifest herself in the tree. The *adhibās*, or welcome of the goddess, is addressed to the divinity in the *bel* tree. The plate of welcome is offered to the tree as if it were the goddess. After this, all the deities represented in the painting—the goddess, her family, and all gods and demons associated with the origin and subsequent history of the goddess—are honoured and served. *Bhog*, cooked rice offering, represents the high point of the ritual. *Bhog* also means 'enjoyment' and 'acceptance'. It is the most sacred offering men can give the goddess, and only a Brāhmaṇ can ask her to accept it.

The Nine Sacred Plants

The *nabapatrikā* consists of nine plants or their leaves, also known as the Nine Durgās. The nine plants are tied together with the vines of the *aparājita* flower, a flower associated with Durgā. The goddess herself is *aparājita*, undefeated. This collection of plants appears only in the Durgāpūjā, entering the festival the evening of Ṣaṣṭhīkalparambha. But in the *rājā's pūjā*, where the *kalpas* (aims) of the three Ṭhākurānīs are celebrated on a more elaborate scale, the *nabaptrikā* is worshipped on each of the *belbaraṇ* nights. Each Ṭhākurānī has a separate *nabapatrikā*, and all three are immersed together on the tenth day. The plants are sacred in the totality of the *nabapatrikā*. Even separately they have great significance in ritual and the everyday life. All nine are valued by men and form basic ingredients of Bengali cooking. Rice is essential for human life, and the others are only slightly less important. These plants are fit representations of the goddess; divinity is comprehended through creation.

Men need images, for they cannot fathom the formless Universal Spirit (*brahman*). If one has the proper *bhakti* attitude, one can recognize the different aspects of divinity in the variety of creation. In a way the *nabapatrikā* also symbolizes human life. It represents all that is necessary for maintenance, well-being, and happiness. The nine plants stand for nine aspects of the goddess, nine kinds of *śakti* (power). Each plant is associated with one of the goddess's *śaktis*, and the goddess encompasses these aspects of her creative energy. Each one of them is a separate manifestation of Śiva. The Nine Durgās are the nine goddesses in the Candīpāṭh (the Debī Māhātma). Durgā is called Caṇḍī in the sacred texts; Caṇḍī is the name of the most powerful, dangerous, and potent aspect of the goddess, the form in which she defeated her enemies, the *āsuras*. Caṇḍī is depicted as a fierce goddess in the full flush of victory, shouting her joy so loudly that even distant mountains tremble. The nine plants and Nine Durgās are discussed below.

Rambhā is banana or *kolā* (the ordinary word is not used in rituals; the Sanskritic name designates the function of this fruit in the ritual). The goddess Brahmānī (Brahmā's *śakti*) is associated with it. Banana is an important item of all rituals; not only is it a favourite raw fruit, it is also cooked when unripe, and the flowers are used in curries. It is regarded as a necessary item of ordinary diet. Its leaves are used as plates for eating because they are pure and sacred. The plant itself is auspicious, being used for the *maṅgalghaṭ* in *pūjās* and life-cycle rituals.

Kacu is the Goddess Kālikā. This is an edible root; when cooked it resembles and tastes like meat. Many use it to supplement the rice diet. It is an important staple but can be eaten only in a cooked form. Kālikā is the consort of Śiva, the Goddess Kālī.

Haridrā or *halud* is the ordinary name for turmeric, an edible root, one of the most important spices. Not only does it appear in all rituals, including life-cycle celebrations (especially weddings), but it is the basic seasoning of any cooked food prepared from vegetables and meat. Mixed with other spices, it is *tarkāri*, the 'curry' of Bengal. It is pure and good for the body; people use it in treating all kinds of stomach upsets. It purifies the body inside and out and is used in the daily bath along with mustard oil—good for the skin, good for health. It is the plant of the Goddess Durgā herself.

Jayanti is the plant of the Goddess Kārttiki, the *śakti* of Kārtik, Durgā's son, the leader of the heavenly armies. It is a tree, but also a name of the Goddess Durgā. Some images in some temples of Bengal are known as Jayanti Debī. It means rejuvenation, celebration, a jubilee. The leaves of the tree are used to prevent and cure fevers.

Bel is one of the most sacred trees in Bengal. It is indispensable for any *pūjā*. The leaves are usually offered to all deities, especially

Śiva and his consorts. They are offered as picked, in clusters of three, symbolizing the *trisūl* (trident), Śiva's weapon. The goddess is invoked in this tree, the *sebā* (service) of the *pūjā*, the many offerings that are not actually on the scene may be symbolized by the *bel* leaf. The longest series of offerings in the *pūjā* are done with water and *bel* leaves, a symbolic service in which the *bel* expresses the same attitudes of worship as the whole *pūjā* sequence. The *mantra* with these offering states that the *jajmān* offers the deities scented flowers for their pleasure. The fruit of the *bel* tree is highly regarded as cooling in the summer, beneficial to health. It is a valuable medicine, used to treat digestive troubles. In a society where dysentery is the most common health problem, *bel* and *halud* are predictably valued. The goddess of this tree is Śaktī, the consort of Śiva.

Dalim, the pomegranate fruit, is also a regular item of offering in most *pūjās*, especially Debīpūjās. It is opened and spread out on a plate, the small red clusters constituting the offering. It is also a summer fruit, cooling and delicious. The tree is worshipped only during Durgāpūjā; the goddess associated with it is Raktadantika.

The *asoka* is another of the most sacred trees. Together with the *bel* tree, the *asoka* is the most often 'established' tree in Bengal. Certain trees (of these species) are selected as objects of worship for a variety of reasons. In a ritual that is similar to the invocation of life in an image of a deity, a god is asked to take up residence in the tree, and from then on the tree is treated as a representation of divinity. *Pūjās* must be offered regularly after that, especially in the month of Boiśakh (April-May), the month devoted to the *pūjās* of divinities as they are manifest in trees. *Asoka* is Viṣṇu's tree; it is also medicinal. Barren women may eat the leaves of this tree, in the course of a ritual, in the hope of becoming fertile. The goddess of the *asoka* is Sokarohita.

Mankacu is the arum plant, a cluster of flowers enclosed by fleshy leaves. The goddess is Cāmuṇḍā, the fearful aspect of the goddess that killed the demons Caṇḍa and Muṇḍa. . . .

Dhān is paddy; the unhusked, harvested rice is the most sacred member of the plant world. It is the basis of life, the central part of any meal. Rice is eaten in many forms, and it is sacred, especially when cooked. Men bathe and offer a portion to the gods before eating cooked rice. Rice is essential to *pūjās* and life-cycle rituals. It is the Goddess Lakṣmī, the goddess of wealth (*dhān* is rice, *dhan* is wealth). The most common representation of the Lakṣmī Debī is unhusked rice in a common measuring pot, the *Lakkhīpai* (*pai*, half-

śeer). The *Lakkhīpai* is worshipped during all Debīpūjās, in temples and *ṭhākurghars*, being placed at the side of the main deity. It is never moved (except in the New Rice festival when the goddess is ceremonially moved into the house), for the Debī is fickle, and wealth may easily leave the house. It is said that no Bengali feels he has eaten anything unless he has had a large portion of rice.

The day after the *belbaraṇs* of the three Ṭhākuranīs, the *kalparambha* in the non-royal Durgāpūjās, the morning ritual is devoted to the bathing of the *nabapatrikā*. The nine plants are regarded as the goddess, and after the bathing they are wrapped in a saffron-coloured *sāri* and worshipped like the goddess herself. On the tenth day the farewell ritual of the *nabapatrikā* is performed. Especially in *baṇgśa* worship (in which the kinship basis of Durgāpūjā is most clearly emphasized), women offer milk products and sweet things to the goddess in the *nabapatrikā* form. During the *pūjā* the *nabapatrikā* stands at the right side of the Durgā image (in the *rājā's pūjā* the *nabapatrikā* and the Durgāpaṭ together are wrapped in a white, red-bordered *sāri*). It is also known as Kala Bou, the banana-tree wife, and is honoured as mother, the Goddess Durgā herself. In the *rājā's* traditional *pūjā* the king himself used to wear this *sāri* on the tenth day, parading through the town, receiving the homage and *praṇām* (prostration) of his subjects. The women of the royal household used to do *praṇām* to the king, touching the sacred cloth. Later they themselves wore it draped around their head and shoulders.

The Vessel of the Gods

The *ghaṭ* is the most essential vessel of the *pūjā*; without it a rite is hardly possible. For the worship of the goddess especially, no image or temple is necessary and no offerings have to be given; the only indispensable items are water, flowers, and the *ghaṭ*. Yet even the *ghaṭ* is replaceable: the *yantra*, or *mātriyantra*, can substitute for the *ghaṭ*. The *ghaṭ* is made of earth (clay) and contains mud and water. It is marked in a special way; across the middle is a wide band painted white and filled with cross-hatching. The shape is that of the ordinary rice-cooking vessel (in other parts of the Bengal delta the *ghat* is painted all over with many-coloured designs, and the shape is also distinctive). The mud and water inside the *ghaṭ* are regarded as *gaṅgāmāṭi* and *gaṅgājal* (earth and water from the Ganges). The items placed on top of the *ghaṭ* (mango leaves, coconut, towel) must be perfect and unmarked. The coconut (*dāb*) must come with the vine that attaches it to the palm tree, for the stem is regarded as a sign of fruition and creation, symbolic of the goddess's function. All these items, including the *svastik* sign painted on the *ghaṭ* and the sacred thread placed around it, are regarded as the most honourable things men can offer (being auspicious, they are fit to be put on a vessel that will become the home of the gods). The *ghaṭ* is a sacred vessel because it symbolizes the body: the body of men is also the house of the goddess. Bhagavan (god) dwells in all men, through the *ghaṭ* men invite the goddess to reside in themselves. Water and earth are elements of the body; the *ghaṭ* is therefore like the living body, the house of the divinity. . . .

Water, whenever it is found in the open, is associated with the sacred Ganges—even a man-made water tank is Gaṇgā herself. Well or tube water is not used, because only open bodies of water have certain qualities beneficial to the health of men. Hence people prefer to bathe in the open; 'natural' water preserves the skin and prevents colds, asthma, and related diseases. The water in the *ghaṭs* comes from the tanks, and the rite of bringing the water is called *ghaṭ-tula* (lifting the *ghaṭ*). This involves processions through the town, usually accompanied by the playing of musical instruments. The procession expresses respect for the gods; the assemblage of *ghaṭ*, priest, umbrella, and fan symbolizes the presence of the gods. The objects associated with the worship are also regarded as potent and worthy of respect. The items carried in the procession are all royal objects; gods are also kings and must be treated as such by men. The vermilion used in painting the *svastik* sign is also auspicious, as are the other items. These 'auspicious things' of the *ghaṭ* are meant to please the goddess; without satisfying her, the worshipper cannot ask for boons. The *svastik* is a symbol of men's desire for auspicious results: let the goddess enjoy her stay, let her remember her devotees, let her mind be fixed on auspicious things, let her fulfill the desires of men.

In the Durgāpūjā a pair of large *ghaṭs* (*jaraghaṭs*) are needed. One is for the goddess herself, the other for Pancadebatā, the Five Gods, who must be worshipped every day. The *ghaṭs* can also mean the consort pair, Śiva and Durgā, or king and queen. Not every deity needs a *ghaṭ* for the worship; the sun is always worshipped directly as a living deity (*sākṣāt debatā*), and Viṣṇu and Śiva are worshipped in sacred stones, the *sālāgrām sila* and the *liṅga* respectively.

The Plate of Auspicious Things

The *prasasta* or *maṅgal* **pātra** is a plate used in the welcome of the goddess. It contains auspicious items used in and found essential for everyday life and also honorific items, symbols of royalty and power, wealth and fertility. These are the best things in the world, hence they are good signs, fit to be offered to the gods as a witness of the good intentions of men. The plate is large and round, made of brass or copper. In welcoming rituals it is waved around the image of the goddess, and then all items are touched to the *ghaṭ* and to the image itself. The plate makes its appearance in many other *pūjās*.

Whenever an image is 'established', given sight and life, the plate is there for the deity to use. It is also used in life-cycle rituals: in wedding ceremonies it is waved around the bride and the groom, then touched to their foreheads (the bride and groom being treated like deities). In the plate all *pūjā* items are collected and offered together to the gods, and in the course of the *pūjā* these items may be used separately, with *mantras* and *mudrās*, to symbolize the different aspects of the goddess.

There are twenty-seven items on the plate, the first being earth, a symbol of the Ganges. Then comes turmeric mixed with oil, especially that of the mustard seed. This oil is very important in *pūjā*; it is mixed with turmeric and, separately, with vermilion before being put on the *ghaṭ*, image, or other representation of divinity. Oil is also used in the daily bath; in water it is a cleaner. Mustard oil is used in cooking to make many kinds of fries eaten with parched or cooked rice. The other items or the plate are 'rock' or parched rice (shaped like small bits of gravel); unhusked rice; scent or perfume, most often sandalwood paste; fruit, a whole banana (unmarked and with its stem intact); and a flower, an indispensable item of worship and a way of expressing joy as well as respect (note the garlanding of elders, guests, and friends). Each deity has a flower particularly suited to his worship, a flower that delights him most. Then there is *dūrba* grass, sacred because a drop of sacred nectar fell on it. The nectar of immortality was rescued by the gods when the demons threatened to capture it after the churning of the ocean. Garuda, the carrier of Viṣṇu, was dispatched to rescue the vessel of nectar, but, being tried, the bird made several stops on his way to the Himalayas. Whenever he put the jug on the ground a few drops fell on the grass. *Dūrba* thus became immortal, and the localities where the nectar fell are still celebrated at the time of the four major *kumbha melās* (jug fairs) involving millions of pilgrims every twelve years. *Dūrba* is used in rites (*bratas*) of women, being tied to the arm with a yellow or red thread (*suta*) as a sign of the goddess's benediction and protective watch over the wearer.

Curds and *ghī* (clarified butter) are the next items, sacred because they are the products of the cow. All these are used in *pūjās*. The cow is regarded as the mother from whom all nourishment comes; Kṛṣṇa himself was the servant of cows in Brindaban. Curds are highly prized as the correct way to end a meal; *ghī* is the purest item of food. Rice boiled with *ghī* is the most sacred food offering; *ghī* is most valuable and highly regarded of all things. It is used in the fire sacrifice; butter burned in the fire goes straight to the gods and incurs their beneficial attention. To please men *ghī* is poured on the rice at mealtime. It is eaten reverently without mixing it with vegetables and pulses.

The next item is the *svastik*, the sign of peace and grace, of welfare and desire for the blessings of the gods. It is to be drawn with rice powder sprinkled on the plate itself. Then comes white starch, the liquid from the first boiling of rice, then vermilion, another important substance. Mixed with oil, vermilion is applied to offerings, *ghaṭ*, images of the goddess, and to anything that is sacrificed and given to Debī. It is necessary for all Debī pūjās. Married women wear it in the parting of their hair, and its application is the central act in the marriage ritual. Red is the colour of the goddess; vermilion is her favourite, symbolizing auspiciousness, victory, joy, and blood in sacrifice. In the same series belong *āltā* and *kājal*; all are accessories of women and therefore indispensable to the goddess. Āltā is the red lacquer women apply to the soles and edges of their feet. It is used to beautify, but it also saves the skin from cracking. Kājal is the black collyrium women put in and around their eyes to beautify and clean them.

Śaṅkha, the conch shell, is another sacred object in the series. As a horn it is used to call and honour deities in the *pūjās* and brides in the marriage ceremony. From this shell, arm bracelets are made that women wear as a sign of marriage. Durgā herself wears these bracelets and holds a conch in her hand. A special artisan caste, the Śaṅkaris, work with this shell. Durgā is held in special respect by the people of this caste. Metals form the next group—gold, silver, and copper—all the pure and precious metals everyone values. These cannot be polluted, hence most *pūjā* vessels are made of copper. Gold and silver are royal as well as pure, and so they ought to be offered to the gods, even if in very small quantities. Copper is less pure than gold, but it can be washed with water and ashes; no pollution is bad enough to make men throw away a copper vessel. Gold is unmarked; copper is less pure because it acquires a green deposit when exposed to humidity. The last metal is iron, not precious but necessary for cultivation and work. Women also wear an iron bangle as a sign of marriage. Then there is the arrow, a weapon of the goddess, a sign of Śiva (also the representation of the Bhairabas). Ascetics carry the arrow and the trident with them all the time. A yellow thread (*suta*) smeared with turmeric is also included as an auspicious sign. Men and women wear this at the time of the different Debī *bratas* when the goddess is worshipped as the one who delivers from danger. The thread is a charm, a lucky sign, protecting men from evil. Threads are worn by children, given at various times after birth to ward off evil spirits and ghosts. But the thread is also a sign of faith; the wearer will fear no danger, because the goddess is watching over him. It is worn at difficult and dangerous rituals like the *gājan,* also as a sign of the goddess's special relation to the devotees.

The final three items are *ārati,* light or flame, and *cāmor* or yak tail. These are all used in the evening *ārati,* a short service of the goddess. They symbolize honour and respect; the *cāmor* is a rare object, for its touch is beneficial and its presence drives away all annoying things of the summer night, such as flying insects and biting vermin. The lamp is a sign of the sun, a witness to worship. A devotee must have a witness, and the sun, light, and flame are the most faithful (Sītā was failed by trees, waters, and animals when she asked for a witness to her devotion to Rāma). The lamp symbolizes knowledge; the goddess who created all things is also the path to knowledge of the world. Through her *māyā* and *līlā* (cosmic play) she hides from the eyes of men the true nature of things, which is oneness beyond seeming multiplicity. *Ārati* is the act of offering these reminders of her nature and power to the goddess, a reminder that serves men as well. It is a final service before the night interrupts the daily cycle of worship.

There are other important *pūjā* objects. The oblations that constitute a major part of a *pūjā* are poured from three vessels; the *kamandala* is the brass water jug in which the Brāhmaṇ keeps the Ganges water and into which he dips the flowers for purification before the offering. From this jug, water is poured into the *kosakusi* (leaf-shaped copper vessels). Water is poured in short streams, repeated three times in the purifications and the bathing of the goddess. These vessels are shaped like the *bel* leaf, the same shape being represented by the two palms cupped in the gesture of offering, *añjali*. The vessels themselves are expressive of offering. The formal flower offerings in the *pūjā*, in which non-Brāhmaṇs may also participate, are made with this gesture. The red or yellow sandalwood paste is made by rubbing the block of wood on a wet stone slab. The stone slab is also used in the kitchen to prepare the spices that go into curry. The *pūjā* ground is often covered by drawings made with rice powder and water. These drawings (*ālpanās*) trace the seats of the worshipper and the priest, the place of the goddess, and her footprints leading to her seat. The priest's mat is placed over the drawn seat, and the offerings are placed on the goddess's *ālpanā* (flower, house, and other signs associated with her are also drawn: footprints, fish, sun, or just a flowerlike abstract design, reminiscent of the more exact and specific *yantra*).

Pradīp (lamp) and *dhūp* (incense) *dhoa* (resin smoke) are also necessary for Durgāpūjā. *Dhup* is scent, always a welcome item, associated with honour even in ordinary life. But it is used especially in *pūjās*, and deities cannot do without it; it is an expression of devotional attitude. Waving a lighted incense stick around a deity is *sebā*, service. *Pradip* is light, knowledge (*jñān*). Out of the darkness comes light, dissolving the darkness. In deep meditation everything becomes dark around the devotee; then lights appear, the expression of pure consciousness. The light becomes more and more intense, dazzling white *cāitanya* (consciousness), which makes men capable of conceiving of the *brahman*. Light is a symbol of *brahman*. In *ārati* a lamp with five branches and five flames is used. Camphor is lit in the five small cups, and the lamp is then waved around the goddess.

Five is a sacred number, recurring time and time again. Many offerings, items expressive of service for the gods and items of purification, come in fives: five product of the cow, five nectars, five grains, and so on. Śiva has five faces, and there are five main gods. The five lights stand for the five paths to god: through desire (*kām*), duty (*dharma*), calculation (*artha*), knowledge (*mukti*), and devotion (*bhakti*). It is also the first item to be waved in the *ārati*, and it sums up the whole little *pūjā*: the goddess is greeted with lights and offered a bath, fresh clothing, and a garland of flowers; finally, she is fanned with the *cāmor*. *Pradīp* also means the power of burning, energy, the energy that drives the five elements and the five vital airs that are the basis of life. *Ārati* also means cessation, rest, and peace, the proper state of Śiva when he is one with the goddess, the time of sleep, of no activity at all.

Time Renewed: *Ratha Jātrā* in Puri

FRÉDÉRIQUE APFELL MARGLIN

The largest festival of the year in Puri is a festival of renewal which ushers in the monsoon in June-July. The car festival (*ratha jātrā*), which takes place annually in the month of *āṣāḍha* (June–July), rejuvenates the deities, thereby renewing the kingship, the people and the land. A much enlarged version of the car festival takes place periodically—every twelve years more or less, whenever the extra lunar month which is added to the year in order for the solar and the lunar year to coincide, happens to be the month of *āṣāḍha*. This festival is called the festival of the new body (*naba kalebara*) and at that time the old wooden images are replaced by new wooden images; the old deities 'die' and new ones are 'born'.

In both these rituals, the main actors are those temple servants who stand in a kinship relationship to the deities. These are the *daitās* and the *devadāsīs*. The *daitās* are considered to be the 'blood relatives' (*rakta samparka*) of Jagannāth [the presiding deity of the famous temple at Puri in Orissa] and the *devadāsīs* are the wives of Jagannāth. These two categories of temple servants are the only ones who stand in a kin relationship to Jagannātha; all the others are servants, not relatives. Here again, as in the case of the left-hand *śākta* ritual, kinship categories are utilized to communicate about time. The communication, as well as the symbolism, is different. Time is not dissolved but renewed, since what is achieved is a rejuvenation. Rejuvenation entails reversing the normal direction of time in which beings grow older, not younger.

These festivals attract hundreds of thousands of pilgrims, mostly from Orissa but also from surrounding provinces. The presence of

Excerpted from Frédérique Apfell Marglin, 'Time Renewed', in *Wives of the God-King: The Rituals of the Devadasis of Puri*, Oxford University Press, Delhi, 1985, pp. 243–63.

the king during these rituals is indispensable. He has to do the sweeping of the chariots before they can leave the temple. I witnessed the festival thrice: in 1976, in 1977 when it corresponded to the festival of the new body, and in 1981. When the Gajapati appears and starts climbing the ramp onto the chariot, the immense crowd shouts with one voice 'Victory to the Gajapati!' One certainly receives the impression at that time, that the Gajapati ideology is not dead and that the kingship and all that it stands for is still very meaningful to a great number of people.

The king is the sacrificer (*jajamāna*) for these festivals as he is indeed for the whole temple. In his capacity of *jajamāna*, the king is the recipient of the fruits (*phala*) of these ritual actions which are the renewal of the prosperity and well-being of the people and the land. . . .

Description of the Car Festival (*Ratha Jātrā*)

The word *ratha* means chariot; by translating the words *Ratha Jātrā* by 'car festival' I am simply following local usage. The name car festival does not refer only to that portion of the festival in which the deities are taken in three huge chariots to another temple but also to what happens before that moment. The festival starts a fortnight before the pilgrimage journey in the chariots, on the full moon day of the month of Jyeṣṭha (May–June)—which is the last day of that month—with the 'Bathing Festival' (*snāna purnimā*; *purnimā* means 'full moon day'). This festival only lasts one day and is followed by the period of illness [of the deities]. Although the great majority of the pilgrims arrive in Puri on the days preceding the pilgrimage journey, the festival of the bath attracts a smaller but not negligible number of pilgrims.

The Bathing Festival

On the morning of the bathing festival, after the images of Lakṣmī and Bhūdevī [consorts of Jagannātha] have been removed from the inner sanctum by brahmin temple servants, the *daitās* enter the inner sanctum and lift the images, one by one and take them in a procession, accompanied by the beating of gongs, large decorative umbrellas and fans, to the bathing platform. This platform is located near the outer wall, facing east, in the north-east corner of the outer compound. The platform is raised so that the images placed on it are visible from the street. In fact the location of the platform makes it clear that the images are on public display; they face the main square in front of the temple. Many pilgrims throng the open space in front of the eastern gate as well as the roofs of the houses just opposite the temple. I myself had rented a seat on such a roof, just across from the bathing platform, which afforded me an excellent view. Pilgrims are also allowed around that platform and many perch themselves on top of the compound wall. Once the four wooden images [of Jagannātha, his brother Balabhadra, their sister Subhadhra, and Sudarśana] are standing on this platform, which is for the occasion shaded with a cloth canopy, the *daitās* along with the *pūjā paṇḍās* and *simhāris* [ritual functionaries] fetch water from a nearby storeroom. This water is placed in 108 pots. It comes from a covered well situated in front of the temple of Sitaḷā, the goddess of fever and pox, near the northern gate of the temple compound. Some of the temple servants climb on the wall at the rear of the bathing platform and pour water on top of the images and some throw water from below. The drenching of the four images occurs simultaneously. The images are discoloured by the water; some of the temple servants collect the water which has run down the images and is blackened by the paint and walk among the crowd which eagerly takes drops of that water as the left-over of the deities. After this bath the pilgrims are allowed on the platform which in an instant is thronged with men and women who all try to touch the images.

Then the platform is cleared of people and the brahmin temple servant who is the representative of the king (called *mudiratha*) or the king himself comes and performs a ritual called 'sweeping' (*cherāpahānrā*). With a gold-handled broom, this man sweeps the bathing platform, while other (brahmin) temple servants sprinkle it with water and sandalwood powder.

Then huge masks in the shape of an elephant's head are brought to the platform and fastened on the images. This is called the 'Ganeś dress' (*Ganeś beśa*). These masks actually hide the images entirely. Thus disguised, the deities are offered the regular sixteenfold offering. The curtain, which in normal worship is drawn at the time of the offering so as to hide the inner sanctum from view, is on that day symbolically represented by a thread which is drawn across the front of the platform. This is the only time that cooked food is offered in public. The most visible and dramatic part of this offering is the bringing and setting out of the food. After the three *pūjā paṇḍās*—who are sitting in front of the three main deities, facing north—have offered the fourteen first offerings . . . the temple cooks (*suāras*) bring the food . . . in earthen pots which are hung on ropes strung to a shoulder pole. . . . The pots are placed on the floor of the platform within four squares which have been drawn just for this purpose. In addition to the pots, three plates of food are set in front of each of the priests. At that time a *devadāsī* used to dance in the presence of the *rājaguru* at the foot of the stairs leading up to the bathing platform. These stairs are situated on the southern side of the platform and the foot of the stairs is not visible from outside the temple. When I witnessed the festival no *devadāsī* danced; the *devadāsīs* told me that when they were still dancing in the temple they used to dance at that time also.

After the offering, the platform is once more made accessible to the public which as before crowd over it. At that time it is late morning and the images are taken back in the same manner as they were brought in to the main temple. They are not returned to the inner sanctum but placed in the corridor which leads from the inner sanctum to the outer sanctum. There they are placed on the floor in a semi-reclining position, propped up by wooden braces.

The Period of Illness (aṇasara)

The moment the deities are placed on the floor in front of the inner sanctum marks the beginning of the period of illness. During the (dark) fortnight of the deities' illness the gate to the dancing hall is closed. No one but the *daitās* and the Pati Mahāpātra can enter the place where the deities are reclining. The Pati Mahāpātra belongs to the cook division (*suāra*). . . . This man is said to have been asked by the *daitās* to do the offering to the deities during the period of illness. Although the cooks have a mixed descent, they are brahmins, but they do not do the offering in the temple. This is done by the *pūjā paṇḍās*. The Pati Mahāpātra is the only brahmin allowed in the place of illness.

During this dark fortnight, the cooking in the great kitchen of the temple is stopped. All 'auspicious' sounds are also stopped. There is no beating of gongs, no sounding of the trumpet or the conch-shell and the *devadāsīs* do not sing and dance. Very few people visit the temple during that time and the temple is silent and deserted.

Although the Pati Mahāpātra is there to do the offering, it is said that the offering is done in 'tribal fashion' (*śabari pūjā*). This means the following: the *daitās* take up residence in the area and bring raw food such as fruits and milk and milk products. They peel the fruits, taste them first to ascertain if they are ripe and then they offer them to the deities. The peels are not thrown outside but remain on the floor. This is said to be the same type of worship that their ancestor, the tribal chief Viśvabāsu performed in the forest. The *daitās* as the blood relatives of Jagannātha sleep and eat right there with their kinsmen.

They also administer an herbal medicine which has been prescribed and prepared by the temple doctor (*baidya*). This man is a brahmin and cannot himself enter in the place where the deities are suffering.

Besides offering raw food and medicine, the *daitās* also repair the body of the images. The drenching during the bathing festival discolours and damages the outer cloth covering of the wooden images. These are removed and replaced with new cloth covering which is then covered with a coat of resin and one of paint. When this outer covering is ready, one of the *daitā*—called the *dutta mukha simhāri*—paints the features of the faces of the deities, except for the pupils of their eyes.

On the twelfth day of the dark fortnight, the *daitās* bring to the king in the palace some plates equal in number to that of the family members of the king, on which they have placed some of the old cloth covering of the deities. These are the left-overs (*praśād*) of the deities and they are offered to the king. The king then orders that some *saris* be brought to the *daitās*. The king first touches these *saris* which are then given to the *daitās*. The latter then go to the main gate of the palace and there tie the *saris* around their heads. This tying of the *sari* is not considered to be the ceremony of 'tying the *sari*' (*sāḍhi bandhana*) which is the temple dedication ceremony. After tying their *saris*, the *daitās* go for a viewing (*darśana*) of the king and they stand in front of him with folded hands and bow down. The king instructs them about the car festival and how to manage it and make it run smoothly. It is only after the *daitās* have given these left-overs to the king that they can give the same left-overs to pilgrims, relatives and friends.

On the thirteenth day of the dark fortnight, one of the *daitās* brings in a silver pot some pasted chalk and gum (*khāḍi*) which will constitute the first coat of paint on the images. This will be offered to the king who in turn will again advise the *daitās* as to the smooth running of the festival. From that night, the work of the painter *daitā* starts. This work is finished on the fourteenth day.

On the dawn of the fifteenth day—the new moon day, *amābāsyā*—the period of illness is over and the gate to the dancing hall is opened. Pilgrims—who have already arrived for the pilgrimage journey—flock to the temple for 'the viewing of the new youth' (*naba jaubana darśana*) of the deities. The deities are still reclining on the floor in front of the inner sanctum and are still pupil-less.

The Pilgrimage Journey (tīrtha jātrā)

After this public viewing the deities and the temple are purified (*mahāsnāna*). After this purification the three *pūjā paṇḍas* of the anthropomorphic deities paint the pupils of the eyes of the three images. This act is called the 'festival of the eye' (*netroścaba*). Once the deities' eyes have been opened so to speak, the representative of the king (*mudiratha*) comes and performs a welcoming ritual (*bandāpanā*).

Once the king, through his representative in the temple, has welcomed the deities in their renewed state, the deities are offered a regular worship. Cooking is resumed in the kitchen and everything proceeds as usual with the important difference that the deities are not reintegrated on their jewelled throne in the inner sanctum but are still reclining on the floor where they just spent a fortnight of indisposition.

The next day, which is the second day of the bright fortnight of *āṣāḍha* (*śukla dvitiyā*), is the beginning of the car festival proper. At dawn the masses of pilgrims all head for the sea to take a purificatory bath. By the time they return to the area in front of the temple, three *śāsan* brahmins are sitting in a pavilion above the main entrance which overlooks the three chariots. There they perform the Vedic fire sacrifice (*homa*) while chanting Vedic verses. This goes on very much on the side and no one pays any attention to this Vedic consecration (*pratiṣṭhā*) of the chariots. The Vedic brahmins then come down and onto the chariots to sprinkle water on the platform where the images will be placed, in order to purify them.

The chariots, which were almost two months in the making, are quite tall structures, the top of the tower-like construction reaching above the walls of the temple compound. The chariots are covered with coloured cloths: red and black in the chariot of Subhadrā, yellow and red in the chariot of Jagannātha and green and red in that of Baḷabhadra. Below the platform on which the *daitās* and other temple servants will ride, which stands some fifteen feet above the ground, are nine niches—about three feet tall—with brightly coloured wooden sculptures of what are called 'side deities' (*pārśva devatā*). The nine images on Jagannātha's car are as follows: (1) Kṛṣṇa holding the mountain Govardhana; (2) Kṛṣṇa on top of the demon Praḷamba; (3) an image of Viṣṇu Nārāyaṇa sitting in the lotus pose and holding his four 'weapons' (mace, discus, conch-shell, and lotus); (4) another image of Nārāyaṇa with eight arms (instead of the four usual ones); (5) a figure of Hanumān, the monkey deity of the Rāmāyaṇa; (6) an image of Nrusingha, the man-lion incarnation of Viṣṇu, with four arms, tearing open a man (Hiranyakaśipu); (7) another image of Hanumān shown with Lakṣmaṇa, Rāma's younger brother; (8) an image of Hari-Hara: half Viṣṇu and half Śiva; (9) an image of Lakṣmaṇa, Rāma and Hanumān.

The images around the car of Baḷabhadra are as follows: (1) Ganeś; (2) Śiva on his bull; (3) an eight-armed Śiva; (4) Lakṣmaṇa on Hanumān; (5) a twenty-two armed Nrushingha; (6) Baḷarāma killing a demon; (7) Baḷarāma; (8) a six-faced image of Brahma riding on the gander; (9) Nārāyaṇa sitting on the serpent Śesanāga.

The nine images around the car of Subhadrā are the following: (1) An eight-armed goddess, Kāḷī, sitting on a corpse; (2) an image of Barāhī, the female boar (Barāha is the boar incarnation of Viṣṇu); (3) Cāmundī, looking 'terrible' with bones strewn around her; (4) Parvatī, four-handed (Śiva's consort); (5) eight-handed Durgā killing the buffalo demon; (6) Kāḷī (?), a goddess with four hands holding the goad, the noose and showing the boon granting and the fear-not gesture; (7) a four-handed Durgā; (8) again Durgā killing the buffalo; (9) Baṇadurgā (Durgā of the forest) showing Kṛṣṇa taking a thorn out of her foot.

The long-awaited moment has arrived and the beating of gongs is heard before the procession emerges from within the temple onto the crowded square outside. The police form a cordon to press back the crowd. The wooden pillar Sudarśana is the first to be brought out. Before being carried up the ramp to the platform of the chariot of Subhadrā, it is made to circumambulate it three times at a run. Then Baḷabhadra is brought out, then Subhadrā and lastly Jagannātha. This is a highly colourful and dramatic moment. A group of twenty or so temple servants actually carry the image. The *daitās* and the cooks (*suāras*) holding the images themselves and the *pūjā paṇḍās* and the *simhāris* holding on to thick silk ropes tied to the images, both in front and in back. The images are decorated with large fan-like flower head dresses which rock back and forth as the men give a slow rocking gait to the deities (this gait is called *pahaṇḍi*). In the front of the images two rows of men from the bell-metal caste (*kansāri*), bare torsoed and their waist adorned with bright red sashes, loudly and rhythmically beat on gongs while with each beat they thrust their bodies forward. The procession is accompanied by umbrella bearers, large fan (*torānas*) bearers and men blowing conch-shells and trumpets. Carrying the huge images up the rather steep and uneven ramp to the chariot is no small task and the crowd cheers the efforts of the *daitās* and the *paṇḍās*. Then the *mahājanas* (brahmin servants in charge of movable images) bring the representative images of Jagannātha, namely Mādan Mohan and of Baḷabhadra namely Rāmakṛṣṇa, onto the chariots of Jagannātha and Baḷabhadra respectively.

Once the deities are properly placed on the chariots everyone waits for the arrival of the king. He is carried from the palace some 100 yards down on the main road, in a vehicle called a *tāmjān* which is an ornamented chair carried by men. He is followed by the palace elephant. The *rājagurus*, agnates, and some feudatory kings accompany him on foot to the chariots. As they ascend the ramp, shouts of *Jay Gajapati*! (Victory to the Gajapati) surge from the pilgrims. The *rājagurus* hand the king a gold-handled broom and the king walks all around the platform three times; once sweeping it (*cherāpahānrā*) and twice sprinkling it with perfumed water. He does this on all the three chariots in the same order as the one in which the deities were brought out. The king returns to the palace in the same manner that he came.

After this ritual the ramps are removed and a team of wooden horses are attached to the front of each chariot. Then a large wooden charioteer is placed on the left side of the platform. The ropes—four to each chariot—are then fastened. The moment that everyone has been eagerly waiting for is approaching. The signal to pull the cars is given by a man, called the car caller (*ratha dāhuka*) who is perched on the front of each chariot and holds a long cane. When he calls loudly out to the crowd,everyone reaches for the ropes. This man shouts out obscenities at the people, challenging them to show their strength and the people laughingly respond.

As the first chariot, that of Baḷabhadra, slowly starts moving, the gong players arrayed in the front of the platform start their loud rhythmic beating. The *daitās* and the other temple servants sit or stand around the images. The huge wheels (as many as sixteen of them) made of wood creak and the chariot moves making a strange roaring noise. From the crowd all kinds of things are thrown onto the chariot. Coconuts come crashing and split open; bananas and mangoes also fly through the air and if aimed right land on the chariot. Money, even jewellery and watches are also thrown from the crowd.

The journey to the Guṇḍicā [a legendry queen devotee of Jagannātha] temple, some two miles down the road, is interrupted by pauses during which large baskets of raw food are brought in front of the chariots and offered to the deities. The food is sent by monasteries (*maṭha*) and by some wealthy private persons as well.

The chariot of Jagannātha, which is the last to leave, makes a stop which the other two chariots do not make. It stops at a temple about mid-way between the Guṇḍicā temple and the main temple. That temple is called the temple of mother's sister (*māusimā*). The name of the goddess enshrined there is Arddhāśinī meaning 'half the ocean'. The priest of that temple offers Jagannātha fried cheese cakes.

When the three cars have reached Guṇḍicā the images are not immediately taken out, but the cars remain until an auspicious hour has been set for the transfer of the deities to that temple. Each time that I witnessed the festival the deities remained on the chariots for about twenty-four hours. Pilgrims settle in around the chariots and chant prayers, offer lamps, fruits or incense, clamber up on the chariots to touch the deities. The *daitās* and other temple servants sit on the chariots and help the pilgrims climb on. The atmosphere is relaxed and suffused with devotion.

While the deities are on the chariots in front of Guṇḍicā temple, the *pūjā paṇḍās* make offerings of dry, raw food (*sukhila bhoga*). This food consists mainly of raw flattened rice (*cuḍa*) mixed with grated coconut and unprocessed brown sugar (*ghur*). Fruits are also offered. The offering is done in the sixteenfold manner as in the temple. The *daitās*, although they do not perform the offering, are around during the work of the *pūjā paṇḍās*. They sit on the chariots but do not touch the food.

The Stay in Guṇḍicā Temple

The deities are carried inside this temple in the same way that they were carried outside the main temple. The Guṇḍicā temple has no image installed in its inner sanctum and is used only during this festival.

After the deities have been placed in the inner sanctum and the *daitās* have left, the temple is purified and the deities are given a purification bath. The *daitās* will not play any role during the seven days that the deities will stay in that temple. Food is cooked in the temple of Guṇḍicā and is offered as usual by the *pūjā paṇḍās*. The ritual day in that temple is the same as that in the main temple. The *devadāsīs* resume their rituals, both at the morning meal offering and at the evening putting-to-sleep ceremony. The only difference with the daily worship in the main temple is that the deities' daily morning bath (*abakāśa*) is more elaborate. The deities are rubbed with sandalwood paste all over their bodies (*sarbānga candan lāgi*). Huge quantities of sandal paste are supplied by one of the monasteries in Puri for this purpose.

On the fifth day of the bright fortnight—which corresponds to the second day of the deities' stay in Guṇḍicā—there takes place a very interesting interlude which involves Lakṣmī and the *devadāsīs*. In 1977 three *devadāsīs*—Amrapalli, Radha and Bisaka—participated in that ritual, which I was able to observe. Lakṣmī, who as we will recall has been left behind, is taken out from the main temple in a palanquin carried by brahmin temple servants. The procession includes torch bearers—since this takes place in the middle of the night—a gong beater, a conch blower and the *devadāsīs* of the outer division, who walk on the left side of Lakṣmī's palanquin. The procession walks at a rather brisk pace to the Guṇḍicā temple and stops in front of the chariot of Jagannātha. There the palanquin is placed on wooden stands and a brahmin temple servant conducts a short worship of Lakṣmī. He offers flowers, incense, perfume, lamp and food. In between each offering another temple servant pours water over his hands. When this is over the *devadāsīs* sing a song called the Herā Pañcami song after the name of this ritual (Herā Pañcami means 'the seeing fifth' when Lakṣmī goes to see her husband on the fifth day). The song sings the anger of Lakṣmī who has been left behind by her husband. While they sing, the *devadāsīs* approach a man, who turns out to be Swaī Mahāpātra, the *daitā* in charge of the image of Jagannātha. They all bend down and take a hold of the end of his *dhoti* (lower garment) and pull on it as if to tear it, while singing [a] song [of separation and craving for reunion]. . . .

After this song the palanquin with Lakṣmī on it is taken around the car of Jagannātha and one of the *devadāsīs* breaks off a small piece of wood on it. The group then proceeds inside the temple of Guṇḍicā. . . . Inside the temple, the *devadāsīs* remain in the audience hall while Lakṣmī is taken into the inner sanctum. There one of the brahmin servants throws the powder that was secured from the temple of Bimalā before Lakṣmī set out from the main temple. As the song says, this magic dust, once thrown in Jagannātha's face, will make him want to return to Lakṣmī. The deity's response to the dust thrown in his face is indicated by his being slightly pushed forward by one of the priests. While this is going on in the inner sanctum, the *devadāsīs* in the audience hall sing again the song of Herā Pañcami. Then Lakṣmī is returned to the main temple and the *devadāsīs* go home.

The day after Herā Pañcami, in the morning three *pūjā paṇḍās* take three 'garlands of order' from the deities (*āgyāmāḷa*) and place these garlands on the three chariots. From that moment the three chariots are turned around to face south in the returning direction. This must be accomplished within three days.

The Return Journey (bahuḍa jātrā)

On the tenth day of the bright fortnight of this same month (*śukla daśami*) the deities start their return journey (*bahuḍa jātrā*). Exactly the same series of events take place that happened during the first journey. The deities are taken out in procession, lifted onto the chariots, the king sweeps the chariots and the pilgrims pull them. . . .

The chariot of Jagannātha makes a stop in front of the king's palace. There takes place what is called 'the meeting of Lakṣmī and Nārāyaṇa' (*Lakṣmī-Nārāyaṇa bheṭa*). The statue of Lakṣmī is carried from the storeroom in the main temple by brahmin servants, to a pavilion placed on top of the outer compound wall on the eastern side, called 'the gazing pavilion' (*cāhāṇi maṇḍapa*). Lakṣmī is accompanied by her *dāsīs*, the *devadāsīs*. From that pavilion Lakṣmī gazes at the chariot of Jagannātha parked in front of the palace. While there the *devadāsīs* sing . . . the *Lakṣmī-Nārāyaṇa bheṭa* song, announcing the return of the god. . . .

Lakṣmī is then carried in a palanquin from the temple to the palace. The *devadāsīs* accompany her. When Lakṣmī's palanquin has left the temple, news is sent to the king who sets out on foot along with the two *rājagurus* and an entourage consisting of some agnates and (erstwhile) feudatory kings. The king meets Lakṣmī's palanquin about midway between the palace and the temple. He takes hold of the right side of Lakṣmī's palanquin—keeping the goddess on his left—and walks towards the chariot of Jagannātha. When the small procession arrives in front of the chariot, the king lifts the small statue of Lakṣmī above his head and makes her face the statue of Jagannātha on the chariot. After replacing her on the palanquin, still holding on to it, the king and his entourage come close to the chariot where the *daitās* of Jagannātha hand to the *rājagurus* the 'garland of order' of the deity and the *rājagurus* give it to the king. After this the king, still holding onto Lakṣmī's palanquin, circumambulates Jagannātha's chariot once. The circumambulation ends right by the palace gate, where the king and his entourage for a moment stand facing the crowd so as the people may have a last *darśan* of the king. The statue of Lakṣmī is returned to the temple.

The chariot of Jagannātha then is pulled to the main temple. There, a sixteenfold offering of raw dry food is done by the *pūjā paṇḍās* on the three chariots. On the evening of the eleventh day (*ekādasi*, especially sacred to Viṣṇu) a special offering is given. It is called 'the lip milk drink' (*adhāra poṇā*). This drink, made of milk, cheese and bananas, is placed in huge earthen wares which reach up to the lips of the images, hence the name. The drinks are offered by the *pūjā paṇḍās* in a fivefold worship, after which the jars are broken and the liquid runs all over the chariots and onto the ground. The pilgrims jostle with each other to catch some of the liquid which they drink as *praśād*. This offering is said to be for the *yoginīs*, who are the attendants of Kālī.

The deities are then given what is called 'the golden dress' (*sunā beśa*). To their unfinished arms and legs are affixed solid gold forearms and hands as well as feet. On their heads golden crowns are placed and they are adorned with gold jewellery. When the deities are so bedecked, the throng of pilgrims circumambulate the three chariots, forming a veritable human river. It is a high point in the pilgrims' journey, for to have a view of this golden dress is considered particularly auspicious.

After the gold has been removed, some two hours later, the deities are taken back inside the temple, in the same fashion as they were taken out. When the images of Sudarśan, Baḷabhadra and Subhadrā are in the audience hall and the statue of Jagannātha is just being lowered down the ramp from his chariot, the small statue of Lakṣmī is carried in the hands of the *mahājanas* from the storeroom to the 'meeting pavilion' accompanied by the *devadāsīs*. After Lakṣmī has been replaced in the inner sanctum, the *devadāsīs* remain in that portion of the temple.

When the image of Jagannātha has reached the audience hall, the other three images are already in the inner sanctum. The *devadāsīs* close Jaya Bijaya Duāra, which is the gate leading from the audience hall onto the outer sanctum. The *devadāsīs* are on the inside and the *daitās* with Jagannātha are in the audience hall. A song dialogue takes place between the *devadāsīs* and the *daitās*. The *devadāsīs* are those of the inner division. Now the ritual is done only by Brundabati. She gave me a lively report of this dialogue which quite obviously she had great fun in doing. The tone of voice in which the dialogue is enacted is loud and lusty. The first two verses are recited in Sanskrit but then both *devadāsīs* and *daitās*, whose main spokesman is Swaī Mahāpātra, shift to a very colloquial Oriya. According to Brundabati, Swaī Mahāpātra first recites a verse in Sanskrit which she was either unwilling or unable to give me. But the same thing is then repeated in Oriya and simply says: 'Oh Dāsīs, are you there? Open the door!' The *devadāsī* replies in Sanskrit (but she gave me only the Oriya version): 'Have you forgotten the road? This is not Guṇḍicā temple. How have you come here? In Guṇḍicā you had singing and dancing and young women, here there is nothing. This is the dwelling of a housewife (*gruhiṇī*). This is the house of one who suffers from separation (*birahiṇī*). It is better for you to return to that Guṇḍicā place. Then follows the song dialogue in Oriya [speaking of reunion and happiness]. . . .

At the end of the dialogue, the *devadāsī* unhooks the gate and she exits through the southern gate which is a side entrance to the outer sanctum.

Jagannātha is brought in the inner sanctum and placed on the dais. After the purificatory rites are carried out, normal temple worship resumes; this is initiated by Lakṣmī being replaced on the dais to the left of her Lord. Thus reunited with his wife, the Lord's pilgrimage is at an end.*

* *Every twelve years, a more elaborate version of the* ratha jātrā *takes place. Called* naba kalebara *(the festival of the new body), it is marked by the replacement of the old by new wooden images ('rebirth' after 'death') of the deities (see Marglin 1985: 263–6). For Marglin's interpretations, see ibid.: 266–81.* Editor.

Mūrtipūjā in Śvetāmbar Jain Temples

JOHN E. CORT

The Śvetāmbar Jain temples of Rāṇakpur, Delvāḍā on Mount Abu, Śatruñjay, Tāraṅga, and Girnār—to mention just a few places in Western India—are justly famous as being among the finest examples of Indian temple architecture. But my intention here is not to dwell on the artistic merit of these temples; rather, I want to convey something of what the Jain worshipper *does* and *feels* when he or she enters a temple and performs *pūjā* to or receives *darśan* of the Jina enthroned therein.

My comments are limited to the Śvetāmbar Mūrtipūjak Jains, but in many respects would be applicable to the Digamber Jains as well. The other two major Jain sects—the Śvetāmbar Sthānakvāsīs and the Śvetāmbar Terāpanthīs—are ideologically opposed to the worship of images. An exploration of Sthānakvāsī and Terāpanthī forms of ritual and devotion would, therefore, lead in very different directions.

Most art historians study the aesthetics of temples and images, but do not study the aesthetics of what people do *to* those images *in* those temples. We have a well developed vocabulary to describe the aesthetics of these temples and images as *things*; we need to begin to develop a vocabulary for an aesthetics of *action in* and *interaction with* those temples. In such an aesthetics one will view the temples and images in a distinctly and necessarily *religious* context, a context that is irretrievably lost for an image taken out of the temple and placed in a museum, or for a temple photographed without any worshippers in it. As the historian of religion Wilfred Cantwell Smith (1976: 166–9) has argued, a temple as a religious structure is a 'living complex constituted by the temple and the worshippers within it.... To appreciate the significance of [a] temple as a temple, we must get inside the consciousness of those for whom it is a sacred space, must know how it feels and what it means to be a worshipper within it.' By ignoring the religious context of temples and images, one also ignores the foundation of any indigenous aesthetics of those temples and images, and ignores the fact that in India aesthetics have been inextricably interwoven with religious emotions. My argument may seem obvious and self-evident; but treatments of Jain images and temples have been surprisingly lifeless and devoid of religious context.[1] This has contributed in no small way to what Paul Dundas (1985: 162) has described as the academic stereotype of the 'relentless asceticism of the Jaina monks and the grim and cheerless probity of the lay community', and of Jainism itself as 'grey and unappealing, as austere as its followers'.[2] This stereotype differs sharply from my own experience of the Jains. In the course of two years of fieldwork I found them warm, open and full of humour as people, and their rituals aesthetically pleasing and profoundly sensual.

Let me now do what Smith advocates, and describe something of what it means to be a worshipper in a Jain temple, and how that worshipper interacts with the space of the temple. To begin with, however, I will briefly describe the temple from the outside, as an object— for a Jain temple as a building is recognizably a Jain temple, a *derāsar*,[3] not a Hindu temple (*mandir*) or a Muslim mosque (*masjid*). The architects (*śilpakār*) of Jain temples are the same as those for Hindu temples;[4] nonetheless differences exist between Jain and Hindu temples.

Flying from the top of the spire of every Jain temple is a distinctive *dhajā*, a red-and-white striped banner which is replaced every year on the *varṣ-gāṇṭh*, the anniversary of the installation of the main image, the *mūḷ nāyak*. Jains enjoy spending their wealth on their temples. In fact, they are encouraged to do so, as *dev dravya*, or money gifted to God, is the highest, most meritorious form of gifting. As a result, the temples are lavishly built. In former times, during Muslim and Maratha rule, when security was a very real concern,

[1] See, for example, U.P. Shah's *Jaina-Rūpa-Maṇḍana* (Shah 1987), and my review (Cort 1988).

[2] Dundas's comments are a description of the negative stereotype presented by Margaret Stevenson in her book. *The Heart of Jainism*.

[3] *Derāsar* is the Gujarati term for a Jain temple; Hindi speakers use the more general term *mandir*.

[4] In Gujarat, the architects for both Hindu and Jain temples are Sompurā Brāhmans.

the temples tended to be plain and unassuming from the outside, but decorated with intricate wood-carving on the inside. In recent decades, with the removal of concerns for security, and with the ready availability of marble, many Jain temples are constructed in part or wholly of marble. Such temples have a cool, soft, white glow, as the light is gently suffused throughout the temple. Many knowledgeable Jains, such as the trustees of Āṇandjī Kalyāṇjī, the trust which manages Śatruñjay, Girnār, Rāṇakpur, and other temples, understand well the connection between the aesthetic appeal of a temple and the attitude of the worshippers: if a temple is ugly, how can one have a truly religious experience? If the temple is beautiful, then one's mind is elevated, and one is filled with the proper *bhāv* or emotion.

On this issue, among others, the major Jain temple trusts disagree with the Archaeological Survey of India on how to manage the older Jain temples. The Jains want the temples to be renovated tastefully and accurately, so that they can continue to be used as places of worship. The Archaeological Survey views the temples as antiquarian monuments, and its goal is the preservation of India's ancient heritage. The Survey tends to view renovation as running counter to the spirit of historical preservation. The Jains tend to view preservation without adequate renovation as disrespect to the Jina and the Jain faith; this is an *aśātnā*, or moral fault.

In Patan, in north Gujarat, on the first three days of every year following *Dīvālī*, a *caitya-paripāṭī*, or 'procession to the temples', takes place. For three afternoons the Jains of Patan go for *darśan* to each and every one of the more than one hundred Jain temples in town. As I went around with one family, they paid particular attention to the 'artistic' (*kalātmik*) aspects of the temples, oohing and aahing over wood carved interiors, painted murals, and images made of quartzcrystal (*sphatik*) or five-metals (*pāñc-dhātu*: gold, silver, brass, copper, and zinc). They especially noticed the *āṅgīs* on the images: a silver cover is placed over the image, and a specialist will spend hours carefully decorating the cover with silver and gold leaf (*varak*), flowers and many colours of sparkling powder. The *āṅgī* combines with the crown placed on the image to create a majestic, royal, and awe-inspiring appearance.

Each temple has its unique personality and its unique *bhāv*, or sentiment. Among older temples, this is created in part by the vagaries of architectural style. Since many temples were fitted into pre-existing buildings, or else built on small plots in residential neighbourhoods, they often do not correspond to the textual norms. But the *bhāv* is also a matter of intention, on the part of both the architect and the temple management. One of the favourite temples in Patan for *darśan*, that of Śāmḷājī Pārśvanāth, was popular in large part because of its *bhāv*. The elongated main room of the temple provided a gradual approach to the Jina. The ceiling had painted depictions of various Jain *tīrths*, and the walls had murals depicting the life of Pārśvanāth, painted in the 1930s in a neo-Ajanta style. The walls of the *gabhāro* (Sanskrit *garbhagṛha*: the central shrine of a temple) were covered with small concave pieces of mirror, so that light rebounded upon the worshipper. The *mūrti* itself was also highly revered, both for its age and for its miraculous sanctity. To visit Śāmḷājī for evening *darśan*, when the temple was filled with soft candle-light reflecting off the *gabhāro* mirrors, the image decorated with an *āṅgī* and a crown, and half a dozen worshippers singing hymns of veneration (*vandan*) in the main temple room, was a religiously moving experience.[5]

As part of the concern for the attractive appearance of the temples, Jains also place great emphasis upon the cleanliness of the temples. A dirty temple is an *aśātnā*, or a moral fault against the Jina. If the temple is dirty, reason the Jains, how can one properly worship God?[6] One of the main functions of the *pujārī* (who is not a Jain) in a Jain temple is to clean the temple every day; unlike in Hindu temples, he does not act as a necessary ritual intermediary between the worshippers and God. In many Hindu temples, the worshipper is beseeched by *pujārīs* to worship at this or that shrine, for only in this way do the *pujārīs* earn any money. In Jain temples, the *pujārīs* are paid employees, whose role is to assist the Jain worshippers, and to keep the temple clean. Jains often proudly contrast the cleanliness of their temples with Hindu temples. When James Burgess visited Girnār in 1869, he was struck by the contrast between

[5] I speak here in the past tense, as the temple building was torn down in 1987 for renovation (*jīrṇoddhār*). Feelings about the renovation were mixed. Most people agreed that the new, spacious, marble structure will lack some of the *bhāv* of the old temple. But renovating a temple is a highly meritorious deed, and people admired the spirit of devotion which motivated the man who organized, and in part paid for, the renovation (although some people did accuse him of caring more for the merit than the *bhāv* of the temple). Everyone admitted that the existing structure was in need of extensive repairs, and not to have repaired the temple would have been an *aśātnā*.

[6] Jains easily and comfortably speak of God in English, and Bhagvān or Parameśvar in Gujarati and Hindi, to refer to both the Jina as symbolized by the *mūrti* in the temple, and to the collectivity of all Jinas. See Cort 1989: 408–25.

the Jain temples and the Hindu temple of Ambājī: 'The Jaina temples are all beautifully clean inside; this of Amba is filthy with smoke, and seems scarcely ever to have been swept since the Buddhists or Jainas had to leave it' (Burgess 1869: 48–9).

Before entering the temple for his[7] morning *pūjā*—performed between six and ten in the morning—the worshipper dons pure *pūjā*-clothes of high-quality cloth.[8] The men wear unstitched *dhotīs* and unstitched upper wraps (*kes*), ideally of silk. The women wear fine *sāṛīs*; many wear their wedding *sāṛīs*. Having bathed beforehand, the worshipper walks to the temple with *pūjā* implements in hand. As he crosses the threshhold into the temple, he utters the word '*nisīhi*' ('it is abandoned') three times, signifying that he is leaving behind all things of the world and will henceforth think only of God. He proceeds to the door into the *gabhāro*, the wombhouse wherein the images of the Jinas are enshrined and enthroned.

A Jina *mūrti* is a carved stone representation of a Jina seated in eternal meditation. Since there are no qualitative distinctions among the liberated souls of the Jinas, *mūrtis* are indistinguishable one from the other. The one exception is that of the most popular of the Jinas, Pārśvanāth, who is depicted with a nine-headed *nāga* arched over his head.[9] The other Jinas can be distinguished only by the identifying symbols carved into the bases of the *mūrtis*, and by the names that are frequently painted on the walls behind the *mūrtis*. Because the liberated Jinas reside in eternal dispassion at the top of the universe, there is no 'real presence' of the Jinas in the *mūrtis*. But the stone *mūrti* is ontologically different from other pieces of stone, as it is marked (*saṁskārit*) both by the rite of 'eye-opening' (*añjan-śalākā*) peformed by a mendicant at the time of the installation of the *mūrti*, and by the daily *pūjās* in the temple. In conversation, Jains will refer synonymously to both the Jina and the *mūrti* in a fusion of signifier and signified.

Standing in front of the *gabhāro* and holding his hands before him in *añjalī*, the worshipper silently receives *darśan* or holy view-

[7] For simplicity's sake, in this paper I use masculine pronouns. It should be stressed, however, that except for the three (or five, depending on family and sectarian tradition) days per month of menstrual impurity (*sūtak*), women are allowed full access to *pūjā* and to the images.

[8] This description of a daily eightfold (*aṣṭaprakārī*) *pūjā* is synthesized from many I observed in the course of twenty-one months of fieldwork from August 1985 to May 1987. For other descriptions and interpretations of Jain temple ritual, see Babb 1988, Cort 1989: 341–425, Humphreys 1985, Jain 1977.

[9] Images of the seventh Jina, Supārśvanāth, also depict the *nāga* heads.

ing of the Jina. With his hands still folded in *añjalī*, he then thrice circumambulates the *gabhāro* (if it is a temple in which the *gabhāro* can be circumambulated), thinking of the Three Jewels of Right Faith, Right Knowledge, and Right Conduct that lead to release from the rounds of rebirth. He sings a *stuti*, a hymn of praise, to the sacred mountain of Śatruñjay, homologizing this neighbourhood *tirth* with that famous one in Saurashtra. After the third circumambulation, he stands in front of the *gabhāro* and sings another *stuti* to the Jina:

Praise to you
    remover of the pain
    of the three worlds
O lord.
Praise to you
    stainless ornament
    of the earth's surface.
Praise to you
    supreme lord
    of the triple world.
Praise to you
O Jina
    you dry up
    the ocean of rebirth.[10]

The worshipper now prepares for *pūjā*. In a small metal bowl he mixes some sandlwood and a small amount of saffron in water. He ties on his *muhpatti*, the cloth—often just a handkerchief—that covers his mouth so that while performing the *pūjā* he does not commit violence against invisible organisms by inhaling or breathing upon them. *Ahiṁsā* (non-harm) is the central Jain ethical precept, and all aspects of *pūjā* must be performed in accordance with *ahiṁsā*. Standing outside the *gabhāro*, the worshipper holds aloft a mirror and performs *kesar pūjā*, dabbing sandalwood paste onto the reflected image of the *mūḷ nāyak*, 'so I can close my eyes and see You in my heart', as one man described, and sings a *stuti*. He now makes a small sandalwood *tilak* on his forehead, to indicate that he obeys the teaching (*ājñā*) of his Bhagvān, his Lord, feeling in his heart the emotion of surrender (*samārpan bhāv*). He enters the *gabhāro* and,

[10] Mānatuṅgasūri, *Bhaktāmara Stotra*, verse 26. In Kapadia 1932: 70.
All translations from Sanskrit and Gujarati in this paper are mine. The worshipper can choose any from the vast repertoire of Jain devotional hymns. I have given examples which I know worshippers to sing.

before commencing the eightfold *pūjā*, bows his head to the feet of the Jina, in further surrender to His teachings.

There, in the centre of the temple, he begins the eightfold *pūjā*. After carefully cleaning the image, he bathes it with water and milk, and then dries it, again with great care. This is first *pūjā*, the water (*jaḷ*) *pūjā* or lustration (*abhiṣek*). Using the ring finger of his right hand, he performs the nine-limbed sandalwood-saffron *pūjā* to the *mūḷ-nāyak*, dabbing the sandalwood-saffron paste onto the (1) two big toes (2) two knees (3) two wrists (4) two shoulders (5) top of the head (6) forehead (7) throat (8) chest and (9) navel. Many images have small silver knobs at these thirteen places, so the worshipper will not in any way damage the actual image—this would also be an *aśātnā*. He then performs the third, or flower (*puṣpa*) *pūjā*, adorning the image with unblemished flowers picked from his own garden, roses if they are available, or perhaps hybiscus or *campak*. He repeats these three *pūjās* to the other images in the *gabhāro*. The *pūjās* of water, sandalwood, and flower are known collectively as *aṅg pūjā*, 'limb *pūjā*', for in them the worshipper physically touches the image. The remaining five *pūjās* are known collectively as the *agra pūjā*, or 'facing *pūjā*': while performing these the worshipper has physically distanced himself from the image, and is offering these *pūjās* in front of the image, not onto the image. The first two of the *agra pūjās* are performed while he is still in the *gabhāro*. He performs incense (*dhūp*) *pūjā*, lighting a stick of sandalwood incense, and then waving a small pot of fragrant frankincense before the images. As he waves the pot of incense, he sings:

Come let us do the incense *pūjā*,
O honourable enchanter of my mind.
The lord is your final refuge,
O honourable enchanter of the mind.[11]

He follows this with the lamp (*dīp*) *pūjā*, waving the ghī-lamp before the images, and singing another hymn.

He now exits from the *gabhāro* and sits on the floor of the temple, with a small table in front of him. For the rice (*akṣat*) *pūjā*, he uses unbroken grains of rice to draw a symbolic form such as the *svastik*, symbol of the four realms of transmigration[12] that one must abandon when following the Three Jewels of Right Faith, Right Knowledge,

[11] From *Śrī Sudhāras Stavan Saṅgrah*, p.5. These are the first and last of the four verses.

[12] The four realms are those inhabited by celestial beings (*devatā*), humans (*manuṣya*), plants and animals (*tiryañc*), infernal beings (*nāraka*).

and Right Conduct on the path to liberation. Onto this diagram he places a piece of fruit (*phaḷ pūjā*), a piece of sugar or other edible item (*naivedya pūjā*), and a coin of small denomination, to symbolize that he gives his all to the Jina. He sings:

In doing the rice *pūjā*
  may I be successful, O Avatār.
I seek this fruit that is in front of you, O Lord;
  save, save, O save me.
In seeking worldly fruits,
  one wanders much in *saṁsār*;
by warding off the eight kings of *karm*,
  I seek the saving fruit of *mokṣ*.[13]

Having finished his eightfold *dravya pūjā*, or physical worship, he now proceeds to his mental worship, or *bhāv pūjā*, in part comprised of the rite of *caitya vandan*, or 'veneration in the temple'.[14] He sings more praise-hymns, thrice prostrates and recites a formula to disavow any intention behind faults committed the previous day, and recites the Nokār Mantra. This is the Jain 'universal prayer' in praise of the Jinas, the other liberated souls, and the mendicant community consisting of *ācāryas*, *upādhyāyas*, and *sādhus*.[15] Picking up the small table, he sweeps the rice and coin into the temple storechest. He returns to the door of the *gabhāro* where, with hands folded, he sings a final *stuti*. He waves the yak-tail fan (*cāmar*) before the image, 'to show his love, respect, and devotion to his Lord', singing (Kuśalcandravijay 1977: 5: 20):

The devotee[16] waves the whisk with a gay mind,
  he waves it with vigour;
He lowers the whisk onto the head of the Lord
  and merit (*puṇya*) rises up.

[13] From *Śrī Sudhāras Stavan Saṅgrah*, pp. 7–8. These are the first two of three verses.

[14] *Caitya-vandan* is one of the six daily obligatory rites (*āvaśyaka*) performed by mendicants of all four sects. It thus constitutes an ancient, core rite of the Jain tradition.

[15] This mantra is:
  Praise to the Liberated Teachers
  Praise to the Liberated Souls
  Praise to the Mendicant Leaders
  Praise to the Mendicant Preceptors
  Praise to all Mendicants in the world
  This fivefold praise
  destroys all sins,
  and of all holies
  it is the foremost holy.

[16] The word actually used here is *sur*, 'god'; I have translated it in the song as 'devotee' for the sake of clarity.

He then rings the temple bell, and leaves the temple for home.

Each of the eight offerings of the *pūjā* has a detailed symbolic meaning. The sandalwood *pūjā*, for example, symbolizes the cooling of the passions that leads to a reduction of *karmic* influx, and the fruit symbolizes liberation as the desired fruit of religious action. Jain theologians in their writings and sermons take care to explain the proper understanding of *pūjā* on the part of the worshipper. The Jina is not in any way embodied in the *mūrti*. The offerings are not to the Jina, but rather to the virtues of enlightenment, liberation, and dispassion symbolized by the *mūrti*. The offerings are not part of any interaction between the worshipper and the Jina, but are symbolic actions indicating a desired change in the ontological status of the worshipper. In this way, Jain temple worship is closer to a form of meditation than to the morphologically similar Hindu temple worship.

This description of the daily eightfold *pūjā* to the image of the Jina shows how the worshipper uses all of the space of the temple, and how the different spaces have different significances. Entering the temple, the worshipper utters '*nisīhi*' three times, to denote a sharp break between the profane realm of *saṁsār* outside the temple and the sacred realm of the *dharm* of the *mokṣa-mārg* inside. The ritual then involves a gradual narrowing in to the centre of the temple: *darśan* of the Jina, thrice circumambulating the *gabhāro*, and further *darśan* before finally entering the *gabhāro*. There, in the centre of the temple, in physical proximity to the Jina, the stone representation of the Jain religious ideal, the worshipper performs the three *aṅg pūjās*. The first two *agra pūjās*, of incense and the lamp, which involve the shift from offering *onto* the image of offering *in front of* the image, are performed while he is still inside the *gabhāro*. For the last three *agra pūjās* the worshipper further distances himself from the Jina, offering the rice, sweets, and fruit from outside the *gabhāro*. The *caitya vandan*, the 'praises in the temple', is also performed while in the main room of the temple, outside the *gabhāro*. Some accounts of the Jain ritual complete the logic of separation from the temple and re-integration into the world of *saṁsār* by having the worshipper thrice utter the word '*āvasihi*' ('it is re-entered')[17] as he exits the temple.

The movement inside the temple, from periphery to centre and back again, accompanies an elaborate sensory involvement of the

[17] My only references to this are Burgess 1884: 193 and Stevenson 1921: 800. I never encountered anyone who uttered or even recognized the phrase.

worshipper in the ritual: the contact with the image itself, dabbing the cool sandalwood paste onto the cool marble; the feel of the silk *pūjā*-clothes on the worshipper's body; the sounds of the worshippers' hymns and the periodic ringing of the bell; and the rich panoply of fragrances from the sandalwood and saffron paste, the sandalwood incense, the frankincense, and the flowers. I have in my possession a book given to me in Patan that had been stored for several years in a cabinet in a temple; whenever I open the pages of this book, the powerful smells of the paper take me back mentally into a Jain temple. Visual stimulae also affect the worshipper: the soft silky white of the men's *pūjā*-clothes, the bright auspicious colours of the women's *pūjā-saris*, the cool white of marble in many temples, the light of the lamp offered to the Jina, the colourful flowers offered onto the Jina, and, later in the day, when *pūjā* is finished for the day, the brightly coloured *āṅgīs* or bodily decorations that cover the image.

Stanley Tambiah (1970: 35) has said of ritual that it 'is for the practical man what philosophy is for the thinker. If the saint and the ascetic act upon themselves—their minds and bodies, and inner states—the layman acts upon the world with the external things of the world'. So we find that *pūjā* as performed by the Jain layman is called *dravya pūjā*, worship with physical objects, in contrast with the *bhāv pūjā*, or mental worship, which is the only form of worship the possessionless mendicant is allowed to perform. As merchants and housewives, the Jain laity are intimately involved with the world of external things, and they manipulate and use these external things in their worship of the Jina. They may not be able to explain the abstract theories of the Jain philosophical teachings; but they do understand the notions of what Lawrence Babb (1988) has aptly called 'giving and giving up' that are embodied in the daily temple ritual. One twentieth century Jain mendicant has described image-worship (*mūrti-pūjā*) as follows (Buddhisāgarsūri 1925: 5):

> The basis for image worship is love. Wherever in the world there is love, there is also image worship. That which is loved is an image, and so it becomes worthy of worship. . . . By love expressed through form, the Lord who has form is worshipped. . . . From worship of the image which has form, love of the formless Lord grows. The image of the one who is loved resides in the heart, and it is from this that the loving person learns. Without love, without the *bhakti* of service [to the Lord], there are no virtues.

Most Jain temples remain closed from mid-morning until late-afternoon. In the evening, many people come for the *āratī*, or evening lamp offering, and for *darśan*. The *āratī* has two parts: the five-wicked *āratī* proper, and the single-wicked Holy Lamp, the *maṅgaḷ dīvo*. During a festival, a brilliant 108-wick *āratī* is also offered. The right to make these offerings is auctioned off to individuals among the assembled congregation. First the *āratī* is offered, everyone singing and clapping their hands, several people playing hand cymbals, and one man ringing the temple bell. Then follows the beloved *maṅgaḷ dīvo*, to which everyone sings:

Lamp O lamp, holy lamp
long life results from raising up the *ārati*.
We sing the lamp in this Kali era,
King Kumārpāl offers up the lamp.
Our house is holy, your house is holy,
may the fourfold congregation be holy.[18]

If the evening falls during a festival, an hour or more of *bhakti bhāvnā*, or 'spirit of devotion', might follow in the temple. People gather in their finest clothes, and professional musicians come to play the harmonium and drums (and nowadays the electric 'banjo') and to lead the singing. The congregation sits in the main room of the temple, singing and clapping along in the songs, 'making a joyful noise unto the Lord'. Some individuals overcome with devotion will take up the yak-tail fan and dance before the Lord. As one dancer finishes and sits down, others murmur, 'such beautiful *bhakti*, such beautiful *bhakti*'.

On evenings without a special *bhakti bhāvnā*, people coming for *darśan* enter the lamp-lit temple, approach the *gabhāro* and, with hands folded before themselves in reverence, quietly sing a *stuti* to the Jina. Some people will go to several different temples for *darśan*. Especially popular are those temples where the image is *camatkārī*, miracle-performing. Devotion to these images is doubly efficacious, and the devotees can recount many instances of miraculous results of such devotion.

One evening in Patan, a man from Maharashtra was receiving *darśan* at several of the downtown temples, going quickly from one to another for as many holy viewings as possible. I met him in the main temple in Patan, that of Pañcāsar Pārśvanāth. As he was talking to me of the beauty of the old images in the temple, and the carvings

[18] 'Maṅgaḷ Dīvo', from *Śrī Sudhāras Stavan Saṅgrah*, p. 96.

on the recently-renovated temple walls, he suddenly stopped. He threw his arms out, and exclaimed, '*Śānti śānti śānti*. The hubbub of the world is not *śānti*. This', he said, indicating the temple, '*this* is *śānti*'.

He expressed what is a central theological notion for the Jains—the sense of inner peace and quietude one gets from being in a temple, doing *pūjā* to the images, and receiving *darśan* of the Lord. Such a peace is totally other from the hubbub of the world. The space within the temple, and the use of lights, incense, and decorations, are all designed so as to contribute to a sense of both awe and inner peace on the part of the worshipper. The atmosphere in a temple is profoundly familiar and reassuring to a Jain. It is conducive to an attitude in which the cares and concerns of the world are left outside, and the worshipper can focus his mind solely upon the Jina in a proper spirit of devotion (*bhakti bhāvnā*). The peace that the worshipper gains is, of course, multivalent—at once a salvific peace that is totally other than the daily life of business and family, and a peace that he can take back to that daily life. Peace refers both to the subduing of passions that lead him astray on the path to liberation, and the subduing of obstacles on the path of worldly success. The intention in the design of space in a Jain temple is in part to generate this peace and contentment in the worshipper.

One of the most popular of all the Jinas is Śāntināth, precisely because of his name: Lord of Peace. Let me conclude with one of the most popular of all *stutis*, addressed to Śāntināth:

Śānti Jineśvar is the true Master,
    you pacify in this Kali era, O Jinjī.
you are in my mind,
    you are in my heart.
I meditate from moment to moment, O Master-jī.
You are in my mind,
    you are in my heart.
Granting *darśaṇ* as I wander in birth after birth,
    in a moment you fulfill my desires, O Jinjī.
You are in my mind,
    you are in my heart.[19]

[19] Jinraṅg, 'śrī Śāntināth Jin Stavan', in *Śrī Sudhāras Stavan Saṅgrah*, p. 51; verses 1–2.

Mangala among the Coorgs

M. N. SRINIVAS

The astrologer selects an auspicious day for the performance of *mangala*, and an even more auspicious part of that day for the performance of *mūrta*, which is the most important part of *mangala*.* . . .

The house in which the *mangala* ritual takes place is cleaned, and its walls are colour-washed, and a decorated booth (*pandal*) of five pillars, one of which is a branch of a milk-exuding tree, is erected in front of the house. Poleyas and Medas [service castes] beat tom-toms and play pipes in front of the house, and Coorg youths dance to the music.

Four Coorgs beat the small Coorg drum called '*duḍi*' and sing some traditional songs at various points during *mangala*. These songs give an account of the ritual that is being performed. The singers also sing the 'road song', while conducting the subject of *mangala* from one part of the house to another, and the road song gives a traditionally exaggerated account of everything that is found *en route*. At night, after dinner Coorg singers sing songs about the groom, bride, their ancestors, and the guests who are present.

The elaborate preparations for *mangala* and the selection of an auspicious day for its performance stress the social importance of the occasion. *Mangala* indicates the movement of the subject from one position in the social structure to another, it marks a change in his social personality. *Mūrta* ritual is the most important part of *mangala*, and, consequently, it is performed during the most auspi-

Excerpted from M. N. Srinivas, 'The Ritual Idiom of the Coorgs', in *Religion and Society among the Coorgs of South India*, Clarendon Press, Oxford, 1952, pp. 72–100.

* *In Sanskrit, maṅgala means 'well-being', and mahūrta, from which mūrta is derived, refers to a precisely calculated period of about an hour which is suitable for auspicious ceremonies such as marriage.* Editor.

cious part of the auspicious day, and the subject undergoes a series of preparatory and purificatory rites before sitting down for *mūrta*.

The subject of *mangala*, if male, is ritually shaved by the barber, after which he is given a bath by three women relatives whose husbands are alive and who therefore enjoy a higher ritual and social status than widows. Only an unmarried girl, and a woman whose first and only husband is alive, are entitled to take part in auspicious ritual. Not only widows, but also remarried widows, are excluded from auspicious ritual, but such exclusion is not as thorough among Coorgs as it is, for instance, among the Brahmins.

After a bath, the subject wears ritual garments, and proceeds to the sacred central hall, where all rituals ought to take place, ideally speaking. In the central hall is the sacred tripod stool on which the subject sits, and on either side of the stool stands a bell-metal lamp. The subject thrice walks round the tripod stool and lamps, and then salutes the lamps and the tripod stool before sitting down on the latter. Circumambulation is clock-wise in auspicious ritual and anti-clockwise in mourning.

In front of the sitting subject is another such stool covered with a red silk cloth. An earthen lamp burns in a metal dining dish which is kept on the stool before the subject. The lamp rests on a thin bed of rice spread inside the dish. A few betel leaves and areca-nuts are also kept alongside the lamp. The dish, rice, lamp, and betel leaves and nuts are all collectively referred to as '*taḷiyakkiboḷuk*' which literally means 'dish-rice-lamp'. It will be referred to as 'dish-lamp' in future, and a dish-lamp is considered essential on all ritual occasions.

At *mangala*, in addition to the earthen lamp, a *kinḍi* full of milk is kept on the dish-lamp. A *kinḍi* is bell-metal vessel with a long spout at the side. At *mangala* every relative performs *vis-à-vis* the subject a series of solidarity rites collectively called *mūrta*. . . .

Each of the assembled relatives singly performs *mūrta*, described below, towards the subject of *mangala*. Three married women, close relatives of the subject, are required to perform it before anyone else. If the subject's mother is alive and not a widow, she is entitled to be one of the three, and what is more, perform it first, even if the other two are her seniors.

The mother, or senior married woman, begins by sprinkling rice on the two bell-metal lamps on either side of the subject, and then salutes them. The sun-god is saluted next after throwing some rice backwards, over the shoulders. This is followed by the relative depositing a little rice successively at the joints of knees, elbows, and shoulders, and on the head of the subject. The relative then holds the spouted vessel before the subject and he sucks in a little milk through the spout. After this she presents the subject with a gold or silver coin. The subject salutes her by touching her feet with both his hands and carrying the latter back to his forehead. This is done thrice. The married woman blesses him by touching his head and saying, 'may you live long', or 'may you live happily'.

It has been mentioned before that *mangala* is an auspicious or good-sacred ceremony and that it has to be performed on an auspicious day. All over India, among Hindus, it is believed that certain periods of time have ritual value while others do not. 'Ritual value' is synonymous with the term 'sacred' in its widest sense, as inclusive of good-sacredness as well as bad-sacredness, auspiciousness as well as inauspiciousness. Certain periods of time are auspicious while others are inauspicious. One occasionally finds in Coorg homes a sheet of cardboard nailed to the wall which mentions the inauspicious periods in each day of the week. Important work is not begun during an inauspicious period.

Adult Coorgs are usually able to read the *panchānga* which may be described as the ritual calender of the Hindus. *Panchāngas* are nowadays printed and sold in towns, and it is customary for a Coorg house to have a *panchānga*. It is frequently referred to as it gives the auspicious and inauspicious periods in each day, the days on which one may have one's face shaved, the days on which one may travel in a particular direction, when an eclipse will occur, and so on. . .

Mangala has not only to be performed on an auspicious day, but also in an auspicious place: a Coorg likes to have it performed in his ancestral house which he regards as sacred and for which he has a strong attachment. Only certain high castes like the Brahmins, Okkaligas, and Gauḍas may enter all parts of the ancestral house. Meḍas and Poleyas, on the other hand, have to stop at the paved yard in front of the house. Castes like the smiths (Airis), washermen (Maḍivāḷa), and Baṇṇas may come to all parts of the house except the kitchen, central hall, and south-western room. If, however, they have to come in to perform their duties on certain occasions like a marriage or an ancestor-propitiation, then the house is purified after their departure.

The sacredness or ritual purity of the ancestral house was better preserved by the fact that a woman was not allowed to stay within it during her periods. Such a woman is in a defiled condition and defilement is contagious. It also cuts off the person affected by it from normal participation in social life. . . .

It is not only places which have ritual value, but also points of the compass. East is a sacred direction because the sun rises there, and Hindus in all parts of India regard the sun as a deity.

The Coorg ancestral house faces east and so does the ancestor-shrine. The lip of the sacred wall-lamp in the central hall faces east. The subject of a *mangala* ceremony sits facing east.

On getting up from his bed in the morning a Coorg salutes the wall-lamp and the sun. The cultivation of rice is accompanied by ritual at every stage, and on all these ritual occasions the subject of the rites begins by saluting the sun.

South is an inauspicious or bad-sacred direction. A corpse is buried or cremated with its head towards south. In Sanskritic Hinduism, south is the abode of Yama, the god of death.

Coorgs, like Hindus in other parts of India, regard east as a good-sacred direction and south as a bad-sacred direction. East is associated with Chūriya (sun-god), and south with Yama. Both these deities have an all-India spread. Coorgs worship these two deities along with other Hindus all over India. The possession of common values binds people together and Coorgs form a single community with Hindus all over India when they worship the same deities.

Mūrta is the crucial part of *mangala*, and the rites performed prior to *mūrta* prepare the subject for it. The subject is shaved by the barber, given a bath by three married women, and dressed in ritual robes and ornaments before sitting down to *mūrta*. Shaving, the first of several preparatory rites, will be briefly considered here.

It is necessary to repeat here that shaving is done by barbers who form a caste. Contact with the barber defiles a member of a higher caste, and consequently shaving is invariably followed by a purificatory bath.

The subject of *mangala* wears a white cotton *kupya* while he is being shaved by the barber. The *kupya* is like a dressing-gown, and it is either black or white. The white gown is of cotton, has long sleeves, and covers the neck up to the throat. This is the traditional ritual dress of Coorgs. The black gown is a Westernized version of the white original: it is of wool, has short sleeves, and a V-shaped neck permitting the display of a collar and tie. The white gown is ritually superior to the black gown. . . .

The subject salutes the lamp in the south-western room, the south-western pillar, and the wall-lamp before sitting on the tripod stool placed on a mat. Near the mat is a dining-dish containing milk, and a harvest-basket containing some rice, a coconut, a bunch of plantains, and betel leaves and areca-nut.

Water may not be used for shaving on this occasion. Milk is used instead. The shavings are put into the dining-dish, and later the barber empties the dish at the foot of a milk-exuding tree.

A distinctive form of shaving prevails at marriage, and perhaps at subsequent *mangala* (it does not, however, prevail at the ear-boring *mangala*). The front of the head is shaved in such a manner that it leaves two 'horns' above the temples, formed by the shaved patches. This mode of shaving is called *'kombanjavara'* which means 'horn shave'.

The harvest-basket containing rice, plantains, and the bell-metal dining-dish, and the scarf at the subject's waist, are given as gifts to the barber.

Two other men get themselves shaved after the subject. All over south India it is common at a wedding for two or four companions of the subject to 'accompany' him (or her) in certain rites. For instance, two men are given a bath along with the groom, and two girls are given a bath along with the bride.

In the south-western parts of Coorg the bride undergoes, before *mūrta*, a rite called *'kūrangodi muripa'*, which is analogous to shaving. The bride's brother's wife removes from the bride's head a thin wisp of hair, and pares her nails. (The barber normally pares the nails after shaving a man.) These are put into a dining-dish containing milk. Later, the dining-dish is emptied at the foot of a milk-exuding tree. . . .

Marriage conferred on a man the right to have his head shaved periodically, and a bachelor was not entitled to it unless be had undergone the ear-boring *mangala*. The latter ritual conferred social adulthood on a male: in the folksong about the hero Kaiyandira Appayya it is seen that he successfully claims to be an adult on the strength of the fact that his friends, all boys tending cattle, performed this ritual for him in the jungle.

The ear-boring *mangala* has now entirely disappeared . . . but it used to be the first of several *mangalas* for a male, and the head was shaved for the first time on this occasion. The performance of this *mangala* conferred certain privileges on the individual in question, one of which being that he could have his face shaved periodically by a barber.

At the various *mangalas,* shaving is a preparatory ritual act. On these occasions it is followed by a bath and by the wearing of ritually pure robes. These preliminary rites make the subject pure, and while in this condition he performs certain rites, or others perform certain rites towards him. . . .

The preparatory, purificatory ritual act which comes after shaving is a ritual bath. It is usual for three[1] married women to give this ritual bath to the subject. The *guḍḍa* or bathroom is a room outside the main building of the ancestral house, and the subject marches in state to it. The procession is headed by pipers and drummers followed by four Coorgs beating a tiny drum and singing the traditional 'road song'. At a wedding, after the groom returns in state from his bath, the best man who must himself be a married person helps to dress him in ritual robes and ornaments.

A Coorg washes his hands, feet, and face before saluting the sacred wall-lamp every day, morning and evening; and on festival day he takes a bath and changes into clothes washed by the washerman. Both bath and change of clothes are preliminary to prayer.

It is usual to approximate physical impurity to ritual impurity. An unwashed state is an impure state, and taking a bath and changing into clean clothes alter the ritual status of the subject. . . .

A ritual bath . . . adds to his ritual purity and makes him fit to pray, or to be possessed by a deity. But sometimes the emphasis is on the bath terminating a condition of ritual impurity. That is to say, instead of a bath adding purity to normal ritual status, it might only be putting an end to ritual impurity, which is a condition inferior to normal ritual status. . . .

That a ritual bath is different from an ordinary bath is made clear from the fact that the confined mother has an elaborate massage and bath every day, beginning with the day the baby is born [rendering her ritually impure for fifty-nine days]. The massage and bath last several hours, but their object is therapeutic and not ritual. It is only on the twelfth and sixtieth days that a bath alters the ritual

[1] Odd numbers have ritual value in Coorg as elsewhere in south India. Number '3' is specially sacred. A person usually walks thrice round a sacred object like a tripod stool, temple, and funeral pyre.

condition of the mother. All baths clean the body, but only some purify as well as clean. . . .

The widower (or widow)* and eldest son go, after the mourning period is over, to Bhāgamandla where the rivers Kāvēri and Kanaké meet. After a shave, they bathe in the confluence of the two rivers, and then offer balls of rice-flour to the dead person's spirit. This is followed by a visit to the temple of Bhagaṇḍēshwara where the mourners offer worship. Subsequently they go to the source of the River Kāvēri, bathe in the larger spring, worship the smaller spring, and then return home.

Two ideas can be distinguished in the above ritual acts: (1) a ritual bath alters the ritual status of the subject; and (2) bathing in a sacred river is not only purifying in a ritual sense, but also removes the sins of the bather. This latter idea is shared by Hindus all over India. . . . Bathing in the Ganges, or in any other sacred river, rids a person of the sins he has committed both in this and in a previous existence. It confers on him spiritual merit (*puṇya*). . . .

After having been given a bath . . . the groom is helped into his ritual robes and ornaments by the best man. He has to wear a white cotton gown for the *mūrta*, and this is worn in such a way that the right side comes over the left side. A red silk sash secures the gown at the waist. The ornamental Coorg knife, *pīché katti*, is tucked into the sash in front, and the broad Coorg sword, *oḍi katti*, hangs from its clasp at the groom's back. The clasp is fixed to a chain which is tied round the groom's waist. The groom also wears a number of ornaments.

The groom wears the Coorg turban (*pāni manḍé tuṇi*) which is flat at the top and also covers the back of the head. He may not wear any sandals, however, as leather defiles. He carries in his hand a staff (*gejjé tanḍ*) with small bells tied to it near the top.

The bride wears a uniform of red silk: a red silk *sari*, a red silk full-sleeved Coorg blouse (*kaḷa kupya*), and a red silk scarf which is tied round her head. She wears bangles, necklaces, ear-rings, and also ornaments on her ankles, feet, and toes.

The best man and matron of honour hold a white cloth umbrella over the groom and bride respectively. . . .

The corpse, which is in some respects treated as similar to the subject of a *mangala*, is dressed in a white gown, but with the under-

* *Like birth death too causes different degrees of ritual pollution among the survivors.* Editor.

side on top if it is going to be cremated, and with the left side over the right if it is going to be buried.

Formerly, mourners also wore the white gown, but in a particular way: the right hand did not pass through the right arm of the gown, but instead it was allowed to hang limp from the right shoulder. The gown was secured at the waist by a black sash instead of a red one.

The white gown is worn on all important ritual occasions. Ritual occasions are either auspicious or inauspicious, and there is need to differentiate between them. Hence, though the subject of *mangala*, corpse and mourner, are all dressed in a white gown, the mode of wearing it is different in each case. The subject of *mangala* wears it in the normal way, while in the case of a corpse it is reversed, and in the case of the mourner the right arm drops loosely from the shoulder. . . .

Red colour seems to have greater ritual value than white, and silk greater ritual value than cotton. For instance, at a wedding, the ceiling of the sacred central hall is covered with white cloths, except for the part just above the bridal seat which is covered with red cloths. All the bride's clothes are of red silk, and according to the ancient marriage song the groom wore a red silk gown and red silk turban.

When a man (or woman) dies his relatives have to carry gifts of white cotton cloths to him. But the dead man's sister's children, or dead woman's brothers' children, have to carry gifts of red silk cloths. Those who bring gifts of red silk cloths are considered to be closer relatives than those who bring white cotton cloths. It is those who bring red silk cloths who take part, along with the dead man's eldest son and widow, in the important pot-breaking rite (*koda kukkuva*) which ritually severs the dead man's connection with his living relatives.

The ritual preference of silk to cotton is widespread all over peninsular India among Brahmins, and it is very likely that Coorgs borrowed the use of red silk from the Brahmins of the west coast. The use of red silk in ritual is not very clearly defined—at least it is not as clearly defined as the use of the white gown.

The turban is worn on very important auspicious occasions like a wedding. On less formal occasions a Coorg ties a scarf round his head. Both men and women tie a scarf round their heads out of doors. But no form of head-dress, turban, scarf, or cap, is worn inside the house. When a kinswoman comes into the house the hostess removes her scarf. Failure to do so would be an insult, as it would amount to treating the kinswoman as a stranger. Absence of head-dress indicates the intimacy that prevails among the members of a household. It is presumably for this reason that everyone, including the senior mourners, has to remove his scarf and sandals before the corpse. Such removal shows that the dead man and mourners are members of one household. They are kindred, and kinship is intimacy. When two people are able to appear before each other without scarves they are intimate, they are members of the same household. It is an expression of the solidarity prevalent between the two.

There is a great social and ritual elaboration of the distinction between a married woman and a widow. A married woman or *garati* is one whose first and only husband is alive. Remarried widows and divorcées have a slightly higher status than widows, but this does not entitle them to be classed as *garatis*.

The Coorg widow's dress consists of a white cotton *sari*, a white cotton blouse, and a white cotton scarf. *None* of these clothes may have a coloured border. The corpse of a widow, too, is dressed in clothes without a coloured border. The corpse of a married woman, on the other, hand, is dressed in a coloured *sari* with a coloured, or silver, or gold, border. . . .

After being dressed in ritual robes, the subject of *mangala* salutes the various lamps in the house before sitting down for *mūrta*. On either side of him is a dish-lamp placed on a tripod stool. The dish-lamp is indispensable on every ritual occasion.

Every day, early in the morning and again just before nightfall, the housewife sweeps the house and sprinkles it with a purifying solution of cow-dung. She then lights the wall-lamp and salutes it. While saluting it she prays to the ancestors of the *okka*, to Mother Kāvēri and Shiva. Every member of the *okka* joint household salutes the wall-lamp after getting up in the morning, and again at night.

The ending of night as well as of day is marked by sweeping and purifying the house, and by lighting and saluting the wall-lamp. The period between the ending of the day and the beginning of night is regarded as a critical time, and children are not given food or allowed to sleep at that time. This is a common south Indian custom.

It is regarded as a bad omen if the lamp goes out while a Coorg is having his dinner. The sudden extinction of the lamp indicates the approach of disaster. The diner gets up from his meal, cleans the dish and washes his hands. He sits down to dinner again a few minutes later. This makes it a different meal altogether and not the one that was interrupted.

A Coorg never says that a lamp has gone out. He says instead, 'the lamp is brighter' (*boḷicha dumb pōchi*). . . .

The ritual attitude prevalent towards the domestic lamp is easily extended to fire generally, and to the sun. These again provide points of contact with Sanskritic or all-India Hinduism.

The kitchen stove is a convenient focus for the general ritual attitude existing towards fire. The kitchen stove, like the domestic lamp, stands for the unity, strength, and protective power of the *okka* and this fact finds ritual expression. When a member of the *okka* is dead and it is decided to cremate his body, the funeral pyre is fired with a torch lighted from embers from the kitchen stove. The torch is made with twigs collected from the domestic burial-ground.

The belief in the protective power of *teḷi nīr* is again the result of a ritual attitude towards the kitchen stove. A few embers from the kitchen stove and a few grains of cooked rice from a vessel on the stove are put into a dining-dish. Water is poured on the embers and rice, and a thick, ashy liquid is formed in the dining-dish. This liquid is *teḷi nīr*, and great protective powers are attributed to it. The mourners returning home on the eleventh day after performing the rites in the burial-ground, a daughter-in-law returning to her conjugal home with her baby born in her natal home, a member of the house returning from a long journey, and a newly bought calf are all sprinkled with it. . . .

The sprinkling of rice on a person or thing is a common ritual act in Coorg, and it is one of the several acts which together form the ritual of *mūrta*. An instance of the ritual sprinkling of rice will be considered now with a view to discovering its meaning.

Birth results in pollution for the mother, the new-born infant, and the *okka* of which the mother is a member. While the other members of the polluted *okka* attain normal ritual status on the twelfth day of birth, the mother herself remains polluted till the sixtieth day. On that day, after a bath which ends her long period of pollution, she performs a certain ritual which signifies her resumption of her normal, pre-pollution duties.

One of her normal duties is the bringing of water from the domestic well into the kitchen, and the resumption of this particular duty is dramatized in *Ganga pūja* (worship of Ganga or Ganges). The confined woman has a bath, after which she changes into ritually pure garments. She then goes to the domestic well accompanied by two married women. First of all she salutes the sun by throwing some rice grains into the air, and this is followed by putting small quantities of rice thrice into the well. She then drops a few betel leaves, with the smooth side on top, into the well, and also empties the milk of a slit coconut into it. Finally, the confined woman and, after her, two companions draw water from the well in vessels and carry the latter into the kitchen. . . .

While white rice is used in auspicious ritual, rice yellowed with turmeric is used in inauspicious ritual. At the very important funeral rite of 'breaking the pot', each of the mourners sprinkles a little rice, yellowed with turmeric, on the corpse before saluting it.

The ritual sprinkling of rice on objects and persons usually accompanies salutation. In *mūrta*, the sprinkling of rice occurs with salutation and with the giving of milk and money presents. All these rites affirm a bond which exists between the subject and all those who perform them to him. These are members of his kin-group, caste-group, and village. They constitute his community. These rites of solidarity which affirm the existence of a bond between the subject and the community serve also to stress the importance of the particular *mangala* the subject is undergoing.

It is entirely proper that rice and not any other grain or article should be used in the most common solidarity rite in Coorg. Even today rice has a very important place in the social and economic life of Coorgs, and formerly, before the introduction of coffee and oranges into Coorg, it was the most valuable crop.

The ritual of giving milk to the subject follows the sprinkling of rice on him. This, like the other ritual acts mentioned earlier, is performed at every *mangala* including marriage. While the structure of every *mangala* is, broadly speaking, the same, there are minor differences between one *mangala* and another. The ritual giving of milk at marriage makes the meaning of ritual milk-giving particularly clear.

On the first day of marriage *mūrta* is performd separately for the bride and groom in their respectice homes. The bride's relatives and the high-caste members of her village perform *mūrta* to her *in her house*, and the groom's relatives and members of his village perform *mūrta* to him *in his house*.

On the second day, the groom's relatives go in state to the bride's house, and the groom's relatives perform *mūrta* to the bride. For this purpose *they carry some of their own rice and milk with them*.

The bride's relatives perform *mūrta* to the groom and, finally, the groom performs *mūrta* to the bride. Later in the day the bride leaves her natal home and accompanies the groom to his home. Relatives of the groom who did not accompany him to the bride's house now perform *mūrta* to the bride.

When a marriage takes place, it is not only two persons who come together but two kin-groups. They come together through the acquisition of two common objects of interest. But before marriage the bride was only an object of common interest to her natal kin-group, and the groom to his natal kin-group. . . .

Like the sprinkling of rice, the giving of milk is a common ritual act in Coorg. At the naming ceremony of a child, the mother puts the infant into the cradle and says, 'Chengappa, get up to eat rice mixed with milk.' She smears the child's tongue with a little cream, using a gold coin to scoop the cream contained in a bowl.

A child is given solid food to eat six months after birth: and this food usually consists of cooked rice mixed with milk and sugar. On the second day after marriage, when the bride enters her conjugal home, her mother-in-law combs her hair and gives her rice mixed with milk to eat. The latter dish is considered a great delicacy.

Milk is used not on good-sacred occasions but also on bad-sacred occasions. When an infant dies, a coconut-shell containing milk from its mother's breasts is placed over the grave; and if it is a few months old, rice mixed with milk is placed there instead.

On the day after the cremation of a corpse, the dead man's son goes to the burial-ground, and on the spot where the dead man was buried he pours successively a vessel of water and a vessel of milk.

Milk is a very valued commodity, and the ritual giving of milk indicates that solidarity is, or ought to be, prevalent between the giver and the recipient. It is also a symbol of pleasure, luxury, and happiness, and consequently mourners abstain from it while they offer it to the spirit of the departed person. The mourners also abstain from other valued objects like curd, honey, mushrooms, meat, and betel leaves and areca-nut, which are again offered to the dead person's spirit. . . .

Everyone who performs *mūrta* to the subject should give a money-gift, and the three married women are expected to give a gold coin (*pombaṇa*) each. At a wedding the mother of the bride (or groom), and the groom while performing *mūrta* to the bride, have to give a purse containing several coins, one of which should be a gold coin.

A money-gift has to be given not only at *mangala* but on other occasions as well: relatives who come to pay their last respects to the dead man perform series of solidarity rites at the end of which they give a money-gift. Again, an infant has to be given a money-gift on the occasion of giving him (or her) a name. In fact, a relative who is seeing an infant for the first time must give a money-gift. On the second day of marriage, when the bride visits the groom's house, she gives a money-gift to every infant in her conjugal *okka*. Later the groom does the same in the bride's *okka* thus sealing the contract.* . . .

* *Srinivas concludes his detailed analysis of the ritual complex of mangala by describing ritual salutations, ceremonial playing of bands, and organization of community dinners. All these activities, he explains, testify to the Coorgs' concern with social solidarity.* Editor

The Pilgrimage to Ajmer

P. M. CURRIE

The goal of the pilgrimage is the mausoleum of Mu'īn al-dīn.* Once they have achieved the inner sanctum of the shrine, the devotees bow low and kiss the tomb. Prayers are offered in thanksgiving for favours received, and petitions made for favours required. The prayers are a form of spiritual bargaining; offerings to the shrine will be made if the devotee's prayers are answered. As an earnest of their offerings, devotees tie strings to the pierced-marble screens that surround parts of the mausoleum. These strings are removed when the prayers have been answered and the offerings submitted. The devotees scatter red rose-petals over the tomb, and the privileged are given petals which have been lying there to keep as *tabarruk* or to eat. Pilgrims also spend time circumambulating the mausoleum, and sitting in its vicinity in passive and receptive silence to absorb the spiritual presence of the saint and to meditate on his life and teachings. There is a special enclosure, immediately adjacent to the mausoleum—the Arhat-i Nūr—where women may sit in silence and read the Quran. The men may read the Quran inside the mausoleum itself.

The pilgrims then visit various other places associated with Mu'īn al-dīn and his family and entourage. The anecdotes of Mu'īn al-dīn's coming to Ajmer are all located and commemorated by monuments. Thus, the pilgrim may go to his *chillā* where he is

Excerpted from P. M. Currie, 'The Pilgrimage to Ajmer' in *The Shrine and Cult of Mu'in al-dīn Chishti of Ajmer*, Oxford University Press, Delhi, 1989.

* *Shaykh Mu'in al-din Chishti of the fourteenth century is one of the most highly revered Muslim Sufi masters of India. He lies buried at Ajmer in Rajasthan. His mausoleum has attracted large numbers of pilgrims from India and abroad for centuries. Currently over 100,000 devotees come to Ajmer for the 'urs (festival) every year. Among them are some Hindus also from the locality. The pilgrimage to the tomb of the Shaykh is indeed a hope in the breast of every pious Muslim of South Asia.* Editor.

believed to have lived before being accepted into the city. Next to this shelter cut out of the rock is the cell where Qutb al-dīn, his *khalīfa* [successor], is believed to have performed his ascetic exercises. The converted [Hindu] *dev's* temple is now the site of a mosque, as is the place where Mu'īn al-dīn immobilized the Rājā's camels. The pilgrim visits the place where Mu'īn al-dīn died, now marked by a building known as the *khānqāh* [hospice]. . . .

Two other major shrines visited by pilgrims are the *dargāh* [shrine] of Mu'īn al-dīn which is situated at the foot of Taragarh hill, and, halfway up the hill, an imposing white edifice known as the *chillā* of 'Abd al-Qādir Jīlānī [a famous Sufi master]. 'Abd al-Qādir never visited India but tradition relates that a faqīr from Ajmer visited his shrine near Baghdad and returned with two bricks from the mausoleum. When the faqīr died these bricks were buried with him and in *c.* 1800 a shrine was built over these relics. Pilgrims then continue up the hill until they achieve the fortifications which crown the summit and house the *dargāh* of Mīrān Husain Khing Sawār, Governor of the fortress, who is believed to have died in an attack by the Rajputs in 1202. . . . His *dargāh* was not built until the reign of Akbar [1556–1605]. The rise of the cult of Mīrān Sahib is clearly associated with the growth of interest in Ajmer as a sacred centre under the imperial patronage of Akbar himself, and perhaps helped by a confusion over the identity of Mīrān Sahib. There is a lively cult of Mīrān Sahib in other parts of northern India, with shrines dedicated to him not only at Ajmer, but also at Amroha, in the Muradabad District, at Banaras and at Bundi. Popular belief regards these shrines as being dedicated to the same Mīrān Sahib, whose identity is further confused with 'Abd al-Qādir Jīlānī. . . .

Returning from the *dargāh* of Mīrān Sahib, pilgrims pass the Adhar Silla. This is a large boulder which is said to have been magically thrown at Mīrān Sahib by his Hindu enemies. Mīrān Sahib saw it coming and spoke to it saying, 'If thou art from God, fall on my head; if magic sent thee, stay there.' But evidently he enjoyed the favour of Allāh, for the missile fell at his feet and the old lady who attends the Adhar Silla shows pilgrims where his fingers and horse came into contact with it.

At all these objects of veneration pilgrims make offerings in cash or kind, and the path between these sacred places is lined by beggars to whom they give alms. Cowries are still negotiable currency here.

At the bottom of Taragarh Hill pilgrims buy a weight of shells and distribute them as they wind their way upwards.

Most parties of pilgrims present a *chādar* at Mu'īn al-dīn's mausoleum. This cloth to cover the tomb varies from the coarsest and cheapest material to richly-worked embroidered silks and velvets costing several thousand rupees. The pilgrims, led by musicians, proceed through the bazars to the shrine, holding the *chādar* above their heads. Others clamour to touch the cloth which will have such close contact with the sacred tomb and impart their personal blessing to it.

It is not only the pilgrims who give to beggars. The *dargāh* administration distributes food to the destitute twice daily from the *langar khāna* [kitchen].... Chishtī foundations have always believed in distributing food to the needy whenever possible. The medieval Chishtī [a Sufi order] *khānqāhs* kept open kitchens and this tradition is continued by the Ajmer *dargāh.** ...

[It is customary for certain people to] loot the *degs*, sell the contents and keep the proceeds. The cooked food** goes to those who can afford it, rather than to the hungry and destitute. This practice is now against the law which states that 'no portion of the food so cooked shall be sold'. However, the *dargāh* authorities lack the executive power to enforce the law and a tradition is recounted to discourage anyone from attempting to do so....

The various families from Inderkot work as teams to secure as much of the food as they can for themselves. When the *degs* are cooked and *fātiha* [the opening verses of the Quran] has been recited, the cloth cover, laden with ghee, is torn from over the contents, and the *deg*-men, wrapped in rags against the heat, begin frenziedly to empty the cauldron by the bucket-load. When the level of food inside the *deg* is such that the emptiers can no longer reach it with facility, they leap into the gruel, eager to salvage as much as they can for themselves. Steam envelops the fighting Inderkotis.... The heat inside the *deg* is intense; some of the Inderkotis collapse and are dragged senseless from the cauldron to be revived when the hectic looting is over. The looters are well rewarded for their struggle.

* *Food was cooked in large quantities in two* degs *which were presented to the* dargāh *for the purpose of providing for the poorer pilgrims.* Editor.

** *According to local tradition, rice and meat used to be the sacred food, but out of deference for the wishes of Hindu pilgrims only sweetened rice is now cooked.* Editor.

They auction oil-drums full of the looted food for as much as Rs 400 (1976 prices) to entrepreneurs who then sell the rice in small bowls or on leaves to pilgrims. The food is regarded as *tabarruk*; in other words it is thought to be laden with *baraka* ['grace'] so that none may be wasted. Those who cannot afford to buy a portion may be seen licking the protective clothing of the Inderkotis. The surrounds of the *degs* are washed and the slops carefully conserved and drunk.

During the *'urs* the most important official function is the *samā'* [literally, 'hearing'] which is held every evening after the *'Ishā* [night] prayer in the Samā Khāna. Whatever Sufi theoreticians have written in the past about the dangers of *samā'* to the spiritually immature, there are no restrictions on attendance at the *samā'* at Ajmer for men. Women are, however, forbidden to attend.

Before the singers (*qawwāls*) begin, a *Fātiha Khwān* ceremony is performed. Hereditary *fātakhwān* officiate; there are seven incumbents of this post at present. They all hold other jobs as well; most are government clerks or railway employees. They start by reciting the *Sūra Fātiha* [from the Quran] once and then the *Sūra Ikhlās* three times. The *Sūra Falaq* and *Sūra Amān* then follow. After this a special sweet, called *dallī*, is distributed among the audience.

The living representative of the former saint (the Diwan or Sajjāda-Nishīn) sits at one end of the Samā' Khāna under a silken canopy (*shamiana*) supported on ornate silver posts. Facing the Diwan's *gadī*, at the other end of the hall, sit the musicians. Between the Diwan and the musicians are ranged the most privileged members of the audience, sitting tightly packed into neat rows, cross-legged on the floor. Two hereditary officials, called *chobdārs*, clad in *angarkhas* (white robes tied across the chest and widening out below the waist into billowing pleated skirts), control the audience and usher respected guests to the best seats. They carry long silver staffs of office. The rest of the audience is kept at bay outside the central area of the Samā' Khāna. The music is relayed by a loudspeaker system to all parts of the *dargāh*, so that women who are forbidden to enter the Samā' Khāna, and those men who were too late to find space in the audience hall, may still have the benefit of hearing the *samā'*.

The group of musicians consists of a drummer, a harmonium player, and at least two other singers. The same musicians do not perform all night. Substitute groups of *qawwāls* are brought on as energy and repertoire begin to fail. When particularly moved or impressed by the musicians' performance, individuals from the audience present money to the musicians through the Diwan. They take their rupees to him, bowing low as they approach. The Diwan puts the money to his forehead and then hands it to an attendant (a son of the *chobdār* who is there to learn his father's business), who takes the offering over to the musicians. Often a member of the audience will not take his money direct to the Diwan, but will use an intermediary in order to show his humility and give another the privilege of approaching the Diwan.

Responses to the music differ. Many appear to be bored by the whole proceeding and there is a constant background of shuffling and whispering. Some evidently find the music and the poetry 'uplifting' and an aid to the contemplation of the essentials of their religion as the *qawwāls* sing of the prophet, his descendants and entourage, and of the exploits of Mu'īn al-dīn and his *murshid* [preceptor] and *murīds* [followers]. Others react ecstatically to the performance [become delirious, go into a trance, and even lose consciousness]. . . . Where ecstasy calms rather than agitates, the devotee remains seated, rocking . . . with the rhythm of the music until he gradually attains the state of *wajd* [ecstasy].

When *wajd* is achieved the Diwan, and the whole audience with him, rise to their feet to honour the ecstasy of the devotee. The *qawwāl* repeats the couplet that has so inspired the ecstatic until the latter's spiritual thirst is quenched and he returns to this world.

The *samā'* is interrupted at 3 a.m. when tea, flavoured with saffron and cardamom, is brought into the Samā' Khāna by servants of the shrine dressed in long velvet dresses. The tea is served only to the Diwan and his party, and VIP visitors who sit in the front rows of the audience. The *qawwāls* continue for another hour, after which the proceedings are brought to an end with the *fātiha* being read again. Bowls containing rose water which has been used to wash Mu'īn al-dīn's tomb are then passed around. A fortunate few are able to sip from them before the rest is sprinkled over the crowd. The Diwan rises, and with him the whole congregation, which then loses all self control, pushing forward in an attempt to gain a position from which the Diwan may be touched on his way out. Officials eventually manage to clear a path for him. The Diwan and his entourage walk down the aisle thus created. The *samā'* is over.

The only official *samā'* is that held every night during the *'urs*, one in the morning on the final day of the *'urs* which may be attended only by invitation from the Diwan himself, and a weekly *samā'* on Thursday evening. However, the *dargāh* is continuously filled with the sounds of *qawwāls* singing for the devotees who gather around them in various courtyards of the shrine. Private *samā'* parties are organized by groups of pilgrims in the houses where they are staying, and by the few *khānqāhs* that still exist in Ajmer out side the *dargāh*.

On the last day of the *'urs*, all the pilgrims gather together in and around the *dargāh* to pray before returning home. Every flat space in the mosques and courtyards of the shrine, on the rooftops and in the streets of the surrounding bazars is occupied by pilgrims. They arrive several hours before the prayers, so they can secure a position close to the centre of the *dargāh* from which the call to prayer is broadcast by a public address system over the whole shrine and adjacent parts of the town.

At the end of this *namāz* a gun is fired, the Jannatī Darwāza of the mausoleum, only opened for the duration of the *'urs*, is closed, and the festival is officially ended. The pilgrims begin to leave the city, but many stay on until the ninth day of the *'urs* (9 Rajab) when the entire shrine is ceremonially washed and cleaned. Only the *khuddām* (servants of the shrine) may wash the saint's grave and the inside of the mausoleum. This they do with rose water which is then sold as *tabarruk*. The pilgrims buy special brooms made from long reeds with which they sweep the rest of the *dargāh*.

This ritual washing (*ghusl*) is the final ceremony associated with the *'urs*. The life of the shrine returns to normal and the population of pilgrims diminishes.

Motive for the Pilgrimage

In order to understand why people in such large numbers visit the tomb of Mu'īn al-dīn, it is necessary to understand that death does not prevent the *shaykh* [spiritual leader] from playing his two roles of healer and spiritual guide. He is believed to live on in the place where he is buried and to continue to help his followers in the way he did during his earthly life. It is this belief which inspires his followers through the ages to continue to make the pilgrimage to his grave.

The specific motives which take devotees to Ajmer fall into two categories which correspond closely to the roles of the *shaykh* as healer, and as guide: the practical or material, and the spiritual or ritual.

Practical or Material Motives

The commonest motive for making the pilgrimage to a saint's shrine is to ask him to fulfil a need or to thank him for help already received. This was certainly the case historically. [Thus] it was through the intervention of a saint that Prince Salīm was believed to have been born, and it was to give thanks that the Emperor Akbar made his pilgrimage on foot to Ajmer. He also travelled to Mu'īn al-dīn's tomb to give thanks for his military victories. . . .

However, in the sample interviewed in Ajmer it was only a minority who came to request specific things or give thanks for specific favours received. The prayers—either of supplication or of thanksgiving—of the majority were on a more general level: thanks for their well-being and prayers for their continued prosperity.

Ajmer is not only a sacred centre, it is also a market place. Many of the visitors come to exploit its commercial possibilities. During the *'urs'* prices of commodities and services soar. Businessmen come for the duration of the festival to sell their wares. Shops in the bazars around the shrine are leased for this short period at a rent which would normally only be paid for a whole year lease. These short-term traders specialize in regional products and objects associated with the cult of Mu'īn al-dīn—pious compilations of anecdotes about him, hats to be worn in the shrine, rose water to be scattered over the mausoleum, petals to be placed on his grave, and embroidered cloth covers to adorn it.

These traders are not necessarily devotees of Mu'īn al-dīn, but there is a class of traders who attend the *'urs* to combine business with piety. Amongst those interviewed, a sherbet-seller, bangle-maker, cobbler, perfume-seller, several prostitutes and tea-stall holders, fell into this category. So too does the large population of itinerant beggars who do the rounds of religious festivals and only come to Ajmer for the *'urs*.

Both sides benefit from these transactions, regardless of the motivation. The saint is believed to perform a service for the devotee in return for which offerings are made. Likewise, the beggars, in return for the alms which they receive, enable pilgrims to observe one of the demands of their faith and earn religious merit. With pilgrim traders the transaction is more strictly of a commercial kind. The religious transactions are of a similar order to the secular ones and appear to be modelled on them.

Ritual Motives

It is frequently mentioned in the literature on the subject of sacred centres that pilgrimages are made at particular times in the life cycle.... No trace of this particular life-cycle ritual could be found....

Spiritual Motives

The shrine of Mu'īn al-dīn is a source of power and pilgrims travel there to establish a relationship with this power. The *baraka* of the saint is contagious and may be absorbed by close contact with his grave and with anything associated with it. The power of the saint is not simply valued for the material and physical help that it can bring, it is also a spiritual power which works by kind of spiritual osmosis. The saint's *baraka* imbues the places and things which are close to him; thus, the pilgrim kisses his tomb, eats the rose petals which have touched it, touches the *chādar* which will adorn it, buys the rose water which has washed it and eats the food which has been cooked near it. The models for such behaviour are to be found in the hagiography where unbelievers are converted by eating food which Mu'īn al-dīn has chewed and by the power of his glance. His power is still believed to be communicated by sight and touch, and benefits all those who come within reach of it.

The possibility of spiritual benefit at the shrine is not limited to a passive absorption through physical proximity to the interred saint. The shrine can be used as an aid to contemplation.... But this, too, is of declining importance and only relevant to the small band of *darvīshes* [mendicants] and Sufis who still pursue the *tarīqa*.... Associated with this is often a belief that prayers offered on such holy ground have a peculiar efficacy. But there is no belief that the saint in some way lives on at his shrine, or that the saint can be used as an intermediary to God.

Thus, there are different kinds of motives depending on the intellectual and religious status of the pilgrim. Only the very orthodox find no justification for pilgrimage to anywhere except Mecca. The diverse motives for the pilgrimage mean that the pilgrims are not drawn from any one class, rank or even religion.

The belief that pilgrimage is an act of penitence provides a further motive for the pilgrimage to Ajmer. The Prophet is traditionally claimed to have held the view that 'Pilgrimage is a sort of punishment', and that 'Pilgrimage effaces the sins committed after the previous pilgrimage. . . .'

Linked with this is the belief that physical misfortune can have a spiritual cause. In this way, the spiritual and physical motives for pilgrimage can become intermingled. Misfortune can be caused by sin; pilgrimage, as a penitential act, can erase the sin and counteract the misfortune.

There is another, subconscious, category of motives for the pilgrimage; the observer who stands outside the belief system involved may search further for these.

An *'urs* offers a holiday. The attraction of the pilgrimage journey, the picnics, the companionship and the music must exercise a considerable pull on the individual bound up in the routine of everyday life. . . .

Pilgrimage offers a means of escape from the hierarchy and obligations of the social structure. The pilgrim leaves behind his social role and 'the role-playing games which embroil his personality in manifold guiles, guilts and anxieties' (Turner 1975: 203). Instead, he associates only with those who share similar values, and who are reaffirming those values by the act of pilgrimage, and through the rituals performed and witnessed at the shrine. The fact that these values are shared is emphasized in the rituals; the differences between the participants are minimized and their equality and relatedness are stressed.

At Ajmer, in spite of differences of caste, class and religion, all the pilgrims get on their knees to sweep and wash the precincts of the shrine—a communal activity particularly remarkable in India where normally only members of an untouchable caste would perform such a menial task. The pilgrims all pray together in public. They eat the same food from the *degs*. At the *samā'* they drink from the same bowl of rose water. They have come, whatever their individual motivations, to venerate the one saint. The contrast between life at home and at the pilgrimage centre is further shown during the *samā'* when normal patterns of behaviour may be abandoned and individuals are encouraged to lose conscious control of their bodies and enter a state of trance. . . . At the shrine the pilgrims behave in a way which would be impossible and unacceptable in their homes. They are freed from the obligatory everyday constraints of status and role. Instead of the hierarchy of social structure the pilgrim lives temporarily in a community governed by the principles of equality and brotherhood. In short, he experiences what Turner (1969: 96) has called *communitas*.

Pilgrimage is, therefore, a journey from *structure* to *communitas* and back to *structure* again. . . .

While the pilgrims travel [this road] occasionally, the mystic attempts to live there permanently. His life style contrasts with that of structured social life. The communities which were centred *on a shaykh* in Indian Islam were characterized by a lack of structure and hierarchy. Ideally they had no property, no privileges, no material pleasures and little or no clothing. They were cut off from the world of commerce and lived on the very fringes of society.

Pilgrims temporarily, and *shaykhs* permanently, inhabit a place peripheral to the social structure. But it is at this periphery that *communitas* is experienced. From here the mystic seeks communion with God and the pilgrim endeavours to experience more directly the sacred. Thus, *shaykh* and shrine occupy a similar structural position mediating between this world and the next, the visible and the invisible, laymen and God. The community surrounding a *shaykh* in his *khānqāh* and the community of pilgrims at a shrine are strikingly similar. Both are set apart from the constraints of social life. In both, the ideals of religion can more easily be lived out, for the community at a *khānqāh* or at a shrine is based on the Muslim ideal of equality and exemplifies the principles of Islam. The *shaykh* and his disciples attempt to live exemplary Muslim lives and pilgrims are scrupulous in their performance of the obligatory prayers and spend time also in supererogatory prayer. The shrine is also a place for alms giving and reading the Quran, and for living as brothers, not as 'superiors' and 'inferiors'. . . . Thus, every step the mystic takes is a symbol of the journey to Mecca. If the Sufi theorists say that the journeys of a pilgrim and mystic have something in common, it is legitimate to deduce that their destinations and life styles there are not dissimilar. . . .

Just as this world (*al-dunyā*) is dominated for the layman by the hierarchical structure of society, so too is his vision of the unseen (*al-ghā'ib*). In this world society is stratified into *ashrāf*, non-*ashrāf*, high- and low-caste converts, and infidels, and social relations are organized hierarchically. Similarly, in the unseen world there are the various ranks of the Awliyā', the prophets, Muhammad and Allāh. To petition Allāh, it is necessary first to approach an intermediary. . . .

The issue is complicated by the fact that this hierarchical vision of this world and the next is opposed to the teachings of the Quran. According to the Quran all men are equal before Allāh and no one approximates to Him in any way. However, such equality does not exist within society, except at its edge—in the *shaykh's khānqāh* for the disciples, and at the shrine for the pilgrims. The *shaykh* is an exemplar of the ideal Muslim, and the community that surrounds him during his life in his *khānqāh* exemplifies ideal Muslim society. The life of the *shaykh* is closer to Quranic Islam than that of the layman, so it is inevitable that he will be regarded as somehow superior to the layman and, therefore, as a suitable intermediary between the layman and Allāh.

As the hagiography of Mu'īn al-dīn developed, he was transformed in popular belief from a *darvīsh* [a religious mendicant], about whom little was known, into an idealized *shaykh*—the 'Prophet of India'. Like-wise, as the cult of Mu'īn al-dīn developed Ajmer came to be regarded as a threshold to the next world—a second Mecca.

Moharram

A. R. SAIYID

The first description below is of the observance of Moharram in the Konkan region of Maharashtra State. The data presented here are, specifically, from a fishing village, Fatehpur, in Ratnagiri District. The village is predominantly inhabited by Mahigir Muslims. The second description is from Chanorba,[1] a medium-sized Muslim majority town in Moradabad District in Uttar Pradesh. The Muslims of Chanorba are divided into well-defined social layers and Moharram appears to largely involve the various service castes. . . .

In Fatehpur, the sighting of the moon which heralds the beginning of the lunar month of Moharram, was a matter of great joy and excitement for the Mahigir Muslims of the village. Young and old were equally eager to see the *Moharram-ka-chand* (the Moharram moon); indeed, their eagerness almost made one feel as if the moon for Ramadan-Id[2] had been sighted! Soon after the moon had been sighted, the *naqaras* (big drums) that had been stored in rooms adjoining the mosques of each locality were brought out and beaten loudly in front of the various mosques. This was done to inform one and all that Moharram had begun. On subsequent evenings, the *naqaras* were beaten after the *Isha ki namaz* (night prayers) until the end of the 'celebrations' on the tenth day of the month. The *naqaras*, incidentally, were played somewhat briefly and perfunctorily from the second till the sixth nights, but thereafter it became extremely ethusiastic, frantic and deafening.

On the first evening, apart from the beating of the *naqaras*, some

Excerpted from A. R. Saiyid, 'Moharram', in Imtiaz Ahmad, ed., *Religion and Ritual among the Muslims in India*, Manohar, Delhi, pp. 118–33.

[1] *Fatehpur and Chanorba are both pseudonyms*. Editor.

[2] *Feast day at the end of the month of fasting by day light called* rozah *(Persian) or* saum *(Arabic)*. Editor.

individuals began digging small pits in front of the mosque of each *mohalla*. In these pits—or *alava*, as they are called—a small *diva* [earthen lamp] was lit every night, and around it the men and children performed a typical dance, which is known as *waye* all over Konkan. The *waye* was performed every night till about midnight to a rhythm set by the *naqaras*. From the seventh night onwards, along with the *naqara* beating, the *waye* too became extremely boisterous. Till the ninth night, the *waye* was danced in front of the *mohalla* mosque only, but on the ninth night and on the tenth and final day it was performed throughout the *mohalla*. One norm pertaining to *waye* is that individuals have to perform it only in their own *mohalla*. If, however, a group is interested in dancing in another *mohalla*, then they have to give an assurance to the *hodekar* (headman) of that *mohalla* that they will not misbehave or create any kind of disturbance or foster an inter-*mohalla* conflict.

It was observed that in these inter-*mohalla* visits, the 'visiting' performers did not limit themselves to dancing but also indulged in various kinds of comic acts and tomfoolery. Some of them wore wigs and fancy dress and acted out various roles for the entertainment of the sightseers/onlookers. It was not difficult to see that there was a spirit of healthy competition in these performances and also that they were a tremendous source of enjoyment for everyone concerned. When questioned, the villagers appeared to feel that such inter-*mohalla* competitions enhanced fellow-feeling and intra-village unity.

As if to enhance the gaiety and enjoyment, at least in one *mohalla* some of the houses were seen to be decorated and Divali-like lights[3] were kept burning near the doors. Some fireworks were also let off. A local *dargah* [shrine] was also illuminated with electric bulbs during this period.

Women, however, did not participate in dancing the *waye* or in the horseplay. But nor were they indoors. While the menfolk danced and played, most women recited *mercias* [*marsiyah*, dirge] sitting in a circle just a few yards away from where the menfolk were dancing the *waye*. In one *mohalla* the women sat in a tent on which all kinds of artistic efforts had been lavished. This tent too was erected opposite the *mohalla* mosque—it was quite spacious and of a squarish shape. There were bulbs of various colours hanging inside. The canvas walls of the tent were painted with colours showing big trees,

[3] *The Hindu festival of Dīvalī celebrates the triumph of good over evil.* Editor.

rivers, grass, etc. Thus, the inside of the tent was made to resemble a garden. In the middle, there was a replica in multi-coloured paper of a monument resembling the Taj Mahal. Beside it there were two other replicas—one of the Kaaba[4] and the other of the tomb of Fatima (the mother of the martyred brothers, Hassan and Hussain). Considerable artistic skills and efforts had gone into making all these things, so that the overall impact was quite impressive and gave evidence of the creative talents of the villagers.

While the dancing went on till midnight, the women kept congregating in the tent, locally referred to as *phool-jhaad* (literally, tree of flowers, but perhaps, more correctly, 'garden'). A number of women brought sweets of various sorts, as well as sherbet, and deposited them by the side of the replica of Fatima's tomb. When the *waye* finished around midnight, *dua* [prayer] was recited over the sweets and the sherbet and these were then partaken of by both men and women. In the other *mohallas* where there were no *phool-jhaad* tents, the women would collect in some spacious house and recite the *mercias*. In all the *mohallas*, the recitation of the *mercias* continued only up to the eighth night. On the ninth night, when the *waye* was performed not just around the *alava* but throughout the *mohalla*, the women moved around with the rest of the procession and served as some sort of 'cheer-leaders'. On the tenth and final day too, the women accompanied the *waye* processionists round their respective *mohallas*. In this way, on the verge of the conclusion of the celebrations, both men and women jointly participated in the 'festivities'.

The next important activity in the community pertained to the *tazziyas*.[5] After the moon had been sighted, meetings were held in each *mohalla* to discuss the details of constructing the *tazziyas*. Specific responsibilities were allocated and financial arrangements made and agreed upon. However, the actual construction began only on about the sixth day and the various *tazziyas* were completed by the ninth. Interestingly enough, the *tazziyas* were constructed on the premises of the mosques. Accordingly, throughout the ten days the mosques became hubs of endless activity. A striking observation in this connection was that the loudspeakers installed in the mosques were used for a variety of purposes. From time to time, individuals would come to the microphone and recite verses

[4] Ka'bah, *the cube-like building inside the mosque at Mecca*. Editor.

[5] Ta'ziah, *a representation of the tombs of Hasan and Husain*. Editor

from the Koran; at other times, records of similar recitations would be played. Shockingly enough, on other occasions, film music also blared from these loudspeakers. Indeed, barring the period of the prayers, these loudspeakers were almost continuously busy.

In Fatehpur, as in other places, the construction of *tazziyas* is facilitated by the fact that the basic wooden structure is never destroyed but is safely preserved in the mosque to be used year after year. Every Moharram, this wooden structure is brought out from its storing place, and the bare frame is beautifully and attractively decorated with coloured paper. The final step is to fix a large paper dome on top of the wooden structure, with the result that the *tazziya* begins to resemble a mausoleum. Inside the Fatehpur *tazziyas*, there were replicas of the graves of Hassan and Hussian. Electric illuminations were also provided inside the *tazziyas* so that at night the coloured lights enhanced their attractiveness, and they became a source of wonder and appreciation for the village children, women and men. Thus, the *tazziya* too are products of artistic creativity and skills. And, as may well be imagined, they were a source of *mohalla* pride and inter-*mohalla* competitiveness.

An inevitable accompaniment of *tazziyas* is the phenomenon of *mannats* [*munajat*, silent prayer]. Men and women, but particularly the latter, visited the *tazziyas* in large numbers and expressed requests for various kinds of favours.[6] Those that came to make these requests appeared to be highly emotionally charged and had a visible air of helplessness. The implorations were made very earnestly, and it was evident that life afforded no other solutions to these simple folk. In return for the grant of favours sought, the favour-seekers promised that they would make cash offerings to the *tazziya* in the subsequent year or years. Obviously, the more acute or intense the emotional state of the favour-seeker, the more lavish he or she is in the promises made. Several informants gave the clear impression that there is a strong feeling that *mannats* made in the presence of *tazziyas* are fulfilled. One interesting observation in this connection was that there were public announcements over the loudspeaker regarding individuals who had donated twenty-five rupees or twenty-five paise in return for the fulfilment of their respective *mannats*. Clearly, such public announcements are

[6] The differing concerns that affect women and men are well reflected here. Women generally seek intervention for, and on behalf of children and ask for marital happiness. For men, employment, success in business and other economic interests are the dominating desires.

supposed to act as encouragement to others. The amount thus collected, it was pointed out, is either spent on the various expenses incurred in connection with the *tazziyas* or split between *tazziya* construction and the maintenance of the *mohalla* mosque. In addition to such contributions, which are a sort of 'thanksgiving' payment, individuals also made voluntary contributions partly in reponse to the appeal made by those responsible for constructing and maintaining the *tazziya* of the locality, and partly as a matter of respect for, and faith in, the *tazziya*. Overall, there existed a deep religious motivation, and satisfaction, in the support given on the *tazziya*; and, there was a general agreement among those questioned that supporting the *tazziyas* was a religious duty and earned, for the supporters, religious merit.

In Fatehpur, the *tazziyas* were found to be popular among the Hindus also and several of them visited the *tazziyas* for *darshan*[7] and made *mannats* and offerings. Thus, insofar as the common problems of life are concerned, Hindus and Muslims were united in seeking solutions through the *tazziyas*. But apart from *tazziyas*, Moharram increased inter-communal interaction. During the entire ten days, Hindus, including Brahmans, were found to be visiting Muslim localities and even houses. The Hindu guests were served . . . various snacks and, in some instances, . . . alcoholic drinks as well.[8] During the nights, the Hindus were present to witness the *waye*, though they did not appear to participate actively in the dancing. (The *waye*, incidentally, is quite similar to the *govinda* dance of the Maharashtrian Hindus, performed in this region on the occasion of Gokulashtami.)

The Moharram 'celebrations' reached their peak on the ninth day. Till the ninth, the *waye* was performed only opposite the *mohalla* mosque, but on the ninth night (as has already been mentioned) the entire *mohalla* became the locale of dancing. By now the *tazziyas* were ready and were taken out in a procession throughout the *mohalla*. These processions went on practically throughout the night and, accordingly, the *waye*, which used to stop around midnight, continued almost non-stop on the ninth night. On this night, many individuals were observed to be wearing new clothes and had also adorned their faces with cosmetics, chief among them being

[7] Darshan *is the seeing of sacred objects as an act of religious devotion*. Editor.

[8] It may, however be added here that inter-communal amity is a special feature of Moharram in Konkan. Traditionally, this region of India has been blessed with exemplary friendliness between the two communities. This friendliness gets further cemented on ocassions like Moharram.

talcum powder! Some males had dressed themselves as females and kept dancing in front of the *tazziyas*. Several women accompanied the procession and appeared to be in high spirits.

On the following day, which was the final day of the Moharram 'celebrations', the unique custom of *posst* was observed. At about ten-thirty in the morning, a group of about six persons were seen to be moving about in the *mohalla*. They had a *naqara* and a *tasha* (a somewhat flat-shaped drum with a metallic base) with them with which they were creating a lot of noise. They would stop at every door and collect one rupee and twenty-five paise. This amount was collected from Hindu homes also. The total collection was later spent on alcoholic drinks,[9] which were consumed in the process of dancing and merry-making. Incidentally, the drinks were supplied to the dancing men by the womenfolk! This custom of *posst*, it was learnt, is also followed during Dussehra and Divali, when the Hindus collect the funds and Muslims donate and drink along with the Hindus. These *posst* donations are not compulsory, but traditionally both Hindus and Muslims contribute.

The tenth day, being the day when the *tazziyas* are disposed of, was also a day of processions. Accordingly, after the *posst*, the *tazziyas* in the various localities were taken in processions at about 2 p.m. round the respective *mohallas*. Each procession was characterized by a peak-of-form *waye*. Drinks were freely consumed. In this stage of intoxication and heightened emotional frenzy, the dancers kept shouting various slogans of both a religious and non-religious nature. The music and dancing created a tremendous din throughout the village. However, the noise appeared to be a source of great joy to everyone. All this continued till sunset. At sunset, the processions began to leave their *mohallas* and head towards a jetty. When all the *tazziyas* reached a point from where they could all be seen simultaneously, the ritual of *salaami* (valediction) was performed. Thereafter the *tazziya* that was nearest the jetty moved towards it first, followed by the others. At the jetty water was sprinkled on

[9] For most Muslims, this information will indeed be very shocking. To be sure, as individuals many Muslims do drink but public consumption of alcohol is too drastic a violation of one of Islam's best known taboos. It may be clarified, however, that the drinking reported here is not a feature or part of Moharram as such. In fact it is a part of the daily life of most, if not all, Mahigirs. Theirs is a very strenuous occupation which takes them out of their homes in the middle of the night. They are out at sea early in the morning and return to the village, utterly exhausted, only around mid-day. Further, most of them are rather poor and lead a dull and drab existence. Due to the fish lying everywhere, the village is full of a horrible stink. In these conditions, drinking has become a way of life.

each *tazziya* to symbolize its 'demise'. The water, incidentally, had been brought from the various *mohallas* for their respective *tazziyas*. After the water was sprinkled, *fatihah* (opening verse of the Quran) was recited. Next, the *dera* (dome) from each *tazziya* was removed and cast into the water. After this coconuts were dashed on the ground and bits of coconut, along with some candy, were distributed among those present. Soon therefore, the *tazziyas* minus their domes were brought back to be stored in the *hujras* (chamber). The coloured paper used to decorate the *tazziyas* was allowed to remain on the *tazziyas* for another two days.

On the twelfth day of Moharram, a *ziarat* ceremony [pilgrimage] was observed. This consisted of holding *mauloods* in the evening. After this recitation, the coloured paper was removed from the *tazziyas*. This step signalled the culmination of the Moharram observances. One detail that has not been mentioned concerns the *alavas* in which the *divas* had burnt throughout the first nine nights. These *divas* were extinguished on the evening of the tenth day after the *maghrib ki namaz* (sunset prayer). The *alavas* were filled with earth. Later, water was sprinkled on this earth and *agarbattis* (joss sticks) were lit and kept burning on the small mounds of earth.

The above description may perhaps have made it evident that the 'celebration' of Moharram is an integral part of the village community's social life, and that it has certain social and psychological meanings to it which are not always evident to the outsider, especially if the outsider is not versed in the task of sociological analysis. In this connection, it is illuminating to know that Moharram continues to attract the villagers even when they live away from the village. Every effort is made by the inhabitants to return to Fatehpur by the seventh day in order to 'play' *waye* and participate in the other proceedings. In one case, an individual,who happened to be only some thirty miles away from Fatehpur and could not get a bus to the village, hired a taxi at a cost of Rs 80 just to ensure that he would be home on the seventh day. In fact, he boasted that had he been away in Bombay (almost 200 miles away), he would have spent whatever was necessary to return to Fatehpur by the seventh of Moharram. This individual, incidentally, was physically decrepit and was unable to really dance the *waye*. Nevertheless, the spirit was stronger than the flesh, and with the help of intoxicants he tried to enjoy the 'festival' as best as he could. Probably there were some others too who had rushed back from as far away as Bombay. According to informants, individuals who made *mannats* while away from the village and whose *mannats* had been fulfilled, invariably returned to the village during Moharram. As for the vast majority that lived in the village, all fishing activities were suspended from the sixth day onwards; thus for full four days enjoyment and merry-making transcended economic interests.

It was observed that even the village *pesh-imams* (those who customarily lead the prayers in the mosque) were unable to escape participation, excepting that they did not consume alcoholic drinks or perform the *waye*. But they could not avoid being a part of the various processions. Indeed, informants revealed that *pesh-imams* who were opposed to such enjoyment were either not appointed, or, if appointed, were dismissed before Moharram. One significant information in this connection was that a popular Hindu doctor of Fatehpur, who enjoys respect among the Muslims as well, was invited a few years ago to address the Mahigir Muslims on the occasion of Moharram. In his address, he criticized the consumption of liquor, the blaring of loudspeakers in the mosques, and the generally boisterous enjoyment of Moharram. He pointed out that such an observance of Moharram was un-Islamic. But he only succeeded in evoking a negative reaction and since then he has not been invited to participate in the Moharram 'festivities'. Indeed, the very practice of inviting guest speakers on this occasion has been abandoned to avoid such unsavoury and conscience pricking homilies.

We shall now describe Moharram as it is observed in Chanorba. In Chanorba, agriculture is the dominant occupation. The Muslim population is divided into various status groups, including such service castes as the Julahas (weavers), Qasais (butchers), Saqqas (water-carriers) and Faqirs (traditionally beggars, but who now also work as casual labourers and domestic servants). In thc upper echelons are the traditional elite, the *moulvis* (literally, scholars, but here landlords), and an intermediary group of peasant farmers, the Chaudharis. Moharram in Chanorba primarily preoccupies the lower status groups, but the elite are not entirely divorced from the various ramifications of the 'celebrations'.

From the day the month of Moharram begins, the Muslims belonging to the various service castes don green *kurtas* (longish shirts) and green caps. This green attire is held to symbolize the fact that with the advent of Moharram all status differences in the community have been obliterated and that all Muslims can participate in the festival without any distinctions. (Of course, this is only a pious hope inasmuch as the elite reveal no such desire and do not participate in the planning and execution of the various Moharram activities.)

From the very first night of Moharram, the residents of the various *mohallas* gather together in their respective localities (after the *Isha-ki-namaz*) to participate in what is known as *maatam* (mourning). While *maatam* generally involves beating of the breast, in Chanorba there is only a slow rhythmic beating of drums. Those present merely sway to the rhythm. The *maatam* gatherings occur every night for the first five nights, and are more in the nature of social get-togethers. From the sixth to the ninth day of Moharram, the community witnesses various kinds of processions. First, in the evenings there are the *alums* (ensigns) processions followed in the night by *mehdi* processions. And finally, there are also the *tazziya* processions. The construction of the *mehdis* and *tazziyas* is an elaborate affair in Chanorba and those involved in these tasks work at them almost throughout the year. The *mehdi* is a local creation. It is the shape of a big *doli*, or palanquin, and is spectacularly decorated with multicoloured and shiny papers which are artistically pieced together in numerous designs and patterns. It rests on two long bamboo shafts and is carried by four persons. In a sense, the *mehdi* is another form of *tazziya* but is all the same a distinct entity with its own norms. Thus, in Chanorba the *tazziyas* are only ready on the tenth day and are taken out in procession later that evening. But the *mehdis* are prepared earlier and they can, therefore, be taken out in processions right from the initial days. They seem to serve the function of building up a tempo from the very beginning. The various *mehdis* are linked with the different occupational groups and in this way they provide an accepted mechanism of inter-group rivalry in terms of creative self-expression. The *mehdis* are taken out in nocturnal processions according to an agreed schedule and each night is designated by the name of the occupational group whose *mehdi* is going to make the rounds that night. As with *tazziyas* so also with *mehdis*, it is considered to be an act of religious merit to give one's shoulder to the *mehdi* during the procession.

Unlike Fatehpur where the various activities pertaining to Moharram had their locus in the locality or *mohalla*, in Chanorba the *alums*, *mehdis* and *tazziyas* are caste-centred. As such, they are linked with specific occupational groups like water-carriers and so on. Accordingly, the competitive spirit underlying the *tazziyas* and *mehdis* is also caste oriented. This inter-group competitiveness, incidentally, is not limited to the *mehdis* and *tazziyas* only; there are two other institutionalized competitions that are a vital part of the Moharram 'celebrations' in this town. First, there s *mercia-goi* and then there is *patey-baazi*. The former refers to a display of competence in the recitation of eulogies in the memory and honour of Hassan and Hussain, while the latter is a pseudo sword-fencing competition which is held with sticks that are carved out as swords. The fencers initiate a small battle scene symbolizing Imam Hussain's battle with his enemies. Both *mercia-goi* and *patey-baazi* have over the years been raised to the status of fine arts which are learnt, practised and displayed with exemplary zeal and dedication. In fact, the potential competitors keep practising one or the other of these throughout the year so as to be in a fit condition when Moharram comes round. While the learning of *mercia-goi* is largely an individual effort, skill and perfection in *patey-baazi* are a matter of training under a skilful *ustad* (teacher). . . .

The opportunity for the public display of talent and skills in these two enterprises comes when the *mehdi* or *tazziya* processions are going round the various localities. It is customary for these processions to halt in front of the homes of the rich and prominent members of the community, who generally limit their participation to the grant of cash assistance for the construction of *tazziyas* or *mehdis*. In token of appreciation, therefore, the processions halt in front of homes of such individuals and performances of *mercia-goi* and *patey-baazi* are given. The intensity of interest and seriousness of these performances is heightened by the fact that the members of the elite group witness and patronize the 'show'. While *patey-baazi* is in progress, there is a continuous and loud beating of drums and blowing of trumpets to a certain rhythm; this accompaniment is infectious inasmuch as the spectators too begin to gyrate their bodies in a slow rhythmic manner. When the *mercia-goi* and *patey-baazi* are over, the participants are given an appreciative pat and are also served with some snacks and refreshments, provided by the individuals who are honoured by the halts and performances in front of their *havelis* (mansions). Thereafter, the procession moves on to its next halt.

From the above, it will be evident that even though the elite members of the Muslim community in Chanorba do not participate in the Moharram 'festivities', nevertheless, in a covert manner, their interest and support are extended; and, it is a matter of personal gratification for them that they are personally recognized and honoured through the performances of *mercia-goi* and *patey-baazi*. In a feudalistic set-up, such recognition and honour are of ineffable value for the self-esteem of the elite. Consequently, the elite too encourage all the traditions of Chanorba's Moharram and this support, obviously, is a source of encouragement and legitimation for lower castes to 'celebrate' Moharram with pomp and pageantry. One interesting point that needs to be mentioned here is that young children of the elite families are especially woken up even at very late hours of the night to witness the various processions. Indeed, this is a part of a child's socialization in these families. In this way, conscious efforts are made to inculcate an interest in, and enthusiasm for, the local Moharram. This practice amply supports the observations concerning the elite.

In the preceding description of Fatehpur's Moharram, it was mentioned that *tazziyas* were instruments of blind faith when it came to illness and other personal crises. In Chanorba too the people have a strong belief that *tazziyas* and *mehdis* can, and do, help overcome illnesses, especially the incurable ones. However, instead of making *mannats*, there is a local tradition whereby children are made to pass from under the *tazziya* or the *mehdi*. This passing through the empty space (under the *tazziya*) is believed to be beneficial for effective cure. In fact, the popular belief is that the more often one goes under the *tazziya* . . . the greater the benefit that one will derive. Accordingly, it is seen that the moment the procession stops somewhere, there is a stampede in which individuals, particularly children, try to get under the *tazziya* or *mehdi*. Mothers of ailing children especially congregate so as to encourage and push their children in the space below. This belief is shared by the Hindus also, and they pass under the *tazziyas* and *mehdis*.

As in Fatehpur so in Chanorba, the excitement begins to mount after the first six days. On the seventh day, the processions have an added feature in the form of a giant black figure which is supposed to represent Jaffar, the mythical king of the Jinns. He is believed to have come to the rescue of Hussain in the blood-bath of Karbala, but Hussain refused to be helped. On the eight day, the duration of the procession is prolonged inordinately because two, rather than one, *mehdis* are on show, and hence there are two processions which take up the entire night. A competition—involving the usual *mercia-goi* and *patey-baazi*—is arranged between the two processions, and the winners have the satisfaction of becoming the toast of the community. For several days after the actual performance, people keep discussing the merits and demerits of the respective performers, and the decision of the panel of judges, which is constituted for this purpose, is supported and criticized in various quarters. . . .

The tenth and final day, as everywhere, is the day of bringing the Moharram 'festival' to an end. As part of the last round of enjoyment and merriment, a small fair is organized and children especially are given money to spend in this fair. The shops and stalls that are set up in this fair belong to the Hindus. In this way, the Hindus benefit economically from this particular feature of Chanorba's Moharram. It may also be mentioned here that since the surrounding villages have a sparse Muslim population, they cannot afford to organize their own Moharram festivities. Consequently, the Muslims from these villages come to Chanorba to participate in its Moharram and thereby increase the scale of Chanorba's 'festivities'. In addition, as in the case of Fatehpur, the residents of Chanorba who have taken up jobs in places as far away as Calcutta try to return home during Moharram and they are often in the mood to spend lavishly. This general influx of individuals during the final days of Moharram serves as a windfall for the Hindu shopkeepers. Not surprisingly, these Hindus help the 'festival' by donating money for the *tazziyas* and by providing illuminations on the procession routes.

The culminating procession on the tenth day provides an interesting commentary on the reality of the social differentiation among the Chanorba Muslims. It has already been mentioned that in Chanorba the *tazziyas* are not constructed by each *mohalla* or residential locality but by occupational groups which, it need hardly be mentioned, are hierarchically organized. Significantly enough, the order in which the *tazziyas* are lined up in the final procession reflects the social hierarchy. Since there is no river or stream near Chanorba the *tazziyas* are not immersed in water but are buried on the premises of the *Imam-bada*.[10] . . .

[10] *Building for the observance of Moharram.* Editor.

Further Readings

Ahmed, Imtiaz, ed.,
1981 *Ritual and Religion among Muslims in India*, Manohar, Delhi.
Based on fieldwork in different parts of India, this volume of papers covers several kinds of performances including life cycle rituals and periodical festivals.

Herman, William P.,
1989 *The Sacred Marriage of Hindu Goddess*, Indiana University Press, Bloomington.
This is a rich ethnographic study of a major Hindu temple ritual of South India. The author highlights the interweaving of the ritual and the social in everyday life.

Jaini, Padmanabha,
1979 *The Jain Path of Purification*. Motilal Banarsidass, Delhi.
Based on textual sources, but also drawing upon observation, this book presents Jain beliefs regarding the notion of 'purity' and describes everyday and periodic rituals connected with the same.

Stevenson, Mrs. Sinclair,
1971 (1920) *The Rites of the Twice-Born*, Oriental Books, New Delhi.
This well-known book by a Christian missionary provides a detailed account of the life cycle rites and other rituals among high caste Hindus, particularly Brahmins, on the basis of information collected in Gujarat. A useful work for assessing the extent and nature of social change in Hindu society over the last two generations.

IV

Sacred Persona

It is a well-known fact that the social distribution of knowledge is uneven, that some people know more, and more deeply, of certain things than others. This is, for instance, true of traditional sacred (or modern technical) knowledge. Access to certain kinds of sacred knowledge is, in fact, severely restricted as it may be obtained only by favour of some supernatural power or agency rather than by individual effort. A typical example would be the knowledge obtained by a shaman in the course of a trance which he then uses for certain purposes such as divination and healing. Compared to the shaman other specialists of sacred knowledge may appear to be rather humdrum, but they have their own importancce, even when they are no more than the lay followers of a religious faith.

Thus, the Hill Saoras of Ganjam and Koraput (Orissa), who are the subject of the first reading in this part, recognize four types of religious functionaries, viz. Buyya (priests), Kuranmaran (shamans), Idaimaran (acolyte-assistants to shamans), and Siggamaran (funeral functionaries). The Kuranmaran are divided into five subtypes of which the most important are the Raudakumbmaran who are married to tutelaries, learn their duties in dreams and trance, and perform at major as well as minor rituals. Also noteworthy are the Regamaran (medicine-men). Corresponding to male Kuranmaran are the female Kuranboi; the Idaiboi are the female counterparts of the Idaimaran, and the Raudakumboi of the Raudakumbmaran. The office of shaman, though not hereditary, runs in families. The shamans and shamanins are, Verrier Elwin informs us, expected to follow a stricter way of life than ordinary Saoras.

Shamans are generally associated with pre-literate societies but they or their counterparts are also found in modern societies though they may not, strictly speaking, belong to them. Many observers have written about the so-called 'god men' of contemporary India, some of whom have an international following. One such 'jet-age holy man', a 'deity-saint' and 'miracle-maker' is Sathya Sai Baba. Lawrence Babb's essay here explores such issues as the biography of Sathya Sai Baba, the nature of his concerns, the significance of his 'miracles', the character of his following and the cult, and the light all this information throws on religion in contemporary India—and indeed in the modern (and post-modern) world.

Besides traditional shamans and modern miracle-makers, there are (as mentioned above) other kinds of specialists who acquire and use sacred knowledge in less dramatic ways. The priests who assist at the performance of rituals, at home and in temple or church, readily come to mind. They may be born into a priestly caste, as among the Hindus, or take on the priestly role by pursuing a course of studies and being formally inducted into it, as among the Christians. In the third reading, excerpted from Christopher Fuller's book on the priests of the famous Hindu temple at Madurai in South India, we read about a situation in which the assignment of the role of religious functionary is shown to be quite complex, and influenced by many factors, including some from outside the strictly religious domain, over a long period of time. Fuller describes different categories of priests, their initiation, consecration and way of life, their rights and obligations, etc. These priests are servants of the deity and are even considered to be his incarnation.

There are several kinds of priests in Hindu society including, notably, family priests who help in the performance of domestic ceremonies, temple priests, and priests attached to centres of pilgrimage. One of India's holiest cities is Gaya, considered sacred by Hindus and Buddhists alike (Gautama attained enlightenment here). Located on the banks of the river Phalgu in Bihar, it attracts Hindus from all over the country for the ritual of feeding the manes and for worship at Vishnupada temple. The priests who officiate at these rituals are called the Gaya *panda* ('learned, wise man') or the Gayawal ('residents of Gaya'). L. P. Vidyarthi discusses various aspects of the life of the Gayawal including a wide-ranging network of relationships. The excerpt from his book included here refers to these relationships as 'extensions' and describes their broad scope. It shows that priests in Hindu society fulfil a variety of roles—as spiritual seekers, ritual specialists, clients, patrons, and professional rivals—which have religious as well as economic aspects. The sacredness or sanctity of the priestly persona is more manifest in some of these roles than in others.

The last essay is of interest as it shows clearly that the lay followers of a religious faith, and not religious specialists or functionaries alone, may come to consider themselves, and be recognized by others, as having acquired a sacred persona. In fact, Sikh society does not have a priesthood, and all Sikhs are believed to be equally capable of achieving spiritual merit if they live by the teachings of their gurus. J. P. S. Uberoi's well-known essay on the symbols of Sikhism (revised by the author for inclusion in this book) clarifies the notion of Sikh identity. Formal initiation into Sikhism was introduced by the tenth and last personal guru of the Sikhs, Gobind, in 1699. It was prescribed but not strictly enforced. Those who went through the ceremony were, however, required to stick to a well-defined way of life which required, among other things, being unshorn and carrying on one's person a *kirpan* or sword (its size was to be a matter of choice) as an emblem of the divinity. The interest of Uberoi's analysis does not lie in its historical accuracy but its method which 'reveals' an unconscious structure linking the five symbols of Sikh identity in one meaningful whole. It is through this analysis of the Sikh sacred persona that Uberoi locates for us the place of Sikhism in the cultural history of India.

The five readings on sacred persona are merely illustrative of the phenomenon and do not attempt to present the full range of typological possibility. The absence of the category of prophet may be commented upon though: it is simply absent in India's indigenous religious traditions. God born as man (*avatar*), as Rama or Krishna, and as the Buddha for that matter, partakes of sacredness in the highest measure. Seekers of the ultimate (*sants*) and devotees of God (*bakhta* and *sufi*) also are holy people and much revered. The spiritual preceptor occupies a place at par with if not higher than that of

God. But the idea of a prophet, such as Moses, Jesus or Muhammad, who brings God's message to humanity, has remained alien to the religious sensibility of Hindus, Buddhists, Jains and Sikhs. There is no sure example even from among the so-called tribal peoples.

Saora Shamans and Shamanins

VERRIER ELWIN

The Kuranmaran, the shaman, is the most important religious figure in a Saora village. He has the power not only to diagnose the source of trouble or disease, but to cure it. He is doctor as well as priest, psychologist as well as magician, the repository of tradition, the source of sacred knowledge. His primary duty is that of divination; in case of sickness he seeks the cause in trance or dream. Every shaman has a tutelary-wife in the Under World, and she comes to assist him in any perplexity and often guides him in his duties. He may inherit his powers, and is generally trained by his father or some other relative, but he is chosen by the direct intervention of a tutelary, and his marriage with her effects his dedication. Once that is done he is continually in touch with the gods and ancestors of the other world, and if he is adept he may develop a wide practice, for he is not confined to his own village, but may go wherever he is summoned. He is regarded with respect and often with affection, as a man given to the public service, a true friend in time of affliction.

The trance[1] occurs, or may occur, as a feature of any ceremony at which the spirits are invited to be present, provided there is a shaman qualified to accommodate them.

But if the ceremony is being conducted by an ordinary priest, or by an Idaimaran, or by a shaman not fully qualified, then it proceeds to its conclusion more expeditiously, but without the excitement

Excerpted from Verrier Elwin, 'Saora Shamans and Shamanins', in *The Religion of an Indian Tribe*, Oxford University Press, Bombay, 1955, pp. 130–1, 469–83.

[1] A trance may either be a cataleptic or hypnotic condition marked by the suspension of consciousness, or a state of mental abstraction from external things, absorption, exaltation, ecstasy (*O.E.D.*). In the Saora trance the shaman is abstracted from external things but not wholly unconscious of them.

and interest that a shaman in trance invariably provides. Shamans may also fall into trance on occasions at which they are performing no official function; I have often seen shamanins fall to the ground in a state of spirit-possession at entirely secular dances or during the processions of a Harvest Festival. On more than one occasion I have been somewhat embarrassed by a shamanin going into trance as a result of listening to my gramophone.

Once a shaman passes into a state of dissociation anything may happen. The belief is that he is possessed by a spirit, or more usually, a succession of spirits who speak and act through him. He is supposed to be completely under their control and to have no knowledge of what he is saying and doing. Yet although there is no programme, and there is endless diversity in detail, there is a remarkable general similarity throughout the whole Saora country in the way the shamans talk and behave at these times.

There is generally great confusion and, as I say, anything may happen. There may be revelations and discussions about matters entirely unrelated to the sacrifice or festival at which the trance occurs. The dead are always breaking in, for—it is said—'at the least sign of love the dead approach'. A ghost may take the opportunity to give instructions about the disposal of his property or to demand a quite different sacrifice later on; a god may give warning of an epidemic or threaten ruin to the crops. The regular course of the proceedings may also be interrupted by visitors who drop in for a consultation. For once it is known that a shaman is in trance, it is economical to consult him, for it is supposed that now the door to the other world is open, the spirits are there thronging to get through, and it is a good time to consult them about one's personal affairs, however irrelevant they may be to the matter in hand.

There is a fairly definite routine of entering on an officially-induced trance (as distinct from those which occur spontaneously), and there are several ways of preparing for it. It is generally preceded by a period of invocation when the shaman[2] squats on his heels before the altar or ikon,* makes offerings of rice and wine, and calls on the spirits to attend. When he feels that 'they are on the way', he changes his posture, sitting upright on the ground with his legs stretched out straight in front of him. He takes a fan of rice in his

[2] All this will apply equally to a shamanin.

* *'Ikon' is used by Elwin to refer to the drawings made on the walls of houses in honour of the dead, to promote fertility, and to celebrate festive occasions.* Editor.

left hand and lights a little lamp which he waves above the rice and places by the altar. Then he begins to rub his right hand round and round in the rice, calling as he does so on his tutelary to come upon him. He continues doing this for as long as perhaps five minutes, and his voice grows fainter until suddenly he gives a start, his whole body stiffens, his arms extend straight before him and both his hands clench themselves tightly over his fan. His attendants at once catch hold of his arms and legs and bend them and unclench his fingers; this sometimes involves a regular struggle to break down the rigour which the trance induces.

Then there is a pause. The shaman sits with head bent, legs straight forward, his arms stretched along them. And then all at once he begins to speak in a high-pitched unfamiliar voice, sometimes using a few Kui or Oriya words; this is the voice of the spirit who has come upon him.

After this there is no programme, no routine. The shaman *becomes* whatever spirit has possessed him for the time being, and within an hour he may play a dozen different parts. He appears to be entirely out of his own control. He weeps, laughs, jokes, curses. Now he is a woman and pretends to give suck to a child; he puts anything given him on his head as a woman does. Now he is an old man, wears a big hat and hobbles round driving imaginary herds before him with a stick. Now he is a tutelary's horse and demands water and drinks it with great noisy gulps. A bawdy ghost comes upon him, and he demands a woman, catches hold of one, and makes a token attempt at intercourse. As an old man he coughs and spits; as an old woman he sheds tears, pats his shrunken breasts and combs his hair. When the ghost of old Jigri came one day at Boramsingi, the shamanin tottered about on a stick complaining of her sore foot just as Jigri used to do in life.

Although a shaman engaged in sacrifice or incantation may be left severely alone, there is always a crowd when he goes into trance. For here is pathos and humour, bargaining and gossip; a good shaman provides first-class entertainment. And there is nearly always a hot discussion, the congregation remonstrating, pleading, arguing; the spirit complaining, abusing, threatening at first, then gradually softening in the face of promise and persuasion.

Normally a shaman's own tutelary comes upon him first, and after that a succession of gods and ghosts. The sign that one is going and another coming is that the shaman's voice falters and dies away; his body jerks convulsively and his hands slide down his legs to his feet; sometimes he scratches his armpits. There is a pause and then he begins to speak in a different voice.

When everything is over, the shaman relaxes; he spits into his hands, rubs them together, rubs them over his face, yawns, stretches himself; he is like someone waking up.

Although the most common way of inducing trance is by the aid of rice in a winnowing-fan, there are several other methods.

A new earthen pot, which will later be dedicated to a spirit, may be used to induce a sort of auto-hypnotism. The wife of Somra, at Taraba, who was a well-known shamanin, affected the use of the pot in preference to any other method. I once watched her in trance for two whole hours as she talked with her tutelary and his relatives. After hanging up two coloured cloths for her daughters in the Under World, she dedicated a pot to the tutelary and began to speak into it, holding it close to her mouth, first to one cheek and then to the other. She threw it up and down, catching it in both hands and all the time calling on her tutelary husband to come to her. For a time he did not come and she wept. Her attendants sat behind her ready to catch her when he did come. Suddenly she stiffened and fell back into their arms. The tutelary refused wine and demanded a little rice beer; the shamanin had to mix some rice flour with water and drink it. Then one by one all her relatives in the Under World came upon her and she talked to them in turn, singing into the pot which she held caressingly to her mouth. Sometimes she held the pot with one hand and rubbed rice in a fan wih the other. When all was over she hung the pot up before an ikon.

The *kurānrājan** and the hide-gong are also used to induce the proper rhythmic atmosphere for trance. The shaman accompanies his invocations on the fiddle, and soon the quiet rhythmic music accomplishes the desired result. The steady beating of a hide-gong serves the same purpose, and so may a dance. The shamans are very sensitive to any kind of rhythmic music or movement.

I can best give some idea of what happens in trance by describing an actual case, one of scores which I have attended. On 22 December 1950, Iswaro the young Chief of Boramsingi, and nephew of old Jigri, fell ill, and an old shamanin, by name Sahadri, was summoned to discover why. The actual period of trance lasted from two thirty to three forty-five in the afternoon.

Sahadri sat with two Idaibois to assist her before a small altar

* *A fibre-string musical instrument of high ritual value made by the shaman himself.* Editor

consisting of a basket of rice and a pot of wine, beneath an ikon for her tutelary. Her patient, Iswaro, sat just behind her. She began in a squatting posture and, taking a pinch of rice between her thumb and forefinger, passed it over the boy's back as she chanted, calling on the ancestors to identify who among them has caused the sickness. . . .

She threw away the rice and, turning to the ikon, offered wine before it. Then she stretched out her legs and took a fan in her lap. One of the Idaibois handed her a small basket of rice. Sahadri lighted her sacred lamp and waved it round and round above the basket; she examined it carefully, smelt it, took out some of the rice and peered at it, passed her hand through the flame of the lamp and then threw a few grains towards the ikon. She poured the rest of the rice into her fan, and began to rub her right hand round and round in it, calling on her tutelary as she did so.

There is a good road. Come quickly and help me discover what is wrong here. Whether it is a big matter or a small matter, it is for you to see to it. Is this boy's pain due to sorcery? Is it the work of a god? Is it a god of this world or of the Under World? Is it Uyungsum? Is it the god who lives in aeroplanes? Gogoji Rajaji, take this matter into your ears and attend to it. Goiyaraji Kararaji [famous old shamans who had become tutelaries], come and help. Whether it be tough or tender, soft or hard, come to us and help. Look in your books and come. Do not trip or stumble on the way; do not stub your toes against stones in the path. You who live with Kittung, come. If there is a rock in the way, break it open; if there is a tree in the way, knock it down; if you are in an aeroplane, descend.

The shamanin continued in this strain for about fifteen minutes, calling on every god, ancestor and tutelary she could remember, and then gradually her voice began to die away; she herself seemed to grow weaker; you could almost see her passing out of normal consciousness. She spoke slowly, then more slowly, until she was silent but for little gasps and cries. She gave a sudden start, her body tensed and stiffened, her hands gripped the sides of her fan.

The Idaibois at once caught her arms and legs, and after a little struggle relaxed them; it was harder to force open the clenched hands. There was then a pause of about a minute of complete silence, and for once there was not so much as a whisper among the onlookers. Then Sahadri jerked her body sharply and picked up some rice, smelt it, threw it up in the air and began to rub the rice in her fan. Suddenly she gave a loud scream, which indicated that her tutelary had come. Through her he cried, 'What are you bothering me for? What is it you want now?' The Idaibois and the others in the room at once began to explain, all speaking at once with a tremendous chatter. 'Tell us', they said, 'was it a god of the forest or a god of the path?' 'Why', asked the tutelary, 'had the boy been somewhere?' 'Yes, he'd been to Jampapur'. 'Then I'll go and find the god who did it and bring him here. But it might have been a plot of your enemies in Boramsingi and Kittim. Personally, that's what I think it was, but I'll go and find out.'

The shamanin jerked forward, her hands slid down her legs, and she remained silent with bent head for a couple of minutes. This was supposed to allow the tutelary time for his inquiries. Another violent jerk announced his return. The shamanin put her lamp beside her and began to rub her rice again. Once more everybody began to shout questions. The tutelary refused to answer till he had a drink. The shamanin took a long draught of wine, but the tutelary (speaking through her own lips) abused her. 'This is water. Get me some proper wine, and in a tumbler. There is a sahib here. That shows that this is an important occasion; I must be treated right.' There was another pause while someone went off to my camp to get a tumbler. When it came, it was filled with wine and the shamanin took a long drink. 'That's better', said the tutelary. 'Now tell me again, what is it you want?' More screaming voices answered him.

'There was a banyan tree', said the tutelary at last, 'on the path to Jampapur, and the tutelaries of Singjangring and Jampapur had put their pots of gruel in its shade while they had a chat with some ancestors from Ladde who were returning home after a sacrificial feast. The boy kicked one of the pots over as he went by. You must give a pig in compensation at once.'

After another drink, the shamanin gave another jerk as a sign that her tutelary had departed. She was then visited by a procession of ancestors. One of them, Iswaro's paternal uncle, admitted that he had been there under the banyan tree, but disclaimed any share in the incident. Then the ghost of the shamanin's own dead husband came and discussed family matters with her sister who was sitting near by. Rather late, for owing to the sore on her foot she could only hobble along, the ghost of Iswaro's formidable aunt Jigri arrived. She demanded to see the pig proposed for sacrifice. She now showed that she had taken with her to the Under World those sound financial gifts which had made her so prosperous in life. The shamanin (in her character as Jigri) took the pig in her lap and carefully examined it. 'It is not very fat', she complained. 'You paid far too much for it. Couldn't you get some of the money back? In any case, it's too small. When we have important visitors in the village, we ought to do better than this. Why don't you sacrifice a buffalo?' The spectators explained volubly, stressing their poverty, their debts, the failure of the crops that year, the endless demands upon them. Jigri laughed derisively. 'I've been watching you ever since I died. You may trick others, but you can't trick me. You can't see me, but I can see you. I know just how well off you really are.'

Then an old man with an obvious hangover, who was not even related to Iswaro, came in and insisted on the shamanin inquiring into the cause of his bad head. Sahadri passed her hands over his body, removed something from it and placed it in the fold of her cloth, then pulled at his fingers and toes. The ghost of a man who had been murdered some years previously came upon her, saying that he was now Uyungsum and that the old toper must give him a buffalo. This was rather more than he had bargained for, and he hastily put some rice in the shamanin's hands and clasped them in his, saying, 'Look, you and I are old friends; we used to go drinking together; you wouldn't want to bother an old friend.' But the ghost swore with an oath that unless he had a buffalo he would take his old friend away.

This interesting discussion was interrupted by the return of Jigri's ghost; she was not satisfied about certain matters concerning the disposal of her extensive property, and in particular insisted that her niece Arari, who had let her down by marrying before her dedication as a Guarkumboi had been completed, should not be given the keys of any of the store-rooms.

The proceedings continued with a score of irrelevancies. Young Iswaro was completely forgotten. Sometimes the talk was homely and good-natured; the spirits laughed and made the people laugh with them. But sometimes they discussed the scandals of this and the other world, and a ghost would be angry and abusive.

At last, when it was approaching four o'clock, the shamanin's tutelary returned and showed an interest in the patient of the day. He made the shamanin blow violently in his nose and ears, feel his ribs, blow on his stomach, stroke his legs and thighs, squeeze his arms. Then he said, 'He's going to be all right. Sacrifice that pig at once, and there will be no more trouble. Give me something to drink and I'll be off.'

The shamanin took a long drink out of the tutelary's special tumbler, jerked violently to show that the spirit had gone, and then relaxed completely as a sign that she was coming out of her trance. She spat on her hands and rubbed them over her face, yawned and sat up. Then without any pause she turned to me with a beaming smile and asked for some medicine for itch!

What are the shaman's own sensations while he is in trance? Some say that they feel intoxicated, as they well may in view of the amount they drink on behalf of their spirit-guests. One shaman compared the trance to his first experience of sexual intercourse: 'Everything went black before my eyes.' Another also compared it to a first intercourse, but one more poetically: 'It was as if the sky and the earth were made one.' A shamanin at Baijalo rubbed her eyes on coming out of trance because, she said, 'Owing to the god everything was dark'. Yet another said, 'My throat is parched and I feel very thirsty. I feel like someone lost on a lonely road.'

All shamans agree that they know of what goes on during the trance, the details of the conversations, which spirits came to them, how they themselves behaved. But some of them say that their inner experiences of a sort of dream would vary according to the kind of spirit that possesses them. The dead, for example, are far more exhausting than other spirits. . . .

[The general opinion about the medley of feelings experienced during a trance is well summed up by] Sondan the shamanin. . . . 'When a god comes, everything looks beautiful to me, and when he leaves me I do not feel at all tired. But when an ancestor comes, everything is dark and when he goes my body is worn out and aches in every bone.'

These experiences compare, of course, with the dreams of the Under World which every shaman has and the general picture compares with those of the ikon paintings. But the sense of exhaustion, and the motif of the pretty girls who would keep the shaman for ever in the world of dream are peculiar to the trance-state.

But whether the shamans know what they are talking about or not, they do in effect give a dramatic exhibition of what the spirits are supposed to be like. The records of these trance-sessions, therefore, throw much light on Saora theology, on the relations of living and dead, of human and divine, and above all on the character of the gods.

The picture that emerges is a curious one. On the one hand, we discern traces of kindliness and amiability, even of love, a willingness to help, a concern for human welfare. On the other, there is greed, temper, selfishness and an extraordinary lack of dignity.

In the first place, the spirits are revealed as very touchy about the order of precedence. At one ceremony I attended, the shaman's tutelary was indignant because some of the ancestors had been called before her. At another, Uyungsum complained that the ancestors were always arriving first and getting the best food.

Then again, the spirits continually complain about the quality of their entertainment. A ghost, speaking through a shamanin at a Name-giving rite, smelt the wine he was offered and said, 'What kind of liquor is this? Did you put your hand into your thing and bring it from there?'

It is not perhaps unreasonable, on the Saora theory, to suppose that the dead will make a good deal of fuss about food. For everyone knows that the unhappy shades live on the frontiers of starvation, and even the ancestors are often hungry in the Under World. But the tutelaries are pictured as doing themselves very well; they have large houses, many servants, are constantly giving parties, and some of them maintain private zoos. Yet a tutelary visiting a shamanin will be as exacting in his demands for food and drink as any ghost. And the gods are as bad, though they have many sources of income.

Indeed a large part of the communion between the spirits and their votaries is taken up by tedious arguments about food.

The unseen visitor invariably finds the wine insipid, the food inadequate, his worshippers lacking in respect.

But when the session continues for some time, and as the shaman grows more mellow with the offerings of wine which he has to consume, his representation of the spirits mellows also. Soon they begin to joke, often obscenely; they show a keen ear for gossip; they themselves let out scandals at which no one living has yet dared to hint; they swear friendship. At a ceremony at Barasingi, a ghost demanded a woman, 'a Dom woman' he insisted, amid roars of laughter. On the same occasion a shamanin threw her arms round the necks of two men at once and banged her head against theirs in token of a spirit's friendship. At Ladde the ghost of a man named Sobha possessed his widow in a dream. The woman fell ill, and when the shaman came to assist her, Sobha's ghost came laughing upon him and said, 'Oho, what a fine time I had with her! She was going to leave my childern and marry someone else. So I had her and made her ill. Now draw an ikon showing what I did.'

And the shaman had to paint what is called a *tutun-ittalan*, a 'copulation ikon', showing Sobha with his widow.

If the behaviour of the spirits during a trance is familiar and undignified, the conduct of the human worshippers is often equally familiar, casual and even frivolus. Death itself becomes a matter for jest. At the Potta Doripur, an old woman joked with a ghost who possessed the shaman. The ghost said, 'I have left my fields and the reaping of my harvest to come here. Everything is in a muddle. Let me go quickly.' The old woman protested, and the ghost said, 'Then why not come with me [die] and help me reap my crop?' 'Not me', said the old woman, chuckling as at an enormous jest. 'I've plenty to do here.'

People are not afraid of abusing the spirits. At a Name-giving ceremony, they said to an ancestor, 'You are always coming here to get things to eat, but you don't really help us at all, and our children always die.' And at another similar ceremony, a sick child's mother cried, 'You gods and ghosts only think about eating goats and pigs and fowls. All you want is liquor. But when it comes to helping us, you do nothing at all.' At a Rogonadur celebration, the shamanin scattered scraps of food on the threshold 'for the spirits that are crowding like dogs outside the house'. And at a Doripur ceremony for a sick boy, his father who had had heavy expenses in the attempt to cure him, cried, 'You are always lying to us, promising that if we give you this or that, you will be content. But you always come back for more. I cannot see gods ghosts, but if I could, I would kick you all.'

But the atmosphere at most ordinary ceremonies is informal and relaxed. I remember that once at Abbasingi, when a shaman fell into trance, his attendants shouted with laughter as they bent his stiffened arms and legs. At Barasingi in January 1951, everyone was very jolly at the Sikunda ceremony. The priest who would have performed this important rite did not bother to turn up at all, and his place was taken at the last moment by an elderly shaman who was completely blind. The congregation found this tremendously amusing, shouted encouragement after every mistake, offered him contradictory advice, and ragged him unmercifully. Later, there was a procession to the burning-ground to dig up the bones of a woman from another village. As these pathetic relics were exhumed, there were roars of laughter from the crowd, and boys and girls chased each other in and out of the throng.

Long before, at a buffalo sacrifice for an ancestor at Karanjasingi on 19 December 1944, I had been impressed by the frivolous behaviour of most of the participants in the rite. The donor of sacrifice, one Leju, was a very casual young man with an indifferent notion of his filial duties, which he had long postponed. But the others present seemed equally indifferent to any danger from the potentially dangerous spirit. Women joked and giggled; bathed their babies and put them to the breast under the very shadow of the ghost. Two little boys led off the dedicated buffalo to its doom with derisive cat-calls; as they went they played at killing it by beating it on the back of the neck with their little sticks. The actual sacrifice was performed by irreverent youths with loud sniggers of amusement; they made dirty jokes about the executioner because he did not kill the unfortunate victim with a single blow. . . .

There are times, however, when everyone is very serious. At the funerary rites after an ill-omened death, there is fear and silence. At the first moment of a trance, when the shaman awaits a spirit to possess him, there is complete quiet. At ceremonies for the dangerous Ratusum or for the smallpox goddess, there is laughter, and no irreverence. . . .

The shaman does his work on an empty stomach, and from his first invocations he begins to take sips of the wine he offers to the spirits. After he has passed into trance, he drinks constantly, perhaps for several hours, as spirit after spirit demands refreshment. For since the spirit occupies the shaman's body, and since after all wine is a material thing, this body is the only channel through which the wine can reach its divine recipient. Sometimes the programme continues long into the night, occasionally even till dawn, and it is little wonder that the shaman, without food or sleep, and alternately stimulated and depressed by the quantities of alcohol he has consumed, should experience functional disturbances of his organs of sense.

The effects of this gradually maturing intoxication is to be seen both in the attitude of the shaman himself, and later in his dramatization of the conduct of the spirits who are supposed to possess him. The shaman approaches his task of divination, sacrifice and trance rather timidly, as becomes one who is about to address beings of incalculable temper in an enterprise where mistakes are easy and quickly punished. But as he proceeds with his invocations, as he drives away now a sorcerer's familiar, now a suicide's ghost, now a tiger-shade, and as he takes sip after sip of the heart-warming fluid in his gourd, his manner changes. Self-criticism and self-restraint fall from him. He is no longer timid. His fears of the unseen are one with the anxieties of yesterday. He no longer bothers his head about ritual mistakes. He is on top of the world, even of the Under World. Where previously he grovelled, declaring his willingness to eat the excreta and drink the urine of the gods, he now commands and threatens. He now feels that he is a great shaman.

By the time a shaman is ready to pass into trance, he is generally slightly intoxicated already, and once has passed out, or rather once a spirit has passed in, his alcoholic exuberance is regarded as characteristic not of him but of the spirit who has possessed him.

For once a shaman is in trance, he is of course no longer himself. Up to this point, he was the repesentative of society and spoke for the people; now he is the representative of the society of spirits and speaks for them. He can no longer say a word for himself. The shaman in trance is no more the mouthpiece of the congregation; the congregation becomes the mouthpiece of the shaman. . . .

When everything is done, the shaman often quietly passes out and spends the rest of the day asleep. When he wakes up, he usually remembers nothing of what has happened; this alcoholic amnesia probably accounts for the fact that most shamans cannot remember anything that they did in trance.

The very entertaining antics of the shamans and shamanins are obviously due to that disappearance of self-criticism and the dulling of inhibitions that is always characteristic of intoxication. . . .

It is impossible to watch one of the greater Saora shamans or shamanins in trance without being impressed by their extraordinary quality. For his work a shaman must not only have a good grasp of theological principles, but a considerable knowledge of local geography, history and economics; he must be acquainted with the circumstances and genealogies of every family in his circuit; and he must also be well aware of village gossip. In the state of dissociation, all his varied knowledge and experience comes to the fore and is expressed in a dramatic performance which often has a genuinely healing effect.

Sathya Sai Baba's Miracles

LAWRENCE A. BABB

A more up-to-date young couple could scarcely be imagined. I met them for the first time on a Christmas afternoon in their impressively appointed house in one of the most expensive residential colonies in New Delhi. Then in their thirties, they were Punjabi Hindus whose families had been uprooted from Lahore at the time of the Partition of the subcontinent between India and Pakistan. The chaos of those grim days seemed very distant from that pleasant sitting room. He was a very successful chartered accountant; she a housewife presiding over a neolocal household with three children. They spoke to me in fluent and expressive English. They had never been abroad, but their outlook was informed and cosmopolitan. They were in every way exemplary of modern Delhi's educated upper-middle class.

It all began, he told me, with his wife's sister's husband in Calcutta. This man was very rich and quite a libertine, an inveterate club-goer and heavy drinker. One evening as his bearer was about to bring his first whiskey, he picked up a copy of a book entitled *Sathyam, Shivam, Sundaram* (Kasturi, probably 1977), which his mother had left on a nearby table. The subject of this book was a deity-saint known as Sathya Sai Baba,[1] whose picture was on the cover. As he opened the book and began idly scanning its pages, his eye lighted on a sentence that read: 'You have not picked this book up by chance; it is by my will that you have done so.' This sentence, my informant told me, occurs nowhere in the actual printed book. His brother-in-law then began to read, and when his

Excerpted from Lawrence A. Babb, 'Sathya Sai Baba's Miracles', in *Redemptive Encounters: Three Modern Styles in the Hindu Tradition*, Oxford University Press, Delhi, 1986, pp. 159–74.

[1] A more correct transliteration of his name would be *satya sāī bābā*. In the text to follow I shall use the nearly universal English version: Sathya Sai Baba.

cronies called, he told them that he had decided to stop drinking for a while. In the end he became a devotee of Sathya Sai Baba and a transformed man. This story was the beginning of their own, my informant continued, for it was their astonishment at the alteration of the character of this incorrigible man that set in motion a chain of events that led them, too, to become Sathya Sai Baba's devotees.

Sathya Sai Baba is modern India's most famous deity-saint. His somewhat heavy, cherubic face, framed by a cloud of curly afro-style hair, almost certainly has the highest degree of recognition (were such a thing ever to be measured) of all modern India's religious figures. In middle-class India, at least, the mere mention of his name usually suffices to elicit some comment, good or bad. As a type he is neither novel nor new. He is not the first living deity to set foot on the soil of India, nor will he be the last. Even in my limited circle of middle-class friends and neighbours in New Delhi, there were social networks that extended to several figures like Sathya Sai Baba, though not of his renown. Thousands of would-be Sathya Sai Babas probably pursue their divine career in the relative obscurity of India's lesser cultural and social byways. But Sathya Sai Baba is the one who has risen to the top, the premier deity-saint of India's English-speaking and generally high-caste middle and upper-middle classes. Though his devotees are not all rich, as a group they tend to be both wealthier and more cosmopolitan than the generality of Radhasoami and Brahma Kumari devotees.* Whatever else this wealth and status may mean, it has provided his cult with vast resources and unparalleled public visibility. The acclaim, however, is not universal. He has many detractors and is frequently accused of fraud and/or favouring only the rich and powerful. However, the size and influence of his indigenous (as opposed to international) following certainly justifies ranking him among the most important of modern India's religious personalities.

He is, at one level, a jet-age holy man. He is often to be found in automobiles and airplanes, travelling to meet his many followers throughout the subcontinent. And his followers, in their turn, are often people who better than any other represent the worldwide culture of middle-class modernity in its Indian form. Nor is the modernity of his cult only veneer. There is indeed something new, or newish, about Sathya Sai Baba's religious style. His personality resonates with the religious yearnings of the cosmopolitan and

* *Discussed in Babb's book* Editor.

wealthy in a way that may not be unique, but is an impressive display of modernized saintliness. At a deeper level, however, there is something very ancient about Sathya Sai Baba's persona. He does the things a deity should: he receives the homage and devotion of his devotees, and he reciprocates with love and boons. And, above all, he performs miracles.

The remainder of that Christmas afternoon was given over to a very lengthy account of this couple's experiences as his devotees. For the most part this was an account of miracles. One of their children had been pronounced dead in the womb by doctors, but was restored to life by the deity-saint. When the wife developed a detached retina, Sathya Sai Baba saved her from blindness. One morning footprints of an infant were discovered before one of the many pictures of the deity-saint with which the interior of the house is filled. This was evidence of a nocturnal visitation by 'Baba'. (He is usually called *bābā* in conversation; also *svāmi*.) Red powder once oozed forth from one of these same pictures overnight. And another time, while they were praying, a garland that had been placed over one of the pictures leaped to the other side of the room. There was much, much more.

Avatār

Who is Sathya Sai Baba? As we shall see, this is a question with complex implications. From an outsider's standpoint he is a man born at a certain place and time with a personal biography. However, the matter cannot end here, since to his devotees Sathya Sai Baba is far more than an ordinary man. Also, as in the case of the Radhasoami gurus and Dada Lekhraj, the trick of recognizing him for what he 'really' is lies at the foundation of the religious experiences cultivated by his followers. Among other things, this means that the 'man himself' (as the outsider would say) is hard indeed to find. The strict facts of his personal biography and manner of life are buried beneath layer upon layer of hagiography. . . . As far as I am aware, no objective account of Sathya Sai Baba's life has been written by anyone close to him. Indeed, such an account may be an inherent impossibility; it is unlikely that anyone who is allowed into his inner circles would *want* to write in such a vein. The word *defended* may be too strong, but the outside world is allowed only certain kinds of interactions with Baba, interactions that deviate very little from rather narrow devotional paradigms. He may be personally isolated even from his most trusted associates. One simply does not know.

Thus Sathya Sai Baba himself cannot be the actual subject of an account of his cult. For now, no supposedly 'real' Sathya Sai Baba can be any more real than an imagined character in fiction. All that is available are his public surfaces, his self as formally presented as an object for the devotional attitudes of his followers. But the humanly real Sathya Sai Baba is not of greatest interest in any case. Whoever he is, he is certainly more than the mere parlour magician many of his critics claim that he is. But even so, the most interesting Sathya Sai Baba, and in a sense the most real too, is the one who is worshipped by his devotees. This Sathya Sai Baba is what is known as an *avatār*, a 'descent' of God to earth. And of this Sathya Sai Baba one can indeed give an account, because his persona is fully available in the public domain of religious symbolism. At this level the extravagances of hagiography are not an impediment, but an important aid, to discovery.

His life story, as it emerges in the available materials, consists of a core of basic facts surrounded by a great deal of elaboration. The facts are but the framework; the real tale is told by the elaborations. At the heart of this tale is the central theme of disclosure, which is also fundamental to the devotional attitudes assumed by his devotees today. As seen from the perspective of his devotees, Sathya Sai Baba's entire life has been one of signs and portents, uncanny occurrences that reveal at successively higher levels what is taken to be the truth about this only apparently human being.

Sathya Sai Baba was born in 1926 to a pious family of modest circumstances belonging to the Rāju caste in the village of Puttaparthi in what is now the state of Andhra Pradesh. Named Satyanarayana, he was the last of four children. We are told that his birth was heralded by miracles. The strings of a *tambūrā* that was hanging in the house were plucked by a magical force just prior to his birth, and a cobra mysteriously appeared under the newborn infant's bedding (suggesting Vishnu's serpent-bed). It is said that during his early childhood he exhibited many signs of his very special character. He was unusually intelligent and an instinctive vegetarian. His character is described as sympathetic towards the poor and destitute, and much given to charitable acts. He was also, we learn, able to materialize food for himself.

Sathya Sai Baba's education began in a rustic village school and culminated at a high school at Uravakonda, some 90 Kilometres from his native village. There is no evidence that he ever distinguished himself as a student. During his school years his main interests seem to have been in singing *bhajans* (devotional songs) and performing in traditional dramas. These dramas were based on episodes from Hindu mythology, and the young Satyanarayana was apparently a skilled actor. During this period there were many more uncanny occurrences. For example, he is said to have once prevented one of his teachers from rising from a chair by causing it to become tightly fixed to his backside. He also materialized sweets and other items for his friends.

The great watershed of his younger years, and the first great disclosure', occurred in 1940 when he was thirteen years old. In March of that year, while at Uravakonda, he fell into a seizure of some kind, which at the time was thought to be caused by a scorpion sting. He recovered quite quickly, but then began behaving very strangely. Long periods of silence would give way to crying, laughing, fainting spells, and intense bouts of singing and scripture recitation. Doctors could do little. After his parents returned him to Puttaparthi, exorcists were employed, also to no avail. Finally on a morning in May he arose and began materializing items for members of his household and neighbours. His father was called, and in a flash of anger at being told to treat his son as a god, he threatened the boy with a stick. In response Satyanarayana said, 'I am Sai Baba. I belong to Apastamba Sutra, the spiritual school of Sage Apastamba and am of the Spiritual Lineage of Bharadwaja; I am Sai Baba; I have come to ward off all your troubles; keep your houses clean and pure' (Kasturi 1977, 47).[2] This was the first time Sathya Sai Baba explicitly declared his true (though partial) identity.

Although it might have meant little to Satyanarayana's (now Sai Baba's) fellow villagers, the name Sai Baba was a famous one at the time. Sai Baba was a much celebrated and rather mysterious holy man who years before had lived at the town of Shirdi in Maharashtra. There is no need here for an extended discussion of this most interesting figure, but a few details are essential. Sai Baba first appeared in Shirdi as a teenaged boy in 1872. He was dressed as a Muslim mendicant but professed to know nothing of his origin. Tradition declared later that he was born of Brāhman parents but had been raised by a Muslim fakir. When he arrived at Shirdi, he

[2] Bharadvaja is one of the mythical Seven Sages (*rishis*), mind-born sons of Brahmā and ancestors of the Brahmanical *gotras* (lineages) . . . but the relevance of this to Sathya Sai Baba's claim is not clear. Apastamba is the putative author of an important body of *dharmashāstra*.

took up residence in an empty mosque (having been expelled from a local Hindu temple), where he remained for the rest of his days. Over the course of the ensuing years he attracted a very large following and continued to be the focus of a widespread cult after his death in 1918. His saintly style was notably eclectic, a blend of Hindu and Muslim elements. His trademark was a perpetually burning fire. He distributed the ashes from this fire to his followers, who ate it or applied it to their bodies. He was famous as a curer and miracle-worker, and the ash he distributed was regarded as a material vehicle for his mysterious powers. This is a theme we shall encounter again.

Having made the astonishing claim that he was a reincarnation of this great Maharashtrian saint, Sathya Sai Baba returned to school, but by now his educational career was in a shambles. He began to create an enormous sensation by materializing sacred ash (called *vibhūti*) and other items and substances. There were many other miracles as well. Finally, in October 1940, he announced to his brother's wife (he was living in his brother's house in Uravakonda) that he was no longer 'your Sathya' (ibid.: 52). This was the decisive break with earthly relatives that marks the career of any holy man. He then returned to Puttaparthi and, living apart from his family, began to accept devotees.

Over the years that followed Sathya Sai Baba's reputation grew very rapidly. The main basis of his fame was the miracles. Materializations, astonishing cures, and much else of the same sort drew increasingly large crowds to Puttaparthi. During the 1940s he also began to travel to Madras and elsewhere in South India, and soon he had a large regional following. In 1950 the construction of his *āshram* at Puttaparthi was completed (it has grown since then), and by this time this once obscure village had become a notable feature of the sacred geography of South India. During the 1950s his fame spread to the rest of the country (partly a result of tours to the sacred centres of the north), and he became firmly established as a religious figure of national (and to some degree international) reputation.[3]

The second great 'disclosure' occurred in June of 1963, and is quite reminiscent of the first disclosure in 1940. On the morning of

[3] Although Sathya Sai Baba has travelled in East Africa, he has not, unlike some of India's other modern deity-saints, put a great deal of emphasis on internationalization. He treats foreign devotees with particular consideration, but his constituency is basically Indian. For a non-Indian devotee's perceptions of Sathya Sai Baba, see Murphet 1975. . . .

June 29th, while at his *āshram*, Sathya Sai Baba had another seizure. A witness (his close associate, N. Kasturi) describes it thus: 'The face twiched and muscles drew the mouth to the left . . . the tongue lolled. The left eye appeared to have lost its sight' (1975b, 79). A physician who was called to the scene diagnosed the illness as tubercular meningitis. The ailing saint was in what appeared to be a coma for part of the time, although there were periods in which he was at least aware enough of his surroudings to refuse injections and to communicate with his grieving devotees by means of gestures and a few indistinct words.

On the sixth day the pain abated somewhat, and on the eighth day he appeared before a large crowd. Still visibly ill, he was propped into position in his chair. He first turned to one of his assistants (N. Kasturi) and asked him to announce to the crowd that the illness from which he seemed to be suffering was not really his, but something he had taken upon himself for the relief of a deserving devotee (a claim he had also later made about his indisposition in 1940). He then sprinkled water on himself, and by so doing, apparently cured himself instantaneously and completely.

In the discourse that followed he reiterated, in full voice, that he had taken on the illness to save a devotee. Then he went on to say that he would disclose something that he had kept to himself for his thirty-seven years of life. He was, he said, actually Shiva and Shakti (Shiva's consort) in embodied form. At a deeper level of significance, his apparent illness was actually that borne by Shakti because she had once neglected the sage Bharadvaja, causing him to become ill. Just as Shiva cured Bharadvaja by sprinkling water on him, Shiva had now cured Shakti in Sathya Sai Baba's body. He further let it be known that there would be a total of three Sai incarnations, all in the lineage (*gotra*) of Bharadvaja. Shirdi Sai Baba was Shakti alone, and Sathya Sai Baba is Shiva and Shakti together. Still to come is an incarnation of Shiva alone. He will take the form of Prem Sai, to be born in Karnataka State.

These pivotal assertions marked the formal completion of Sathya Sai Baba's publically available identity. One notable feature of this rather complex statement is the promise of a third incarnation. As D. A. Swallow points out, this assertion has important organizational implications: Sathya Sai Baba's promise that he will be reborn yet again obviates, at least in theory, potentially difficult succession rivalries that might arise within the cult (1982: 136–7). None of those in his immediate circle can have any basis (in the prevailing theory of Sathya Sai Baba's identity) for preparing the ground for claiming his sacred authority after his death.

But what is central is the claim to be an *avatār* of Shiva (and of course, of Shakti too). Moreover, this claim is quite overt. Unlike the Radhasoami *sant satgurus*, Sathya Sai Baba's assertion of divine status is expressed in the first person; he states it boldly and repeatedly. He has come in the present age of wickedness and misery, he says, not merely to alleviate individual misfortunes (though he does do this for his devotees), but to set the whole world right, to usher in a 'Sai Age'. In the form of Shirdi Sai Baba his mission was to establish Hindu-Muslim unity; in his present incarnation he will reestablish Vedic and Shastric religion. As Prem Sai he will bring all of this work to completion. His present incarnation, he says, has four phases. For the first sixteen years he engaged in playful pranks (*bālalīlās*), and during the second sixteen years he displayed miracles (*mahimās*). The third sixteen-years period is reserved for teaching (*updesh*) and further miracles, and the remainder of his life will be devoted to the intensive teaching of spiritual discipline (*sādhanā*) to restricted groups. He will die at the age of ninety-six, but his body will stay young until then.

Because all the gods are ultimately one, Sathya Sai Baba is all the gods (and goddesses too) of the Hindu pantheon—and, indeed, in his view he is the deity of every religion. His devotees call him *Bhagavān*, which is to say, simply, 'God'. But his dominant identity is Shiva, and it is around the traditional image of Shiva that some of the most important symbolic accouterments of the cult are centred (on this see esp. Swallow 1982). Iconographically he is frequently portrayed in association with Shiva or the *linga*, which is Shiva's principal material representation for purposes of worship. In popular prints he is often represented standing inside a *linga*. In the cult's sacred year the most important occurrence is the festival of *mahāshivrātri*, 'the great night of Shiva'. On this occasion he materializes vast quantities of sacred ash from his hand inside an inverted pot. The ash then pours over a silver image of Shirdi Sai Baba (in parallel with the bathing of the deity, *abhisheka*, in a temple rite), after which it is distributed to devotees. On the same occasion he materializes *lingas* within his body, which he then ejects, with signs of pain and difficulty, from his mouth.

In many ways at the symbolic centre of the cult, this sacred ash is a particularly unambiguous link with Shiva. Ash is basic to Shaivite ritual; markings of it are worn by Shiva's priests, and it is distributed to his worshippers from his altar. Ash is also associated with Kāma (Kāmdev), who was reduced to ashes . . . by Shiva's fire of anger. It embodies Shiva's ascetic powers, and is associated with the burning grounds, one of Shiva's favourite haunts. Sathya Sai Baba's use of ash also recalls the figure of Shirdi Sai Baba, who distributed ash to his followers from his perpetually burning fire.

Since the revelations of 1963 the cult has continued to grow. Although national in scope, it has only one true centre—the person of Sathya Sai Baba himself. Its *raison d'être* is the worship and service of this living deity. As already noted, the cult has a rather narrow—but socially and culturally very influential—constituency, which is basically drawn from urban India's English-educated elites. Since there are no formal ties of membership, it seems unlikely that we will ever know how many devotees there actually are. The cult has no well-defined boundaries in any case. Among my neighbours in New Delhi there were some who did not identify themselves as actual devotees, but who nonetheless considered Sathya Sai Baba to be in some sense a living deity. Of course there were also many who regarded him as a fraud and worse. But all of my neighbours at least knew of him; in middle-class India one would have to be asleep not to.

The Cult in the World

One of the most remarkable features of Sathya Sai Baba's cult is that he has managed to preserve the imagery and atmosphere of a purely personal constituency, despite the fact that many of his devotees see him rarely, and then often only from a distance. Though rooted in the South, his cult is far less regionally focused than the Radhasoami or Brahma Kumari movements. He is a frequent traveller to various parts of India where he meets groups of devotees, and many followers travel to Puttaparthi to see him. But there are obvious physical limits on the degree to which his person can be accessible to followers. Nonetheless, despite its size and complexity, the cult expresses, and is energized by, Sathya Sai Baba's personal charisma. The cult-in-the-world is a kind of devotional empire, far-flung but totally dependent on the authority of its sovereign.

Baba, I was told, does not accept donations of money and does not own property. However, donations are accepted and property held by a legal entity known as the Central Shri Sathya Sai Trust. Donations to the trust can be made at any branch office of the Canara

Bank (a large concern with branches all over the subcontinent). In each Indian state there is also a State Trust with its own Council of Management. The councils of management are composed of distinguished and prominent persons from a variety of backgrounds. Sathya Sai Baba himself, I was told, is the sole trustee of the various trusts.

Under the umbrella of the trusts is a vast organization, the cult's infrastructure, that engages in a number of quite diverse activities. These activities include the support and management of the cult's various devotional epicentres. Sathya Sai Baba's main *āshram* (known as Prashanti Nilayam) is at Puttaparthi, but he also has a colony at Whitehead (near Bangalore) and maintains residences at Bombay, Hyderabad (in Andhra Pradesh), and Madras. Through its Educational and Publication Foundation, the cult publishes a monthly magazine called *Sanathana Sarathi* in English, Hindi, and Telugu. This same organizational arm also publishes and distributes numerous books dealing with Sathya Sai Baba or containing collections of his discourses.

Social service is another major emphasis of the cult. With junior and senior branches, the *sevā dal* (service corps) sponsors a variety of charitable and philanthropic activities: feeding the poor, assisting the authorities in relief work during disasters, visiting the sick, and so on. During the Delhi flooding of 1978 the local *sevā dal* was involved in distributing food to victims.

Education is another field in which Sathya Sai Baba's organizations are quite active. In 1979 four 'Sathya Sai Colleges' existed: three for girls (at Anantpur, Bhopal and Jaipur) and one for boys (at Bangalore). Plans were afoot for a college in each state of the Indian union. The educational arm of the cult also sponsors summer courses in 'Indian culture and spirituality' for college students. Major efforts are devoted to what is called the *bāl vikās* (child development) programme. The purpose of this programme is to supplement the secular education of children with 'spiritual' instruction. The classes are held once a week for an hour or so, usually in individual homes. There are said to be over eight hundred such classes taking place in India.

The *bāl vikās* classes exemplify well some of the most characteristic features of the general outlook of Sathya Sai Baba's cult. In consonance with a common doctrine of most forms of neo-Hinduism, Sathya Sai Baba interprets his message as religiously universal. Therefore, the *bāl vikās* programme is deemed to be 'nonsectarian'.

Nonetheless, the symbolism deployed in the classes is distinctly Hindu. Classes take place before an altarlike arrangement consisting of a picture or pictures of Sathya Sai Baba and an empty chair (actually occupied, in spirit, by the deity-saint himself). Classes begin with the chanting of the sacred syllable *om*, followed by a prayer (in Sanskrit) and the singing of devotional songs (*bhajans*). Then follows a lecture. The one I heard was on guruship: just as the deities Brahmā, Vishnu, and Shiva preside over creation, preservation, and destruction—the children were told—so a guru creates a new person, preserves the goodness in him, and destroys the bad. Then follows an interlude of meditation on Sathya Sai Baba's form. At the conclusion of the class each child receives a *tilak* of sacred ash on the forehead' (a standard Hindu practice). What Muslims make of this kind of ecumenism I do not know; I was told that there were three or four Muslim children in the class of sixty-five that I attended. Even if some concessions are made to other religions in these classes, they are clearly locked into essentially Hindu devotional patterns.

The cult of Sathya Sai Baba does not make great demands on its adherents. This is not to say that a devotee might not make considerable demands on himself or herself, but the imposition of rigid rules is foreign to the spirit of Sathya Sai Baba's teachings. He favours a moderate and *sāttvik* (in essence, vegetarian) diet, and avoidance of alcohol and smoking. These are not radical injunctions in a Hindu context. Though celibate himself, Sathya Sai Baba does not advocate the celibate life for his devotees. He holds the householder's (*grihastha's*) life in high esteem, and encourages celibacy only after the age of fifty. One of my devotee-informants happened to have nearly destroyed his marriage by vowing celibacy without consulting his spouse (also a devotee), but this was on his own, not because of any teaching of the cult.

In contrast to the Radhasoami and Brahma Kumari movements, the cult does not consider itself to be in tension with the religious usages of the surrounding community. The cult does not have prescribed rites that might conflict with other ceremonial requirements, nor does it see its tenets as at odds in any way with what is said to be the true essence of other religions. Given Sathya Sai Baba's divine identity, all worship of God—in whatever form—is actually worship of him in any case.

One can participate in the cult at practically any level. Placing a picture of Sathya Sai Baba in one's family shrine (or a statuette on the dashboard of one's car) is participation of a kind. More committed devotees are likely to attend sessions of devotional singing, which are held on a regular basis (usually monthly) in devotees' homes. Special sessions are also held in conjunction with major Hindu festivals such as *mahāshivrātrī*, *gurupūrṇimā*, *dashehrā*, and *janmāshṭamī*. These events take place in the presence of the usual altarlike display of an empty chair (actually occupied) and numerous pictures of Sathya Sai Baba, Shirdi Sai Baba, and various deities. Attendees tend to be well dressed and obviously affluent, and I suspect that in some circles these events carry a certain social cachet. The main event is the singing of devotional songs, most of which are overtly addressed to Sathya Sai Baba himself. A book containing suitable *bhajans* is owned by many devotees. The singing is followed by a period of silent meditation, and then *āratī* is performed in the usual fashion before the altar. Devotees receive *prasād* as they leave.

At a higher level of commitment devotees not only participate in these observances but are actively involved in the educational and social service activities of the cult. Such individuals are also likely to be frequent visitors to Puttaparthi, and might even have purchased some form of permanent accommodations there. One of my informants, for example, joined two other devotees to pay Rs 12,000 for permanent rights in a place to stay during visits to the *āshram*. Hard-core devotees are often easily identifiable as such by the interior decor of their houses. The houses of strong devotees are usually stuffed with pictures of Sathya Sai Baba and other cultic bric-a-brac: books, recordings of Sai *bhajans*, busts, life-sized plaster replicas of his feet, and so on. Highly committed devotees use the phrase *sāī rām* as a salutation.

Sathya Sai Baba is, among other things, a teacher. He is a frequent giver of discourses, now compiled in several volumes. He usually speaks in Telugu, and before a Hindi-speaking audience an interpreter is required. One of his most characteristic rhetorical devices is the ad hoc (and often false) etymology. For example, he has stated that *Hindu* means 'one who is nonviolent' by the combination of *hinsā* (violence) and *dūr* (distant).

In the case of Sathya Sai Baba's teachings we are not, as in the case of the Radhasoami and Brahma Kumari movements, dealing with an elaborated and internally rationalized doctrinal system of which an extended account has to be given. Sathya Sai Baba's doctrines are basicaly an eclectic blend of elements drawn from a variety of well-known philosophical and devotional traditions. Virtually everything 'spiritual' is accorded its own value, including non-Hindu religions too. His ethics are basically common coin in the Hindu world, though certainly not to be dismissed on that account. Tolerance, gentleness, and kindness toward others are among his most frequently stated values. Whatever else he or she might feel, a Hindu auditor or reader of Sathya Sai Baba's discourses would probably not react to any of his teachings with surprise.

Nor does Sathya Sai Baba teach anything resembling the distinctively rationalized systems of disciplined introspection we have encountered in the Radhasoami and Brahma Kumari movements. That is, he does not have a meditational 'system' of his own. In fact, although he pays due respect to matters of salvation, the atmosphere of his cult is really not very soteriological at all. My informants dwelt little on questions of ultimate salvation; what mattered mainly to them was Sathya Sai Baba himself, and what he did or did not do to alleviate the misfortunes of life in this world.

Nonetheless, Sathya Sai Baba does strongly encourage his followers to engage in *sādhanā* (spiritual discipline). Identification with the body, he says, is a delusion; the reality of the person is the self or 'soul', the *ātmā*, encased within five material sheaths (*koshas*). By means of the repetition of the Lord's name, and meditation (*dhyān*) on his form, one can remove the effects of past *karmas* and directly experience the true reality of the self within. He urges daily meditation, preferably at 3:00 or 4:00 a.m. Recommendations on technique, not distinctive in any way, are scattered throughout his discourses and are also a prominent feature of the *bāl vikās* curriculum. Devotees should meditate on Sathya Sai Baba's form or on the flame of a lamp. If a lamp is used, the meditator should stare at the flame, mentally fix its image between his or her eyebrows, and then imagine its light filling up the body. The light is the Lord, and by experiencing oneself as the light, one realizes one's identity with God, who all along has been within. The final goal, therefore, is merger with God, who is, in fact, Baba. The result will be the eradication of harmful motives and tendencies, and feelings of deep inner peace (*prashānti*).

Under the rather cluttered eclecticism of Sathya Sai Baba's teachings are a few very consistent themes. One is a persistent note of cultural nationalism of a kind that sometimes verges on nativism. Although he welcomes foreigners as followers, he regards Western cultural influences as highly destructive in India. He believes that many Indians have sold themselves to the West and have become alienated from their own heritage. How, he asks, can Western values be applicable in any sense to Indian life? Though India has won its freedom, he says, 'The attitudes and the habits of the West still dominate the mind of the educated and the leaders' (Kasturi n.d.a: 147). 'Indians should not try to imitate others, but should adhere to the folkways that have been preserved by the folk-mind of this land' (Kasturi n.d.b: 43). He particularly deplores what he regards as the prevailing ignorance of the Hindu textual tradition, which is indeed true of many of his followers. Instead of being taught Sanskrit *stotras*, he says, Indian children are made to recite such nonsense as 'Baa, baa black sheep'. Correcting all of this is a major goal of his educational ventures. Sathya Sai Baba's harsh judgement of the Westernization of India, which is expressed repeatedly in his discourses, is not a minor theme. These are obviously matters that touch with particular directness on the life experiences of his English-educated, middle-class followers.

However, his discontent with the state of present-day India does not mean that he advocates radical reform of existing economic or social institutions. On these matters his views are in many ways profoundly conservative. For example, he is adamantly against strikes: for him the ideal social order is one based on noncompetitive complementation, a view deeply conditioned by the ideology of caste. 'The owner', he says, 'is the heart of the organization; those who work in it in the various fields of activity necessary to carry out its objectives are the limbs. The heart has to keep the limbs active; the limbs have to sustain the heart' (Kasturi 1975a, 80). It is true that God showers his grace on all, and is indifferent to caste distinctions, but this does not mean that all human beings are the same. Innate capacities differ: 'The cry of equality now being used as a slogan is a vain and meaningless cry; for how can man, inheriting a multiplicity of impulses, skills, qualities, tendencies, attitudes, and even diseases from his ancestors and from his own history [Karmic history] be all of the same stamp?' (Kasturi n.d.c.:29). Sathya Sai Baba urges his followers to treat others with decency and charity, but he does not advocate the upsetting of existing hierarchies.

He is no feminist, but by his own lights he has a deep concern for the welfare of women, as evidenced by the attention he has given to women's education. There are many women among his most ardent devotees in Delhi. He keeps a somewhat wary distance from his female followers, or so I am told. This is only prudent, given endemic suspicions about relations between male gurus and female followers. His views on the innate characteristics of women are of a piece with his views on caste, and are hardly enlightened, at least from a feminist point of view. Women are trusting, compassionate, humble, and shy. They are also weak (in some ways) and quick to petty anger. A virtuous woman is a treasure, but she has a circumscribed place in the order of things: Women should strive to realize *strī-dharma*, the inherent virtues of womanhood, which means that they should not be 'seen or talked about' and should stay 'away from the public gaze'; they should be 'silent invisible partners and inspirers, and teachers' (ibid.: 65).

But anyone familiar with the cult of Sathya Sai Baba will know that this discussion of doctrines and teachings is, though not irrelevant, to a considerable degree beside the point. As far as I know, not one of my informants became involved in the cult because of Sathya Sai Baba's teachings as such, nor did many of them advert to doctrinal matters when describing their experiences as devotees. It is of course important that Sathya Sai Baba pronounces and teaches, and the content of what he says has its importance too. But for most devotees Baba's teachings are little more than a *tambūrā*-like background drone. For them what is important about what he says is not its content, but the fact that *he* is the one saying it.

When devotee-informants talk about Sathya Sai Baba, what one hears is not theology, but account after account of their personal experiences as devotees. What emerges as one general theme in these accounts is the same kind of visual, tactile, and alimentary intimacy that is so central to devotional Hinduism in general, and what we have seen exemplified with particular clarity in the Radhasoami materials. His devotees long to see him, to hear him, to be near him, to have private audiences with him, to touch him (especially his feet), and to receive and consume, or use in other ways, substances and objects that have been touched by him or that originate from him. But above all, what one hears about are the miracles. In this respect, the account with which this account began is entirely typical. It is largely because of the miracles that devotees are drawn to him in the first place. The miracles, moreover, seem to play a vital role in sustaining the allegiance of his devotees. Miracles are the staple of any conversation about Sathya Sai Baba among his devotees, and are the principal topic of the literature concerning him as well. Any attempt to understand this cult, therefore, must try to come to terms with the miraculous.

Knowing Better

It would be easy not to take the cult of Sathya Sai Baba seriously. Because of its surfaces of modernity and the apparent estrangement of its many wealthy and English-educated adherents from 'grass-roots Hinduism', it would be tempting to dismiss the cult as in some sense inauthentic, a less-than-best avenue to an understanding of anything truly Hindu. But in my view this would be a mistake. Not only is this cult deeply and authentically Hindu . . . but the very cultural alienation of its main constituency sets in bold relief certain features of the Hindu tradition that we might not otherwise see as clearly.

In its emphasis on the miraculous the cult of Sathya Sai Baba seems to invert what common sense would lead us to expect. There is certainly nothing new about the miraculous in the Hindu world. Indeed, in this world the credibility of miraculous occurrences is never really the main issue; what matters most is what such events, in specific instances, actually *mean*. But Sathya Sai Baba's following is notably cosmopolitan, consisting of many people who at least outwardly are as strongly attuned as anyone to the more international cult of scientific rationality. These people, we are inclined to think, really 'ought to know better'. And yet the miraculous is absolutely central to what the Sai Baba phenomenon is about. This circumstance pushes to the fore questions that we might not otherwise ask. From what, exactly, do these miracles derive their convincingness, a convincingness so great that it seems to pull people into convictions ostensibly at odds with what their own subculture deems to be common sense and considered judgement? What is the source of the energy of Sathya Sai Baba's 'magic', an energy that is apparently strong enough to have life-transforming effects on his devotees? Does it arise from cunning theatrics? Or is its true source something else?

Hindu Temple Priests

C. J. FULLER

Introduction

As the principal servants of [the goddess] Mīnākṣī and [her divine consort] Sundareśvara, the priests are closer to the god and goddess than any other group in the Temple* and in its hierarchy they occupy, after the deities themselves, the first rank. This discussion is mainly devoted to analysing that hierarchy, and connectedly the division of ritual labour between the priests and other officiants, as well as the position of the devotees. In broad terms, the Temple's hierarchy may be labelled 'Āgamic', for it reproduces the superiority accorded to Ādiśaiva priest in the texts known as the Āgamas, although, as I shall show, the Āgamic model is actually qualified in several significant respects. It is also important to note that the hierarchy I describe here is only manifested within a particular field and from a particular standpoint. The field is the Temple as a ritual domain and the standpoint is its centre. Imaginarily, the perspective is that of the god and goddess themselves, to whom the priests are uniquely close by virtue of the services that they alone can perform for the deities in close proximity to their image. The hierarchy analysed here is important partly because it is embedded and expressed in the ritual organization of the Temple—the aspect of the Temple as a total institution that has to do with its principal *raison d'être*, communication with the deities—and partly because it has a central place in the priests' own understanding of

Excerpted from C. J. Fuller, 'The Priests and Hierarchy within the Temple', in *Servants of the Goddess: The Priests of a South Indian Temple*, Cambridge University Press, Cambridge, 1984 (OUP, 1991), pp. 23–35, 185–7.

* *This is in Madurai in Tamilnadu, South India.* Editor.

their collective identity and the patterning of their relationships with the deities, as well as with other people in the Temple and the wider society. . . .

Categories of Priests

In the Minaksi Temple the priests are known as *paṭṭar* (Skt. *bhaṭṭa*), a Tamil word normally anglicized as 'bhattar'.[1] The term is used by the priests as a caste 'surname'. The same term is employed for the priests of other Saiva temples in the Madurai and Ramnad regions, including the Śiva temple at Rameswaram although in other parts of Tamilnadu, Śaiva temple priests are usually known as *kurukkal* (from Skt. *guru*). In Vaiṣṇava temples, priests are commonly called *arcakkar* (Skt. *arcaka*), although *paṭṭar* can also be heard (Rangachari 1931: 99; Thurston 1909, 1: 330). *Arcakkar*, like *ācāriyar* (Skt. *ācārya*), is, however, often employed to refer to the entire category of Śaiva and Vaiṣṇava temple priests.

The Minaksi Temple priests, like those of other Śaiva temples in Tamilnadu, belong to the Ādiśaiva subcaste, generally considered to be Brahman, but ranked below all the ordinary, non-priestly Brahman subcastes. In Vaiṣṇava temples, there are two distinct systems of worship, the Pāñcarātra and Vaikhānasa, according to the texts that are followed. In Pāñcarātra temples, any married Brahman can officiate as a priest, but in Vaikhānasa temples, only qualified priests, the Vaikhānasa *arcakkar*, can perform the rituals (Rangachari 1931: 99). Amongst Vaiṣṇavas, an entirely separate subcaste equivalent to the Ādiśaiva does not appear to exist. Nonetheless, Vaiṣṇava priests do not intermarry with ordinary Brahmans and they are accorded a low rank by the latter. . . .

The priests at Śiva's and Viṣṇu's major temples are clearly distinguished from two categories of priests: the Brahman domestic priests and the non-Brahman priests of the non-Sanskritic, 'village deities' temples. Domestic priests, the subject of Subramaniam's study, are the classical *purohita*; in Tamilnadu, however, they are generally known as *cāstiri* (cf. Skt. *śāstri*) (Subramaniam 1974: 12). They act as priests in the homes, mainly carrying out rituals at festivals and rites of passage. In Madurai, however, some of them also work as chanters, primarily responsible for reciting the Vedas in the Minaksi Temple, and their role will be considered shortly.

[1] *Puṭṭar*, an honorific plural, is a reference term. Devotees normally address the Temple priests as *cuvāmi*, 'lord', the term also used to refer to and address Sundaresvara.

(How widespread is the custom of employing as chanters men who are also domestic priests, I do not know.) The Minaksi Temple priests never work as domestic priests; nor, to the best of my knowledge, do their colleagues at other major Śaiva temples and the same probably applies to Vaiṣṇava temple priests as well. In small towns and villages, however, individual priests often do work in both temples and homes. There are various status distinctions amongst the domestic priests; nonetheless, all of them, as priests, rank below their caste-fellows who do not take on the role.

The second category, the priests of the non-Sanskritic temples, are generally referred do as *pūcāri* (from Skt. *pūjā*). They serve the 'village deities' . . . goddesses . . . and their male equivalents, such as Aianār and Karuppacuvāmi (Dumont 1970b: ch. 2). *Pūcāris* are almost always non-Brahmans and therefore rank unequivocally below all Brahman priests in the caste hierarchy. No *pūcāri* has an important role in the Minaksi Temple and I shall therefore be making few references to them.

The Priests' Way of Life

In July 1980, fifty-six priests were working more or less regularly in the Minaksi Temple. There are a few others who are entitled to work there, but because they have alternative employment, they do not do so. They are divided into two groups: the Vikkira Pantiyas and the Kulacekaras. Vikkira, correctly Vikkirama ('valorous'; Skt. *vikrama*), and Kulacekara ('head of the tribe'; Skt. *kulaśekhara*) are the names of two of the legendary Pāṇḍyan kings. Of the fifty-six, thirty-three priests belong to the Vikkira Pantiya group and twenty-three to the Kulacekara group (although some of the latter strictly belong to a third group that has recently acquired rights in the Temple.) The different rights and duties, and the internal constitution of the two groups, which comprise several clans and clan-branches, will be briefly discussed below.*

All the priests live in houses close to the north tower of the Temple, on North and South Bhattamar Streets and on North Āvaṇi Mūla Street, which links the other two. It is said that they used to reside near the east tower, but were moved to new houses in the seventeenth century in order to provide space for a new hall (Palaniappan 1970: 14). Some priests live in extended families, while others live in nuclear families. Some of them occupy old houses, while others

* *Also see chapter 4 of Fuller's book*. Editor.

live in modern buildings; many of them live in small, cramped rooms, whereas a number have quite spacious residences, and one or two live in large, well-equipped homes. With the exception of some of the youngest, most priests live in the style of traditional, orthodox Brahmans and all of them, of course, are vegetarians. However, it is generally held, by themselves and others, that they are less fastidious about rules of purity than are many Vaiṣṇava Brahmans. All the priests wear the sacred thread (*yajñopavīta*; Tam. *pūṇūl*) given to them at the Brahman male initiation ceremony (*upanayana*) undergone in early adulthood.[2] One Brahman domestic priest serves all of them at their rites of passage. He is hereditarily linked to all the priests, but is now paid each time he comes to serve them. He also has other clients elsewhere in Madurai. Some of the younger priests shave themselves, but most continue to rely on the services of a barber, who is hereditarily linked to all of them and continues to serve them at rites of passage and various other ceremonies. Nowadays, he is paid in cash for each job. Previously, the priests also had an hereditary washerman, but this is no longer the case. In the traditional manner, many priests continue to dip their clothes in water to purify them when they are returned by the washermen whom they now employ.

The Ādiśaivas form an endogamous subcaste, and informants told me that they knew of no marriages between Ādiśaivas and other Brahmans (or non-Brahmans) in the Madurai region. Like other Tamil Brahmans, they pay dowry at marriage and the preferred marital partner is a cross-cousin, an elder sister's daughter (for males) or another affinal relative. Informants, however, denied that there was any preference for a partner from the paternal as opposed to the maternal side, or vice versa. Intermarriage between the various clans of priests attached to the Minaksi Temple is frequent, so that there is a high degree of interrelatedness amongst them.[3]

2 A priest acquires the first three strands of his sacred thread at the initiation ceremony, the next three at his marriage, a further three at his consecration and a final three when his wife is pregnant with her first child. Ordinary Brahmans usually wear only nine strands (i.e. they omit the three for the consecration).

3 Of the 56 working priests and 7 other married males belonging to their families, 28 have married women from the Vikkira Pantiya or Kulacekara groups (although in some cases they now have second wives from elsewhere after being widowed), 25 have married women not belonging to the two groups, and for 10 recently married priests I lack information. Only a small number actually married cross-cousins or other genealogically close relatives, but the principle of marrying affines is nonetheless reflected in the high rate of intermarriage within and between the groups. Some marriages to outsiders were also to affinally linked relatives.

When working in the Temple, all the priests must wear the white cotton cloth (Tam. *veṣṭi*) of the Tamil male, tied between the legs in the traditional Brahman style. Over the top of this cloth, they wrap a piece of coloured cloth (Tam. *paṭṭu*, 'silk') which is ideally silk, to form a kind of cummerbund. Because it is believed that silk does not transmit pollution, the coloured cloth is said to protect the priests from polluting contact with devotees in the Temple.[4] Tucked into the cloth is a small bag in which priests keep a supply of white ash (*vibhūti*). Another cloth or a towel is usually carried over the shoulder. At home, some priests (mainly younger ones) retie their loincloths in the style favoured by all younger Tamils and non-Brahmans, that is hanging straight from the waist, and some don a shirt (which is never worn in the Temple). A few occasionally put on footwear, but many never do. The majority wear some jewellery, usually earrings and necklaces, the latter almost always incorporating the *rudrākṣa* beads sacred to Śiva; such ornaments are nowadays seen on only a minority of Tamil males.[5] The coloured cloth, the bag for white ash and the *rudrākṣa* beads are said to be indispensable for the priests, their ritual 'uniform'. Except for a couple of young priests, all of them wear their hair long and tied in a knot, and all of them shave their foreheads in the manner of orthodox Brahmans. On the forehead, they always place the three horizontal stripes of white ash sacred to Śiva (the Śaiva 'sect-mark'), usually with a dot of red powder (*kuṅkuma*), sacred to the goddess, above the bridge of the nose. The priests also place the three stripes on their arms, shoulders and chest. In the Temple, they always carry a plate (either brass or alloy) on which they keep ash, powder and camphor, and onto which offerings are placed. The plate, together with the rest of their 'uniform', enable devotees easily to identify the priests.

The priests' wives also mostly lead the lives of traditional Brahman women, dressing in the nine-yard sari tied between the legs that is favoured by orthodox Brahmans. (Other women wear six-yard saris tied to hang from the waist.) They all observe regular menstrual pollution periods and very few of them have any employment

[4] Amongst Brahmans in Madurai, the Tamil term *maṭi* describes the specially heightened state of purity demanded for domestic rituals. Although the priests say that they must be in a state of *maṭi* for rituals in their homes, the term is never used in the Temple. However, I was told that a priest ought to be in an equally pure condition when officiating there.

[5] The *rudrākṣa* ('Rudra [Śiva]-eyed') is the dried black berry of *Elaeocarpus ganitrus*: it often has five divisions, said to represent Śiva's five 'faces' (Stutley 1977: 254).

outside the home. The priests' children nowadays dress like other Tamil boys and girls, in shirts and shorts or blouses and skirts, and they all attend school. More emphasis is still placed on the education of sons than of daughters, and most priests . . . hope that their sons wiil obtain the educational qualifications needed for good jobs outside the Temple. Of the priests now working in the Temple, one has a degree and another has the Pre-University Certificate required for university entrance, but most have few formal educational qualifications, although several adult male members of the community, who could have worked as priests, do have higher qualifications and posts outside the Temple. One priest working regularly in the Temple also has a job with the state electricity board. One priest is widely held to be illiterate, but I do not know if the jokes made at his expense are well-founded. To the best of my knowledge, all the others can read and write Tamil; one or two also have some English and a few have an elementary knowledge of Sanskrit.

The Ādiśaivas

In any temple, the priests' principal role is the performance of rituals. As we shall see, there are a number of ritual tasks that they cannot or do not do in the Temple, but the central acts in all important rituals can only be performed by them. . . . In the public worship these include particularly the bathing, decorating, food-offering and lamp-waving rituals, and in private worship they perform the equivalent task on behalf of devotees. However, in the Minaksi Temple, some of the priestly work is actually done by others, and there are also differences between the roles taken by Vikkira Pantiya and Kulacekara priests. . . .

The priests who alone can perform the public worship in a Śiva temple have two particular qualifications that distinguish them from all other categories of the population: they are males who belong to the Ādiśaiva subcaste and who have been appropriately consecrated. . . . These two qualifications will now be discussed in turn.

The Ādiśaivas, the 'first Śaivas', are also sometimes known as Śivācāryas ('Śiva priests, masters'), Śivabrāhmaṇas ('Śiva Brahmans') or Śivadvijas ('twice-born of Śiva'). The Āgamic texts differ on the precise definition of the Ādiśaiva category and its relation to the rest of the population. However, the texts agree that Ādiśaivas rank second to Śiva himself, and are thus above other Brahmans and members of lower castes. The Ādiśaivas are said to be the lineal descendants of five sages (*ṛṣi*), who emerged from the mouths of the five faces of Sadāśiva. These sages were called Kāśyapa, Kauśika, Bhāradvaja, Gautama and Ātreya (or Agastya). All descendants of one sage are members of one eponymous *gotra* (patriline) and the priests of the Minaksi Temple all belong to one or other of the five *gotras* (the fifth being Ātreya). Intermarriage within the *gotras* is proscribed, and the groupings also have some significance in adoption, because adopting a son born in one's own *gotra* requires less elaborate rituals than taking him from another *gotra*. Otherwise, however, *gotra* membership is of little practical significance. According to the Āgamas, the Ādiśaivas' most vital quality is that they alone can properly perform the public worship of Śiva in his temples, an ability said to derive directly from their unique descent from the god himself. Through initiation (*dīkṣā*), which is open to everyone, ordinary people can become identified with Śiva and competent to perform his worship on their own behalf, but, because they are not, unlike Ādiśaivas, descended from Śiva, they cannot be consecrated and cannot carry out his public worship, 'for the well-being of the world', in the temples.

In the Minaksi Temple, some of the priests are able to recount, more or less closely, the myth of their origin as explained in the Agamic texts. Others, however, are more vague and content themselves with the simple assertion that, according to both the Āgamas and Tamil tradition, only Ādiśaivas are competent to perform Śiva's public worship in temples. The claim is not questioned by other personnel in the Temple, nor by the vast majority of devotees, although . . . it has been challenged by modern Tamil politicians. For most people familiar with the organization of temples, however, it is a given 'fact', sanctified by tradition, that only Ādiśaivas can work as priests in Śiva temples, although many ordinary folk, particularly non-Brahmans, probably know nothing of Ādiśaivas and simply assume that they are a category of Brahmans. Because Ādiśaivas alone can perform Śiva's public worship, the Minaksi Temple priests naturally claim that Ādiśaivas are closest to the god and that they, in their own Temple, are closest to Sundaresvara and his consort, Minaksi. As a first approximation, the hierarchy within the Temple may be described as Āgamic, the critical feature being that Ādiśaivas occupy the first rank above ordinary Brahmans and, of course, the lower castes.

Initiation and Consecration

To perform the public worship in a Śiva temple it is not, though, sufficient to be born an Ādiśaiva; a man must also be consecrated. The consecration is known as the *ācāryābhiṣeka*, 'consecration of an *ācārya*', a *guru* or master. Only an *ācārya* can perform Śiva's public worship and consecrate other priests. A form of the consecration ritual is also carried out for the heads of Śaiva monasteries, but in the temples it may only be undergone by Ādiśaivas. Before a man can be consecrated, he has to receive the three Śaiva initiations: the 'regular initiation' (*samayadīkṣā*), the 'special initiation' (*viśeṣadīkṣā*) and the 'liberating initiation' (*nirvāṇadīkṣā*). Unlike the consecration, these initiations, which must be taken in the above order, can be undergone by ordinary people.

I have discussed the initiation and consecration of Minaksi Temple priests in some detail elsewhere, and I have particularly drawn attention to the difference between Āgamic textual prescription and contemporary practice in the Temple (Fuller 1985). Here I shall only briefly summarize my earlier discussion. In the Āgamic texts, the central act of the regular initiation is the conferment of Śiva's blessing on the neophyte, which is by the major authorities considered to qualify him to worship the god. In the special initiation, the neophyte is reborn as a son of Śiva. In the lengthy and highly complex liberating initiation, the soul of the neophyte is purified and freed from the fetters binding it, before it is replaced, transformed, into his body. The initiate is now potentially liberated, although final liberation comes only after death and is conditional upon the regular worship of Śiva throughout the initiate's lifetime. In the texts, the initiations, and especially the liberating initiation, are seen as the great rituals that transform a devotee's soul, so that he himself becomes the god; the essential condition for worshipping him because, in the Āgamic tradition . . . 'only Śiva can worship Śiva'. The consecration, on the other hand, is a relatively simple ceremony, in which the central act is the besprinkling of the neophyte with water into which the power of Śiva has been invoked by the chanting of *mantras*. The god's power is thus devolved on to the new priest, who is then given the emblems of his office and can begin to perform the public worship.

In the Minaksi Temple, however, the rituals deviate considerably from the Āgamic prescriptions that I have just summarized. The initiations are treated as rather unimportant rituals; they are done hastily and often carelessly, and their Āgamic significance is mostly unknown. They are seen as little more than the necessary preliminaries for the consecration, which in the Temple immediately follows them. This ritual is a very elaborate spectacle accorded far more importance than the initiations. Its most striking aspect is the way in which worship is performed for the new priest by his *guru* (an older priest) in almost exactly the same form as it is for the images; he is bathed in a variety of substances (culminating in the 'holy' water into which Śiva's power has been invoked) and, after he has dressed in new clothes, food is offered before him and lamps are waved in front of him. In the consecration, therefore, new priests are publicly displayed as becoming forms of Śiva, whereas in the texts this transformation occurs during the initiations. The consecration as performed in the Temple, I have argued, is to be understood primarily as a public ritual of office that admits a man into the Temple priesthood. It serves to legitimate the priests' exclusive rights to conduct worship in the Temple, and it is this function that is seen as important rather than the spiritual transformation at the heart of the Āgamic initiation rites. Moreover, the consecration is a ritual conducted by the priests to create new priests from their own community, and it thus stresses the fact that they form a self-perpetuating body, endlessly able to legitimate themselves and answerable only to the god of whom they are themselves earthly forms. The consecration ritual, attended by the Temple administration's officials, other Temple officiants and priests from elsewhere, as well as a large crowd of devotees, provides the public sanction for the priests' act of self-legitimation and the public display of their unique relationship with the deities.

In the past, priests did sometimes start work in the Temple before being consecrated, although in such cases they apparently never carried out the public worship. In some other Śaiva temples in the region, I believe that this is still so, but in the Minaksi Temple the administration has insisted, since the 1930s, that all priests be consecrated before carrying out any kind of ritual work in the Temple. The administration has also given itself the power to approve candidates for the consecration. In some respects, however, these changes are relatively unimportant, because it is the public worship that is of primary significance, not the private worship, and the evidence suggests that public worship, at least since the mid-nineteenth century, has probably never been carried out by unconsecrated priests. An Ādiśaiva who has not been consecrated, although potentially able to become a priest, is therefore in practice in the same position as an ordinary devotee and is unable to perform any of the rituals.

The Problem of the Priests' Wives

There is, though, a further qualification required of a priest. Before he can be consecrated, he must be married. Today, young men intending to work in the Temple are usually consecrated in their twenties and they marry shortly before the ritual is held. In the Minaksi Temple, a priest can only perform the public worship if he has a living wife, although informants say that he may do private worship (and possibly some less important parts of public worship) even if he is widowed. But in practice, widowed priests rarely do continue to work; they either remarry or—usually if they are elderly—retire. In some other Śaiva temples in the region, I was informed, the insistence on a living wife is less strictly enforced.

The demand that a priest has a living wife apparently has no sanction in any Āgamic text. However, since Vedic times, there has been a general precept in Hinduism that husband and wife should co-operate in all religious acts, for they alone represent a unity. Possibly, the rule about the priests' wives has been introduced into Āgamic ritual in imitation of the widespread Vedic norm, or possibly it has always persisted despite the lack of any Āgamic stipulation. It is in terms similar to the Vedic precept that informants themselves explain the rule. One informant (not a priest) argued that a priest is only 'complete' if he is married, but amongst the priests themselves this general formulation gives way to a more specific one. They stress particularly that they must have access to *śakti*, the divine power personified as feminine that is required in order to worship Minaksi properly. A priest can only legitimately gain access to this power, incarnated in the goddess but also inherent in all women, through sexual relations with his wife. This notion is reminiscent of the Tantric doctrine that in ritual intercourse the female incarnates the goddess's power, but it also has Tamil antecedents. More pertinently and specifically, though, it mirrors the conceptualization of Śiva in the Temple rituals; just as the god must almost always be accompanied by his consort, his *śakti*, in rituals . . . so must his human incarnations, the priests, be united with their consorts, even though the latter do not actually accompany them to the Temple. But the fundamental idea is the same: a male is quiescent unless he has access to feminine power and the complete unity of the god, as of his servants, is only attained through the conjuction of the male and female opposite principles. Correspondingly, the priests emphasize too that they are sexually active householders (*grhasta*), unlike the monks and other ascetics, who are celibate renouncers (*sannyāsin*). The contrast is, typically, symbolized by the hair, because the priests should not cut theirs, whereas monks are tonsured. . . .

There is, however, a further difficulty here pertaining to the priests' wives themselves. The initiations and consecration are held for neophyte priests accompanied by their wives, so that both of them undergo the same ritual transformations. The priests and other informants all aver that the rituals effect the same changes in both the priests and their wives, so that the latter do possess the ability to perform the public worship in the Temple. This is explained as a kind of residual right; if all the priests were somehow incapacitated, they say that their wives could replace them. This is evidently hypothetical, but informants do claim that the priests' wives used to conduct worship in the Temple for the Nāyaka queens, who are said to have observed purdah. I have found no documentary confirmation for this. However, it certainly is believed in the Temple that priests' wives are capable of performing the worship in extreme circumstances, even though in practice (and in law) . . . they never do. Whether this belief about the wives' abilities is peculiar to the Minaksi Temple and is connected with the pre-eminence of the goddess there, I do not know.

The Priests' Hereditary Rights

So far, we have seen that three qualifications are required of a priest: he must be an Ādiśaiva, he must have been consecrated and he must be married. The first two of these are specified by the Āgamas and they—and possibly the third condition as well—are general in Tamil Śaiva temples. On these criteria, it would appear that any consecrated Ādiśaiva with a living wife should be able to perform the rituals in any Śaiva temple. This does indeed seem to be close to the position set down in the Āgamic texts, inasmuch as they define succession to the office of *ācārya*, or priest, in terms of the master-pupil line. There is no stipulation that a master's successor should belong to his own descent group.[6] However, in all major temples in south India, priestly rights are *de facto* hereditary and, in the Minaksi Temple, belong exclusively to members of the Vikkira Pantiya and Kulacekara groups. . . . A brief glance at the priests' history is . . . required here.

When the Sultan of Delhi's Muslim general, Malik Kāfur, raided and sacked Madurai in 1310, the Pāṇḍyan king abandoned his capital. The temples were plundered and the Minaksi Temple priests are said to have closed it and fled to Nanjinad (now in southern Tamilnadu). Before leaving, they placed a substitute *liṅga* in front of the sealed sanctum of Sundaresvara. The deities' festival images were removed to Kerala. The Musl'ms eventually established an independent Sultanate in Madurai, but this was overthrown in 1378 by Kumāra Kampana, who incorporated Madurai into the newly expanding Hindu empire of Vijayanagara (centred in modern Karnataka). Legend has it that when the Vijayanagara commander entered the Minaksi Temple, one Kulacekara Pĕrumāṉ opened Sundaresvara's sanctum, whereupon it was discovered that the lamp left inside nearly seventy years before was still burning, the silk cloth round the *liṅga* was still clean, and the sandalpaste and flowers were still fresh. Seeing this miracle, Kumāra Kampana appointed Kulacekara Pĕrumāṉ the Temple's *stāṉikar* (Skt. *sthānika*), a term that I translate as 'chief priest'. . . . Kulacekara Pĕrumāṉ was also granted lands and, having been consecrated as a priest, began with other members of his family to perform the rituals.

After a few years, however, the Vijaynagara regent of Madurai, Kumāra Kampana's son, became dissatisfied with the conduct of Kulacekara Pĕrumāṉ and his family (i.e. the Kulacekara group), only one of whom was still working in the Temple, and so he invited one Sadāśiva to work there.[7] Sadāśiva was consecrated, given the

[6] Brunner-Lachaux (1977: xxvii-xxx, xliv-xlv, 486–91, n. 47) argues that the Āgamic texts clearly specify that a master (*ācārya*) should retire after consecrating his pupil, as he has transferred his powers to his successor.

[7] Kulacekara Pĕrumāṉ is clearly a Kṣatriya name, which could suggest a non-Brahman origin for the Kulacekaras although no one ever mentioned this to me in the Temple. Sadāśiva, on the other hand, is a Brahman name and he is said to have come 'from the north', as are the priests—north Indian Gauda Brahmans—said to have worked in the Temple before Malik Kāfur's invasion. In the Temple's legend, too, Benares is claimed as the home of the original priests. Even today, the priests maintain, though with little conviction, that they all originated in Benares, and similar claims are widespread in south Indian Śiva temples, for example, Chidambaram. These claims obviously have to be interpreted as assertions of priestly legitimacy, as given by the link with the Aryan Brahmans' northern homeland and its holy Śaiva city, Benares.

title Vikkira Pantiya and appointed the first chief priest of the Temple. Kulacekara Pĕrumāṉ became the second chief priest. Sadāśiva then invited priests from five other nearby villages to assist him in the Temple, and the putative descendants of these priests, together with those of Sadāśiva himself, form the Vikkira Pantiya group. Over the following decades, the influence of the Vikkira Pantiyas expanded at the expense of the Kulacekaras and, throughout the Nāyaka period, conflicts between the two groups periodically erupted. Various Nāyaka kings, including the great Tirumala Nāyaka (who reigned from 1623–59), attempted to settle the disputes and from time to time errant priests (and other officiants in the Temple) were disciplined or dismissed for misconduct by the kings or their ministers responsible for the Temple (*dharmakartā*). After the final collapse of the Nāyaka dynasty in the early eighteenth century, Madurai came under the intermittent control of Muslim chieftains, until the region was ceded to the English East India Company in 1801. The new rulers took over many of the function's of their predecessors, and the British Collector of Madurai was soon involved in trying to settle disputes between the priests in the Temple.[8]

The accuracy of the historical account that I have just summarized is certainly not beyond doubt, although there is little reason to question its main outline. However, the precise facts are not especially important here. It matters more that the account is set down in documents that are considered authoritative and that its key elements are widely known and generally believed in the Temple. . . .

The conflict between the Vikkira Pantiyas and Kulacekaras was principally about their different rights to perform various types of ritual and, almost certainly, about the emoluments linked to those rights. . . . During the Nāyaka period, the Vikkira Pantiyas—the more recently appointed priests—established a superiority that they retain to this day. Only Vikkira Pantiyas can perform the daily worship, only they may be appointed as *nampiyār* (Tam.), the priests given sole charge of the six major festivals and Navarātrī, and only they can offer food and wave the lamps during public worship; moreover, only they may touch the main images of Minaksi and Sundaresvara. The Kulacekaras' principal task is bathing and decorating the movable images at festivals, although they may

[8] The *dharmakartā* was the equivalent of the Vijayanagara *dharmasanādhikārī*, the minister in charge of law and religious endowments; the office apparently existed in all south Indian kingdoms (Mahalingam 1955: 122).

touch any of the images except the two main ones. In practice, at minor festivals, Kulacekara priests do sometimes offer food and wave the lamps, but they never do so at important festivals and they never perform any of the daily worship. Priests from either group may carry out all types of private worship, unless it involves touching the main images (including bathing and decoration of them), in which case it must be done by Vikkira Pantiyas.

The Vikkira Pantiyas claim that if anyone other than themselves, including the Kulacekaras, were to touch the two main images, the latter would be polluted, and it is by reference to this assertion that they defend their monopoly over the daily worship carried out in the main sancta. But it is, I think, plain, as the Kulacekaras argue, that the Vikkira Pantiyas' logic merely rationalizes in the ubiquitous idiom of pollution the latters' monopoly. As we have seen, both groups of priests belong to the same subcaste, they regularly intermarry and all of them undergo an identical consecration. Therefore no criteria of relative purity or ritual qualification serve to distinguish them, although some Vikkira Pantiyas do claim that Kulacekara priests used to undergo a different, less elaborate consecration—a claim for which no evidence seems to be available. Nor can the argument about purity really explain why only Vikkira Pantiyas may be apointed as *nampiyār* in charge of festivals, or offer food and wave the lamps during the public worship. As Kulacekaras emphasize and Vikkira Pantiyas do often admit, the principal explanation for the latters' superior rights in the Temple is that they were granted them by the Nāyaka kings and have been able to keep them ever since. It is, however, equally important that Kulacekara objections to the Vikkira Pantiyas' superior rights could also be raised against the Kulacekaras' own position in almost identical fashion, for that too is owed to royal appointment. If Vikkira Pantiyas are not ritually superior to Kulacekaras, nor are the latter ritually superior to other consecrated Ādiśaivas into whose families they also marry.

The critical importance of the king and royal appointment for the understanding of priests' rights in the Temple, together with the effects of developments since the collapse of the Nāyaka kingdom, [are discussed elsewhere in Fuller's book]. At this stage, the vital point to be stressed is that, in practice, Adiśaiva priests are not servants of the universal Śiva and his consort, but of the particular local manifestations of the god and goddess in the temple in which they have their rights. Possession of such rights is, in reality, another qualification needed to perform the public worship in a temple of Śiva. The Vikkira Pantiyas and the Kulacekaras are the servants of Sundaresvara and Minaksi, the former being the first servants and the latter their second. They are not the servants of other local manifestations of the god and goddess; nor are Ādiśaivas working elsewhere the servants of Sundaresvara and Minaksi. In fact, some Minaksi Temple priests do have rights in other temples as well. But that does not affect the vital general principle that a priest is only a servant of the god and goddess in a temple in which he has rights. The Āgamic model, which relates Ādiśaivas collectively to the universal Śiva, has to be modified at this level, for as Śiva is localized in his many Tamil temples, so his Ādiśaiva servants are segmented into distinct groups possessing exclusive rights in their particular temples.*

** Fuller follows up the foregoing account of the temple priests with a discussion of other ritual officiants including temple servants (pp. 35–9), and the musicians and the dancing girls (pp. 39–41). The various categories of ritual specialists serve not only the deities but also the devotees (pp. 41–2).* Editor.

Gaya Priests and their Social Networks

L. P. VIDYARTHI

GURU-SHISYA RELATIONSHIP AMONG THE GAYAWAL*

The first, the *guru-shisya* type, refers to the relationships that the Gayawal caste as a whole, or its members individually, enjoy with the spiritual teachers, religious leaders, and holy ascetics. Some of these spiritual leaders who are followers of Vaishnavism of the Madhava sect stay at Gaya permanently and are revered by the Gayawal as *jati-guru* or caste-teachers. Others known as Vairagi, or Vaishnava *sadhu* (ascetics), and Dasnami, or Shaiva *sadhu* of ten orders, visit Gaya, stay at their respective monasteries, and hold 'sacred sessions' (*satsang*) with the Gayawal and other Brahmans living in Old Gaya. All such spiritual teachers, directly or indirectly, raise priestly morale and the quality of the religious life of the Gayawal in particular and other groups of people associated with the Gayawal in general. Moreover, visits of outstanding holy persons and their *satsang* attract large gatherings from the city as well as the neighbouring villages. When these holy persons visit other places of pilgrimage or other parts of India, they hold similar sacred sessions, formally or informally, and speak about the sacredness of Gaya as a place for ancestor worship and [about its association with the Vaishnava cult], thus helping to keep the current of pilgrimage flowing.

In the neighbourhood of the Vishnupada temple there are three

Excerpted from L. P. Vidyarthi, 'The Sacred Specialists: Extension', in *The Sacred Complex of Hindu, Gaya*, Asia Publishing House, Bombay, 1961, pp. 66–85.

* *The Gayawal, a priestly caste attached to the bathing ghats and temples of Gaya, enter into a variety of relationships with people of several castes. Five of these are particularly noteworthy, and are discussed below.* Editor

monasteries—one dedicated to the Madhava sect, the second to the Shankara sect, and the third for accommodating any holy ascetics or religious leaders. In the course of my fieldwork (1952–6), I found the Madhava *math* an active institution, whereas the Shankara *math*, while having a good collection of Sanskrit books, appeared on the whole to be desolate. I found some *sadhus* engaged in meditation in the third *math*.

The Madhava *math* is maintained by the Gayawal, and the Madhava *jati-guru*, who is a full-time worshipper, scholar, teacher, and philosopher, is very well looked after by them. He teaches Sanskrit texts and the Gayatri hymn to the Gayawal, addresses private and public religious sessions at the Vishnupada temple, and holds disputations with such pandits and priests who come to him for these purposes. He keeps himself aloof from the factional disputes that arise from time to time among the Gayawal, but always tries to lift their morale with spiritual advice. In many ways he is a 'sacred policy maker' and thus links himself with the religious intelligentsia who have visited Gaya in the course of its long history and, perhaps, have been instrumental in developing priestly groups by, first, converting selected people to the priestly way of life, and second, providing them a living by popularizing Gaya pilgrimage in the Hindu universe.

It is unfortunate that we do not have even scanty documents for understanding the role of such . . . intelligentsia in developing a group of literati as well as in communicating the great traditions to the masses. However, it can be conjectured with a certain amount of confidence that Gaya has been attracting religious intelligentsia from the time it became universally known in India as the birthplace of Buddhism in the fifth century BC. Subsequently . . . there emerged in Gaya a large group of Buddhist literati, and in successive years several monasteries, temples, railings, etc., were built there. Gaya attracted pilgrims not only from different parts of India but also from foreign Buddhist countries. Among them, two Chinese travellers, Fa-heien (AD 399–414) and Hiuen Tsiang (AD 629), visited Gaya during the period of decline of Buddhism and have left the earliest accounts about Gaya as a sacred place of pilgrimage.

Shankaracharya, the eighth century savant from South India, is said to have visited Gaya during his great religious conquest over Buddhism. He is believed to have had a great part in establishing the importance of Gaya as a place of pilgrimage for *shraddha* sacrifice. He is also said to have converted the Buddhist monks to the

Hindu priesthood and popularized them throughout India under the name of the Gayawal during his tour . . . popularly known as Shankara Digvijay. Recently a park, along with his image, has been laid in memory of his historic visit to Gaya. The desolate *math* with hundreds of Sanskrit books also reminds us that Shankara had great influence at Gaya. There are numerous priests and householders who consider themselves to be the followers of Shankara.

A third religious leader who has had tremendous influence on the Gayawal is Madhavacharya who flourished during the twelfth century AD. The Gayawal caste as a whole is a follower of the Madhava Vaishnava sect, and, as we have noted earlier, the Madhava *math* is a living religious centre that wields a powerful influence on the Gayawal. It is believed that wherever Madhava went, especially in the south and west of India, he popularized the efficacy of *shraddha* and Vishnu worship at Gaya for earning spiritual merit and salvation. Some educated Gayawal suspect that the Dakhini (South Indian Brahman) first became the spiritual teacher of the Gayawal caste at that time. It is customary for one of the celebrated *acharyas* of the Madhava sect hailing from South India to reside at Gaya and act as spiritual teacher of the Gayawal.

A fourth outstanding member of the sacred intelligentsia stayed at Gaya and was converted to Vaishnavism here. This was Mahaprabhu Chaitanya (1485–1527). . . .

According to his biographers, Chaitanya, during his pilgrimage to Gaya . . . met Ishwar Puri, a Vaishnava monk of the order of Madhavacharya, evidently the *jati-guru* of the Gayawal, and accepted him as his spiritual guide. His acceptance of the *bhakti* cult and abandonment of the *yajna* cult brought 'a complete change over his spirit, his intellectual pride was gone, he became a *bhakta* (devotee instead of a philosopher) and whatever subject he lectured on, the theme of his discourse was love of Krishna'. The great master travelled for six years from Gaya to Banaras, Prayag, Mathura, Jagannath, and many other places of pilgrimage . . . .

Chaitanya thus took with him the sacredness of Vishnu at holy Gaya whose sight (*darshan*) produced such a wonderful change in his sensitive nature, and Gaya became more widely known for its sacredness among the millions of followers of Chaitanya. . . . The Chaitanyaite call themselves Madhava Gaudiya and consider themselves a section of Madhavas. At Gaya they have a Gaudiya *math* dedicated to Hari, the eighth incarnation of Vishnu, and it attracts numerous followers of Chaitanya, Madhavacharya, and other Krishna worshippers. . . .

Ramananda in the thirteenth century and Vallabha in the sixteenth century, the other two great spiritual teachers of Vishnavism of north India, are believed to have visited and stayed at Gaya in the course of their extensive religious tours. It is quite likely, that they might have talked about the significance of Gaya pilgrimage in the course of these tours.

In a later account, Buchanan (1811–12:12, 93) refers to several *sannyasis* (ascetics) whom he met at Gaya. He makes mention of one 'Dandi swami who adhered to the rules of Madhava as practised in the South from whence he came and retained all the pride of his country'. Evidently, Buchanan is making reference here to the *jati-gurus* of the Gayawal who are usually quite orthodox and adhere to all the religious codes of conduct. He also writes about twenty-five other *sannyasis* who abstained from marriage. He further mentions three orders of Dasnami *sannyasi* (ascetics of Shankara's order) who act as shrine priests for the Gayeshvari temple. But he fails to give any detailed account about them as he was not allowed to enter into the *math* of many of these *sannyasis*. Monier-Williams (1891:88) describes the severe austerities and bodily mortification of Urdhava-bahu (a type of Shaiva ascetic) which he saw in the course of his visit to Gaya.

In recent times, the Gayawal have informed me about the visits of modern religious leaders like Ramakrishna, Dayananda, Vivekananda, and Guru Govind Singh, whose writings they claim to preserve in their professional record books. . . . The life-history of one of my Gayawal informants reflects the influence of modern religious movements like Arya Samaj and Brahma Samaj upon his religious thinking, although in the end he accepts his own traditional Sanatan Dharma (eternal religion) as the best among them. . . .

PANDA-JAJMAN

The *panda-jajman* or priest-sacrificer type refers to the hereditary relationship and mutual obligations that have come to exist between the Gayawal families and many families of clean castes of different parts of India whose members come to Gaya for ancestor worship [*shraddha*]. Traditionally the whole of India has been parcelled out among the several lineages of the Gayawal, and as a rule the pilgrims start from their houses knowing the names of their respective

Gayawal *pandas* or priests. The caste organization of the Gayawal also provides an effective mechanism to identify and regulate the priest-sacrificer system from generation to generation. Such mechanisms are (1) the inheritance of lineage designations and hereditary nicknames, and (2) maintenance and ownership of record books (*khata*) containing the genealogical details of all the sacrificers (*jajman*) who fall under Gayawal jurisdiction.

The lineage designation . . . regulates the inheritance of property as well as of the sacrificers in the patrilineal line. Second, such lineage designations (*vanshnam*) act as professional titles and thus enable the sacrificers to identify their hereditary *panda*. In case a lineage becomes extinct for want of a male heir, its title as a piece of property is inherited by another collateral relative who, in addition to his own lineage designation, also bears the adopted one. In other words, the lineage designations through which the *panda* are identified by the *jajman* theoretically never become extinct, and thus the *panda-jajman* relationship under such *vanshnam* is always maintained. . . .

In general and common practice, the patrilineally inherited *vanshnam* is more important than the adopted one. But when the adopted title comes from a rich lineage or family, the patrilineal *vanshnam* becomes subservient or in some cases is completely abandoned for professional purposes. . . .

As far as my investigation goes, fifty-five such professional titles have been recorded. Among the fifty-five titles, about twenty have either become extinct, or are incipiently associated with other lineage titles, or survive in small dying families. The origin of the names of these titles is not known in detail. . . .

These *vanshnam* or *paddati* (names of lineages and families), if considered in broader perspective, can be categorized in several ways. Out of fifty-five *vanshnam*, fifteen refer to certain religious, social, and political offices of their bearers within the caste group or pilgrimage organization. Thirteen of them come from the nicknames or other personal characteristics of individuals after whom the lineages were named and known. Nine of them are derived from the titles borne by several castes of Brahman *varna*, while six are after the caste titles borne by Vaishya castes in Bihar. Seven of the *vanshnam* might be identified with certain villages and regions from where their bearers are believed to have migrated to the city. Some of the titles . . . might belong to more than one category. . . .

The second mechanism that facilitates establishment of the rightful claims of the Gayawal on their *jajmans* is the record book (*khata*) in which the names of the *jajman* and their villages are carefully entered. When a lineage or a joint family . . . breaks into two or more, the area of jurisdiction as well as the number of patrons are likewise divided by the pages of the *khata*. When disputes arise over the claim to a pilgrim, these *khatas* prove a ready reference. In this way, the *khata* of the Gayawal is their most important property and it enables them to regulate the working of their 'sacred estate'. In the event of inheritance of the 'sacred estate' of some collateral relatives, which actually means the transfer of *khata* from one lineage to another, or in case of partition in a joint family, the members concerned keep at least their rich *jajman* informed about the changes. This was done in the past by touring in the area of jurisdiction by the Gayawal themselves or by sending their representatives. Now they also take recourse to writing letters to them. . . .

In spite of all these arrangements, however, every year some non-committed pilgrims whose *jajmani* relationship is not identified with any *panda* come to Gaya. According to one arrangement, such pilgrims are regarded as the *jajman* of the entire caste and all the sacred and secular services are provided to them by a Gayawal organization called Vishnu Ashram (the resort of Vishnu). Profits received from such pilgrims go for the general welfare of the caste. A separate record book is maintained for such pilgrims, and the pilgrim is asked to transfer this temporary arrangement to a *panda* whom he likes. This is one of the many arrangements made to solve the conflicts that arise among the competing priests over the non-committed pilgrims. . . .

The *panda-jajman* relationship based upon several obligations primarily finds expression on two occasions: first, when a *panda* and his party or his representatives make a visit to his *jajman*; and second, when a *jajman* and his relatives and attendants come on Gaya pilgrimage to observe *shraddha* sacrifice or offer special worship at the temple of Vishnupada.

The purposes of a *panda* in making a visit or sending representatives to the *jajmans* are manifold: to raise religious consciousness among the *jajman* for making a pilgrimage to Gaya; to renew relationships with old *jajman* and receive gifts . . . to approach the rich *jajman* for help in some domestic financial crisis; to recruit new *jajmans* and to guide all those *jajmans* who are willing to come on Gaya pilgrimage.

In the past when transportation facilities were limited and impediments in making journeys were many, it required elaborate preparations for a Gayawal to make a visit to the *jajmans*. A rich *panda* who made visits only to his wealthy *jajmans* was always accompanied by a host of attendants, guards, and musicians. He would take with him personal deities (*thakurji*), whose worship on the way and wherever he stayed would be a special feature. He would also take with him . . . sweets as *prasad* (token of blessings) from the Vishnupada. . . .

Though the *panda* would be especially inclined to contact rich *jajmans* during his *jajmani yatra* (visits to sacrificers), he would never lose sight of communicating with the common *jajmans*. In addition to his own trips, he would send special groups of his representatives to meet them, to persuade them to make Gaya pilgrimage, and then to escort them home safely. For these many purposes he used to have several grades of servants, travelling staff, and guides. . . .

With the introduction of cheap means of transportation, the trips by the representatives of the Gayawal have become almost out-of-date. They are no longer needed now to escort the pilgrims nor are the pilgrims desirous now of waiting until a large company of the *panda's* representatives arrives to accompany them. They can easily come to Gaya from any part of India without any transportation difficulties or without any fear of being robbed or harassed on their way. Owing to this development, the work of the *panda's* representatives has become concentrated at the railway and bus stations in the neighbourhood of Gaya. They also travel in the trains coming to Gaya and sort out the pilgrims belonging to their respective masters.

The *panda*, however, sometimes makes *jajmani yatra* for which he has to make very little preparation. Some of the life-histories of the old and young *pandas* also point out the emergence of a new type of *jajmani* trip wherein a *panda* takes along his wife, combines pilgrimages with *jajmani* trips, or conveniently goes alone from place to place within a few weeks and comes back with whatever gifts he can get from the poor and rich *jajmans*.

The second type of *jajmani* obligation occurs when the *jajman* and his relatives arrive in Gaya for the performance of *shraddha* sacrifice.

The *panda* makes all possible arrangements for accommodation, cooking, and ritual performances with a feeling of cordiality, familiarity and age-old attachment. The *panda* tells him about the visits as well as the good qualities of head and heart of the *jajman's* ancestors who visited Gaya in the past, and how they gave him 'so much' in gift. The *jajman*, thus, in a homely atmosphere performs all the rituals under the guidance of his hereditary family *panda*. He is entertained by musical performances for which the Gayawal in general are famous. He attends and participates in religious gatherings like *sankirtana*, *katha* and other types of devotional recitations. He also may be advised to go to see some religious films that are usually shown in the local cinema houses. In addition to making the rounds of the sacred centres and participating in other secondary performances, some of the *jajmans* may choose to help in other types of religious activities—construction and repair of temples, feeding of Brahmans and beggars, giving gifts to *sadhus* and priests, and maintaining or aiding some religious institutions. Such actions are believed to bring additional spiritual merit to the *jajman* and, moreover, also add to the prestige of his *panda*. . . .

Such close and constant contacts between the *panda* and the *jajman* have influenced the lives of both. The *jajmans* of the Gayawal come into contact with many other types of priests from other places of pilgrimage, as well as with the local and regional priests. Similarly, a Gayawal, though not always in contact with the same *jajman*, remains in close association with some *jajman* throughout the year, and his way of life is evidently influenced by them. . . .

Mixed Jajman-Pauniya

This type (master-servant) refers to the semi-hereditary relationship that the Gayawal themselves have entered into with several caste specialists primarily to provide adequate sacred and secular services to their *jajman*, and also to facilitate the smooth running of their priestly organization. The relationship between these caste specialists and the Gayawal is not merely that of employees and employers. Several socio-economic factors have brought them into closer association, and some of these 'employees' have become part of the family organization and, thus, have influenced the Gayawal way of life.

A Gayawal family needs the services of several caste specialists in the organization of the priesthood as well as in the priestly way of life. First, in order to maintain his contacts with his *jajmans* and receive them at the railway and bus stations, he needs a group of attendants and travelling staff. Again, when these *jajmans* are housed, he needs several male and maid servants to provide them menial services. Moreover, for his own domestic work and comforts, he requires several attendants.

In order to meet all these requirements, a Gayawal employs several families of servant castes (especially of Kahar and Dhanuk castes). Cash payments are nominal, but these families enjoy many other privileges of free food, free clothes, free housing, special rewards during the celebrations at their master's house or from his *jajmans*, and financial aid when some celebration of rites takes place at their (servant's) houses. Several families of servant castes become attached to a Gayawal family and continue their relationship with the same family generation after generation. . . .

The life-histories of the Gayawal are full of examples of initimate relationships that they have developed between them and the families of their servants. In general, a Gayawal child is reared by the maid servants; when he grows up he plays with his servants' children; and when he becomes an adult, in some cases, a closer relationship might develop with the girl servants. Concubinage is more or less a recognized institution among the Gayawal, although persons maintaining concubines are usually looked down upon. Such concubines, coming from servant castes, for many practical purposes become part of the family, though they occupy an inferior position both in the family and in the Gayawal caste. In general, the [presence of servants] has been a powerful influence in the domestic life as well as the priestly life of the Gayawal.

Second, the *acharyas* conduct the *jajmans* to the various sacred centres and guide them in the performance of rituals. They are mostly Brahmans of Sakadvip, Kanauj, Shrotriya, and Maithil castes. Brahmans from different linguistic regions—Marathi, Bengali, Tamil—also live in the neighbourhood of Vishnupada and are employed by those Gayawal who serve *jajmans* from these linguistic areas.

Some Gayawal who receive many pilgrims employ three to ten *acharyas*; on the other hand, one *acharya* may serve two to three Gayawal families who receive fewer pilgrims. During the *pitripaksha* fair [annual 'feeding' of the manes lasting a fortnight], the Gayawal families employ many *acharyas* temporarily.

The relationship of the *acharya* with the Gayawal has become more or less contractual. The *acharya* employed on a permanent basis receives regular salary, though free clothes and occasional monetary rewards are also given. The families of the *acharyas* are usually on a formal relationship with their masters' families, but there is more frequent social intercourse with them than with other families in the neighbourhood. Exchange of visits, gifts, invitations, and mutual help is usual at the family level. The *acharya* continues to serve the same master for his whole life, and there are even cases in which several generations of an *acharya* family serve the same master family. But the element of hereditary service is not so strong with the *acharyas* as it is with the menial servants. Cases of frequent change of masters are not uncommon. The *acharyas* are also paid by the Gayawal for specific services rendered to their *jajman*.

Third, the *munshiji*, who belongs to Kayastha caste, maintains the Gayawal's *khata* (record book) and does other clerical jobs that may be needed for domestic and professional purposes. In case of disputes among the Gayawal over the claims of a pilgrim, he helps his own Gayawal master with ready reference. I was told that the entries of genealogical names are so complete and comprehensive that the *khata* has sometimes been required in court in order to establish rightful descent. . . .

Fourth, the *pauniya* class includes the Nai (barber), Mali (florist), Kumhar (potter), and Pindabechva (rice-ball seller). *Pauniya* means 'one who receives', and such caste specialists provide service for annual payment along with special payments to be made on the occasion of festivals, *rites de passage*, and the annual *pitripaksha* fair. However, at the present time, instead of annual payment, piece work payment is also made by the Gayawal. One or two families of such specialist castes provide service to a group of Gayawal families. These caste specialists render services both to the Gayawal and to their *jajmans* who come to observe *shraddha* and require their services. Usually for both the services (rendered to the Gayawal as well as to his *jajmans*), payment is made by the Gayawal. The *jajman*, however, may make some present to a *pauniya*, especially of the Nai caste who performs the ritual shaving. When a Gayawal family needs more services than its *pauniya* can supply, the *pauniya* is asked to make further provision for rendering service. Such a situation is usually encountered in the case of the Nai caste who are required in large numbers for the ritual shaving of the thousands of *shraddha* sacrificers during the *pitripaksha* fair. On such an occasion, the family barbers bring their distant relatives to work for them. . . .

Gayawal-Dhami

The Gayawal also maintain professional relationships with another caste of priests, usually called the Dhami or the Dhamin. The Dhami are guardians of the two sacred clusters—Ramshila and Pretashila hills—where *shraddha* sacrificers are escorted by the *acharyas* to make offerings in the name of Yama [God of death], his infernmal dogs, and several gods and goddesses and ghosts and spirits. At these places, rituals are conducted by the Dhami who are entitled to three-quarters of the gifts that are made.... The remaining one-quarter goes to the Gayawal *panda*. Thus, the relationship between these two priestly groups is one of partnership.

The Dhami comprise a community of about twenty-seven families who live in the rural setting of the foothill zones of Pretashila.... As they are associated with shrines devoted to ghosts and spirits, they call themselves 'Pretiya Brahman', or Brahmans associated with ghosts. However, I was told that the Dhami fall far short of what is expected of Brahman priests....

It is generally believed by the Gayawal and the local citizens that the Dhami are non-Brahmanical priests. Some citizens identify them with the florist caste that inhabits a locality of Gaya named after the Dhami (Dhami Tola). Buchanan (1811–12: 323, 335) identifies the Dhami with the Dhanuk, low caste agriculturists, and suspects the present Dhami were their priests in ancient times....

Unfortunately, there is no way of knowing how this compromise between the Brahmanical and the non-Brahmanical priesthood evolved and came to be linked within the single ritual of Gaya *shraddha*.... The Dhami, though without much result, still continue to raise *jajmans*, maintain *khata*, and carry on an independent priestly profession. In such efforts they come into conflict with the Gayawal, and several cases to this effect have been instituted in the local courts. To the thousands of pilgrims, however, who come here to offer *shraddha*, the two priesthoods are of equal importance in their respective contexts. Traditions have established that the Dhami should be revered and given gifts at the hill-shrines, and to many they are as important and as sacred as the Gayawal. They are an inseparable part of the same ritual complex.

Pujari-Darshaniya

In the preceding four sections, we noted the structural relationship of the Gayawal with the outside world in respect to their roles as *shraddha* priests. In addition to their status as *shraddha* priests, the Gayawal are also shrine priests, *pujari*. The *pujari-darshaniya* type refers to the relationship that a Gayawal, as a shrine priest, enters into with those local and regional worshippers [seekers of *darshan*] who make ritual visits to a sacred centre at which he officiates.

The main temple at which the Gayawal officiate and which is largely attended by the worshippers is that of Vishnupada. Every Gayawal enjoys equal rights in entertaining worshippers and in receiving gifts from them during daytime. In the evening, however, the right is restricted to the Gayawal of Bhaiya lineage. A representative of every family of this lineage, by rotation, goes to the temple in the evening, pays for the special evening worship, and is entitled to receive all the gifts that are made there by the worshippers during his presence in the temple.

During daytime, those Gayawal who want to escort visitors to the Vishnupada temple (which entitles them to receive the offerings made by the visitors at the shrine) assemble at the raised platform (*darvani*) at the gate of the temple. Here the Gayawal shrine priests watch for the arrival of the visitors. The priest who is first to see a visitor and prompt enough to declare his identity according to his dress or other such characteristics is entitled to serve as his shrine priest. At times, disputes and conflicts follow among the competing shrine priests on the issue of establishing rightful claims over a worshipper.

Ideally, the Gayawal in general do not like this job of shrine priesthood. Shrine priesthood is characterized by poor income, scanty gifts, continuous waiting, and undesirable competition. Moreover, the Gayawal, especially in the past, were so well off as *shraddha* priests that they cared very little for their rights as shrine priests. Only boys and a few adults of poor families attended to this job. Due to economic depression, however, the temple has attracted large crowds of competing Gayawal youths.

For the Gayawal boys, the temple provides a place for apprenticeship in the profession of priestcraft. Every day a Gayawal boy gets up early in the morning, takes his bath, decorates his forehead with sandal paste, puts on the typical priestly dress, and hurries up to the temple to 'hunt' *darshaniya* to get gifts. His attraction to the sacred temple is always greater than his attraction to school. . ...

Five Symbols of Sikh Identity

J. P. S. UBEROI

Every emancipation is a *restoration* of the human world and of human relationships to *man himself*
KARL MARX *The Jewish Question (1843)*

THE STRUCTURAL METHOD

The custom of wearing long and unshorn hair (*kes*) is among the most cherished and distinctive signs of an individual's membership of the Sikh Panth, and it seems always to have been so. The explicit anti-depilatory injunction was early established as one of the four major taboos (*kuraht*) that are impressed upon the neophyte at the ceremony of initiation into Sikhism, and unshorn hair is one of the five symbols that every Sikh should always wear on his person. Yet there exists hardly any systematic attempt in Sikh studies to explain and interpret the origin and significance of this custom.[1] As a religious system, Sikhism is anti-ritualistic in its doctrinal content and general tone, so that a study of the few obligatory rites and ceremonies that are associated with it in its institutional or social aspect should be of considerable interest for their own sake. Moreover, if our investigation of the connection between the nature of Sikhism as a whole and its five symbols, including the specific custom of being unshorn, were to be made in a comparative and empirical spirit and according to rules of method capable of universal application, we may expect that the solution of this particular problem would also illumine certain general problems of the sociology of religion, for example, regarding the nature of religious innovation and its social institutionalization.

This is a revised version of my paper published in *Transactions of the Institute of Advanced Study*, vol. 4 (Simla, 1967). I am grateful to the authorities of the Institute for allowing it to be reprinted in the present form.

[1] A noteworthy exception is Kapur Singh (1959), especially chs. 4 and 5.

I am not myself able to adequately investigate the problem at present since I do not possess the requisite linguistic proficiency to study the original Punjabi sources and without enquiring into them at first hand one cannot proceed satisfactorily. The argument and interpretation presented in this paper will be based solely on the information available in English; and for my reliance on second-hand sources that are incomplete and liable to error I owe an apology in advance. I shall hope nevertheless that the sociological method or scheme of interpretation that I shall adopt might invoke some interest. For the results achieved, or capable of being achieved, in a line of enquiry depend not only on the evidence examined and its authenticity, but also on the method of analysis and interpretation followed.

The particular method adopted here, which may be called the structural method, implies that, for a proper theoretical understanding or explanation, the ceremonial custom or rite in question must be viewed from two interrelated aspects. We should attempt to determine (1) its ideological meaning within a particular system of symbolic thought, and (2) its social function within a particular social system of groups and categories. The first aspect, which we may call explanation at the level of culturally conditioned thought and belief, is a matter of examining the ceremony or rite as a condensed statement, the symbolic expression of certain characteristic cultural ideas and values. In the second aspect of our study we move to the level of institutionalized behaviour or social action, and seek to relate the rite and the social occasion of its performance to the wider social system of the group or category of persons who recognize the obligation to perform it. In neither case do we consider the particular rite in isolation but bearing in mind the context of the other rite with which it is associated in reality, and at either level of analysis our understanding proceeds by seeking to relate the part to its larger whole, the piece to the pattern. Only after these necessary steps have been accomplished in the context of a particular culture and society may we rightly proceed further to compare the meanings and social functions of similar rites observed in two or more different cultures, or even of the same rite in a single culture at different historical periods.

Combining these two aspects or levels of thought and behaviour, which it is convenient to distinguish for analysis, we may state the central assumption of our procedure in the form that all ceremonies and rites are constitutive, expressive and affirmative in character, that is, they embody and communicate abstract meanings and values in concrete shape. The obligatory and oft-repeated social performance of a body of rites serves to give definitive expression and form to a people's collective life and thought. It constitutes and affirms to themselves and to others the structural coherence of their particular pattern of culture, thought and social organization as an ordered whole, and contributes to maintain and develop that pattern from generation to generation. These effects together constitute, according to our chief theoretical assumption, the *raison d'être* of ritual behaviour and symbolic thought.

It will be apparent to anyone who has made the attempt that an investigation of the exact meaning and social function of a rite is a complex and difficult task. It is a process like that of ascertaining the grammar and syntax of a language, its structure as against its lexicon, which cannot be done by simple enquiry from a native speaker or informant. For ritual is capable by its inner nature of encapsulating several abstract meanings and social references, and moreover these generally do not lie readily accessible at the conscious surface of life but require to be extracted, as it were, from the sub-conscious. It is therefore specially necessary in this field of study to avoid all easy inferences from intuition or deductive reasoning or commonsense and to adhere to explicitly formulated rules of method.

Symbols, Sects and Initiations

The cultural association of male hair, specially long hair, with magical or sacred ideas is known from many parts of the world. It is well recognized in general terms to be a symbol of manliness, virility, honour, power, aggression and so on. For example, in very early Europe the Achaeans, who conquered Greece, customarily wore their hair long and wild. The Semitic story of Samson and Delilah as told in the Old Testament well illustrates the virtue of remaining unshorn. We can readily locate many similar examples in classical Hinduism. The Institutes of Manu specify that: 'Even should a man be in wrath, let him never seize another by the hair, when a Brahmin commits an offence for which the members of other castes are liable to death, let his hair be shaved off as sufficient punishment.'

We should, however, be careful to remember that, like all sacred or tabooed objects, long hair can also equally carry the opposite connotation. It can be regarded, especially when unkempt, as signifying something unclean, dangerous or abandoned. We must thus refer, according to the rules of our method, to the actual context and situation in order to determine which of these two elements is predominant in a particular case.

That the precise physical state of the hair is always relevant to its symbolic meaning, but is never by itself the deciding factor, can be made clear from the example of the Chinese pigtail, which superficially resembles the Hindu *shikha* (scalp-lock) in appearance. The Manchus, a foreign dynasty, in fact first instituted the pigtail among the Chinese in AD 1644 as a sign of their subjection. It later became accepted as a characteristic Mandarin custom, even as a sign of honour. In the mid-nineteenth century the Taiping rebellion and in the early twentieth century Sun Yat-sen's movement and others sought to dispose of it, remembering its original significance. The Taipings did so by wearing all their head hair long and so became known as the 'long-haired rebels', whereas the twentieth-century revolutionaries proceeded to cut all their hair short, literally throwing the pigtail away. The complete contrast between these two outcomes of a single impulse is not without interest for our study.

In Sikhism the injunction to remain unshorn is expressly associated with the ceremony of initiation, and it is in that context that we must primarily explain it. Now every initiation rite evidently possesses the nature of an investiture or conferment, since through it some new status or role with its consequent rights and obligations is conferred symbolically upon the neophyte and he or she enters upon a new mode of existence. But every initiation rite necessarily also contains a much less obvious element, namely that of renunciation or divestiture, whereby the neophyte symbolically discards or has taken away from him attributes of his old status and mode of existence. One must ritually first abandon the previous course or phase of social existence in order to properly enter the new. Admittedly, the positive element of investiture or conferment generally predominates in initiation rites, but the element of renunciation or divestiture is always present to some degree. This negative element may even be uppermost in certain cases, for example, in initiation to monkhood or the monastery.

I want now to draw attention to a class of initiation rites of this latter kind that were widely prevalent in the Punjab at the time that Sikhism took its origin. These were rites of renunciation (*sannyas*) through which an individual obtained entrance to one or other of the medieval mendicant orders (Sannyasis, etc.). It is my contention that an examination of this class of rites with the details of the Sikh initiation rite borne in mind, shows a remarkable relation of structural inversion to exist between the two. I want to suggest that, in terms of the symbolic language and ritual idiom of the times, at least one cultural meaning of the Sikh initiation rite was that it stood as the antithesis or the antonym of the rites of Hindu renunciation.

A Sannyasi is a person who, having passed through the first three statuses (*ashramas*) of Brahminical Hinduism, renounces the world and is cared for by others. It may perhaps be that the Sannyasi religious orders were older than the Brahminical institution of *sannyas*, the fourth and last stage of life. At any rate, the orders seem to have been open to entry by the individual person of almost any physical age. The Sannyasi orders had decayed significantly during the Buddhist period and then split into sub-orders with heterodox creeds. They were reformed by Shankaracharya, whose four disciples instituted four *maths* (orders) that later developed into numerous *padas* (sub-orders). Each sub-order was said to have two sections, one celibate and mendicant, the other not. All Sannyasis were further graded according to four degrees of increasing sanctity (Kavichar, Bahodak, Hans, Paramhans).

The Sannyasi initiation rite was and continues to be essentially as follows.[2] The candidate intending to attain renunciation must first go on a pilgrimage to find a *guru*, who should be a Brahmin; and then the latter satisfies himself as to his fitness and proceeds to initiate him. The neophyte commences with the *shraddha* (obsequies) to his ancestors to fulfil his obligations to them. He next performs the sacrificial *baji hawan* and gives away whatever he possesses, severing all connection with the world. His beard, moustaches and head are entirely shaved (*mundan*), retaining only the scalp-lock (*shikha*), and the sacred thread is put aside. He then performs the *atma-shraddha* or his own death rites. (An initiated Sannyasi is thus counted as socially deceased, and when he dies is not cremated but buried in a sitting posture without further ceremony.) The scalp-lock is now cut off and the neophyte enters the river or other water with it and the sacred thread in hand and throws both away, resolving 'I am no one's, and no one is mine'. On emerging from the water he starts naked for the north but the *guru* stops him and gives him a loin-cloth (*kopin*), staff (*danda*), and water vessel (*jalpatra*) kept

[2] The material presented on the succeeding pages is derived from Rose (1911 and 1914), which is based on the Census Reports for the Punjab, 1883 and 1892.

out of the neophyte's personal property. Finally, the *guru* gives him the *mantra* (spiritual formula) in secret and admits him to a particular *math* (order), *sampraday*, etc. (Rose 1914: 358).

The initiation rite of the Jogi order, which was also widespread in medieval Punjab, is very similar. According to the *Punjab Census Report*, 1912, 'Jogi' is a corruption of *yogi*, a term applied originally to Sannyasis well advanced in the practice of *yogabhyas*. 'The Jogis are really a branch of Sannyasis, the order having been founded by Guru Machhandar (Matsyendra) Nath and Gorakh Nath Sannyasis, who were devoted to the practice of Yoga and possessed great supernatural power. The followers of Guru Gorakh Nath are absorbed more in the Yoga practices than in the study of the Vedas and other religious literature, but between a real good Jogi and a *yogi* Sannyasi there is not much difference, except perhaps that the former wears the *mudra* (rings) in his ears. The Jogis worship Bhairon, the most fearful form of Shiva (P. Hari Kishen Kaul, *Punjab Census Report, 1912*, quoted in Rose 1914: 361.) Their main subdivisions are stated to be the Darshani or Kanphatta (split-eared), known as Naths, who wear the *mudra* (ear-rings); and the Aughar, who do not.

In Jogi initiation the neophyte (*chela*) is first made to fast for two or three days. A knife is then driven into the earth,[3] and the candidate vows by it not to (1) engage in trade, (2) take employment, (3) keep dangerous weapons, (4) become angry when abused, and (5) marry. He must also scrupulously protect his ears, for 'a Jogi whose ears were cut used to be buried alive, but is now only excommunicated'. The neophyte's scalp-lock is removed by the *guru* and he is shaved by a barber; his sacred thread is also removed. He bathes and is smeared with ashes, then given ochre clothes to wear, including the *kafni* (shroud). The *guru-mantra* is communicated secretly, and the candidate is now a probationer (*aughar*). After several months' probation his ears are pierced and ear-rings inserted by the *guru* or an adept, who is entitled to an offering of one-and-a-quarter rupee. 'The *chela*, hitherto an *aughar*, now becomes a *nath*, certain set phrases (not *mantras*) being recited' (Rose 1911: 400).

According to an account of the Ratan Nath Jogis, the intending candidate is proffered a razor and scissors by the *guru* to deter him from entering the order. If he perseveres the *guru* cuts off a tuft of his hair and he is shaved by a barber. He is made to bathe, smeared

[3] The Jogis hold the earth and everything made of it in great respect. 'The earthen carpet, the earthen pitcher, the earthen pillow and the earthen roof,' is a saying that describes their life. Like the Sannyasis, Jogis are buried in the earth and not cremated.

with ashes and then given a *kafni* (shroud), a *lingoti* (loin-cloth) and a cap to wear. 'The ashes and *kafni* clearly signify his death to the world.' After six months' probation his ears are pierced and earthen ear-rings inserted in them (ibid.: 401n).

After initiation, a Jogi may either remain a celibate and ascetic mendicant (called Nanga, Naga, Nadi, Nihang or Kanphatta), living on alms; or he may relapse and become a secular Jogi (called Bindi-Nagi, Sanyogi, Gharbari or Grihisti), having property and a spouse. A Jogi usually joins one or other of the various *panths* or 'doors' (sub-orders), whose traditional number was twelve.

I mention finally the initiation rite of the Dadupanthi order, stated to have been founded by Dadu, a Gaur Brahmin who died in AD 1703.[4] In this rite the *guru* in the presence of all the *sadhus* shaves off the neophyte's scalp-lock and covers his head with a skull-cap (*kapali*) like the one that Dadu wore. He dons ochre clothes and is taught the *guru-mantra*, 'which he must not reveal' (Rose 1911: 216). The rite concludes with the distribution of sweets.

The Sikh Initiation and its Five Symbols

In my view, there can be little doubt that the anti-depilatory taboo (*kuraht*) of the Sikh initiation rite is to be understood as a specific inversion in structural terms of the custom of total depilation enjoined by the Jogi, Sannyasi, etc. initiations. The element of symbolic inversion, as I see it, is in fact much more pervasive, but it has been entirely overlooked before owing to the prevalence, among students of religions, of the scholarly method of endlessly adducing parallels and similarities to the neglect of significant relations of contrast, counterpoint, inversion and apposition.[5] In contradistinction to the Jogi and Sannyasi ritual of nakedness or smearing with ashes, the Sikh neophyte is made to come tidily clothed to the ceremony. The ear-rings affected by the Jogis are specifically forbidden to him (Teja Singh 1938: 113). Instead of requiring the Sannyasi's resolve, 'I am no one's, and no one is mine', the Sikh rite, emphasizing a new birth, requires the neophyte to reply in answer to questions that his father is Guru

[4] See Rose 1911: 215, where it is said that other accounts make Dadu contemporary with Dara Shikoh, and still others with Guru Gobind Singh. The Gur Bilas gives an interesting story about Guru Gobind Singh's meeting with a Dadupanthi (see Banerjee 1962: 94–5).

[5] This neglect is apparent, for example, in van Gennep (1960: 97). The same method is followed by Kapur Singh (1959), chs. 5 and 7.

Gobind Singh and his mother Mata Sahib Kaur, and that he was born in Kesgarh and lives in Anandpur. Even more significantly perhaps the initiator, instead of being the individual *guru*, is a collective group, the Five Loved Ones or the Five Lovers, composed of any five good Sikhs. Instead of the *guru-mantra* being communicated secretly to the neophyte, as with the Sannyasis, Jogis and Dadupanthis, the Sikh Gurus' word is spoken loud and clear by the initiators. Finally, in contrast to the Jogi vow never to touch weapons, the Sikh neophyte is invested ritually with the *kirpan* (sword) as one of the five *k*'s which he must always wear thereafter.

I think we may safely say that the Sikh initiation rite contains a marked theme of inversion in relation to the rites of social renunciation established by the medieval mendicant orders that preceded Sikhism. Like them, Sikhism was instituted as a religious brotherhood open to all who sought salvation, but its spiritual and social aims were in direct contrast to what theirs had been. Whereas they had sought to obtain emancipation and deliverance through individual renunciation, as their rites signify, of what amounted to social death, the Sikh community was called to affirm the normal social world as itself the battleground of freedom. That is why, in my opinion, its initiation rite makes the positive theme of investiture prevail wholly over the negative theme of divestiture, and taking certain widely established customs of renunciation, emphatically inverts them. The meaning of being unshorn, in particular, is thus constituted by the 'negation of the negation': it signifies the permanent renunciation of renunciation.

This hypothesis, however, is not yet complete; it requires a further consideration regarding all the five *k*'s. We have so far concentrated our attention on the initiation rite itself and attempted to understand the meaning of *kes* in that context, but the five symbols of Sikhism are worn for life. Now, following initiation, the Sannyasi custom is to either wear all their hair or shave it all. The *jatadhari* Jogis follow the former course—though among all Jogis the signification of renunciation seems to be borne primarily by their pierced ears and ear-rings. The important order of Bairagis also keep long hair (Rose 1911: 36), whereas the Uttradhi Dadupanthis shave the head, beard and moustache (ibid.: 216). The Rasul Shahis, a Muslim order founded in the eighteenth century, also shave completely the head, moustaches and eyebrows (ibid.: 1914: 324). In all such instances where long hair is worn, it is worn as matted hair (*jata*), frequently dressed in ashes. According to Sikh custom, on the other hand, unshorn hair (*kes*) is invariably associated with the comb (*kanga*, the second of the five *k*'s), which performs the function of constraining the hair and imparting an orderly arrangement to it. This meaning is made even clearer by the custom of the Sikh turban, enclosing both the *kes* and the *kanga*. The *kes* and the *kanga* thus form a unitary pair of symbols, each evoking the meaning of the other, and their mutual association explains the full meaning of *kes* as distinct from *jata*. The *jata*, like the shaven head and pierced ears, symbolizes the renunciation of social citizenship; the *kes* and *kanga* symbolize its orderly assumption.

The *kirpan* (sword) and the *kara* (steel bracelet) similarly constitute another pair of symbols, neither of which can be properly understood in isolation. Without going into the evidence, I merely state that in my view the bracelet imparts the same orderly control over the sword that the comb does over the hair. The medieval ascetic order of the Kara Lingis indeed wore on a chain a similar ring over the naked penis. The *kirpan*, in its conjoint meaning with the *kara*, is a sword ritually constrained and thus made into the mark of every citizen's honour, not only of the soldier's vocation. Finally, the *kachh*, a loin and thigh garment, the last of the five *k*'s is also to be understood as an agent of constraint, like the comb and the bracelet, though the subject of its control is not stated. This unstated term, I think, can only be the uncircumcised male member. The *kachh* constitutes a unitary pair of meanings with it, signifying manly reserve in commitment to the procreative world as against renouncing it altogether.

In case it might be objected that I am merely profaning the mystery in advancing the last hypothesis, I hasten to quote Guru Gobind Singh himself on the subject:

> Ajmer Chand inquired what the marks of the Guru's Sikhs were, that is, how they could be recognized. The guru replied, 'My Sikhs shall be in their natural form, that is, without the loss of their hair or foreskin, in opposition to ordinances of the Hindus and the Muhammadans' (Macauliffe 1909: V, 99).

We can now formulate the proposition that the primary meaning of the five symbols, when they are taken together, lies in the ritual conjunction of two opposed forces or aspects. The unshorn hair, the sword and the implicit uncircumcised male organ express the first aspect. They are assertive of forceful human potentialities that are of themselves amoral, even dangerous, powers. The comb, the steel bracelet and the loin and thigh breeches express the second aspect, that of moral constraint and discrimination. The combination of the two aspects is elaborated in the form of three pairs of polar opposites (*kanga*/*kes*: *kara*/*kirpan*: *kachh*/uncircumcised member), thus generating, with one term left unstated, the five Sikh symbols. The aspect of assertion and the aspect of constraint combine to produce what we may call for want of a better word the spirit of *affirmation*, characteristic of Sikhism.

Sikhism and Hinduism

So much then for the structural explanation of cultural meanings, the logic of symbols. We must now turn, although very briefly and simply, to the second level of analysis required by our method, and consider the wider social context of Sikhism's origin and growth. I do not here give all the evidence or make every qualification but state the problem in broad and general terms as follows. The Hindu system of social relations called caste, using that term to include *varna* as well as *jati*, is in fact only the half of Hinduism. The whole Hindu *dharma* is better described by the term *varn-ashramdharma*, that is, caste as well as the institution of the four stages, statuses or roles of individual life (*ashramas*). If sociologists have hitherto concentrated on the institution of caste to the exclusion of the latter institution, I cannot claim to understand their reasons. For the social system of caste was always surrounded in reality by a penumbral region, as it were, of non-caste, where flourished the renunciatory religious orders whose principles abrogated those of caste and birth; and the fourth *ashrama* (*sannyas*) constituted a door through which the individual was recommended to pass from the world of caste to that of its denial. The mutual relation of the two worlds, and I have no doubt that it was mutual, is of the greatest significance to a full understanding of either of them.[6]

The hierarchical system of local caste groups, predetermined by birth, on the one hand, and the contrasted system of voluntaristic cult associations or orders and sects, on the other hand, cut across one another, forming the essential warp and woof of Hinduism.

[6] Caste (and particularly the position of Brahmins) was stated by Max Weber to be "the fundamental institution of Hinduism" (see Gerth and Mills 1948: 396). This purely one-sided view is especially curious in the German sociologist since he was the first to make use (in 1916) of the "partly excellent scientific Census Reports" (Ibid.: 397) which also form the basis of Rose (1911 and 1914) and of the present paper.

The third structural feature, territorial kingship, necessary to uphold *varnashramdharma*, possessed its own relations with the two contrasting worlds of the Brahmin and the Sannyasi. Thus the total ideological and social structure of the medieval Hindu world, including its political institutions, rested upon a tripartite division and a system of interrelations among the three worlds symbolized by the King, the Brahmin and the Sannyasi. The domains or roles of (1) the rulers, the world of *rajya*, (2) the caste system, *varna* or *grihasta*, and (3) the orders of renunciation or *sannyas*, formed the three sides of the medieval triangle. Moreover, the same total underlying structure can perhaps be seen in the Islamic culture of the period in the division and interrelations among the three respective spheres of *hukumat* (the state power), *shar'iat* (the social order) and *tariqat* or *haqiqat* (the Sufi sect as a way of salvation). These are all sociological problems for future investigation, when broken down into suitable units for study.

An order like the Aghor-panthi Jogis, who appear to have smeared themselves with excrement, drunk out of a human skull and occasionally dug up the body of a newly-buried child to eat it, 'thus carrying out the principle that nothing is common or unclean to its extreme logical conclusion' (Rose 1911: 404), evidently constituted the truly living shadow of caste orthodoxy. The theme of antinomian protest could hardly be carried further (unless it was by the Bam-margis who added sexual promiscuity to the list!). Yet it could be reliably said of other Jogi sub-orders that 'in the Simla hills the Jogis were originally mendicants, but have now became householders', and that the secular Jogis, called Sanyogis, 'in parts of the Punjab form a true caste' (ibid.: 399n., 409). We can resolve this seeming contradiction only if we regard both these Jogi conditions as forming the different stages or phases of a single cycle of development. According to this view, we should say that any particular order or sub-order that once renounced caste with all its social rights and duties and walked out into the ascetic wilderness through the front door of *sannyas*, could later become disheartened or lose the point of its protest, and even end by seeking to re-enter the house of caste through the back door.

Of course, as a particular order or section fell back, so to speak, from the frontier of asceticism and abandoned its non-procreative, propertyless and occupationless existence, its function with the total system of *varnashramdharma* would be fulfilled by some other order or section, since the ascetic or protestant impluse itself remained a constant feature. During its ascetic period, an order or sub-order may occupy one or the other of two positions, or pass through both of them successively. It may either adopt a theory and practice completely opposed to those of caste, like the Aghor-panthis and Bam-margis, and be for that reason regarded as heterodox and esoteric; or it might remain within the pale and link itself to the caste system through the normal sectarian affiliations of caste people. A 'heterodox', left-handed or antinomian sect, we should say, is one opposed to caste as its living shadow; an 'orthodox' or right-handed sect is complementary to the caste system, its other half within Hinduism.

I would not say that all historically-known orders of renunciation in fact passed through these various stages of development, but I maintain that we must construct some such analytical scheme of their typical life-history with reference primarily to their origin, function and direction of movement in relation to the caste system. For that would enable us to classify the vast number of known orders and sub-orders into a limited number of sociological types, and obviate many difficulties in our study of them. In particular, until we can fully understand the development cycle of medieval mendicant orders we cannot place the political phenomena of the 'fighting Jogis' of the sixteenth and seventeenth centuries, the long contemporaneous militant struggles of the Islamic Roshaniya sect,[7] the Satnami Revolt of 1675, or the plunder of Dacca in 1763 by Sannyasis, etc., in their proper structural perspective. The analytical paradigm proposed must account under one and the same theory for cases or phases of political quietism as well as of political activism and conflict.

As a social movement early Sikhism no doubt possessed many features in common with other religious brotherhoods of a certain type. If Sikhism as a whole nevertheless broke free from the convoluted cycle of caste versus non-caste that overtook other protestant or antinomian brotherhoods, to what cause or causes did it owe its freedom? It is true that Sikhism, as we noted earlier, barred the door of asceticism and so did not lose itself in the esoteric wilderness, but we have also to explain why it did not duly return, as so many others did, to the citadel of caste. The new departure of Sikhism, in my structural interpretation, was that it set out to annihilate the categorical partitions, intellectual and social, of the medieval

[7] Founded by Bayazid, Pir-i Roshan, b. Jullundur, 1525.

world. It rejected the opposition of the common citizen or householder versus the renouncer, and of the ruler versus these two, refusing to acknowledge them as separate and distinct modes of existence. It acknowledged the powers of the three spheres of *rajya, sannyas,* and *grihasta,* but sought to invest their virtues conjointly in a single body of faith and conduct.

The social function of the Sikh initiation rite is, I think, precisely this: to affirm the characteristic rights and responsibilities of the three spheres as equally valid and to invest them as an undivided unit in the neophyte. The new Sikh, therefore, takes no Jogi vow to renounce his procreative power and never marry; instead he dons the *kachh* of continence. Instead of vowing like the Jogi never to touch weapons or take other employment or engage in trade, every social occupation is henceforth open to him, including that of soldiering, householdership or political command, and save only that of renouncing productive labour and taking alms. The single key of the 'renunciation of renunciation' was thus charged to unlock all dividing doors in the mansion of medievalism. Whether it succeeded in doing so, and to what extent, is another matter.

The structural method of analysis and interpretation, of which I have attempted to provide an example, shows that we can establish a definite connection between the five symbols of Sikhism and its whole nature as a religion. If my previous pairing of symbols and the assumption of an unstated term be accepted, then the five symbols of Sikhism may be said to signify, in their respective pairs, the virtues and the roles of *sannyas yoga (kes* and *kanga), grihasta yoga* (*kachh* and the uncircumcised state), and *rajya yoga* (*kirpan* and *kara*). As the authenticating sign and seal of Sikhism, the five *k*'s together affirm the unity of man's estate as being all of a piece: this we may take to be the final meaning and function of remaining forever unshorn in the world. Our analysis would also lead to the conclusion that the total human emancipation of religious man, and not merely any ideal of a synthesis or reconciliation of Hinduism and Islam, was the faith and endeavour of Sikhism from its inception. The institutionalization of that faith and endeavour surely marked the opening of the modern period of history in the Punjab.

Further Readings

Ghurye, G. S.,
1953 *Indian Sadhus*, Popular Book Depot, Bombay.

This classic work presents a historical-sociological account of asceticism in India and of several monastic orders and sects. It discusses the development of 'sadhuism' from individual asceticism into a socio-religious institution.

McLeod, W. H.,
1989 *Who is a Sikh? The Problem of Sikh Identity*, Clarendon Press, Oxford.

The book traces the history of Sikh identity, highlighting the interplay of religious and political factors and of 'objective' or documented history and tradition.

Schomer, Karine and W. H. McLeod, eds.,
1987 *The Sants: Studies in a Devotional Tradition of India*, Motilal Banarsidass, Delhi.

A valuable collection of papers, written from several perspectives, it discusses the beliefs, practices, and the impact of the 'Sant' tradition in north and western India. The book includes papers on various religious communities and sects including the Kabir Panthis, Sikhs and Sufis.

van der Veer, Peter,
1988 *Gods on Earth: The Management of Religious Experience and Identity in a North Indian Pilgrimage Centre*, Oxford University Press, Delhi.

A study of Ayodhya, sacred city and pilgrim centre, in a historical setting, this book includes detailed discussions of the Brahman priests (*pandas*) who serve the pilgrims and of the monks of the devotional-ascetic Ramanandi order.

V

Reorientations to the Sacred

The eighteenth century saw the flowering of the Enlightenment—the so-called Age of Reason—in Europe. Religious notions such as 'revelation,' and 'redemption' were questioned and even completely rejected by many. The world mankind lived in was regarded as good and worthwhile and man was considered not only capable of **but also obliged to, as Kant put it, daring to know it, and shape** his own present and future in it.

Secularization as the process which brings more and ever more areas of human life under human control, and loosens the grip of religious beliefs and institutions on mankind, has now proceeded apace for over three centuries. The total displacement of religion has not, however, occurred anywhere, not even in countries such as modern Turkey where the authority and power of the state were employed to secularize public life. Church bells ring again at Christmas in Moscow and Beijing.

The twentieth century has seen many instances of the reassertion of the place of religion in human affairs. This has taken many forms, including restatements of religious traditions in the light of contemporary constraints and possibilities, or an alleged return to traditional doctrines and practices in the garb of religious fundamentalism. Such developments, particularly in the recent past, have led many people to call for a re-examination of the concept of secularism in the West itself, but more so in other parts of the world where religious traditions other than Christianity have been dominant.

The fifth and final part of this book explores the aforementioned themes. The first reading is intended as a backdrop for those that follow it. It explores the complex character of religious communalism in India. Communalism has been defined as an ideology which envisages the religious community as a political group commited to the protection and promotion of its social and economic interests and cultural values. It is thus a substitute for nationalism. The territory occupied (or sought to be occupied) by the group is seen as 'holy land', or 'the land of the pure', which is what the words *pākistān* and *khālistān* mean. As has been pointed out by Louis Dumont, 'the religious element that enters into the composition of communalism seems to be but the shadow of religion, i.e. religion taken not as the essence and guide of life in all spheres, but only as a sign of the distinction of one human, at least virtually political, group against others' (1970b; 90–1). Attempts to explain the emergence of communalism in South Asia have tended to over stress the role of colonialism ('divide and rule') or of the conflict of class interests. Satish Saberwal's essay on the elements of communalism argues for a more comprehensive approach.

Communalism is not a characteristic only of interreligious community relations but may also arise within such a community, emphasizing the distinctiveness of a particular sub-group. The second reading is a discussion of the transitional strategies of contemporary Untouchables in the city of Lucknow (in north India) to carve out for themselves a place of honour in society without completely breaking away from the available religious traditions. Indeed, they draw upon the Hindu, Buddhist and social reformist traditions in attempting to improve their social status. These resources are supplemented by an appeal to their civic rights and duties as citizens in a modern state. Their approach is adaptive and eclectic and the key cultural performer in this situation is the 'ascetic' who is generally honoured by all Hindu castes. The Untouchable Chamars are thus not only changing themselves but also the other Hindus and, indeed, the 'detached' ascetic too is transformed into a 'worldly' ascetic. A whole series of reorientations are shown by R. S. Khare to be under way.

Lionel Caplan's essay highlights religious 'fundamentalism' as a mode of reorientation, as 'counterculture'. His data are drawn from Protestant Christians of South India, particularly those living in Madras. Like Christian fundamentalists elsewhere, the fundamentalist sects here emphasize the centrality of the Bible in the life of the Protestant as also the value of piety and prayer. They set themselves up in opposition to 'modernism'. Reaffirmation of true Christian faith hinges for them on the acceptance of miracles, on the healing power of the 'word of god'. All this has inevitably resulted in the emergence of charismatic prophets and the organization of 'crusades', and threatens to undermine traditional eccelesiastical structures. Fundamentalism as a form of resistance to not only modernity but also conventional religious world views is both unifying and divisive. While it draws like-minded people together into a tightly-knit but narrow circle, it also distinguishes them sharply from others, including their coreligionists, who do not share their fundamentalist convictions. This tension is well illustrated in Caplan's essay.

Religious fundamentalism in recent times has been associated with violence and terrorism in many parts of the world including India. In fact, it may well be argued that fundamentalism will always entail some form of coercion if not also violence. Mark Juergensmeyer, author of the third essay, poses the question of why violence needs religion and goes on to suggest that, basically, no religion depends upon violence as its primary mode of appeal. Religious traditions such as Hinduism and Sikhism entertain the notion of 'righteous war' for the eradication of evil and evil-doers. The followers of Islam have not hesitated to use the sword in their struggle (*jihad*) to spread the faith. And yet even these religions express abhorrence of violence, although not in the same measure as Jainism and Buddhism, and extol peace and non-killing as the general moral order.

Juergensmeyer argues that violence is generated by the conflict of political and economic interests. It is not religious traditions as such which generate violence but the politically organized followers of religions who do so. They use (misuse) religion to sacralize non-religious concerns. A favoured means of doing so turns out to be the equation of mundane conflicts with cosmo-moral struggles. By fighting other people, it is argued, one is actually fighting evil. Acts of violence are thus elevated to the plane of moral virtue and a cosmic meaning is bestowed on them.

The concluding essay raises the question as to whether the notion of secularism, which was the product of the dialectic of religion (Christianity) and science in Europe, may be readily transferred to other places and incorporated in other cultural traditions. Drawing upon the experience of India during the last forty-odd years with the establishment of a secular state, the essay highlights the obstacles that this endeavour has encountered. It draws attention to the dangers of 'dogmatic' secularism, which is like religious faith itself. If fundamentalism is a perversion of religious faith, secularism may well be described as its subversion. It is thus that secularism may be, ironically, seen to provide unintended and indirect support to fundamentalists. The critical question that then emerges is whether religion itself may provide us with an answer to the excesses and violence of fundamentalism? This is not an idle question to ask in a country like India where followers of all the major religious traditions of mankind have lived for millennia.

Elements of Communalism

SATISH SABERWAL

Hindus and Muslims have to be seen at several levels, ranging from a village to a ruling class. Such a phenomenon cannot be unitary or homogeneous, yet it might be possible to analyse any of its specific expressions over common conceptual ground, provided its categories have strategic fit. Here, as elsewhere, it is useful to consider the framework of *interests* separately from, as well as in relation to, the realm of *ideas*, which appear in this case as religious *traditions*.

Both these realms, of interests and of ideas and traditions, are of course part of every social situation; and each has its own distinctive logic—of meaning, of coerciveness, and of the resources available for renewal; yet their separation is an analytic artifact. On the ground, all these usually constitute unseparated experience. In that experience, the religious traditions are transmitted and renewed in processes, social and cultural, which are both conscious and unconscious; and the latter is especially important for such societies (and persons) as do not habitually bring their own unconscious to the inquiring gaze of consciousness.

Framework of Interest

Let us begin with the central Marxian recognition of the sociological reality—call it coerciveness—of the context in which human beings labour and of the mechanisms whereby the product of their labour is appropriated. For reasons that will become clear, however, we have to keep in mind not merely the work situation, agrarian or industrial, but the broader question of access to a mode of making a living, and of the defence of one's hold on that living; and for these

Excerpted from Satish Saberwal, 'Elements of Communalism', in *India: The Roots of Crisis*, Oxford University Press, Delhi, 1986, pp. 58–78.

one uses certain relationships which may thereby separate one's social universe into allies and adversaries and neutrals. This separation may be done in terms other than those of material interests alone. . . .

Interests may come to be defined in several ways. During the early twentieth century, the cultivators in certain parts of Malabar and in eastern Bengal were Muslim, their landlords Hindu; and the conflict of *class* interests between them tended, or could be made, to look like communal conflict. (On Malabar: Dhanagare 1977, Panikkar 1979; on Bengal: R. Mukherjee 1973, Sarkar 1973: 443 *et al.*) In certain parts of late nineteenth-century Punjab, differences of economic interests tended to coincide with differences of caste and also sometimes of religion (van den Dungen 1972). More generally for the nineteenth century, P. C. Joshi (1980: 172–5) speaks of Muslim landowners steadily losing out to Hindu merchants and moneylenders; and this interface was not unknown during the medieval period. Situations of this kind express variously the common historical tendency in India for occupation to correspond with caste or ethnicity, with the proviso that in any particular case the link could have begun from the end either of occupation or of ethnicity. That is to say, *either* persons entering a particular occupation may constitute themselves into a caste—as in the historic cases of Rajputs and Kayasthas—*or* persons of a particular caste may move into the same occupation, as in a Punjabi town during the 1960s—the erstwhile leather-workers moving into lathework (Saberwal 1976: Ch. 5).

Change of religion has usually been not an individual but a collective matter, tending to associate caste with religion in any locality. Consequently, the internal social cement for occupational groups in adversary economic relations often consists indistinguishably of caste and religious ties. Where the two identities, say of Hindus and Muslims, are separated by the coincident boundaries of occupation, caste, and religion, the religious symbols may come to the fore by virtue merely of their mobilizational potential; but, as in the Moplah conflicts, men of religion may also be catalytic, or more active, in channelling what may otherwise seem to be 'purely' class interests.

Communal identities may however be implicated not only in *class* conflict but also in what, for want of an established term, may be called the *competitive* conflict of interests within a 'class'. It arises over access to a given array of opportunities. . . . Bipan Chandra sees the competition for government jobs in the late 1800s as pivotal to the later emergence of communalism in colonial politics. The boundary seen to be activated here is the religious one (and similar anxiety is reported for the late 1500s and early 1600s among certain elements of the Mughal nobility). However, to attribute this to 'false consciousness' (Bipan Chandra 1984: 18–22 and *passim*) seems to me to be an evaluation, not an explanation. A search for explanation merely turns the attribution into a further question: namely, what were the historical antecedents that made the 'false consciousness' emerge along this particular boundary much more than along others associated with such criteria as caste, region, rural/urban differences and so forth?

Religious Traditions

Religious identities . . . tend to get implicated in conflicts of interest, whether of the class or the competitive sorts; but why should religion be implicated in identities at all, and why should these identities engage each other so often in antagonistic terms? . . .

I see religion in the following pages as part of culture, viewed anthropologically. While a religious tradition can be integrative, of a social group as well as of the individual psyche, its symbolic order sometimes persuades its believers in various ways to set themselves apart from the followers of other traditions, laying the basis for communal identities. The transmission of religious traditions is associated with religious experience which is commonly not verbalized or even conscious. And where the religious identities have come to adversary arrays, their antagonisms are stored in the unconscious, in addition to their presence in individual consciousness and enactment in more or less public settings. The run of my analysis will thus force me to point towards the importance of the unconscious, however distant the latter be from my limited competence.

Culture and Religion

Culture here refers to the totality of more or less changing conceptions concerning nature and society, self and others, past, present and future, which any functioning human group possesses, renews, and lives by. All cultural conceptions are ultimately man-made but most are inherited from one's own or others' ancestors, substantially organized into complexes of ideas and social relations; except in acutely disrupted societies, these complexes of ideas and relationships are received by the next generation carrying the marks of 'transcendental law-like necessity'. . . . Much of the scepticism of our time is itself a cultural complex of ideas and relationships.

The human perception of whatever is observed is almost invariably mediated by culturally given conceptions. What is culturally organized may be deliberately so by consciously acting human beings, resorting to culturally derived preferences and routines; but central to the modern understanding of society is the recognition that a great deal of this organization at any time may in fact be *un*conscious. Cultural conceptions are subject to continuous patterning and selecting, part of an often unconscious process of cultural integration.

The principles underlying the integration of culture are too varied to be considered here; I need only make a few simple points. Modern societies organize road traffic, *inter alia*, by specifying the side that the traffic should keep, but these rules are neutral to the travellers' states of ritual purity.[1] The Hindu tradition employed ideas of ritual purity and pollution to organize a great deal of the social traffic, but it tended to be neutral to a vast range of social observances, leaving the caste group largely free to manage its own affairs. Islam came to stress the importance of the *sunnah*, the beaten path of Islamic tradition, and expected its observance by every Muslim, by the entire *umma*, the entire community; but there is no Islamic law for organizing road traffic. Through time and cumulative experience a culture comes to be centred upon certain key ideas which have served recurrently in meeting a wide range of contingencies; these key ideas together may be said to constitute a culture's integrative core.

Until the secularist growth of the last two or three centuries, this integrative core in complex premodern societies invariably claimed transcendental origins, and the sanctions behind this core were widely believed to have transcendental legitimacy. Modern historiography is beginning to show that, at the time of the initial promulgation, the early ideas of some of the great religious traditions arose in sharp intuitive insight into the prophet's own social milieu, showing for example how to re-order the framework of social relations so as to accommodate the changing structures of

[1] My choice of traffic rules to illustrate the cultural integration of modern societies is deliberate. It is characteristic of 'rationality' in these societies to devise rather simple rules to regulate various sorts of dense traffic—on rails, on radio waves, in the mails, in the air, and so forth.

interests more adequately.[2] In the prevailing struggle between competing sets of ideas, the evidence of a prophet's extraordinary experiences, possibly of the supernatural, would give his message an edge, sometimes decisively.

Later generations would amplify and systematize the prophet's message, but certain core symbols would run through and recognizably unify the inevitably vast diversities of the community of believers. Thus in Islam we have the Prophet as the Messenger of God; his sayings and actions as the roots of Islamic law; the sacred core in the Meccan shrines; the unity of the *umma*, the religious community, guided by the *ulema*, the religious scholars. When, say, the Haj brought together Muslims from Djakarta and Rabat, or from Calicut and Agra, they would recognize in each other a certain sharing of religious sensibilities, a bond that made them brothers in faith. This bond would be sensed by their neighbours at home, too, who only heard about the pilgrimage, and could not themselves make it.

This bond, we have to concede, is *not* commonly subjected to empirical judgements as to whether or not the mutual commonalities outweigh the mutual differences. It arises, rather, in faith, in the implicit acceptance of the symbolic order, which acts much of the time at more or less unconscious levels of experience: such elements as purity and pollution, the sanctity of the cow or the power of the Mother, the importance of conserving one's semen . . . these elements are suffused through and are expressed in numerous seemingly unconnected areas of belief and experience. Each element in the symbolic order acquires its meaning within a psychological universe, which is also an experienced universe; and this meaning is created by the ceremonial, by recurrent experiences, and by its confirmation by others during and outside these ceremonies and experiences. In a phrase, this experienced universe is also a moral order. Its meanings are not available immediately outside such a universe; but for the believer these are often critical in intra-psychic integration, and their effectiveness is the greater for their being unconscious.

Religion and Communal Identity

In premodern societies the sense of community fostered in the religious traditions would give direction to much of the prevailing life-style. Imprinted on the child's mind is the sanctity of worship, its place, words, gestures, sounds, smells, and personnel. Religious

[2] For the rise of Islam, see Rodinson (1971). For Buddha, likewise, D. D. Kosambi (1965: 104–13).

acts and functionaries attend many of the critical episodes in life: birth, illness, marriage, death. There are dietary injunctions: be a vegetarian, eat only *halal* meat, beef may or may not be prohibited. Key complexes of religious belief, with their organizing symbols, are thus implanted during the *pre*-reflective years of childhood, when one has little option but to accept one's elders' ideas without question. It would not have happened equally for everyone; but it did happen in enough families to set the temper in their social group. To one born into and surrounded by a faith, its *shared* experiences, meanings, and gestures have the taken-for-granted quality which underlies social ease; and therefore nearly all marriages would have been made within the faith. It would have also been an important basis for *separation* from the followers of another faith—in worship, in religious education, in residence—within the local community and, when the need arose, for a set of potential supra-local links for those who reached out.

A religious tradition, put otherwise, is or used to be like a compass, helping one chart a course through life. It used to be a sanctified manual, listing the do's and dont's for coping with the universe. Members of a multireligious society, however, would work with different manuals, listing divergent codes for life. Where people lived by different manuals, one way to anticipate the other's behaviour, attitudes, and intentions would have been to reckon with the other's manual, the other's religion. Social unease could furthermore be obviated by signalling one's own manual, through various diacritical marks: clothing, hairstyle, facial marks, perhaps one's language and manners. Religiously rooted social identities would thus be established and be mutually acknowledged.

Awareness of the socio-religious identities, then, would help one constitute useful social maps in one's mind, demarcating the social territory into sacred, friendly, neutral, hostile, etc. These social maps are sometimes expressed in, and validated by, myths and legends. Marc Gaborieau (1972: 92f) reports the transformation of a seventh-century event in central Iraq into a religious myth in the hills of Nepal:

> . . . in the central hills, the martyrs Hasan and Husain are venerated during the ten first days of the lunar month of *Muharram*; further west the fair of Ghazi Miyan is held in the beginning of the solar month *of Jesth*. . . . In actual history, Hasan and Husain were killed by Muslims, Ghazi Miyan by Hindus; but in the mind of the hill Muslims, the two legends blend curiously, and the story of the former is shaped on the same pattern as that of the latter: it runs briefly as follows.

The heroes are Muslims: their marriage is going to take place and the rejoicing has begun to the sound of auspicious music. Suddenly there is news that the enemies, who are Hindus, are coming to attack; the auspicious music is changed into a martial music and the heroes, mounting their horses, rush to fight the enemies. They are finally killed and the story ends in lamentation and the funeral music.

. . . During *Muharram* and Ghazi Miyan fair [they] can express successively joy in evoking the marriage, aggression when they commemorate the battle in a sham fight, finally grief when they sing lamentations, for this legend tells of the greatest sorrow: death on the day of marriage. And one should emphasize that the main theme of those festivities, where Muslims express themselves without restraint, is an irreducible enmity between Hindus and Muslims.*

A traditional account undergoes transformation in the course of meeting the conscious and unconscious needs of those who recite it and thus comes to reflect the social maps of their universe. A traditional recital defining a group as hostile thus renews its status as an adversary, and such definitions persist when the corresponding expectations are confirmed episodically in experience.

These social maps remain much in use even when the latter-day secular understandings of nature and society, of life and death, and of one's inner world make one sceptical of the received religious manual and its transcendental aura.

Religious Traditions and the Unconscious

Religious grounding used to be, and often continues to be, important for identities which constitute the social maps for regulating *public* social relations; and it so happens that similarly grounded devices also provide the means for coping with and for organizing the *inner* worlds.[3] I proceed now to sketch the connections in the latter direction.

While the exigencies of life are infinitely variable, some of the key themes in any society arise as its cultural resources and constraints are used for canalizing instinctual impulses—including those of sexuality—and for coping with the trauma left over from childhood. The enormous importance of these devices for the individual psyche is being attested by the slowly growing psychoanalytic work on Indian cultural materials (Kakar 1978). These historically

* *See the essay on* Muharram *in this volume.* Editor.

[3] There is also the tiny minority able to live largely by the modern, secular understanding of these matters.

created devices—austerities, devotions, pilgrimages—are options available *within* a tradition; and just as many of the traumas and instinctual difficulties arise in the ongoing functions and malfunctions of society, so too their bearers take to these devices selectively, recurrently. The point to note here is that a great many of these devices for creating order within one's private self appear to be embedded intimately in the meanings and symbols associated *contrastively* with the several religious traditions. These core psychological and cultural devices also would sustain the social separation.

The use of communal identities by the unconscious at another level was called to my attention by Sudhir Kakar, the psychoanalyst, drawing upon his own fieldwork at Balaji's temple, off Bharatpur in Rajasthan. From various parts of North India—Bihar, Punjab, Rajasthan and elsewhere—persons with mental disturbance, usually considered to be possessed by a spirit, a *bhuta*, come to the temple for its curative rituals. During these rituals, the spirit, 'speaking' through the patient, is persuaded to reveal its own identity and attributes. In the culture surrounding the temple, 'Muslim *bhutas* are considered to be the strongest and the most malignant of evil spirits, indicating perhaps the psychological depths of the antipathy between Hindus and Muslims' (Kakar 1982: 63). In the categories of this social context, the Muslim belongs with the untouchable:

> *bhangiwara* . . . specializes in dealing with the Muslim *bhuta* and [spirits from] the untouchable castes. When a parent comes out of the *bhangiwara* enclosure after having exorcised one of these *bhutas*, it is imperative that he take a ritual bath to rid himself of the pollution. Otherwise it is held that if the patient touches someone else after his *bhangiwara* sojourn, it is almost certain that his *bhuta* will be transferred to the other person (1982: 60).

Translating the healing, exorcising routines at the temple into modern psychotherapeutic terms, Kakar sees these as strengthening

> attempts to transform the patient's belief into a conviction that his bad traits and impulses are not within but without; that they are not his own but belong to the *bhūta*. The fact that fifteen out of twenty-eight patients were possessed by a Muslim spirit indicates the extent of this projection in the sense that the Muslim seems to be *the* symbolic representation of the alien in the Hindu unconscious. Possession by a Muslim *bhuta* reflects the patient's desperate efforts to convince himself and others that his hungers for forbidden foods, tumultuous sexuality, and uncontrollable rage belong to the Muslim destroyer of taboos and are farthest away from his 'good' Hindu self (1982: 87).

Interpreting the unconscious is a highly specialized field, one for which I have no credentials; yet nearly a century after Freud the sociologist must willy-nilly come to terms with this domain. He has to reckon with the interconnectendness of the social, the conscious, and the unconscious; and this applies to the phenomenon of communal separativeness too. The analysis continues with the social organization of religious traditions and communal identities.

Social Organization of Tradition

It is not merely beliefs and symbols and myths but also . . . social organization that makes a tradition: religious specialists, temples, traditional schools, ceremonies and recitations, sacred centres, networks, pilgrimages and the like. Important for us are the links between localities which arise in this social organization. In a world of small, often defensive communities, the religious specialist, itinerant or resident, with his literacy and wider connections and awareness of the sacred and sometimes secular literature, has been the man interpreting new situations, appealing to prior categories and symbols, and sometimes re-sacralizing hitherto dormant ones. My illustrations of these inter-local connections, actual and potential, come from the colonial period. Mushirul Hasan has reviewed how the *ulema* helped to get the Khilafat Movement going:

> They took the lead in voicing Muslim concern over Turkey and the Holy Places and, after 1918, they seized the initiative from the Muslim League leaders, thus unleashing forces of vast political consequence. Fired by religion and buoyed up by their romantic sympathy for the Turkish *Khalifa* they carried pan-Islamic ideology to town and countryside where in mosque and *maktab*, Muslim artisans, weavers, and peasants were susceptible to their religious exhortations. They used the Quran and the *Hadith* as powerful weapons to gain adherence of the faithful who accepted them as infallible. They also forged an alliance with Muslim professional men and utilized their experience in agitational politics to further the cause of Pan-Islamism (1979:307).

Or consider the late nineteenth-century campaigns in Lahore and Allahabad in support of reviving the Vedas, encouraging *shuddhi*, protecting the cow, and propagating Hindi (K. Jones 1976: Bayly 1975). Meanings and symbols—Quran and *Hadith*, Vedas and the cow—emotionally charged and exclusively bounded. Such potent, symbolic elements lie across the psychic, the social, and the cultural, and, for many, at the core of social identities and religious traditions. We have noted earlier that these traditions are maintained and renewed in complexes of specialists, institutions, pilgrimages, literature, and so forth. These socio-religious webs have vast inter-local spreads, but few inter-connections *across* the religious boundaries. Altogether, these tend to be separative.

The Rise of Communalism

Let us take stock of the argument. I have outlined the experiential bases of religious belief and identity, the use of religious identities to organize one's social space, the play of religiously embedded mechanisms in the run of one's inner life, and finally the separativeness of the inter-local networks within what have been called the Great Traditions of the historic civilizations. In settings where the religious symbolic order pervades the daily round, there would seem to be a widespread tendency for religious traditions to try to insulate these symbolic orders from each other by way of both residential separation and careful social routines. This tendency would be expressed categorically at the core of religious experiences and activities and more or less ambiguously in the more secular pursuits.

I move now to the milieu of the 1700s and the 1800s and consider the rise of communalism during this period, trying merely to indicate the major processes which appear to have fostered this growth.

I begin with everyday social relations. To the general tendency to religious separativeness, noted earlier, medieval India appears to have added the following:

1. The inter-cultural social distance between non-Indian immigrants and the natives, until time and circumstance combined to induce a measure of intimacy, at least in the ruling circles; and
2. The stigma of untouchability carried by the lower castes, whose conversion to Islam would scarcely remove that stigma, especially in their localities of origin. On the contrary, it seems that for Hindus both the general tendency to religious separativeness and the specific antagonisms, consequent to loss of power, came to be set in the idiom and the routines of this untouchability.

From the medieval encounter there seems to have been inherited a social separation, sometimes hardened into patterns of residence, commensality, dress, and other acts of daily living. Yet the village community or the small town had relatively stable populations, and the marks of separation would have been taken for granted in an easy, daily round of life, where the caste order accommodated other sorts of separation too. This situation prevailed until, as we shall see, the setting began to shift in the 1800s.

Secondly, it is important to remember that Hindus, in numbers which grew with time, had high places in the ranks of the later medieval nobility (Athar Ali 1968). In this political structure there were numerous relationships between Muslims and Hindus wherein the differences of their religious affiliations were in some measure set apart from the secular political and administrative tasks at hand. The sense of religious affiliation, which has commonly been central to the sense of one's identity, is ordinarily acquired during childhood, in the course of *primary* socialization, as we saw earlier. Affiliation in political, administrative, economic and similar contexts, in contrast, is ordinarily learned much later, during adolescence or adulthood in the course of *secondary* socialization. During the 1700s, the Mughal politico-administrative structure got dismantled, and its constitutive relationships tended to lapse; and in so far as these had previoulsy acted in counterpoint to the separative religious and social relationships, rooted in primary socialization, which continued relatively undisturbed, henceforth the separative relationships would come into play without this secondary set of moderating influences.

Thirdly . . . during the 1800s, *the social framework was beginning to grow in scale*. This process was embodied in part in the expanding metropolitan centres. In the older localities—villages and small towns—the social separation of various caste-like groups was cross-cut by the necessity for co-operation in agriculture, commerce, and so forth, and a corresponding involvement in mutual ceremonials (Aggarwal 1971: Ch. 9; Mines 1972: 102f); but migrants into the metropolitan centres have commonly travelled along the social corridors of kinship, caste, etc. (Timberg 1978: Sec. C). The metropolis of the 1800s and early 1900s appears to have been organized so that rather large areas were relatively homogeneous as to religious community. The prior sense of social separation carried by the migrants with them tended to be confirmed as they settled into these larger, relatively homogeneous areas.[4] This pattern of metropolitan residences is important not only for the consciousness of religious community fostered in them, but also for the long-run, fitful influence of metropolitan models and messages on the lesser communities over the next century and more.

[4] On Calcutta, Bose (1968); on Bombay, M. Kosambi (1980: 121–36). On Allahabad, a *much older* city, Bayly (1975: 39–46) suggests for the late 1800s a considerable admixture of Hindus and Muslims.

To sum up, I am suggesting that the rise of communalism during the colonial period should perhaps be seen in relation to the long-standing separativeness of religious networks, the acute social distance expressing a high level of social antagonism between Muslims and Hindus, the lapse of formerly functioning, integrative political and administrative ties, and the growth of communally homogeneous neighbourhoods in the new metropolitan centres.

It is in this historic context that we notice the conflicts of interests—class or competitive—which have in numerous localities often pitted, or been seen to have pitted, groups of different religious affiliations one against the other.[5] When, during the 1800s, with expanding scales of some social relations, the inter-local linkages of a *secular* sort began to expand vastly, this process built upon the pre-existing social matrices, realigning these for their resources and their influence in the changing milieu (Saberwal 1979). This process did not often violate the boundaries of exclusion which had been associated with the religious identities, and had been built into vast regions of the prevailing styles of life. In ever changing manifestations, it was this combination of interests with inherited, antagonistic, social separation which became the basis for the *social organization of communal identities*. This social organization includes such elements as educational institutions, social service organizations, political and quasi-political formations, journals, ceremonies, and so forth. Somewhat detached from religious belief, yet religiously rooted, these 'communal' identities gathered strength as the wider social and political arenas came into being.

With older restraints weakening, and newer linkages forming separately in an era of unprecedented economic shifts, what had once been relatively stable, largely local interfaces between Hindus and Muslims tended to become much wider and more active oppositions. Of this situation, the colonial regime was at times more than willing to take advantage (e.g. Sarkar 1973: 8–20).

[5] *Within* the social organization of a religious tradition or of a communal identity, too, there are interests to defend: those of the specialists in the organization, or of outsiders able to influence or control them, or, more likely, of both. In defence of these more limited interests too, the specialists may try, covertly if necessary, to mobilize the believers. It would be wholly wrong, however, to dismiss such organizations simply as groups of self-servers. It is characteristic of any enduring complex tradition, and of the associated identities, that these can generate individuals and groups committed to defending the integrity of the tradition, and of identity, regardless of personal cost: that is very much the stuff of martyrdom—a prolific source for fresh symbols!

The Radical and Protesting Ascetic

R. S. KHARE

The contemporary Untouchable ascetic pursues a varying mixture of Hindu monism (*advaita*), Buddhist 'vacuity', the later Hindu notions of 'public service' (*jana sévā*, where *janatā* is Janārdana, god), and the Indian reformist's notions of 'humanism' (*mānava dharma*). Such a range of ideas gives the Untouchable and his ascetic a large (and heterogeneous) cultural ground from which not only to manoeuver and rebut the resistance of the traditional caste Hindu but also to introduce himself to civil rights and social obligations obtainable under the Indian version of democracy. With independence, the Untouchable ascetic's ideological manipulations have become increasingly receptive to a social radicalism that questions the entire traditional socio-economic order and its practices.

This radical ascetic usually derives his strength from the close contact he keeps with a scattered but devoted group of followers. He may attract and influence the young and the old, and men as well as women, especially under the conditions of emotional strain and social distress. When a cluster of Chamar ascetics, for example, was systematically investigated for its social influence in the Baudhabagh [pseudonym] neighbourhood of Lucknow , a whole range of ascetic radicalism, from mild to militant, became evident.

A resident ascetic in the Baudhabagh neighbourhood was generally regarded as a veritable social crutch. He served either in the absence of, or to strengthen, a family elder, a locality leader, and a religious inspirer. A childless wife, a long-unemployed man, a

Excerpted from R. S. Khare, 'Transition II: The Radical and Protesting Ascetic', in *The Untouchable as Himself: Ideology, Identity and Pragmatism among the Lucknow Chamars*, Cambridge University Press, Cambridge, 1984, pp. 79–92.

troublesome or troubled youth, a maiden awaiting a suitable groom, the chronically sick, quarrelsome neighbours, a devout householder, and a person surrounded by miseries (*gardish mein parā ādmī*)—all usually sought, sooner or later, the advice and inspiration of this ascetic. He performed rites like a Brāhman to please gods and to produce charms, amulets, and 'blessed fruits' for the distressed. He was the healer of the mental as well as the bodily sores of the deprived. As a soothing and supportive advisor to the distressed, a spiritual staff for the aged and the dying, an astrologer for the one fallen on bad times, a stern master for erring and indolent disciples, and an activist reformer for locality leaders, the ascetic, despite his failure to bring about a total social revolution, served as a wide-ranging social linchpin for the Lucknow Chamar.

The Baudhabagh ascetics had acquired such multiple roles in a socially prominent manner. They had often replaced the Brahman priest. Usually, each ascetic had also developed at least one specialized role within the community and was known for it. The local Chamars had a clear idea of whom to approach for a specific problem, and what generally to expect from him in response. The ascetics were popularly rated as 'effective', 'ineffective', or 'indifferent' in relation to a specific issue or practical problem. For example, a resident Chamar would know who was best suited for family problems and who for the issue of social and political reform. Mismatching them was usually the sign of a person's social ignorance, and he was quickly offered the required information.

All the resident Baudhabagh ascetics had simultaneous contacts with several households, and all had cultivated a nucleus of specially favoured disciples, once these ascetics had performed a mélange of spiritual, religious, and reformist services for them. To a reformist ascetic, for example, a better-employed, activist youth was his spiritual heir. To a staunch Buddhist reformer, his ascetic-guru had taken the place of a Brāhman priest, an astrologer, and a tantrist (i.e. *tāntrika*). In all, there were four such cases in Baudhabagh. To the two local politicians, their spiritual guru was also their reformer-guru. Neither these leaders nor the ascetics found anything anomalous in this because the ascetics were expected to unite the contraries. If anybody, they should be able to do so most genuinely. Two ascetics told me that all of their efforts, whether it was their sudden reproach or praise, or commitment or withdrawal, or traditionalism or radicalism, were designed to reflect and respond to their disciples' conditions within Baudhabagh and outside.

Baudhabagh also had ascetic-like householders and householder-like ascetics. Both inspired and advised the common Chamar under social adversity, but in their own way. Anantananda (a pseudonym) had become an ascetic-like householder under the influence of his own guru. Though he regularly worked for his living, and worked harder than others in his neighbourhood, he practised renunciation in his daily life. He detached himself from his family, he claimed, though he lived in a small thatched cell outside his main dwelling. He read books in Hindi on yoga, spiritualism, and non-dualism (*advaitavāda*). He delivered discourses in the evening at least two times a month blending the concerns of spiritual and social awakening. In his view, if the second was impossible without the first, both were impossible without doing hard, disinterested work for the betterment of others (*niṣkāmakarma*) . . . he tried to eschew Brahmanic ritualism from within Hindu philosophy and spiritualism, and to replace it with Buddhist ideas.

Gyanananda (a pseudonym) was a householder-like ascetic. He realized by his late fifties that, though an ordained ascetic, his mission lay in selfless social service to his own deprived 'brethren'. He had therefore settled *within* a community. He encouraged people to come to him with their troubles, including when his physical help was required. Though he lived alone and subsisted on alms, he liked social congregations and talked regularly to small groups of men and women within Baudhabagh. He had physically helped Chamars in thatchwork, tending the sick, and cremating the dead. He had looked after the children of a working couple.

In short, the Baudhabagh ascetics demonstrated how they comprised the picture of 'All-Workers' for the ordinary Chamar. It was this All-Worker who thought, willed, and acted for the welfare of the Chamar, irrespective of whether he was against the caste Hindu.

Such examples build on the point made earlier that the Indian ascetic acquires a full range of culturally allowed locations within the society. He can also easily radicalize himself for morally appropriate aims. A radical ascetic in modern India usually transforms himself into a political radical—a worldly ascetic who actively tries to convert his ideological rhetoric into political action. A radical ascetic starts this conversion when he encourages a protest, first usually sporadically and later on a sustained basis. Undoubtedly, to do so means to award a distinctly new dimension to the moderate Chamar ascetic we have discussed so far. But this has been indeed so.

A radical ascetic is easily turned into a protesting ascetic once he presses his demands for reform through direct, whether spontaneous or planned, protests. But he represents a milder variety as long as he does *not* resort to organized, representational politics and regards spiritual or personal influence as the backbone of his intended social reform. He is an ascetic first and a social or political radical second. However, a type stronger than the protesting variety appears when the ascetic is a *de facto* professional politician. He may jump into political frays and arenas with the full resources of a professional politician, even though he is an initiated ascetic. Under the final circumstance, as we will see later, even this ascetic may be found to be deficient, and he has to relinquish this increasingly demanding work to professional politicians and parties.

Although we will discuss other varieties later on, we will consider the ascetic reformer first. He is a critical stepping-stone for the Untouchable's entry into the hectic political events of this century. Because Ravidas is so scantily known and lived several centuries ago, and Ambedkar* is too late in the century and too remote (in training and education) from the ordinary Lucknow Chamar to demonstrate the *beginning of their* demands for moral and social reform, our example should preferably come from the region at the turn of the century. Ideally he should be a radical reform ascetic who turned into a protesting one.

Achchutananda, a regional reformer from Uttar Pradesh working at the turn of this century, best fits our requirements. Not only was he a social reformer, but he also showed all the signs of offering a radical pragmatic ideology to his community. He had a cohesive cultural argument as well as viewpoint. As far as I know, Jigyasu's** efforts to restructure the Untouchable ideology are strongly influenced by Achchutananda's insights and cultural enunciations. This remains true even though it was Jigyasu who gave to his formulations the needed broad cultural interpretation and justification.

Achchutananda was an initiated ascetic and a social reformer rolled into one. He was neither a politician nor a political reformer. In Jigyasu's account, he always stood for 'just' protests, offering a radical rhetoric to go with them. Actually, he was sometimes so radical that even his community members would back out. His life

* *Dr B. R. Ambedkar, the most renowned leader of the Untouchables in the middle of the twentieth century and political opponent of Mahatma Gandhi* Editor.

** *Jigyasu was a reformist Untouchable writer—a householder—also from Lucknow.* Editor.

experiences were the main source of his estrangement from the caste Hindu and a driving force behind the formulation of his protests. When protest was essential to his cause, he did not hesitate to become a protesting ascetic. But he was not merely a protester; most important, he advocated a profound reform of the entire culture order that bred social discrimination. In this last context, he offered the *ādi*-Hindu ideology to his community, making them residents—autonomous autochthons—of India even before Aryan times. I have labelled this ideology elsewhere 'autochthonous radicalism' (Khare 1979). We will present here a short biographical account of Achchutananda, followed by his ideology, and finally its extensive reproduction in an illustrative list of radical cultural theses to which contemporary Chamar reformers increasingly resort. I will depend on Jigyasu (1968) for Achchutananda's biography and ideolgy (with some unattributed quotations from the Lucknow Chamar ascetics), and on Sagar (1965) [a sociologist] for the illustration of certain derived theses, of cultural radicalism.

He was born in 1879 at his mother's home in a village called Umari in Mainpuri District in the state now called Uttar Pradesh, and he was given the name Hiralal. His father was then living in his wife's village 'since he and his brothers had quarrelled with the Brāhmans and other twice-born castes of their village' (Jigyasu 1968: 9). After Hiralal's birth, the family moved to a military cantonment, where Hiralal received his intial informal education. By the age of fourteen he was in the company of ascetics and had learned to read and write some Urdu and English in the cantonment. He was inquisitive and precocious, with a flair for religious studies. During his itinerant phase as an ascetic, he learned several more languages (Sanskrit, Bengali, Gujarati, and Marathi), gathered wide-ranging experiences, and acquired a (presumably Hindu) guru called Sachidananda. The reforming Arya Samaja* attracted him early and he became Harihարananda from Hiralal. However, since he had soon discovered a wide gap between the Arya Samaja's stated equalitarian ideals and actual social behaviour, he left the Arya Samaja (an organization, notes Jigyasu, that continued to hinder his activities long afterwards). A long and intensive period of self-education followed, helping him see through the designs of the caste Hindus. This ordinary ascetic and erstwhile *swami* of

* *The Arya Samaja was established in 1874.* Editor.

Arya Samaja thus became an ardent social reformer who undertook to awaken members of his deprived community.

By 1922, the year of the visit of the Prince of Wales, this ascetic had hit upon 'the principle of the *ādi*-Hindu', and had acquired a political name for himself by siding with the British on the controversy of the royal visit. Soon his independent *ādi*-Hindu movement was also started in some parts of northern India, demanding social equality and justice for the Untouchable. However, this movement meant Achchutananda's confrontation with both the Arya Samaja and the caste-Hindu organizations. Internally, the Untouchables were divided between those who wanted to better their lot *within* the Hindu system (Lynch's [1969] account of Jatavs handles this position in Agra), and those, more radical, who attempted to leave the system. Jigyasu (1968) noted in his biography how this disunity brought lifelong troubles for Achchutananda. (His name itself indicated rebelliousness to the caste Hindu, and it was enigmatic for the ordinary Untouchable, for it meant the one who was blissful in being Untouchable. It was perhaps an attempt to invent that type of symbolic turn that I consider, more generally, an essential feature of Indian reformers.) He was several times so completely forsaken by his friends and community members that he had to go without food and shelter. But he persisted in his goals.

Jigyasu has noted how Hariharananda became 'Sri 108 Swami Achchūtānanda'. In 1928, during a public meeting of the *ādi*-Hindu Sabha in Lucknow, Dr Ambedkar had addressed him so in the middle of the meeting, and prolonged applause followed. However, Jigyasu claimed that this history needed to be corrected. He pointed out that this title had, in fact, come to Achchutananda several years before in 1921, when he had 'won it from the Hindus themselves by defeating a Brāhman scholar in a debate in Shahdara' (near Delhi). It is symbolically significant that he had become the 'world conqueror' as a result (Jigyasu 1968: 16–17).

It was repeatedly made clear in Jigyasu's account that Achchutananda continued to encounter unrelenting resistance and rejection at the hands of upper-caste Hindus. His term *ādi*-Hindu in particular irritated them: if it deftly linked the Untouchable to the autochthons of India and the caste Hindus to the immigrant, invading Aryans, it also made the former the rightful, peaceful, and original owners of the *Bharat bhūmi* (India). The Hindus were considered 'intrigue-filled, ruthless conquerors'. This way the caste Hindu's moral right to belong to Bharat was directly questioned. 'It reminded the Hindu leader of his ancestors' cruelty and suppression', according to Jigyasu (1968: 19). To Achchutananda, however, such resistance from the Hindus was all the more reason for not giving up use of the term *ādi*-Hindu.

This leader indulged in similar symbolic contests. When some Chamars and caste Hindus, for example, refused to call him 'Swami Achchūtānanda' (implying that he did not deserve the honorific prefix of *swāmi*), he began to call himself 'Achchūtānanda Swami' or 'Achchūta Swami', incorporating the title in his actual name as a suffix. (Jigyasu argued on this point that his detractors could not have called him merely 'Achchūta', since it was not a proper noun.) Achchutananda would himself explain his name by observing that the word *achchūta* meant something entirely opposite to what the conventional usage conveyed. It meant to him *a* (meaning 'not') and *chchūta* (meaning 'polluted'), yielding 'the one who was in a state of purity'. The word *sachchūta* for him meant 'the impure'. So understood, the monthly magazine he brought out was called *Achchuta Prācīna [Ancient] Hindu* (later on simply *ādi*-Hindu), while Achchutananda became (under yet another variation) Sri Harihar [taken from one of his earlier names] Swami 'Achchūta'. Here the main name became his *nom de plume*.

In its final phases Achchutananda's movement began to organize itself in two distinct forums—one predominantly political and the other devoted to spiritual reform. 'He participated in both as best he could', according to Jigyasu, but he identified himself more strongly with the latter as independence politics heated up. A consistently ideological recognition of the *ādi*-Hindu, we are told, guided this ascetic leader's movement, and its enunciation was held by his followers to be so original that he was compared to Marx. Jigyasu saw in it a basis for 'original socialism', based on Indian ideas and values, run by Indians, and grounded in the spiritualism of Indian ascetics.

Some aspects of Achchutananda's ideology will complete our account (Jigyasu 1968: 113–14):

> I believe that God is only one and . . . formless. . . . Neither is there any book of His; nor does he incarnate, nor is there any image of His. . . .
>
> I believe that I am an autochthon of Bharat, hence I am an *ādi*-Hindu. . . .
>
> I believe that the religion of saints [*santon dā dharma*] is the original religion [*ādi dharma*] of Bharat: being full of humanism, it is beneficial to mankind. Spiritual experiences [*ātam-anubhava*—a favourite popular term of Achchūtānanda] of such ascetics as Sadashiva, Rshabhadeva, Mahavira,

Buddha, Kabir, Ravidas, Dadu, Namadeva, and Tulsisaheb can deliver me. . . .

I believe that all human beings are equal, and brothers . . . the feeling of high and low is an illusion. Humans become high and low by their own [individual] virtues and vices. Human heart alone is God's temple, hence to practice equality toward the entire humanity is the 'supreme religion' [*paramadharma*].

I believe that giving up lust, greed, attachment . . . is one's [true] personal religion. . . .

I believe that according to the teachings of Kabir all the Brāhman's scriptures (*dharma gr̥ntha*) are based on selfishness, falsehood, and injustice . . . I will [therefore] never have our rites of birth, tonsure ceremony, marriage, and death performed by a Brāhman [priest].

The cultural import of this autochthonous radicalism, still being discussed in popular publications in Lucknow, can best be reproduced in terms of an illustrative list of the cultural theses that several contemporary Chamar literati and reformers in Lucknow continue to emphasize. Some of the points are straight repetitions of Achchutananda's ideology. I quote directly and in full from the Chamars' statements.

The Untouchables, the so-called Harijans, are in fact the '*ādi*-Hindu' (i.e., the original or the autochthonous Nagas or the Dasas of the North and the Dravidas of the South) of the subcontinent, and they are the undisputed, heavenly owners of Bharat.

All others are immigrants to the land, including the Aryans, who conquered the original populations not by valour but by deceit and manipulation of the whole society by usurping others' rights, subjugating the peace loving, and rendering the self-sufficient people indigents and slaves. Those who ardently believed in equality were ranked, and ranked lowest.

The Hindu and Untouchables have since always remained poles apart. They could never really come together in a major way, despite the best efforts of such reform movements as Bhakti, Arya Samaja, Sikhism, and Brahmo-Samaja. They remained as distinct as oil mixed in water.

The cobweb of Hindu scriptures, deities, incarnations, temples, and Brāhman priests is so intricate and pervasive that it has imprisoned the Hindu within his family and *jātis*, and consigned the Untouchable to the bottom. Since there have been no *true* exits in this cobweb—from Manu down to Gandhi, the Untouchable has to take the lead on his own. And this means that he has to examine the Hindu social tactics very closely to get his freedom.

The Hindus have suppressed and destroyed all critical literature produced by the Untouchable intellectuals from ancient times until recently. Hence, the Untouchable must start rebuilding his knowledge, moving carefully from the recent to the remote past. At present, one knows little about anything other than the Hindu's side of the story.

Marriage, commensality, occupation, *Gītā-Rāmāyaṇa*, and extended family are the five most important sacred domains where the Untouchables encounter maximum discrimination and resistance. The radical solution must therefore reject totally and exactly those reasons the Hindus accept and value.

To discriminate against Untouchables on the basis of (beef or) meat eating is an ancient trick of the Hindus for down-grading the *ādi*-Hindu. Such ploys should be clearly recognized and exposed by the available textual and historical evidence.

As a logically related need for the propagation of this knowledge, there also appeared publishing houses devoted to reform literature on the Untouchable's condition, refuting and rejecting the major pillars of traditional Hindu ideas and society. . . . A book (Sagar 1973) recently involved in a legal case offers a 'sociological' study. Written by a trained sociologist, it lists one hundred ancient, preindependence, and modern references to support the argument for the autochthonous status of the Untouchable. This book, incidentally, also contained two tongue-in-cheek testimonials by prominent Hindu functionaries of the Congress party and was dedicated to the renowned Indian Untouchable leader, Jagjivan Ram. In conclusion (pp. 272–6), among other things, Sagar asks his readers not to be taken in by 'the Hindu's four Gs'—the *Gangā* (the sacred Ganges), *Gau* (the sacred cow), *Gāyatrī* (the sacred verse), and the *Gītā* (the sacred Hindu song of God). He lists six ideological features of the Hindu religious system (*dharma*) that should be rajected in order to establish the autochthonous argument: (1) belief in Hindu 'theism' (*āstiktā*), and (ranked) hell and heaven; (2) Hindu ideas of (incomplete) renunciation and 'spiritualism'; (3) the Hindu orders of *varṇa* and *jāti* (caste) ranking; (4) Hindu philosophy based on fate and resignation; (5) Hindu practices of violent sacrifices and 'rituals' (*karmakāṇḍa*); and (6) Hindu faith in karma orthodoxy and resultant 'narrow-minded social views'.

The seven cultural theses of the Lucknow Chamar literati and Sagar's six diagnostic cultural features converge but are not the same. Together, however, they offer a picture of what the Untouchable literati culturally plan to do to regain their autochthonous status. It can be shown from the Untouchable's standpoint that this cultural position is not simply an inversion of the Hindu's position but rather offers flexible platforms of political protest that could be used to express opposition or contradistinction or even ambiguity on some occasions.

With the preceding transitional picture of the Untouchable culture and its reforming ascetics, the first part of our discussion, the cultural structure of the Pariah ideology, is brought to a climax. As a radical cultural alternative is offered, an incipient transition is made toward organized protest, competition, and politics on the one hand, and an ideological commitment to individual equality and justice on the other. To disregard any part of this reformulation is to miss the entire significance of the Untouchable ideologist's contemporary exercise. This context of cultural radicalism is not to be dismissed as merely sociologically insignificant and improbable; it is, instead, a gathering and direct culmination of the work of those protest processes that have perhaps repeatedly waxed and waned with the Indian Untouchable over the centuries.

The cultural ideology of Achchutananda, even if it has a cogent social basis, is actually given varied social reception among the Lucknow Chamars. It might still be too radical for some, too mild for others, and even irrelevant for some others. Modernganj generally expressed all three views, while Baudhabagh was ideologically mild. Karampura,* on the other hand, found Achchutananda's ideology either too radical or irrelevant. Such varied responses help show why a reformer and a politician need diverse political rhetoric, essentially to convince the majority of continuing social injustice. The reception of this rhetoric is also empirically uneven. If some view it as part of a genuine, all-out effort to blunt the discriminatory caste order, thus also matching and defeating today's Hindu thinker at his own game, others find it a hollow exercise, unless the Chamars really unite and commit themselves to reforming their own community first. Yet to be rhetorical is to be doing something; to publicly protest is to be increasingly serious in practice about one's aims.

Sociologically, the Lucknow Chamars demonstrated a generally patterned response to a radical alternative, depending both on where they stood socially and on their practical experiences, needs, and expectations. For example, those who were repeatedly mistreated at the hands of a caste Hindu and were unable to better their lot through regular networks of personal position, political influence, and social patronage generally became radical in their views. A bitter shoe-shop owner from Baudhabagh, who had lived near a big (25-foot-wide) open drain for years, observed:

When flooded, this drain sweeps off an entire row of our shacks, killing some. It has repeatedly infected our water supply since a broken water-

* *Karampura and Modernganj are two other Untouchable neighbourhoods of Lucknow, besides Baudhabagh, studied by Khare. All three are pseudonyms.* Editor.

pipe runs through it. It always remains [for cleaning and repair] at the mercy of indifferent municipal workers on one side, and certain local caste Hindu politicians on the other.

But nobody does anything for us, including even our own political leaders. We increasingly know what Achchutananda, Ambedkar, and Jigyasu talked about, and why. Nothing will change unless the entrenched caste-Hindu interests are uprooted. But this will happen only when we are united.

By comparison, in Moderngan), a better-off locality of the Lucknow Chamar, radicalism is appreciated verbally but with much less emotional edge and social immediacy. A well-paid railway engine driver observed:

It will be good indeed to have those days come to us when social insult and discrimination will not come our way at all. But all the same we earn most ever and share our joys and sorrows among our own people, expecting little from the caste Hindus or politicians and doing little at their bidding. We know that they are ultimately after their own interests more than anybody else's.... Despite the *ādi*-Hindu ideology of our reformer Achchutananda, about whom I have heard and read with appreciation, we just cannot change the whole world so quickly. Then, why should we? We are generally much better off than before and do not want to risk the present arrangement for an unknown upheaval. Instead, we want to improve slowly but surely.

Other wage earners in the same locality were passive; one reasoned: 'I do not concern myself with these matters; I am busy earning my day-to-day livelihood and raising my family... [*apné kāma sé kāma*]'. But a draftsman denied promotion at his office felt cheated and helpless. His reasoning was:

Our own community is so divided that everybody is for his own safety and interests. Whom do I complain to? Who will hear? Rather, I stand the risk of offending my caste-Hindu superiors if I make too much of it with my own political leaders. All powerful people, whether Chamars or caste Hindus, work together among themselves to secure their own interests, and take care of their supporters.

An intellectual, a professor at the local university, who did not reside in any of the three localities but who was in close touch with them, responded, as expected, much more eloquently in a language of social reform. He lamented the ignorance of his community members, the opportunism of his political leaders, and the lack of commitment to social fairness among the educated caste Hindu. He professed Ambedkar's idea of Buddhist identity, confronting, if necessary, the caste Hindu to stop his techniques of 'social subversion'. He organized a reform society, wrote on social reform, and lectured on these issues as often as he could. 'But after all, this is not the work for a lone voice', he reasoned. 'Tell me, what more can I do?'

This response, which the radical ideology had begun to receive as I reached the Chamar intellectual, was readily popularized by the glib speeches of a Moderngaj politician. He harangued in the ethnographer's tape recorder to convince himself (and a few other locality members drawn to his high-pitched soliloquy from his front veranda) of how true and profound his advocacy of the Achchutananda and Ambedkar ideas for uplifting the Chamar community remained. Also, it was done as if to say that this was what he did best as a leader of the neighbourhood. One of his sycophants capped it for him: 'You have never said it any better.'

However, despite the diverse reception given to radical reform, a general point was made: There is no doubt anymore that cultural radicalism is already integral to the self-definition of the contemporary Lucknow Chamar, and that given an appropriate circumstance, it could be translated into prolonged (even militant) protest to respond to any severe social stress or threat. But, over time and space, social radicalism remains variable. What most Chamars considered radical reform at the beginning of this century is today often commonplace and ready to be bypassed.

A relatively varied reception, interpretation, and significance of the radical ideology were also clear within the three Lucknow Chamar settlements. The cases of Moderngaj, Baudhabagh, and Karampura were likened to 'three glasses, one inside the other', according to the priest at the Ravidas temple where Moderngaj was the outermost and socially most open nighbourhood and Karampura the innermost one. The radicalism of Moderngaj had resulted in, among other things, more school education, diverse modern occupations, better brick houses, and an active cluster of local leaders. More residents as a result read newspapers, discussed local, state, and national political affairs, and followed the fluctuating fortunes of the Untouchables in India. Their greater social awareness, in turn, translated into outgoing social expectations and relationships. Their attitude towards 'Hindu injustice' showed disgust and impatience. News of violence against the Untouchable in any part of India would make many faces in the neighbourhood anxious, tense, and angry. These emotions were repeatedly evident to me during my fieldwork. On such occasions, the Chamars spontaneously talked in groups about the news, especially during evenings. Some were angry, some despondent, and some scheming, but few totally indifferent or passive. The Moderngani resident, having received more from society, readily translated his radicalism into democratic social action—everyday activism at the work place, in the city streets, and in the neighbourhood. Their radicalism was less bottled-up, its interpretation was activist, and its overt significance more directly tied to the goals of democratic civil rights.

By comparison, Baudhabagh's radicalism was vocal and involuted; its interpretation was inspired by religious antagonism (including Buddhist reform) but remained mired in social pessimism and political discord. Though its significance was evident for everyday practical issues, it went largely unrealized since the Chamars there bickered among themselves. A Baudhabagh Chamar summed it all up:

> We have a need for major change but feel helpless. We cannot bring it about ourselves because we are too quarrelsome and weak; others do not help us because they know we are weak and disunited. Still since we realize how badly we need the improvement, we feel suffocated and helpless, both at the same time. A reformist ascetic makes the conditions tolerable for many of the Baudhabagh Chamars. He gives them hope, though his opponents think that he only dilutes our resolve to do better.

Karampura, on the other hand, was socially isolated, traditionally passive, and politically neglected. Its radicalism was often limited to occasionally singing of old songs in praise of Ambedkar (and even the traditional Hindu gods such as Hanuman and Bhairava). The interpretations of radicalism were, however, diversifying (especially with Karampura youth getting more education) and were being brought closer to the practical problems of Chamar life. Yet its social significance remained sporadic and remote. There was room seen for major improvements here but since the residents themselves did not consciously feel the need as acutely as did the Baudhabagh Chamars, the sharp sense of helplessness and suffocation was largely absent.

More generally, we may observe that the Chamar radical ideology often shows a transition to the mild position upheld by civilizational constraints. The ideology remains shy of radical political options; it also disallows easy ground to any alien political ideology and its values. Actually, a radical foreign ideology has yet to seriously influence the Untouchable movement at an all-Indian level. Ambedkar, no doubt, favoured and set this course most recently.

He decided to uphold the general civilizational constrains and let the indigenous cultural radicalism develop its way through the secular—economic, legal, and political—arenas of a democratic state. What it has meant is no less significant: The secular achievements of the Indian Untouchable must prove their *real* worth against his needed cultural emancipation from within. Otherwise, he would always feel robbed of the real significance of what he gains in the material world.

The Lucknow Chamars reflected this point in several different ways. An office employee from Moderngan j, for example, complained about the lack of social acceptance among caste Hindus of what the Chamars have achieved, and a hotel bearer criticized the self-deprecating attitude of his community members. The Chamars generally sought approval most from those quarters (and in those terms) where they had lacked it most—from their own (often fractious) peers and from the caste Hindu. A resident ascetic in Karampura exhorted his followers one day:

> Respect yourselves for what you really are and people will respect you. You will thus prove yourself equal to others. If you now have a bicycle while a caste Hindu has a scooter or a motorcyle, you may like to acquire the latter but it will not suffice, for you must also be sure of *your worth to yourself*. Only then will the Hindu change his attitude. But if you imitate him by buying the things he has in order to seek his approval, he will never give it.

Overview

This and the previous chapter [of Khare's book] trace some of the dimensions of a practical transition that the Lucknow Chamar, with the help of the ascetic reformer, All-Worker, tries to bring about for improving his daily life. There are two views to keep in focus in such an exercise, one external and the other internal. Externally, the democratic provisions of independent India are impinging more and more on the Lucknow Chamar, prompting and challenging him to reformulate his traditional cultural values as effectively as he can. As already indicated here . . . the Chamar is responding to this challenge in a more comprehensive manner as he 'totalizes' himself. Despite all that can be said in favour of the entrenched Hindu caste order (and its ideology), the Chamar is consolidating and connecting himself socially. Variously overlapping and sharing a vastly pliable culture among themselves, the Chamars and the caste Hindus know that they can change now only in relation to each other. Chamars also increasingly realize that all significant change is slow change. But yet the depth and the reach of this slow change in either direction (i.e. toward the Brāhmans as well as the Chamars) may impress an observer; he cannot overlook the radically significant social trends initiated in the previous decades of this century.

Under an objective evaluation, therefore, both the caste Hindu and the Chamar are now involved in changing each other in Lucknow. Both are, it seems, engaged in a significant cognitive re-mapping and re-evaluation in relation to each other and in the way they view Indian society at large. In such an exercise, for example, the ideal ascetic must first get translated into the worldly ascetic, and the latter into the routine, resident ascetic of Baudhabagh (cited earlier). The democratic urban ethos must strengthen the Chamar's equalitarian idealism, and the traditional cognitive processes of self-image and social (i.e. of caste and extracaste) evaluation must redirect themselves. The Lucknow Chamar finds himself in the middle of all these vital exercises, as does the caste Hindu. Both apprehend that this time much more is fundamentally changing than perhaps ever before, and both are displaying an increasing seriousness. . . .

Christian Fundamentalism as Counter-Culture

LIONEL CAPLAN

The Western missionary presence in India was intimately connected with the expansion of the Anglo-Indian empire. To concentrate their limited resources, and preserve some measure of harmony among the various organizations, each mission tended to focus its efforts in a limited number of areas. While the larger urban centres were regarded as common property, the rules of 'comity' required that one mission should respect and refrain from entering the field of labour of another. Denominational affiliation for the average convert was therefore not so much a matter of personal choice or conviction, but of the missions' territorial claims.

As they became more mobile, Protestants in South India found themselves living, working and worshipping alongside persons of other mission backgrounds. In the course of time a number of developments, not least the rise of nationalism, further mitigated, blurred and even abolished the lines separating the different denominations. In 1908 Presbyterian and Congregational churches were brought together in the South India United Church (SIUC), and 1947, the year of India's Independence, the Church of South India (CSI) federated the SIUC, Anglicans and Methodists. With well over one and a half million adherents, or just under a third of all Protestants in India, it is today the largest Protestant body in the country. While there were inevitable compromises of dogma and liturgy in the course of negotiating the amalgamation, the outcome was recognizably Western and orthodox Protestant: synods and

Excerpted from Lionel Caplan, 'Fundamentalism as Counter-Culture: Protestants in Urban South India', in Lionel Caplan, ed., *Studies in Religious Fundamentalism*, Macmillan Press, London, 1987, pp. 156–76.

dioceses, a hierocratic order including episcopally ordained bishops, a selected and trained male clergy, formal rites of (child) baptism, marriage and death, as well as agreed procedures for all other ritual occasions. My own fieldwork in Madras was mainly among members of this united church—the CSI.

While the early denominational communities were more or less homogenous in terms of socio-economic criteria, by the late nineteenth century some differentiation was already apparent. This was occasioned, in part, by the limited benefits which the missions were able to offer, and the unevenness of their availability to adepts. Inequalities of education, skills and opportunities therefore arose within and between mission congregations. The gradual expansion of administration, commerce and industry in South India intensified these differences as Christians from the rural areas as well as smaller urban places began migrating to metropolitan centres like Madras city.

With the dramatic growth of industry and infrastructure in and around the city during the Second World War and even more so after 1947, this migration reached significant proportions. A minority of migrants came to acquire advanced educational qualifications, to pursue professional careers, or to assume senior positions vacated by Europeans at the time of Independence or created in the wake of post-Independence expansion and industrialization. The majority, however, entered the capital to meet the demand for skilled and semi-skilled workers in newly established concerns, for teachers in the expanding school system, for clerks and assistants in the burgeoning administration and commercial sector. Many also came to establish or attach themselves to the innumerable petty enterprises of the 'informal sector' which arose in its shadow.

But the numbers of migrants more than outstripped the pace of growth, and as economic expansion halted—indeed was reversed in the 1960s—the situation for those at the lower levels of the occupational order grew increasingly difficult. Their prospects now seem, if anything, less bright than in the past; their material conditions have, and are felt to have, deteriorated. The missionary institutions (now part of the indigenous church) which had once provided education, training and employment to a fairly wide cross-section of the Protestant population, can no longer meet the overwhelming demands made on them, and have become the preserve of the well-to-do, who seek to intensify their hold on recently-won privileges in the educational and occupational fields.

Social arteries have considerably hardened; mobility has become a thing of the past.

Not surprisingly, the dominant voice in the church is that of the new middle class, which provides both its ecclesiastical and lay leadership. In addition to its formal religious concerns, the church has responsibility for the operation of a variety of educational, medical and other social service institutions. The proper functioning of these enterprises relies to a large extent on lay persons voluntarily contributing their time, knowledge and experience. Because of their special managerial skills and professional qualifications, their wide contacts built up over many years, and because only the better-off can contribute their time in this way, the lay leadership tends to be drawn from those belonging to the dominant segment within the community. Many of these elites worship, moreover, in a handful of grandiose churches built by and for Europeans during the colonial period, where rites are still conducted in English. By contrast, Protestants among the lower class—who attend mainly Tamil churches—do not possess the qualifications and previous work experience to be invited to assume positions of responsibility in these organizations. Nor do they possess the kinds of resources—contacts, finances, personal transport—which would enable them effectively to donate their services even if called upon to do so.

The CSI leadership, like that of the other main Protestant churches in Madras, has a strong commitment to the 'social gospel'. This is a direct legacy of the dominant liberal theological emphasis within missionary circles which gained the ascendant in the early twentieth century, and especially during the run-up to Independence. By the 1930s, writes one opponent of this tendency, modernism had spread 'like cancer' through Christian colleges and high schools, sowing 'unbelief in the word of God' and turning denominational churches into 'moral and spiritual graveyards' (Daniel 1980: 89–90). In the context of contemporary South India the social gospel means a concern for economic development (as defined by regional and national governments) as well as for the alleviation of individual poverty and hardship. The CSI originates and/or participates in, among other things, programmes for the relief of drought-stricken regions, the improvement of water resources in rural areas, the provision of agricultural extension services, industrial and craft training, the betterment of urban slum sanitation, and the building of low-cost housing in the city. Kurien remarks that 'they are the *avant-gardes* of the modern age and of the social gospel of the church', and have won for the latter 'a certain respectability in this land' (1981: 4). Funds are also directed to a host of welfare enterprises which, though run by Christian organizations, benefit the poor irrespecive of religious affiliation.[1]

One obvious corollary of this kind of intense engagement with the 'world' is that relationships to persons of other faiths are conceived in a more positive light. The ecumenical tendency finds expression in a greater readiness to acknowledge a common Dravidian culture wih Tamils and other South Indians irrespective of religious affiliation and to acknowledge the need for co-existence with other faiths. The CSI's Bishop in Madras writes of 'spirituality in other religions', and the need to learn from them, even to incorporte certain of their qualities, for example, 'devotionalism' (*bhakti*), and to find Christ 'in the lives of men and women of other Faiths'. He calls for dialogue which will 'lead . . . to knowledge of other religions which is so lacking in the Indian Christian community' (Clarke 1980: 95–8).[2] Such views are frequently heard from the pulpits of elite congregations, and are widely shared by those, mainly within the dominant class, who are regularly engaged in welfare and development activities as part of their commitment to the social gospel.

While there is recognition of the obligation of Christians to spread the message of the gospel, it is regarded as most effectively communicated by the example of 'social work', and therefore implicit rather than explicit. People in the congregations of the well-to-do, I was told by a leading member of one, 'are not very much in favour of standing on the pavement and preaching to people'. Another related how, during a hospital visit, he and several other members of his congregation were appalled and embarrassed when one of their members refused to distribute the light magazines they had collected and brought along. 'He felt that these sick people should be given evangelical literature, so that they would see the error of their ways before it was too late.' This kind of 'vulgar evangelism' is not thought suitable for members of elite congregations.

[1] To its critics in the church's radical wing, the social gospel is a form of institutional philanthropy which does not seriously challenge the existing social hierarchy.

[2] In 1980, Protestant leaders in Madras met with representatives of the Tamil Nadu branch of the RSS, a militant Hindu organization, to hear and examine 'the impressions and grievances [of] influential Hindus concerning the work and life of the Christian Church in India' (*Christian Focus*, 15 July 1980).

The vast majority—those outside the tiny power bloc—neither benefit from these welfare programmes, nor take any part in their planning and execution. It would not be accurate to relate a weak commitment to the social gospel among ordinary Protestants entirely to their own material circumstances. Liberal doctrines now, as in the past, are seen to threaten the pietism which, for the better part of two centuries, has formed the core of popular South Indian Protestantism. It is frequently suggested that the price of the social gospel is the neglect of people's 'spiritual needs', that it replaces 'salvation through faith' by 'salvation through social concern', as one lay preacher phrased it. The social ministry is misguided, it is said, because 'people will only agree to follow Christ if they get something in return'.

Even those who are not totally opposed to welfare efforts on behalf of the less fortunate are convinced, nevertheless, that these should be accompanied by intense evangelism, so that people of other faiths can be brought to see the 'light of Christian truth'. The missionaries are thought to have arrived at a perfect balance between their social concerns and their promulgation of the Christian message. But the social gospel, it is protested, has come to mean 'giving without preaching the world of God'. . . .

The reference is to a policy meant, in part, to take account of the Indian government's extreme suspicions of the motives underlying Christian aid, but one which also reflects liberal Protestant respect for the sensitivities of people of other faiths, and, as already noted, a less aggressive and overt approach to evangelism (see also Clarke 1980: 96–7).

In brief, then, it is not simply that the conservative evangelicalism—what Barr (1977) would label 'fundamentalism'—of the early missionaries has been overtaken by the social gospel favoured by those who now dominate the structures and shape the discourses of the church. It is also that the beliefs and practices of ordinary people have for some years been effectively demoted, left behind in the wake of a confident, modernist, development-orientated ecclesiastical whirlwind. Those so excluded from the exercise of influence within the church as within society, and denied the authenticity of their own religious preferences by the dominant segment within the church and community, are precisely those most attracted to and by the new fundamentalism.

Miraculous Fundamentalism

The fundamentalist sects which have entered Madras recently insist on the centrality of the Bible, on piety, prayer and worship, in Protestant life. They inveigh against the 'infidels of modernism'. They are indifferent if not opposed to inter-faith dialogues and ecumenism, social and political activity on behalf of the poor, church involvement in development programmes, and the whole paraphernalia of social action. They are therefore very much in tune with the kinds of views and practices favoured by most Protestants outside the dominant class, as well as having much in common with the earlier conservative evangelical, pre-modernist tendency within the missionary fold.

But what seems even more to account for the attraction of the new fundamentalist movement is its stress on the authenticity of miracles—one of the 'essential' doctrines of Christianity which has all but disappeared from Western Protestant orthodoxy. It refers to and stems from the Biblical episode when on the occasion of Pentecost the Holy Spirit descended on the original Christian community with the charismata. The fundamentalist claim is that the gifts of the Holy Spirit—tongues, prophecy and healing, among others—were not meant for the early Christians alone, as the mainline Protestant view would have it, but are immanent in every period, if people are but ready to receive them. Moreover, they assert that the devil and all his legions are still abroad in the world and, if anything, Christ is needed as never before to save people from these malignant powers. One hears on fundamentalist platforms or reads in its press that hundreds of thousands of people in India are under the influence of demons' (Sargunam 1974: 130). Or, as one statistically-minded young man told me, 75 per cent of all hospital cases in Madras are due to possession by spirits. Here, fundamentalists are in tune with popular theodicies: that the sources of human affliction may be located in occult evil forces.

Sorcery (*suniam*), for example, is popularly thought to account for various kinds of misfortune—by Hindus and Christians alike. The human agents responsible are the *suniakaran*, sorcerers who are thought to have access to secret knowledge and mystical powers which they employ on behalf of paying clients. The persons who are thought to engage the services of such experts for harmful ends bear personal grudges against the intended victims or their close kin. Thus, rejected suitors, clerks who fail to obtain promotion against less experienced colleagues, dissatisfied heirs, unsuccessful job applicants, or political rivals, may turn their anger and frustration against those whom they feel are responsible for their misfortunes.

Sorcery in its aggressive aspect implies a variety of ritual techniques to inflict harm, including the utterance of spells or their inscription on copper plates, which are then buried in the victim's house or place of work. Sorcerers also perform contagious or associative magic. The latter may include the making of clay figures or dolls (*bomai*) as likenesses of the intended prey, on which all manner of simulated injury may be inflicted to produce a similar effect on the human subjects. These practitioners are associated with graveyards, where they are said to obtain the skulls of eldest children (especially sons) who have died young, from which to prepare their pernicious medicines (*mai*). They are also assumed to control a number of spirits whom they can despatch to bring a variety of afflictions to their victims. Some are simply poltergeists, impish and clown-like, creating havoc wherever they go—causing stones to fall around houses, food to turn to excrement, dishes to fall off shelves or people out of their beds. Most superhuman assistants of the *suniakaran*, however, are portrayed as considerably more malign, and their principal means of attacking victims is through possession. These are the evil spirits known in Madras, as in Tamil Nadu generally, as *peey*. Further, the most malignant of these *peey* operate outside human control, in an entirely capricious and destructive manner (see Caplan 1985).

Fundamentalists do not deny the reality of such (evil) forces which, by intention or otherwise, bring adversity. In this respect, they provide a strong contrast with the orthodox churches and their missionary predecessors. In South India, as in virtually every part of the missionized world, Protestant evangelists long ago turned their backs on such concerns. The essential Christian doctrine of belief in the authenticity of miracles was suspended. Whereas Hindus had resort to a variety of deities and ritual specialists to protect them, the missionaries refuted and eliminated the agencies by means of which converts to Protestantism and their descendants sought protection from these dangerous powers (see Wilson 1973; Norman 1981). They discredited popular beliefs in the existence of evil spirits and the efficacy of magic and sorcery, and any practices which acknowledged such forces were condemned.

Protestants looked in vain to their missionaries and later their indigenous clergy for a satisfactory response to these popular conceptions of affliction, and so were denied the authenticity of such forms of knowledge. These were ridiculed, explained away and disqualified by ecclesiastics who had long since rejected their own thaumaturgical legacy. Thus, the Anglican Bishop of Tinnevelly (in Tamil Nadu), reporting on the widespread belief in the activities of demons, assured a meeting of the Anthropological Society of Bombay in 1886 that he had 'never yet had an opportunity of being present where symptoms, that seemed to me to be incapable of being explained by natural causes, were exhibited . . . and this has been the experience, so far as I have heard, of all English and American missionaries' (Caldwell 1886: 96–9). In Europe, by the seventeenth century, the devil had been severely downgraded. It was not the growing scientific community, moreover, but the church itself which was keen to extirpate magical practices which were thought 'superstitious' (see Hill 1983; Macfarlane 1985). By the era of Protestant expansion throughout what we now call the Third World, belief in the contemporary factuality of miracles had virtually disappeared from orthodox Protestantism. Neither in their own theological education nor in that given to indigenous candidates for the ministry were those aspects of Christian tradition seriously considered. CSI clergymen with whom I discussed these questions could recall no occasion during their training or subsequently as ordained pastors when issues of this kind were even raised within orthodox circles.

Fundamentalist doctrine confirms the existence of evil forces, thereby providing evidence both of satanic influences in the world, and the power of the Holy Spirit to defeat them. These themes emerge time and again in the various contexts where people meet to 'hear the word of God' as they put it. I want to dwell for a moment on such contexts, for they constitute an important site within which Protestants belonging to the main churches are addressed by fundamentalist discourses.

Cells and Crusades

The existence of 'prayer cells' is a widespread phenomenon in the Protestant world, and they are certainly evident in Madras. These informal groups, usually composed of persons who feel that Sunday worship alone is insufficient, constitute a self-selected religious elite, who meet regularly in each other's homes to pray, read the Bible, give 'witness' to their faith, and so on. Members of the CSI churches situated in the neighbourhoods of the lower class now take part in numerous rites organized by and around cell leaders with fundamentalist leanings. These attract not only adherents of different CSI congregations, but persons belonging to other orthodox denominations as well as to different sectarian groups.

Such gatherings do not follow a precise pattern, but almost certainly include gospel songs, and a 'strong message', as the Bible-based, heavily didactic and exhortative sermon is termed. There is ample scope for individual expression and enthusiasm, through impromptu prayer, Bible readings, exegesis, and personal testimonials. Considerable time is also given to the detailed submission by participants of their personal problems. While women are preponderant among attenders, and certainly among those volunteering problems for the group's attention and concern, it is not only their own individual difficulties which they present, but their husbands' and children's as well. Generally, these are dealt with by a patient and sympathetic hearing, and collective prayer. Persons whose wishes have been fulfilled, or whose troubles resolved, 'witness' to the Lord's grace and, more especially, to the power of the Holy Spirit.

Those who organize and lead such groups invariably claim one or more gifts of the Holy Spirit, and almost certainly the gift of healing. This involves the ability to diagnose the causes of affliction—which can mean anything from infertility to cancer, from unemployment to examination failure—and to prescribe suitable remedies, which may include intensive fasting and prayer, or the imbibing of substances blessed in the name of Jesus. They also deal with the effects wrought by a plethora of maleficent human and superhuman agents who are identified as the sources of misfortune.

A few charismatic prophets earn a reputation beyond their own congregations, and attract followings from outside their immediate neighbourhoods. The more miraculous their achievements, the wider their notoriety. Some develop 'specializations', that is, they become known for dealing effectively with particular kinds of problem: certain prophets in Madras are thought to have a singular gift for finding lost property, identifying thieves, exorcizing spirits or even predicting whether a particular marriage proposal is likely to lead to a happy and successful union. Those who achieve supra-local fame do so because they are seen to stand above the innumerable local healers in terms of their charismatic powers. They are also acknowledged to be strong orators, able to hold an audience for (sometimes) hours at a time, to present the word of God in a compelling and convincing way.

There are a handful of prophets whose reputations extend throughout the city and even beyond, in certain cases to other parts of the world (for example, South East Asia, Sri Lanka) where there are large numbers of Tamil-speakers. Though the core of their adherents may be found in a particular congregation, their popularity ensures a much more widely based support. Some in fact do not have an established congregation at all, and are therefore not closely associated with any particular sectarian organization, though the ideology they foster is no less fundamentalist.

The attainment of this level of recognition requires a strong public persona, one which is not simply established in the context of regular interaction with, and validated in terms of experiences within, a small group of followers. The achievement of such a status seems to require evidence of a special and ongoing relationship with the divine. Because such prophets are removed to a very great extent from those who seek their assistance, their links with the supernatural must be reiterated continually. The biographies of these prophets, which become public knowledge through print as well as by word of mouth, emphasize not only the acquisition of charismata, but the dramatic circumstances in which these are obtained. The literature they issue recounts the life histories of the prophets, with special emphasis on miraculous events. What is also stressed is the contrast between their lives before and after receiving the Holy Spirit. In the period immediately prior to this experience these prophets portray themselves as being at the brink of spiritual if not physical death. (In the case of one prophet, the official biography has her actually summoned back from the dead.) They write and speak of being plagued by incurable illness, long and hopeless unemployment, in a state of total despair and near suicide, and frequently engaged in a life full of 'sin' (drinking, smoking, cinema-going, and political activity). Conversion and the Holy Spirit changes their lives totally and brings them into regular contact with Jesus, who thereafter guides them in all their undertakings, and channels his power (*vellamai*) through them. Their reported struggles with satanic forces are hair-raising in the extreme, taking on mythic dimensions, and their victories all the more amazing for it.

The main contexts within which the public encounters these

popular prophets are 'crusades' or 'conventions'. These take the form of open meetings which may extend over a period of several days, and which can attract thousands. Each evening includes entertainment by gospel singers, sermons by lesser personalities, and to crown the evening, the appearance of the prophet, who gives his or her 'message', and concludes with a healing session. At these gatherings, God is said to give them sight of the malignant forces at large in the audience, and the drama of the occasion seldom fails to produce cures and converts, demonstrating again and again the power of the Holy Spirit (and of course, of the prophet). There is usually a hierarchy of assistants on hand, trained by the prophet, to deal with those individuals who may, while attending a meeting, undergo such an experience.[3]

The most successful prophets travel throughout the south, and increasingly to other parts of Asia, where the local Tamil communities organize crusades. The best-known charismatic in south India has established an organization to produce and distribute his sermons and songs on tapes, using sophisticated electronic equipment imported from Japan and the west. It deals with upwards of 500 letters daily (usually asking for help and advice), produces a monthly magazine, and runs a 24-hour a day telephone service which, in reply to the supplicant's stated problem, plays an appropriate recording of the prophet's voice.

The Challenge of Charisma

Charisma, as Weber (1947) pointed out, challenges orthodoxy. As Msgr Cauchon, the Bishop of Beauvais in Shaw's *Saint Joan*, puts it: 'The church's accumulated wisdom and knowledge and experience, its council of learned, venerable pious men, are thrust into the kennel by every ignorant labourer or dairyman whom the devil can puff up with the monstrous self-conceit of being directly inspired from heaven. . .' (Shaw 1946: 95). Few topics have been as vigor-

[3] The evangelical potential of this demonstration is overtly acknowledged in fundamentalist writings and statements. 'The people who blame most sickness on evil powers', writes one historian of Pentecostalism,

> do not find any difficulty in believing that [the Christian] God is the One who has the supernatural power and that He can and will help sick people. Divine healing campaigns will attract many people . . . [and] when people get healing . . . some of them accept Christ as their personal saviour. The divine healing ministry has helped the growth of the Pentecostal churches all over the world (George 1975: 54).

ously debated in the sociological literature as charisma. Weber applied the term to leaders whose authority rests upon the recognition in him, by his followers, of 'supernatural, superhuman, or at least specifically exceptional powers or qualities...' regarded as of divine origin...'(1944: 358–9). He understood charisma as non-institutional, even anti-institutional: the prophet is seen as the ideal opponent of hierocratic institutions. While Berger (1963), Worsley (1970), Kiernan (1982) and others have challenged and qualified certain of Weber's views and emphases, his general statement still has a wide credibility, and can certainly be applied to the situation I have been describing.

In the Madras Protestant context the charismatic prophet threatens to undermine ecclesiastical structures based on an authoritative, episcopally ordained ministry. The majority of those who are members of the CSI readily compare their priests—'the bishop's employees', as I have often heard them called—with the prophets who are, in their view, especially chosen by God to do his work. An explicit contrast is drawn between the kinds of knowledge invested in these two figures. Protestants from the orthodox churches who flock in their hundreds and thousands to hear the word of God from the prophets frequently stress how awesome are the insights conferred by the Holy Spirit as against the insignificance of the formal theological training undergone by their own priesthood. They are quick to note that no education, birth (caste) or gender qualifications are necessary for divine selection, not even a Christian commitment. Indeed, if any particular set of qualities appears to count more than anything else, it is—as the public biographies of the prophets suggest—poverty, unhappiness, despair, even a life of sin and godlessness. The appropriation of prophecy by the disprivileged and the dominated within the Protestant community is evident. The strong representation of women among the category of charismatics also illustrates the careful separation made between these two forms of knowledge. The acceptance of a male monopoly within the orthodox clergy contrasts sharply with the gender blindness exhibited by those who seek prophetic inspiration or assistance. The very people who submit themselves to and sing the praises of a female charismatic might oppose, with equal ardour, the ordination of women in the church.

In so far as the gifts of the Holy Spirit—especially those which bestow miraculous competences—remain outside the control of the institutional churches, they constitute an insidious threat to the dominant element within the Protestant fold. The miracle is, after all, a manifestation of power on the part of individuals who are not fitted by their place in the social order, nor designated by human authority, to hold and exercise it. Gilsenan notes how, in a different (Muslim) context, the miracle becomes a 'weapon or refuge of the dominated, an essential part of the discourse, hopes, expectancies and creations of the poor' (1982: 77). It is no surprise that Christian miracles have for so many centuries been denied by the orthodox churches through being consigned to the age of Christ and the Apostles.

The European missionaries and their indigenous successors in the mainline churches have all along been hostile to the beliefs held by the majority of people—Christian and Hindu alike—regarding the aetiology of affliction, as well as to the fundamentalists and their thaumaturgical solutions to these problems. Until quite recently those found associating with the handful of fundamentalist groups in the city were threatened with excommunication. The post-Independence ecumenical church has been generally contemptuous of the fundamentalist enterprise. Prophets have been constantly ridiculed, stigmatized, denied CSI pulpits, or even the use of church grounds for their meetings. The dominant elements within the Protestant community speak disdainfully of their less-privileged co-religionists who 'chase miracles'. The well-educated, well-to-do, well-connected and well-employed on the whole regard fundamentalist views as the 'superstitions' of the ignorant. The Protestant middle class does not see popular beliefs about affliction as a coherent and authentic system of knowledge. It is, rather, a regrettable, if understandable, failure due mainly to ignorance on the part of the uneducated masses, to comprehend and accept a religious world-view based, like their own, on 'rationality'. They see this 'superstition' as clear evidence of irrational thinking. Popular notions about misfortune therefore constitute the people who hold them as backward and subordinate.

Discussion and Conclusion

In the context of a Christian population characterized for several decades by growing economic and social divisions, the privileged minority has, through its control of ecclesiastical structures, effectively determined what was to be the dominant theological emphasis. The social gospel, which the early twentieth-century missionaries introduced to south India, has remained the principal doctrine in the post-Independence indigenous church, and the favoured discourse of the dominant section within the community. But for the majority of ordinary Protestants, to whom this gospel has no appeal, it is a precept which is simply 'unconvincing, despite [its] authoritative source and stamp' (Turton 1984: 64). For some years they have pursued a sober, exclusive, devout and pietistic Bible-based faith, one, moreover, which maintains a firm trust in the literal truth of scripture, and refuses to compromise with those who have not accepted its message. This is the legacy of their nineteenth-century conservative evangelical missionary forebears, a kind of religiosity which Barr (1977) would regard as 'fundamentalist'.

During the last two decades there has been a dramatic explosion of interest in charismatic forms of Christianity, in south India as in many parts of the Third World. This 'new fundamentalism' has, in large part, been encouraged and funded by American organizations, and may be seen as part of a global Cold War strategy. The spread of such ideas and practices in Madras, however, has also coincided with a large-scale influx of migrants, rapid industrial growth followed soon after by stagnation and retrenchment, and the consequent sharpening of class polarization within the Protestant community as within the city's population at large. While remaining firmly planted in the CSI, those belonging to the congregations of the lower class increasingly participate in the prayer cells organized by local evangelists and healers, where enthusiasm, emotion and direct communication with the divine prevail in place of the liturgical coolness and priestly mediations of the orthodox congregations. They also flock to the crusades of the popular prophets who claim to heal with the power of the Holy Spirit.

Protestant fundamentalism in urban south India, therefore, must first of all be seen as a historical category, in the sense that it has emerged in the context of particular social and political circumstances, though this is not to suggest that it can or should be explained entirely by them. It is defined, moreover, in terms of its opposite: the reformism and modernism of liberal theology and its social gospel, which are seen to challenge Biblical veracity in the most profound way. Scripturalism, however, is not all of a kind, and does not necessarily imply exegetical uniformity. An emphasis on different Biblical doctrines by conservative evangelicals, on the one hand, and those who stress the charismata, on the other, identifies quite distinct varieties of fundamentalism. The charismatics accommodate the principle tenets of conservative evangelicalism, but revive and focus on a particular 'essential' of Protestant dogma, namely the authenticity of Christian miracles. This canon has obvious affinities with widely-held popular ideas—among both Christians and Hindus—concerning the nature of affliction, and the means of dealing with it.

Certain of these 'fundamentals', it might be noted, appear to contradict, or, at any rate, sit uneasily alongside one another. For example, a predisposition to perceive the 'world', the mundane experiences of everyday life, as a domain set apart from and potentially contaminating to the spiritual domain, confronts an outlook which differentiates little between the domains, so that many human and superhuman agents (for example, sorcerers and *peey*) continually cross the dividing line and partake of both. The Bible, as Hollenweger points out, 'does not speak in terms of a sphere of nature, governed by natural laws, and a sphere of the Spirit, governed by supernatural laws. . . .' (1972: 373). Again, while one set of views may be seen as an ideology demanding acceptance of personal responsibility for adversity—its 'interiorisation' (Taylor 1985)—the other displaces helplessness in the face of suffering by projecting it on to external mystical beings. But the contradiction is never resolved, because it is not perceived as such and because it does not and is not allowed to emerge so starkly. This is itself partly attributable to the constant negation of popular ideas and practices relating to affliction on the part first of missionaries and later the indigenous church and community leadership.

The manner in which certain kinds of knowledge are disqualified by being labelled 'superstitious' or 'irrational' encourages us to move away from a primary concern with core doctrines towards a more careful consideration of how 'truth' is produced and contended for. In the context we have been considering the emergence and popularity of charismatic forms of Christianity cannot be adequately understood without taking into account the exercise of and resistance to power, which concerns appropriate religious views and observances no less than scarce jobs and control of property. While there can never be a wholly autonomous popular knowledge which 'lies outside the field of force of the relations of cultural power and domination' (Hall 1981: 232), there are cultural (including religious) formations which may be seen to represent the perceptions, outlooks and ways of acting upon the world of those excluded from circles of privilege. The popular version may emerge as a somewhat mediated rendering of the dominant mode, which is how we might see the strongly pietistic, conservative evangelical Protestantism brought to south India by the European missionaries, and which still largely characterizes the religious predilections of the majority in post-Independence Madras. Or, it can express the more authentic experience of the disprivileged majority, which is how I would interpret the new fundamentalism. This movement is frequently portrayed by its proponents, I think accurately, as a counter-theology, or, in the wider sense, a counterculture. It represents an instance of what Foucault terms an 'insurrection of subjugated knowledges'—popular knowledges which have been muted and downgraded—and through whose reappearance 'criticism performs its work' (1980: 81–2). After all, it accords with and authenticates widely-held theodicies, and offers true believers a way of confronting and overcoming the affliction in their lives. While radical theologians and Christian activists may, with some justice, see the movement as an American-inspired attempt to *defuse* popular protest, paradoxically, in the local context, it may be read as a form of resistance to the dominant minority and the dominant theology within the church and community.

The Logic of Religious Violence

MARK JUERGENSMEYER

Why Does Violence Need Religion?

One reason often given to explain why religious symbols are associated with acts of real violence is that religion is exploited by violent people. This explanation, making religion the pure and innocent victim of the darker forces of human nature, can be overstated; yet it contains some truth. Religion in fact is sometimes exploited, and it is important to understand why that is the case—why people who are engaged in potentially violent struggles at times turn to the language of religion. In the case of the Sikhs, this means asking why the sort of people who were exercised over . . . economic, political and social issues . . . turned to preachers like Jarnail Singh Bhindranwale* for leadership.

One answer is that by sacralizing these concerns the political activists gave them an aura of legitimacy that they did not previously possess. The problem with this answer is that most of the concerns . . . the inadequacy of Sikh political representation, for instance, and the inequity of agricultural prices—were perfectly legitimate concerns, and did not need the additional moral weight of religion to give them respectability. And in fact, the people who were primarily occupied with these issues—Sikh businessmen and political leaders—were seldom supporters of Bhindranwale, at least early on. Even when they became drawn into his campaign, their relations with him remained ambivalent.

There was one political demand, however, that desperately

Excerpted from Mark Juergensmeyer, 'The Logic of Religious Violence: The Case of the Punjab', *Contributions to Indian Sociology* (NS)22, 1, 1988, 65–88.

* *Bhindranwale was killed in 1984 when the government used military force to drive out armed Sikh militants from the precincts of the Golden Temple (see Tully and Jacob 1985).* Editor.

needed all the legitimization that it could get. This was the demand for Khalistan, a separate Sikh nation. Separatist leaders . . . were greatly buoyed by such words . . . as. . . . 'When they say the Sikhs are not separate we'll demand separate identity—even if it demands sacrifice' (Bhindranwale 1987).

Bhindranwale himself, interestingly, never came out in support of Khalistan. . . . Whatever his own reservations about the Khalistan issue, however, his appeal to sacrifice made his rhetoric attractive to the separatists. It also raised another, potentially more powerful aspect of the sacralization of political demands: the prospect that religion could give moral sanction to violence.

By identifying a temporal social struggle with the cosmic struggle of order and disorder, truth and evil, political actors are able to avail themselves of a way of thinking that justifies the use of violent means. Ordinarily only the state has the moral right to take life—for purposes either of military defence, police protection or punishment—and the codes of ethics established by religious traditions support this position. Virtually every religious tradition, including the Sikhs', applauds non-violence and proscribes the taking of human life. 'For a Sikh', Bhindranwale explains, 'it is a great sin to keep weapons and kill anyone'. But he then goes on to justify the occasional violent act in extraordinary circumstances, and says that 'it is an even greater sin to have weapons and not to seek justice' (1983: 21; also see Cole and Sambhi 1978: 138). Many other religious leaders, be they Christian or Muslim or native American, might agree. The rule against killing may be abrogated in unusual circumstances when social or spiritual justice is at stake (see Juergensmeyer 1987).

Those who want their use of violence to be morally sanctioned, but do not have the approval of an officially recognized government, find it helpful to have access to a higher source: the meta-morality that religion provides. By elevating a temporal struggle to the level of the cosmic, they can bypass the usual moral restrictions on killing. If their struggle is part of an enormous battle of the spirit, then it is not ordinary morality but the rules of war that apply.

The parties in a religious war may often claim a higher degree of loyalty to their sides than parties in a purely political war. Their interests can subsume national interests. It is interesting to note, in that regard, that the best known incidents of religious violence throughout the contemporary world have occurred in places where there is difficulty in defining the character of a nation state. Palestine and Ireland are the most obvious examples, but the revolution in Iran also concerned itself with what the state should be like, and what elements of society should lead it. Religion provided the basis for a new national consensus and a new kind of leadership.

There are some aspects of social revolution in the Punjab situation as well. It is not the established leaders of the Akali party who have resorted to violence, but a second level of leadership—a younger, more marginal group for whom the use of violence is enormously empowering. The power that comes from the barrel of a gun, as Mao is said to have remarked, has a very direct effect. But here is a psychological dimension to this power that may be even more effective. As Frantz Fanon (1963) argued in the context of the Algerian revolution some years ago, even a small display of violence can have immense symbolic power: the power to jolt the masses into an awareness of their potency.

It can be debated whether or not the masses in the Punjab have been jolted into an awareness of their own capabilities, but the violent actions of the militants among them have certainly made the masses more aware of the militants' powers. They have attained a status of authority rivalling what police and other government officials possess. . . . The radical youth are even said to have set up their own courts and governmental offices.

By being dangerous, the young Sikh radicals have gained a certain notoriety, and by clothing their actions in the moral garb of religion they have given their actions legitimacy. Because their actions are morally sanctioned by religion, they are fundamentally political actions: they break the state's monopoly on morally-sanctioned killing. By putting the right to kill in their own hands, the perpetrators of religious violence are also making a daring claim of political independence.

Even though Bhindranwale was not an outspoken supporter of Khalistan, he often spoke of the Sikhs' separate identity as that of a religious community with national characteristics. The term he used for religious community, *qaum*, is an Urdu term that has overtones of nationhood. It is the term the Muslims used earlier in this century in defending their right to have a separate nation, and it is the term that Untouchables used in the Punjab in the 1920s when they attempted to be recognized as a separate social and political entity (see Juergensmeyer 1982). Another term that is important to Bhindranwale is *miri-piri*, the notion that spiritual and temporal power are linked. It is this concept that is symbolically represented by the two-edged sword and that justifies Sikh support for an independent political party. Young Sikh activists are buttressed in their own aspirations to leadership by the belief that acts that they conceive as being heroic and sacrificial—even those that involve taking the lives of others—have both spiritual and political significance. They are risking their lives for God and the Sikh community.

Not all of the Sikh community appreciates their efforts, however, and the speeches of Bhindranwale make it clear that disagreements and rivalries within the community were one of his major concerns. Some of Bhindranwale's harshest words were reserved for Sikhs who he felt showed weakness and a tendency to make easy compromises. . . .

While he was alive, Bhindranwale continued to preach unity, but it was clear that what he wanted was for everyone else to unite around him. He and his supporters wished to give the impression that they were at the centre, following the norm of Sikh belief and behaviour, and that the community should therefore group around them. This message had a particular appeal for those who were looking for a centre to Sikhism and wanted to be associated with it: Sikhs who were socially marginal to the community, including Sikhs from lower castes and those who had taken up residence abroad. Some of the most fanatical of Bhindranwale's followers, including Beant Singh, the assassin of Indira Gandhi, came from an Untouchable caste (Beant Singh was from a sweeper caste), and a considerable amount of money and moral support for the Punjab militants came from Sikhs living in places as far away as London, Houston, and Los Angeles.

These Sikhs gained from their identification with Bhindranwale a sense of belonging. The large expatriate Sikh communities in England, Canada and America were especially sensitive to his message that the Sikhs needed to be strong, united and defensive of their tradition. Many of Bhindranwale's supporters in the Punjab, however, received a more tangible benefit from associating with his cause: politically active village youth and small-time clergy were able to gain a measure of popular support. In that sense Bhindranwale was fomenting something of a political revolution, and the constituency was not unlike the one that was garnered by the Islamic revolution in Iran. Insofar as Bhindranwale's message was taken as an endorsement of the killings that some of these fundamentalist youth committed, the instrument of religious violence gave power to those who had little power before.

When Does Cosmic Struggle Lead to Real Violence?

The pattern of religious violence of militant Sikhs could be that of Irish Catholics, or Shi'ite Muslims in Palestine, or militant Christian fundamentalists in the United States. There are a great many communities in which the language of cosmic struggle justifies acts of violence. But those who are engaged in them, including the Sikh activists, would be offended if we concluded from the above discussion that their actions were purely for social or political gain. They argue that they act out of religious conviction, and surely they are right to a certain degree. As we have noted above, destruction of evil is a part of the logic of religion, and virtually every religious tradition carries with it images of chaos and terror. But symbolic violence does not lead in every instance to real bloodshed, and even the eagerness of political actors to exploit religious symbols is not sufficient to turn religion towards a violent end. Yet the fact remains that at some times religion seems to propel the faithful more easily into militant confrontation than at other times: the questions for us are when and why?

The current resurgence of religious violence around the world has given an urgency to attempts to answer these questions, and to identify those characteristics of religion that are conducive to violence. The efforts of social scientists have been directed primarily to the social and political aspects of the problem, but at least a few of them have tried to trace the patterns in religion's own logic. David Rapoport, for instance, has identified several features of Messianic movements that he believes lead to violence, most of which are characterized by a desire for an antinomian liberation from oppression (see Rapoport 1984: 658–77 and Rapoport and Alexander 1982).

My own list of characteristics comes directly from our discussion of the religious language of cosmic struggle. It is informed by my understanding of what has happened in the Sikh tradition, but it seems to me that the following tenets of religious commitment are found whenever acts of religious violence occur.

The Cosmic Struggle is Played out in History

To begin with, it seems to me that if religion is to lead to violence it is essential for the devout to believe that the cosmic struggle is realizable in human terms. If the war between good and evil, order and chaos, is conceived as taking place in historical time, in a real geographical location, and among actual social contestants, it is more likely that those who are prone to violent acts will associate religion with their struggles. This may seem to be an obvious point, yet we have some evidence that it is not always true.

In the Hindu tradition, for instance, the mythical battles in the Mahabharata and Ramayana epics are frequently used as metaphors for present-day struggles, just as are the actual battles in Sikh and Islamic history and in biblical Judaism and Christianity. Hindu politicians are as fond of making allusions to religious and literary tradition in their speeches as are Muslim and Christian politicians. Like them, they are apt to characterize their worldly foes by associating them with enemies in legendary battles. It might be remarked that the difference between Hindu and other politicians is that their references are to mythology rather than to actual historical events. But in religious language, the boundaries between myth and history are blurred. The 'historical' events of ancient Christianity and early Islam are told with all the piety and elaboration of mythology, while the 'mythology' of Hinduism has an aura of factuality to many pious Hindus. To them, the stories in the epics are no less real than those recorded in the Bible or in the Sikh legends. There are Hindus who can show you where the great war of the Mahabharata was actually fought, where Krishna was born and where he danced. Moreover, history is more important in Hindu consciousness than many Christians suppose: the great cycles of time allow for a cosmic destruction to take place in this world, at the end of the present dark age. For these reasons the Hindu tradition may be considered as one of the historical religions—it is not as devoid of images of divine intervention in worldly struggles as European and American writers sometimes assume.

The major tradition that appears to lack the notion that the cosmic struggle is played out on a social plane is Buddhism. But this would appear to be an exception that proves the rule, for it is a tradition that is characteristically devoid of religiously sanctioned violence. There are instances in Thai history that provide Buddhist justifications for warfare, and it may be that there are religious elements in the Buddhist involvement in conflict in present-day Sri Lanka—I do not know the Sri Lankan case well enough to say. But even if this were the case, it and the Thai example are rare for the tradition as a whole. In general, Buddhism seems to have no need for actual battles in which the pious can prove their mettle.

Believers Identify Personally with the Struggle

The Buddhist tradition does affirm that there is a spiritual conflict, however: it is the clash between the perception that this imperfect and illusory world is real and a higher consciousness that surmounts worldly perception altogether. And even then the struggle does take place in this world in a sense, in that it takes place in the minds of worldly persons. This kind of internalization of the cosmic struggle does not in itself lead to violence, however, and for that reason Buddhists are not ordinarily prone to violent deeds. Nor are Sufis, the Islamic mystics who have reconceived the Muslim notion of *jihad*. To many Sufis, the greater *jihad* is not the one involving worldly warfare, but the one within: the conflict between good and evil within one's own soul.

This idea that the cosmic struggle is something inside the self might seem to be quite different from the conception of the struggle as taking place in history, but in Sikh theology, including the rhetoric of Bhindranwale, the two ideas go hand in hand. 'The weakness is in us', Bhindranwale explained, as he described the causes of the current crisis, 'we are the sinners of this house of our Guru' (1983: 7). Shi'ite Muslims are similarly racked with a sense of personal responsibility for the moral decadence of the world, and once again their tendency towards interiorization does not necessarily shield them from acts of external violence. The key to the connection, it seems to me, is that the cosmic struggle is understood to impinge about the inner recesses of an individual person in a simultaneous conjunction with its occurrence on a worldly, social plane. Neither of these notions is by itself sufficient to motivate a person to religious violence. If one believes that the cosmic struggle is primarily a matter of large contending social forces, one is not likely to become personally identified with the struggle; and if one is convinced that the struggle is solely interior there is no reason to look for it outside. But when the two ideas coexist, they are a volatile concoction.

Thus when Bhindranwale spoke about warfare in the soul his listeners knew that however burdensome that conflict is, they need not bear it alone. They may band together with their comrades and continue the struggle in the external arena, where the foes are more vulnerable, and victories more tangible. And their own internal struggles impel them to become involved in the worldly conflict: their identification with the overall struggle makes them morally responsible, in part, for its outcome. 'We are the ones who are ruining Sikhism', Bhindranwale told his congregation, and recounted the story of how, when Guru Gobind Singh asked an army of 80,000 to sacrifice their heads for the faith, only five assented. Bhindranwale implied that the opportunity was still at hand to make the choice of whether they were to be one of the five or the 79,995 (1983: 13). He reminded them that even though the cosmic war was still being waged, and that the evil within them and outside them had not yet been purged, their choice could still make a difference.

Sikhism is not the only tradition in which this link is forged between the external and internal arenas of the cosmic struggle. One finds it is Christianity, Judaism and Islam as well. As I have mentioned, Shi'ite Muslims bear a great weight of communal guilt for not having defended one of the founders of their tradition, Husain, when he was attacked and martyred by the vicious Yazid. During the Iranian revolution some of them relived that conflict by identifying specific foes—the Shah and President Jimmy Carter—as Yazids returned. There was no doubt that such people should be attacked. Radical Shi'ites in Iran were not about to compound their guilt and miss a historical opportunity of righting an ancient wrong.

The same sort of logic has propelled many Christians into a vicious antisemitism. It is a mark of good Christian piety for individuals to bear the responsibility for the crucifixion of Jesus: the theme of Christians taking part in the denial and betrayal of Jesus is the stuff of many a hymn and sermon. Some Christians believe that the foes to whom they allowed Jesus to be delivered were the Jews. Attacks on the present-day Jewish community, therefore, helps lighten their sense of culpability.

The Cosmic Struggle Continues in the Present

What makes these actions of Sikhs, Shi'ites and antisemitic Christians spiritually defensible is the conviction that the sacred struggle has not ended in some earlier period, but that it continues in some form today. It is a conviction that also excites the members of the Gush Emunim, a militant movement in present-day Israel, who have taken Israel's victory in the Six-Day War as a sign that the age of messianic redemption has finally begun (see Sprinzak 1988).

Not all Israelis respond to this sign with the same enthusiasm, however, just as not all Christians or Shi'ite Muslims are convinced that the apocalyptic conflict prophesied by their tradition is really at hand. Many of the faithful assent to the notion that the struggle exists within, for what person of faith has not felt the internal tension between belief and disbelief, affirmation and denial, order and chaos?.But they often have to be persuaded that the conflict currently rages on a social plane, especially if the social world seems orderly and benign.

Bhindranwale took this challenge as one of the primary tasks of his ministry. He said that one of his main missions was to alert his people that they were oppressed, even if they did not know it. . . .

In Bhindranwale's mind the appearances of normal social order simply illustrated how successful the forces of evil had become in hiding their demonic agenda. His logic compelled him to believe that Punjabi society was racked in a great struggle, even if it showed no indication of it. Long before the Punjab was torn apart by the recent rounds of violence, Bhindranwale claimed that an even fiercer form of violence reigned: the appearance of normal order was merely a demonic deception. Bhindranwale hated the veil of calm that seemed to cover his community and felt that because of it his own followers were often perplexed about what he said: 'Many of our brothers, fresh from the villages, ask, "Sant Ji, we don't know about enslavement". For that reason, I have to tell you why you are slaves' (1983a: 2).

The evidence that Bhindranwale gave for the oppression of Sikhs was largely limited to examples of police hostility that arose after the spiral of violence in the Punjab began to grow. Some of his allegations, such as the account he gave of the treatment meted out to followers who hijacked Indian airplanes, have a peculiar ring:

> If a Sikh protests on behalf of his Guru by hijacking a plane, he is put to death. . . . None of the Sikhs in these three hijackings attacked any passenger nor did they damage the planes. But the rule is that for a fellow with a turban, there is the bullet. . . . For a person who says 'Hare Krishna, Hare Krishna, Hare Rama', there is a government appointment. Sikh brothers, this is a sign of slavery (1983a: 3).

Those who attempted to combat Bhindranwale could not win against such logic. If they responded to Sikh violence they would be seen as oppressors. If they did not respond, the violence would escalate. And even if there was neither violence nor repression, the absence of the overt signs of conflict would be an indication to Bhindranwale of a demonical calm.

The Struggle is at a Point of Crisis

On a number of occasions when Bhindranwale referred to the immediacy of the struggle he seemed to indicate that the outcome was in doubt. His perception of the enormity of the evil he faced and of the torpor of the Sikh response made his prognosis a dismal one. Sometimes he felt that the best efforts of a few faithful Sikhs were doomed: 'today', he darkly proclaimed, 'the Sikh community is under threat' (1987). But on other occasions he seemed to hold out a measure of hope. Things were coming to a head, he implied, and the struggle was about to enter 'the decisive phase' (ibid.).

What is interesting about this apocalyptic rhetoric is its uncertainty. If the outcome were less in doubt there would be little reason for violent action. If one knew that the foe would win, there would be no reason to want to fight back. Weston LaBarre (1972) describes the terrible circumstances surrounding the advent of the Ghost Dance religion of the Plains Indians: knowing that they faced overwhelming odds and almost certain defeat, the tribe diverted their concerns from worldly conflict to spiritual conflict, and entertained the notion that a ritual dance would conjure up sufficient spiritual force to destroy the alien cavalry.

LaBarre concludes that sheer desperation caused them to turn to religion and away from efforts to defend themselves. But by the same token, if they knew that the battle could be won without a struggle, there also would be little reason for engagement. The passive pacifism of what William James calls 'healthy-souled religion'—mainstream Protestant churches, for example, that regard social progress as inevitable—comes from just such optimism (1985: 71–108). Other pacifist movements, however, have been directly engaged in conflict. Menno Simmons, the Anabaptist for whom the Mennonite church is named, and Mohandas Gandhi are examples of pacifist leaders who at times narrowly skirted the edges of violence, propelled by a conviction that without human effort the outcome they desired could not be won.

In that sense Gandhi and Bhindranwale were more alike than one might suspect. Both saw the world in terms of cosmic struggle, both regarded their cause as being poised on a delicate balance between oppression and opportunity, and both believed that human action could tip the scales. The issue that divided them, of course, was violence.

Acts of Violence have a Cosmic Meaning

The human action in the Sikh case is certainly not pacifist, for Bhindranwale held that there would be 'no deliverance without weapons' (1983: 10). He was careful, however, to let the world know that these weapons were not to be used indiscriminately:

> It is sin for a Sikh to keep weapons to hurt an innocent person, to rob anyone's home, to dishonour anyone or to oppress anyone. But there is no greater sin for a Sikh than keeping weapons and not using them to protect his faith (ibid.).

Contrariwise, there is no greater valour for a Sikh than to use weapons in defence of the faith. Bhindranwale himself was armed to the teeth, and although he never publicly admited to any of the killings that were pinned on him personally, Bhindranwale expressed his desire to 'die fighting', a wish that was fulfilled within months of being uttered (1987).

According to Bhindranwale, those who committed acts of religiously sanctioned violence were to be regarded as heroes and more. Although he usually referred to himself as a 'humble servant', and an 'uneducated fallible person' (1983: 14), Bhindranwale would occasionally identify himself with one of the legendary Sikh saints, Baba Deep Singh, who continued to battle with Moghul foes even after his head had been severed from his body. He carried it manfully on his palm. In Bhindranwale's mind, he too seemed destined for martyrdom.

To many Sikhs today, that is precisely what Bhindranwale achieved. Whatever excesses he may have committed during his lifetime are excused, as one would excuse a lethal but heroic soldier in a glorious war. Even Beant Singh, the bodyguard of Indira Gandhi that turned on her, is held to be a saintly hero. Perhaps this has to be: if Indira was such a demonic foe, her assassin must be similarly exalted.

It may seem a terrible contradiction that some of the most pious people—those who most value the sense of order that religion provides—are sometimes the same ones who cheer the activists in an arena of religious violence. But keep in mind that religious struggles are seen by those involved in them as fights for the good, and for that reason their goals are seen ultimately as conducive for peace, even if there must be bloodshed along the way.

But not all religious people may recognize that a struggle of divine proportions is in the air, and it is the objective of many religious activists, as prophets and agents of a higher order of truth, to engage in deeds that necessarily startle. Their purpose is to awaken good folk, mobilize their community, insult the evil forces, and perhaps even to demonstrate dramatically to God himself that there are those who are willing to fight and die on his side, and to deliver his judgement of death. The great promise of cosmic struggle is that order will prevail over chaos; the great irony is that many must die in order for certain visions of that victory to prevail and their awful dramas be brought to an end.

Secularism in its Place

T. N. MADAN

We live in a world which we call modern or which we wish to be modern. Modernity is generally regarded as both a practical necessity and a moral imperative, a fact and a value. When I say this I am not using the word 'modern' in one of those many trivial senses which I trust we have by now left behind us. Thus, by modernity I do not mean a complete break with tradition. Being modern means larger and deeper things: for example, the enlargement of human freedom and the enhancement of the range of choices open to a people in respect of things that matter, including their present and future life-styles. This means being in charge of oneself. And this is one of the connotations of the process of secularization.

The word 'secularization' was first used in 1648, at the end of the Thirty Years' War in Europe, to refer to the transfer of church properties to the exclusive control of the princes. What was a matter-of-fact statement then became later, after the French Revolution, a value statement as well: on November 2, 1789, Talleyrand announced to the French National Assembly that all ecclesiastical goods were at the disposal of the nation, as indeed they should have been. Still later, when George Jacob Holyoake coined the term 'secularism' in 1851 and led a rationalist movement of protest in England, secularization was built into the ideology of progress. Though nowhere more than a fragmentary and incomplete process, it has ever since retained a positive connotation.

'Secularization' is nowadays generally employed to refer to, in the words of Peter Berger, 'the process by which sectors of society and culture are removed from the domination of religious institutions

Adapted from T. N. Madan, 'Secularism in its Place', *The Journal of Asian Studies*, Vol. 46, No. 4, November 1987, pp 747–58. This is the text, with a few verbal modifications, of the Fulbright 40th. Anniversary Distinguished Lecture delivered on the occasion of the 1987 meeting of the Association of Asian Studies in Boston.

and symbols' (1973: 113). While the inner logic of the economic sector perhaps makes it the most convenient arena for secularization, other sectors, notably the political, have been found to be less amenable to it. It is in relation to the latter that the ideology of secularism acquires the most salience.

Now, I submit that in the prevailing circumstances secularism in South Asia as a generally shared credo of life is impossible, as a basis for state action impracticable, and as a blueprint for the foreseeable future impotent. It is impossible as a credo of life because the great majority of the people of South Asia are in their own eyes active adherents of some religious faith. It is impracticable as a basis for state action either because Buddhism and Islam have been declared state or state-protected religions or because the stance of religious neutrality or equidistance is difficult to maintain since religious minorities do not share the majority's view of what this entails for the state. And it is impotent as a blueprint for the future because, by its very nature, it is incapable of countering religious fundamentalism and fanaticism.

Secularism is the dream of a minority which wants to shape the majority in its own image, which wants to impose its will upon history but lacks the power to do so under a democratically organized polity. In an open society the state will reflect the character of the society. Secularism therefore is a social myth which draws a cover over the failure of this minority to separate politics from religion in the society in which its members live. From the point of view of the majority, 'secularism' is a vacuous word, a phantom concept, for such people do not know whether it is desirable to privatize religion, and if it is, how this may be done, unless they be Protestant Christians, but not if they are Buddhists, Hindus, Muslims, or Sikhs. For the secularist minority to stigmatize the majority as primordially oriented and to preach secularism to the latter as the law of human existence is moral arrogance and worse—I say 'worse' since in our times politics takes precedence over ethics—political folly. It is both these—moral arrogance and political folly—because it fails to recognize the immense importance of religion in the lives of the peoples of South Asia. I will not raise here the issue of the definition of religion: suffice it to say that for these peoples their religion establishes their place in society and bestows meaning on their life, more than any other social or cultural factor.

Unable to raise the veil of its illusions, the modernist minority in India today is beset with deep anxieties about the future of secularism in the country and in South Asia generally. Appeals are made day in and day out to foster a modern scientific temper, of which Jawaharlal Nehru is invoked as a principal exponent. Books are written and an unending round of seminars held on the true nature and significance of communalism and how to combat it. In fact, there is much talk these days in the highest political quarters about the need for stern legislative and executive measures to check the rising and menacing tide of majority and minority fundamentalism and revivalism, and this even as the so-called Hindu society continues to splinter.

An astonishing (or should one say impressive?) consensus among Indian Muslims about preserving the Shari'a, or 'holy law', against what they consider the legislative onslaught of a godless state but others call the indispensability of a common civil law, as a foundation of the modern state, was witnessed in 1986 in connection with the rights of Muslim divorced women (The Shah Bano Case). This was . . . followed by the biggest-ever public protest by Muslims since independence forty years ago, held at New Delhi on March 30, 1987, to demand full possession of a sixteenth-century mosque in the city of Ayodhya in north India, which was built after Babar's invasion at what Hindus believe to have been the birthplace of godincarnate Rama and at which they want to build a temple after demolishing the mosque. By October 1990 passions had become inflamed and widespread communal riots took place in not only Ayodhya but also in other cities, particularly in north India. Meanwhile, Sikh fundamentalists and terrorists in Punjab, and Muslim fundamentalists and militants in Kashmir continue to battle security forces, and kill innocent people of all three communities. Social analysts draw attention to the contradiction between the undoubted though slow spread of secularization in everyday life, on the one hand, and the unmistakable rise of fundamentalism, on the other. But surely these phenomena are only apparently contradictory, for in truth it is the marginalization of religious faith, which is what secularization is, that permits the perversion of religion. There are no fundamentalists or revivalists in traditional society.

The point to stress, then, is that, despite ongoing processes of secularization and deliberate efforts to promote it, secularism as a widely shared worldview has failed to make headway in India. Obviously what exists empirically but not also ideologically exists only weakly. The hopes about the prospects of secularism raised by social scientists in the years soon after independence—recall the well-known books by Donald Eugene Smith (1963) and Rajni Kothari

(1970)—have been belied, notwithstanding the general acceptability of their view of 'Hinduism' as a broadly tolerant religion. Acute observers of the socio-cultural and political scenes contend that signs of a weakening secularism are in evidence, particularly among the Hindus. Religious books, a recent newspaper report said, continue to outsell all the others in India and, one can be sure, in all the other South Asian countries. Religious pilgrimages attract larger and ever larger congregations counted in millions. Buildings of religious worship or prayer dot the urban landscape. New Delhi has many new Hindu temples and Sikh *gurudwaras*, and its most recent modern structure is the Bahai temple facing the old Kalkaji (Hindu) temple, thrown open to worshippers of all faiths late last year. God-men and gurus sit in seminars and roam the streets, and American 'Hare Krishnas' take the initiative in organizing an annual *ratha yātrā* (chariot festival).

While society seethes with these and other expressions of a vibrant religiosity, the feeble character of the Indian policy of state secularism is exposed. At best, Indian secularism has been an inadequately defined 'attitude' (it cannot be called a philosophy of life except when one is discussing the thought of someone like Mahatma Gandhi or Maulana Azad) of 'goodwill towards all religions', *sarvadharma sadbhāva*. In a narrower formulation it has been a negative or defensive policy of religious neutrality (*dharma nirpekshtā*) on the part of the state. In either formulation, Indian secularism achieves the opposite of its stated intentions; it trivializes religious difference as well as the notion of the unity of religions. And it really fails to provide guidance for viable political action, for it is not a rooted, full-blooded, and well-thought-out weltanschauung, it is only a strategem. It has been so self-confessedly for fundamentalist organizations such as the Muslim Jama'at i Islami (see Mushir-ul-Haq 1972: 11–12). I would like to suggest that it was also so for Jawaharlal Nehru, but let me not anticipate: I will have more to say about Nehru's secularism in a short while. Just now, let me dwell a little longer on the infirmity of secularism.

What exactly does the failure of secularism mean? For one thing, it underscores the failure of the society and the state to bring under control the divisive forces which resulted in the Partition of the subcontinent in 1947. Though forty years have passed and the Midnight's Children[1] are at the threshold of middle age, tempers

[1] Salman Rushdie refers to people born around independence day 'midnight's children' in his novel bearing that title. The independence of India was proclaimed at midnight, August 15, 1947.

continue to rage, and occasionally (perhaps too frequently) even blood flows in some places, as a result of the mutual hostility between the followers of different religions.

What produces this hostility? Surely not religious faith itself, for even religious traditions which take an uncompromising view of 'non-believers' (that is, the followers of other religions) speak with multiple tongues and pregnant ambiguity. The Qur'ān, for example, proclaims that there should be no coercion in the matter of faith (2:256). Even an agnostic such as Nehru acknowledged this before the burden of running a secular state fell on his aging shoulders. As long ago as 1936 he said, 'The communal problem is not a religious problem, it has nothing to do with religion' (1972–82, 7:82). It was not religious difference as such but its exploitation by calculating politicians for the achievement of secular ends which had produced the communal divide.

It is perhaps one of the tragedies of the twentieth century that a man who had at the beginning of his political career wanted above all to bridge religious differences should have in the end contributed to widening them. As is well-known, the young Muhammad Ali Jinnah was a non-practicing Muslim in private life and a secularist in public, but later on he (like many others, Hindus and Sikhs as well as Muslims) played with the fire of communal frenzy. Inevitably, perhaps, he became a victim of his own political success of, as Ayesha Jalal puts it, 'an unthinking mob, fired by blood lust, fear and greed' (1985:216). I should think he too realized this, for, without any loss of time, four days before the formal inauguration of Pakistan, he called upon his people to 'bury the hatchet' and make common citizenship, not communal identity, the basis of the new state (see Sharif ul Mujahid 1981:247). And within a month he reiterated: 'You may belong to any religion, or caste, or creed—that has nothing to do with the business of the state' (Jinnah 1947–8:8). How close to Nehru he was, and, though he pulled himself far apart for the achievement of his political goals, he obviously remained a secularist.

Tolerance is indeed a value enshrined in all the great religions of mankind, but let me not underplay the historical roots of communal antagonism in South Asia. I am not wholly convinced when our Marxist colleagues argue that communalism is a result of the distortions in the economic base of our societies produced by the colonial mode of production and that the 'communal question was a petty bourgeois question par excellence' (Bipan Chandra 1984:40). The importance of these distortions may not be minimized, but these analysts should know that South Asia's major religious traditions—Buddhism, Hinduism, Islam, and Sikhism—are totalizing in character, claiming all of a follower's life, so that religion is constitutive of society. In the given pluralist situation, both tolerance and intolerance are expressions of exclusivism. When I say that South Asia's religious traditions are 'totalizing', I am not trying to argue that they do not recognize the distinction between the terms 'religious' and 'secular'. We know that in their distinctive ways all four traditions make this distinction. I wish I had the time to elaborate on this theme, but then there is perhaps no need to do so here. What needs to be stressed, however, is that these religions have the same view of the relationship between the categories of the 'religious' and the 'secular'.

My studies convince me that in Buddhism, Hinduism, Islam, and Sikhism, this relationship is hierarchical (in the sense in which Louis Dumont uses this term). Thus, though Buddhism may well be considered as the one South Asian religious tradition which, by denying supernatural beings any significant role in human life, has the most secularist potential, yet this would be an oversimplified view of it. What is important is not only what Emile Durkheim so clearly perceived, namely the central importance of the category of the 'sacred' in Buddhism, but also (and more significantly in the present context) the fact, so well documented for us by Stanley Tambiah (1976) that the *bhikkhu*, or the world renouncer, is superior to the *chakkavatti*, or the world conqueror, and that neither exists by himself. Similarly, in every Sikh *gurudwara* the sacred sword is placed for veneration at a lower level than the holy book, the *Granth Sāhab*, which is the repository of the Word (*shabad*), despite the fact that, for the Sikhs, the sword too symbolizes the divinity or, more accurately, the inseparability of the spiritual and the religious functions.

I will like to dwell a little on the *Rig Veda* of three thousand years ago, for the reason that it presents explicitly, employing a fascinating simile, the hierarchical relationship between spiritual authority and temporal power. It would seem that originally the two functions were differentiated, but they were later deliberately brought together, for the regnum (*kshatra*) could not subsist on its own without the sacerdotium (*brahma*) which provided its principle of legitimacy. Says the king to the priest: 'Turn thou unto me so that we may unite. . . . I assign to you the precedence; quickened by thee I shall perform deeds' (see Coomaraswamy 1978: 8). The very word used for the priest, *purohita,* points to precedence. What is more, the priest and the king are united, as husband is to wife, and they must speak with one voice. This is what Dumont would call hierarchical dyarchy or complementarity. Even if one were to look upon the king and the *purohita* as dissociated (rather than united) and thus contend that kingship had become secularized (see Dumont 1980: 293), the hierarchical relation between the two functions survives and is even emphasized. The discrete realm of economic interest and power (*artha*) is opposed to and yet encompassed by Dharma.

Let me move on to the Kautilya Arthashāstra (? fourth century BC/AD), which has been said often enough to present an amoral theory of political power. Such a reading is, however, contestable. What I find more acceptable is the view that emphasizes that the Arthashāstra teaches that the rational pursuit of economic and political ends (*artha*) must be carried out in fulfilment and not violation of Dharma. More broadly, '*artha* must be pursued in the framework of *kāma, dharma* and *mokṣa* . . . the principle remains that *artha* to be truly *artha* must be part of a larger totality, individual and social' (Shah 1982: 72).

I might add here parenthetically that in traditional Brahmanical political thought, cultural pluralism within the state was accepted and the king was the protector of everybody's Dharma: *that* was *his* Dharma. Only in very exceptional circumstances, apprehending disorder, might the king have used his authority to abrogate certain customs or usages (see Lingat 1973: 226). Hence the idea of a state religion was not entertained.

I will say no more about the ancient period but only observe that some of these traditional ideas have reverberated in the practice of Hindu kings and their subjects all the way down the corridors of time into the twentieth century (see Mayer 1982). Even today, these ideas are relevant in the context of the only surviving Hindu monarchy of the world, Nepal, where the king is considered an incarnation of God and yet has to be consecrated by the Brahman royal priest.

In our own times it was, of course, Mahatma Gandhi who restated the traditional point of view in the changed context of the twentieth century, emphasizing the inseparability of religion and politics and the superiority of the former over the latter. 'For me', he said, 'every, the tiniest, activity is governed by what I consider to be my religion' (see Iyer 1986: 391). And, more specifically, there is the well-known early statement that 'those who say that religion has nothing to do with politics do not know what religion means' (Gandhi 1940: 383). For Gandhi religion was the source of absolute value and hence constitutive of social life; politics was the arena of public interest without the former the latter would become debased. While it was the obligation of the state to ensure that every religion was free to develop according to its own genius, no religion which depended upon state support deserved to survive. In other words, the inseparability of religion and politics in the Indian context, and generally, was for Gandhi fundamentally a distinct issue from the separation of the state from the Church in Christendom. When he did advocate that 'religion and state should be separate', he clarified that this was to limit the role of the state to 'secular welfare' and to allow it no admittance into the religious life of the people (see Iyer 1986: 395). Clearly the hierarchical relationship is irreversible.

Let me now turn briefly to Islam. Traditionally Islam postulates a single chain of command in the political domain; God-Prophet-caliph-king. God Almighty is the ever-active sovereign of His universe, which is governed by His will. In his own life Muhammad symbolized the unity of faith (*dīn*) and the material world (*dawla*). His successors (*khalīfa*) were the guardians on whose authority the kings ruled. They (the kings) were but the shadow of God on earth, holding power as a trust and answerable to their Maker on the Day of Judgment like everybody else. In India, Ziya-ud-Din Barni, an outstanding medieval (mid-fourteenth-century) theologian and political commentator, wrote of religion and temporal government, of prophets and kings, as twin brothers, but without leaving the reader in any doubt about, whom he placed first (see de Bary 1970: 459–60).

In the twentieth century, Muhammad Iqbal occupies a very special place as an interpreter of Islam in South Asia. Rejecting the secularist programme of Turkish Nationalists, he wrote: 'In Islam the spiritual and the temporal are not two distinct domains, and the nature of an act, however secular in its import, is determined by the attitude of mind with which the agent does it. . . . In Islam it is the same reality which appears as Church looked at from one point of view and State from another' (1980: 154). Iqbal further explains: 'The ultimate Reality, according to the Quran, is spiritual, and its life consists in its temporal activity. The spirit finds its opportunities in the natural, the material, the secular. All that is secular is therefore sacred in the roots of its being. . . . There is no such thing as a profane world. . . . All is holy ground' (ibid.: 155). In short, to use the idiom adopted by me, the secular is encompassed by the sacred.

An autonomous ideology of secularism is ruled out. This is how Fazlur Rahman (a most distinguished South Asian scholar who wrote on such subjects) puts it: 'Secularism destroys the sanctity and universality (transcendence) of all moral values' (1982: 15). If secularism is to be eschewed, so is neo-revivalism-to be avoided for its 'intellectual bankruptcy' (ibid.: 137). Rahman argues that a modern life need not be detached from religious faith and should indeed be informed by it, or else Muslims may well lose their very humanity.

This excursus into South Asia's major religious traditions was important for me to make the point that the search for secular elements in the cultural traditions of this region is a futile exercise, for it is not these but an ideology of secularism that is absent and is resisted. What is important, therefore, is the relationship between the categories, and this is unmistakably hierarchical, the religious encompassing the secular. Louis Dumont recently reminded us that the doctrine of the subordination of the power of kings to the authority of the priests, enunciated by Pope Gelasius around the end of the fifth century, perhaps represents 'simply the logical formula for the relation between the two functions' (1983: 15). Indeed, the world's great religious traditions do seem to speak on this vital issue with one voice. Or they did until the Reformation made a major departure in this regard within the Christian tradition.

Scholars from Max Weber and Ernst Troeltsch to Peter Berger and Louis Dumont have in their different ways pointed to the essential linkages among Protestantism, individualism, and secularization. Max Weber's poignant statement that 'the fate of our times is characterized by rationalization and intellectualization and, above all, by the "disenchantment of the world" [is well known]. Precisely the ultimate and most sublime values have retreated from public life either into the transcendental realm of mystic life or into the brotherliness of direct and personal relations' (see Gerth and Mills 1948: 155). Or, to put it in Peter Berger's succinct summing up, 'Protestantism cut the umbilical cord between heaven and earth' (1973: 118).

This is not the occasion to go into the details of the well-grounded idea that secularization is a gift of Christianity to mankind, but it is important for my present concern to note that the privatization of religion, through the assumption by the individual of the responsibility for his or her own salvation without the intervention of the Church, is very much a late Christian idea. The general secularization of life in the West after the Reformation is significantly, though only partly, an unintended consequence of this religious idea. Luther was indeed a man of his times, a tragic medieval figure, who ushered in a modern age that he would hardly approve of.

But let us not stray too far. How does all this bear upon my present theme, namely the prospects of secularism in India? The idea of secularism, a gift of Christianity, has been built into Western social theorists' paradigms of modernization, and since these paradigms are believed to have universal applicability, the elements, which converged historically—that is in a unique manner—to constitute modern life in Europe in the sixteenth and the following three centuries, have come to be presented as the requirements of modernization elsewhere, and this must be questioned. Paradoxically, the uniqueness of the history of modern Europe lies, we are asked to believe, in its general applicability.

To put what I have just said in other words, secularism as an ideology has emerged from the dialectic of modern science and Protestantism, not from a simple repudiation of religion and the rise of rationalism. Even the Enlightenment—its English and German versions in particular—was not against religion as such but against revealed religion or a transcendental justification for religion. Voltaire's 'dying' declaration was of faith in God and detestation of 'superstition'. Models of modernization, however, prescribe the transfer of secularism to non-Western societies without regard for the character of their religious traditions or for the gifts that these might have to offer. Such transfers arc themselves phenomena of the modern secularized world: in traditional or tradition-haunted societies they can only mean conversion and the loss of one's culture, and, if you like, the loss of one's soul. Even in already-modern or modernizing societies, unless cultural transfers are made meaningful for the people, they appear as stray behaviouristic traits and attitudinal postures. This means that what is called for is translation; mere transfer will not do.

But translations are not easily achieved. As Bankim Chandra Chatterji (that towering late nineteenth-century Indian intellectual) put it, 'You can translate a word by a word, but behind the word is an idea, the thing which the word denotes, and this idea you cannot translate, if it does not exist among the people in whose language you are translating' (see Chatterjee 1986: 61). It is imperative, then, that a people must themselves render their historical experience meaningful: others may not do this for them. Borrowed ideas, unless internalized, do not have the power to bestow on us the gift and grace of living.

In this regard, I should like to point out that once a cultural definition of a phenomenon or of a relationship (say, between religion and politics, or society and the state) has crystallized, it follows that subsequent formulations of it, whether endogenous or exogenous, can only be *re*-definitions. Traditions posit memory. Given the fact of the unequal social distribution of knowledge and the unequal impress of social change, it is not at all surprising that some elements of tradition should survive better and longer among the ordinary people, who may not think about it but live it, and others among the intellectuals.

In short, the transferability of the idea of secularism to the countries of South Asia is beset with many difficulties and should not be taken for granted. Secularism must be put in its place: which does not mean rejecting it but of finding the proper means for its expression. In multi-religious societies, such as those of South Asia, it should be realized that secularism may not be restricted to rationalism, that it is compatible with faith, and that rationalism (as understood in the West) is not the sole motive force of a modern state. What the institutional implications of such a position are is an important question and needs to be worked out.

I am afraid I have already said enough to invite the charge of being some kind of a cultural determinist, which I am not. I am aware of the part that creative individuals and dominant minorities play in changing and shaping the course of history. As a student of cultural anthropology I know that even in the simplest of settings cultures, ways of life, are not merely reproduced but are also resisted and changed, more in some places and times and less in others, more successfully by some individuals or groups than by others. In this connection, I must now return to Jawaharlal Nehru as the typical modern Indian intellectual.

It has been argued well by many scholars that while Gandhi put his faith in the reformed, ethically refined individual, in creating a better if not ideal society, Nehru considered the shaping of suitable institutions as the best means to achieve the same goal. And of all the modern institutions it was the state which he believed would be the principal engine of social change. Hegel, you will remember, said that the Hindus were a people and did not constitute a state: this judgment (and similar others) have informed Western social science thinking about India, expressed recently, for instance, in the contrast between primordial bonds and civic ties made by Edward Shils and Clifford Geertz, and others.

Nehru, like many other modern Indians, imbibed the same point of view and obviously wanted to remove the deficiency. The Nehruvian state was first and foremost democratic, but in an economically poor and culturally diverse country it could hardly be truly democratic without being socialist and secularist. I am not here concerned with the course of democracy and socialism in India, but I must make some observations about the difficulties encountered by the secular state established under the Constitution.

I will not enter into the controversy whether the Indian state is at all secular in the sense in which the American state is, or whether it is only jurisdictionalist (see Luthera 1964). We do not, of course, have a wall of separation in India, for there is no church to wall off, but only the notion of neutrality or equidistance between the state and the religious identity of the people. What makes this idea important is that not only Nehru but all Indians who consider themselves patriotic and modern, nationalist and rationalist, subscribe to it. What makes it impotent is that it is a purely negative strategy. And as you know, in the history of mankind, nothing positive has ever been built on denials or negations alone.

An examination of Nehru's writings and speeches brings out very clearly his conviction that religion is a hindrance to 'the tendency to change and progress inherent in human society' and that 'the belief in a supernatural agency which ordains everything has led to a certain irresponsibility on the social plane, and emotion and sentimentality have taken the place of reasoned thought and inquiry' (Nehru 1961: 543). Religion, he confessed candidly, did not 'attract' him for 'behind it lay a method of approach to life's problems which was certainly not that of science' (ibid: 26). But, then, he did not worry too much about religion or its political expression, namely communalism, because he passionately believed that these epiphenomena would 'vanish at the touch of reality' (1980: 469). Hence his insistence that, quoting from a 1931 speech, 'the real thing to my mind is the economic factor. If we lay stress on this and divert public attention to it we shall find automatically that religious differences recede into the background and a common bond unites different groups. The economic bond is stronger than the national one' (1972–82, 5: 203).

Nehru insisted that his conclusions were not speculative but based on practical experience. Many years later, after mature reflection, he wrote that once the national state came into being it would be economic problems that would acquire salience; there might be 'class conflicts' but not 'religious conflicts, except insofar as religion itself expressed some vested interest' (1961: 106). It is not, therefore, at all surprising that until the very end Nehru was puzzled and pained by Muslim separatism and was deeply distrustful of politicians who exploited religion for political purposes; and yet he was contemptuous of those who took the religious question seriously. Not for him Iqbal's insistence that the cultural question was as important as the economic (see Malik 1963: 253). The irony of it is that Iqbal too considered himself a socialist!

In the end, that is in 1947, Nehru knew that the battle at hand, though not perhaps the war, had been lost, that the peoples of the subcontinent were not yet advanced enough to share his view of secular politics and the secular state. A retreat was inescapable, but it was not a defeat. Sorrowfully he wrote in 1961, just three years before his death: 'We talk about a secular state in India. It is perhaps not very easy even to find a good word in Hindi for "secular". Some people think it means something opposed to religion. That obviously is not correct. . . . It is a state which honours all faiths equally and gives them equal opportunities' (see Gopal 1980: 330).

Having thus described Indian secularism, he proceeded in line with his own earlier thinking on the subject: 'Our Constitution lays down that we are a secular state, but it must be admitted that this is not wholly reflected in our mass living and thinking. In a country like England, the state is . . . allied to one particular religion. . . . Nevertheless, the state and the people there function in a largely secular way. Society, therefore, in England is more advanced in this respect than in India, even though our Constitution may be in this matter more advanced' (ibid.: 330–31). It is obvious that Nehru had not given up his trust of the secularization process, that his view of religion remained unchanged.

What is noteworthy, therefore, is Nehru's refusal (or failure) to use the coercive powers of the state in hastening this process. In this regard he invites comparison with Lenin and Ataturk, and, if you allow dictatorship, he suffers by it. I do not have the time to discuss in any detail this instructively fascinating comparison or pose the question as to the conditions under which a part (state) may dictate to the whole (society), but let me say a few words about it, very briefly.

Take Lenin's position. Continuing the Feuerbach-Marx line he asserted that the religious question must not be advanced to 'the first place where it does not belong at all' (see Dube and Basilov 1983: 173). To match this by action, he played an active and direct part in the formulation of the 1918 decree on 'the separation of the church from the state and of the school from the church'. While every citizen was in principle free to profess any religion, or none at all, he could not actively propagate it; what is more, the educational function of the Communist party ensured that 'senseless ideas' arising from a false consciousness would be countered.

Similarly, Ataturk proceeded by one deliberate step after another, beginning with the abolition of the Caliphate in 1924, of the religious orders in 1925, of Shari'a courts in 1926, and of Islam as the state religion in 1928. The process of secularization was continued thereafter, and the changes effected were enforced strictly, with Kemal himself often setting the example in even minor points of detail (see Lewis 1968: 239–93).

Contrast the internal coherence and sense of urgency of these two experiments with the uncertainties of the 1949 Indian Constitution, which sought to establish a secular state (article 15) in a society which it allowed and even encouraged to be communally divided (articles 25–30). Under the rubric of 'freedom of religion', it allowed citizens not only the profession and practice of their respective religions but also their propagation. Besides, it allowed the establishment of educational institutions along communal lines. A direct reference to secularism had to wait until 1976, when it was introduced into the preamble of the Constitution by the Forty-fourth Amendment.

It must be admitted here that the pluralistic situation which Nehru and the other framers of the Constitution faced was immensely more complex than anything that Lenin, and far less Ataturk, faced; yet the fact remains that Nehru did not use his undoubted hold over the people as a leader of the freedom movement and his vast authority as the head of government to bring communal tendencies under strict control. It is often said that he was too much of a liberal and a cultured aristocrat to think of strong-arm methods; I think he was also too optimistic about the decline of the hold of religion on the minds of people. He did not seem to take into consideration the fact that the ideology of secularism enhances the power of the state by making it a protector of all religious communities and an arbiter in their conflicts.

No wonder, then, that secularism as an alien cultural ideology which lacks the strong support of the state, has failed to make the desired headway in India. Instead what have made great strides are, apparently and by general agreement, Hindu revivalism and Muslim and Sikh fundamentalism. This brings me to the last of the observations I want to make, and I will also do this briefly.

Contrary to what may be presumed, it is not religious zealots alone who contribute to fundamentalism or fanaticism, which are a misunderstanding of religion, reducing it to mere political bickering, but also the secularists who deny the very legitimacy of religion in human life and society and provoke a reaction. This latter realization has been slow in coming to Indian intellectuals, but there are some signs of change in this regard. It is thus that old, familiar questions begin to be reformulated. The principal question of this address could be considered to be not whether Indian society will eventually become secularized as Nehru believed it would but rather in what sense it should become so and by what means. The limitations of secular humanism (so-called) and the falsity of the hope of secularists—namely, that all will be well with us if only scientific temper becomes generalized—need to be recognized. Secularized man can confront fundamentalism and revivalism no more than he may empathize with religion.

Maybe religion is not as fake as Marx asserted; maybe there is something eternal about it as Durkheim maintained. Perhaps men of religion such as Mahatma Gandhi would be our best teachers on the proper relation between religion and politics—values and interests—underlining not only the possibilities of interreligious understanding, which is not the same as an emaciated notion of mutual tolerance or respect, but also opening out avenues of a spiritually justified limitation of the role of religious institutions and symbols in certain areas of contemporary life. The creeping process of secularization, however, slowly erodes the ground on which such men might stand. As Ashis Nandy puts it, 'There is now a peculiar double-bind in Indian politics: the ills of religion have found political expression but the strengths of it have not been available for checking corruption and violence in public life' (1985: 17). My question is, Is everything lost irretrievably?

I must conclude; but I really have no conclusions to offer, no solutions to suggest. Let me hasten to say, however, that I am not advocating the establishment of a Hindu State in India—not at all. It simply will not work. Should you think that I have been sceptical about the claims that are made for secularism, scientific temper, etc., and that I have suggested a contextualized rethinking of these fuzzy ideas, you would be quite right. You would also be right in concluding that I have suggested that the only way secularism in South Asia, understood as interreligious understanding, may succeed would be for us to take both religion and secularism seriously and not reject the former as superstition and reduce the latter to a mask for communalism or mere expediency. Secularism would have to imply that those who profess no religion have a place in society equal to that of others, not higher or lower.

Should you think further that the scepticism to which I have given expression has been easy to come by, cultivate, and accept, you would not be, I am afraid, quite right. Secularism has been the fond hope of many people of my generation in South Asia. But, then, that is my personal problem, and therefore let me say no more about it. I will end simply by recalling the following words of the young Karl Marx, spoken, of course, in a very different context: 'Ideas which have conquered our minds . . . to which reason has welded our conscience, are chains from which we cannot break away without breaking our hearts; they are demons which man can vanquish only by submitting to them' (see Lowith 1982: 23).

Further Readings

Beckford, James A., ed.,
1986 *New Religious Movements and Rapid Social Change*, Sage Publications, London.

Nine essays covering eight countries (including India and Sri Lanka) spread all over the world, examine new religious and counter-movements and their roots in conditions of rapid social change. Social composition, organizational structures, beliefs and practices of the movements are discussed.

Bjorkman, James W., ed.,
1986 *Fundamentalism, Revivalists and Violence in South Asia*, The Riverdale Co., Riverdale, Maryland.

A symposium covering the contemporary situation in India, Pakistan and Sri Lanka written mainly by historians and political scientists but of interest to sociologists also.

Luthera, Ved Prakash,
1964 *The Concept of the Secular State and India*, Oxford University Press, Calcutta.

An early assessment of the future of the secular state in India. Argues that secularism in the sense of the separation of the church and the state is not relevant in India and that the best that the Indian state can strive for is impartiality in its dealings with citizens professing different faiths.

Martin, David,
1978 *A General Theory of Secularization*, Basil Blackwell, Oxford

A broad-based work examining the sociological and political aspects of religious change and secularization in a variety of historical settings falling within the Christian tradition. Attempts to build an empirical theory of secularization.

Marty, Martin and R. Scott Appleby, eds.,
1991 *Fundamentalism Observed*, University of Chicago Press, Chicago.

A collection of papers analysing fundamentalist movements within different religious traditions, including those of South Asia.

Smith, Donald Eugene,
1963 *India as a Secular State,* Oxford University Press, Bombay.

A pioneering and comprehensive work which explores India's religious traditions and the contemporary socio-political scene for assessing the chances of the success of the secular state. Optimistic in tone, the book also identifies the danger posed by Hindu communalism.

Appendix

Appendix

Parsi Zoroastrian Myth and Ritual: Some Problems of their Relevance for Death and Dying

CYRUS R. PANGBORN

. . . The Zoroastrian Parsis[1] share with all others of the human race the heightened feeling associated with passing from life to death and many of their ritual acts are not sufficiently different to set them apart from other religious communities. Some specific con-

Excerpted from Cyrus R. Pangborn, 'Parsi Zoroastrian Myth and Ritual: Some Problems of their Relevance for Death and Dying', in Frank E. Reynolds and Earle H. Waugh, eds., *Religious Encounters with Death: Insights from the History and Anthropology of Religions*. The Pennsylvania University Press, University Park, 1977, pp. 125-40.

[1] Parsis are the Zoroastrians whose ancestors migrated from Persia and took refuge in India rather than convert or suffer the disabilities of being 'infidels' to the Muslim Arabs who imposed on the land their religion as well as their rule. Today, this Indian community, centred principally in the cities of Bombay and Poona and the state of Gujarat, constitutes about four-fifths of the world's approximately 120,000 Zoroastrians. Its practices, therefore, may be regarded as essentially normative for the faith.

The name, *Parsi*, like *Persia*, derives from *Pars*, the name of the province from which came the first rulers strong enough to create the nation state of Persia and, after that, an empire, in the sixth century BC.

cerns, however, are focal points for the intense feelings of the Parsis. It is those that strike the non-Zoroastrian as unusual or atypical that I shall describe.

The Parsi rituals associated with death should begin before the last breath is drawn and continue, according to defined frequency, until the respectful memory in which descendants hold the deceased has faded. The usual summary of these rites retains few of their curious features except, notably, the use of the *dakhma* (Tower of Silence) for the deposition of corpses. More descriptive accounts, however, reveal the intense anxiety occasioned by death. The dead and the living survivors alike are threatened by evil, and anxiety is felt for both. But, as other writings show, every single death also kindles afresh another fear among Parsis—the fear of their corporate extinction.

The cultic ceremonies designed long ago to allay fears for the soul of the dead and the welfare of the living may be presumed efficacious. On the other hand, it may be that these archaic rituals promote fears and anxieties among contemporaries that have no basis in present-day Parsi experience. That, however, is another question. If the ceremonies are effective in accommodating the total range of anxiety, then they must be deemed acceptable, even if a more economical response could allay fears on a smaller scale. The fear of Parsi extinction is a different matter. The Parsis, as well as observers, agree that the cultus is not presently an effective solvent for this problem. But whereas the orthodox regard the cultic regulations for religious observance and daily life as ineffective only because they are not rigorously followed, critics believe that it is precisely because the rules are too well applied that Parsi survival is problematical. The question of which argument possesses greater merit need not be settled here. My concern is to show that the cultus which provides the rites for assuaging the fear of death has not been effective in dealing with the burgeoning anxiety engendered by the prospect of corporate extinction.

Tracing Anxiety to Its Source

An understanding of why Parsis do what they do to deal with their fears, whether effectively or not, depends on knowing the considerations which originally gave rise to fear. Thus the inquirer asks if the source could have been Zoroaster, the founding prophet of the faith; and noting that protection of basic natural elements from pollution is a central concern of funeral ceremonies, he turns to the *Gathas*, the hymns of the founder-prophet, to find the germ of contemporary concern for the holy purity of fire, air, earth, and water. There are only five surviving *Gathas* of the many credited to Zoroaster by tradition. But these at least, although containing admonitions enjoining stewardship, yield no clues that would make him accountable for his later followers' notions about innumerable ways of cultically corrupting the physical bases of life. Nor is the *Yasna*, a priestly composition postdating Zoroaster but including his five *Gathas*, of any decisive importance for the inquiry. In the *Videvdat*, however, Zoroaster's morally sensitive concern for the gifts of nature has been transformed into obsessive anxiety about pollution of sacralized elements.

The *Videvdat*, the first ecclesiastical law book of the Zoroastrians, was another priestly contribution to their canonical scriptures, the *Avesta*, all—the *Gathas* alone excepted—in a language called simply Avestan. Characterized by Karl F. Geldner (1904: 8) as 'the Leviticus of the Parsis,'[2] the *Videvdat* is a compendium of profanations to be avoided, which, if not avoided, must have their effects cancelled by rites of purification, penance, and atonement. Here, then, appear for the first time the rules for preventing the pollution of earth by dead bodies, having the dog gaze upon the dead during funeral rites, and disposing of corpses by exposure in a *dakhma*. These are only a few of the many prescriptions for which Zoroaster's authority was claimed, but which in all probability were more congruent with aboriginal beliefs and cultic practices swept away in his reform and then reintroduced by the Median Magi.

Native Persian culture, including religion, languished during the half-millennium of foreign rule after 330 BC. Then the accession to power in AD 220 by the Sassanids, who claimed hereditary continuity with the Achaemenids, provided the opportunity for a renaissance that included the transcription of whatever could be remembered (about one-fourth) of the *Avesta* by priests generations removed from those who had composed it.

The renaissance continued for Zoroastrianism even after the Muslim conquest brought defeat to the Sassanids in AD 641. But

[2] See also Dhalla (1963) and Zaehner (1961) for detailed analyses of Zoroastrian origins during the first millennium BC, the adoption and transformation of the religion by Median priests (the Magi), and the composition and fate of the Avesta up to the time when Cyrus the Great's Achaemenid empire (founded in 550 BC) fell to the Greeks in 330 BC.

restrictions on non-Muslims made a group of Zoroastrians restive; they decided to seek refuge elsewhere and eventually reached India in the eighth century. Others endured their disabilities and wrote in the then-vulgate language of Pahlavi such works as the *Dinkard*, *Nirangistan*, and *Dadistani-i-Dina*. Much of this dates from the ninth century and provides not only extended commentary on the *Videvdat's* prescriptions but also a much expanded treasure of theology, mythology, legend, and eschatology.

Non-Muslims in Persia continued to suffer political disabilities for centuries, but Muslim religious fanaticism had abated by the fifteenth century so that Persian and Parsi Zoroastrians re-established communication. Thus the Parsis became joint heirs, with the Persians, of the Pahlavi literature and the possessors as well of a series of letters called the *Rivayats*. Dating from the early fifteenth through the eighteenth centuries, these were written by Persians in response to questions from the Parsis who feared that in their isolation they might be forgetting or pragmatically adapting, and therefore corrupting, the faith as it obtained in Persia.

Suffice it to say that from the early nineteenth century, the Parsis have been guided in all things essential by the same body of scripture, commentaries, and tracts as have the native Persian Zoroastrians. And although much of the literature may be of the Pahlavi period, the basic lineaments of thought and practice have been consistently Avestan. Thus such Parsi deviations as occurred before the *Rivayats* were acquired and by choice have not been corrected are too minor to require Mary Boyce to qualify her dictum that 'Zoroastrianism is characterized by immense conservatism. Essentially and in details, therefore, the later religion is unchanged from that of ancient Iran' (1971: 211).

The Myth as Context for Ritual

Thus the anxieties that the death rituals are designed to allay have their ideological basis not so much in anything known to have been taught by Zoroaster as in the remythologized soteriology of the later Avestan period. The *Gathas* presented a relatively unadorned picture of life after death. It would be the souls that survive this life, since they are created immortal and, at birth, are pure and innocent. The souls of men who choose *Ahura Mazda* and walk by choice in his ways of truth and righteousness (or, as the Zoroastrian

'Golden Rule' puts it, by *humata, hukhta,* and *hvarshta*—good thoughts, good words, and good deeds) as taught by Zoroaster, will successfully negotiate the crossing from this world to paradise. The image of a bridge, called *Chinvat,* is used to aid in conceptualizing the transition. Judged by their own consciences, the righteous will be helped across by Zoroaster and so enter into the bliss and felicity of heaven, *Garo Demana.* But the wicked, likewise so judged, will fall into perdition and misery, a fate lasting at least until some final resurrection at the end of history.

From this simple plot, the later *Avesta* developed (or reconstructed) an elaborate scenario in which *Fravashis* have prominent places. *Fravashis* are the prototypal heavenly beings or spirits to which the souls of men correspond. Having their origin in eternity or prehistory, they come to earth by choice, each to serve as a human soul's 'higher double' (Dhalla 1963: 237; see also pp. 234ff.). Apparently entering into the person, the *Fravashi* serves its analogue, the soul, as its lifetime guardian, guide, and admonisher. At death, 'the Fravashi . . . remains hovering over the soul' (Dabu 1959: 64). For three days it remains on earth, then it accompanies the soul through Judgment and during its ascent through the lower heavens (the new lower levels ancillary to *Garo Demana* that were supplied by post-*Gathic* imaginations). In the event that the soul has been wicked, the *Fravashi* parts company with it, returning to highest heaven while the soul goes instead to hell, *Drujo Demana.*

The subsequent activity of the *Fravashi* and its corresponding soul appears to be variously conceived. On the one hand, there is the traditional belief that *Fravashis* in general, whether of souls now in heaven or of souls yet unborn, 'wield great power in both the worlds, rendering great help to those who invoke them, and [in the case of those who have already made their descent as doubles for living souls and have returned] keeping watch and ward about the abodes in which they once had lived (Dhalla 1963: 239). They delight in being remembered by the living and 'seek their praise and prayer, sacrifice and invocation' (ibid.: 240). They are thought to descend for the last ten days of the Zoroastrian year, the rituals of which period are dedicated to them and to all departed souls. But failure to attend to them is to invite their curse and lose their blessing. Departed souls, according to this conception, do not return once they are across the bridge, since they are bending their efforts toward reaching highest heaven, and the grateful prayers of the living help them in their ascent just as they please the *Fravashis*. On the other hand, in popular thought, distinctions are often blurred and the functions of the *Fravashis* and departed souls confusedly conceived. Then, says Dhalla, 'The intermingling [of the forms of ancestor-worship] becomes so complete that the souls and not the *Fravashis* are supposed to come down to the rituals even on the days originally consecrated to the *Fravashis*' (ibid.: 243).

Many heavenly characters in the Avestan and Pahlavi mythopoeic elaborations of the drama of death have no place now in the script. Modern Parsis have found the stage crowded with minor characters too numerous to remember and too suggestive of polytheism to be credible. The Avestan texts used as funeral liturgy, however, perpetuate by invocation the belief in several of the ancient dramatis personae, particularly the angels (*yazatas*) of judgment: *Mithra* (the judge, known also as *Meher*), *Rashnu* (angel of justice), *Ashtad* (angel of truth), and a fourth *yazata*, *Sraosha* (the enemy of night's darkness, temptation, and all evil, and the guardian of obedience and discipline), who remains with a righteous dead person as the divine helper and protector of his soul into the fourth day and until *Chinvat* has been crossed and *Mithra* and *Rashnu* have rendered judgment. To *Sraosha*, therefore, are addressed the prayers and litanies of the death ceremonies for those days.

When account has been taken of the current tendency toward demythologizing the soul's pilgrimage after death, there remains a puzzling residue of belief in the need of extraordinary aid from divine agents. Why should such aid be so important if, as Parsis also say, the passport to paradise is reasonable fidelity in life to the ideals of good thoughts, good words, and good deeds in response to divine love and grace? The resolution of apparent discrepancy depends on distinguishing between theoretical claims and *de facto* realities. The funeral rites—which are what Parsis *do*—remain virtually unchanged despite the pruning of the traditional mythology. Here is a clue that the world of the *Videvdat* may not have been left far behind after all. The dangers threatened by the demonic 'opposite numbers' of the angelic forces apparently remain as real as ever in the Parsi imagination. The name of the fear is pollution.

The Rites for the Dead

The rituals of protection begin if possible even before the moment of death. Relatives, and the dying person too, if able, should recite a *patet* (a confession of sin) and, especially, the *Ahuna-Vairya*, a short prayer believed to be Gathic in origin. It is commonly believed that 'if this prayer is repeated properly even once in the correct rhythm and intonation, and with a clear understanding of its meaning, it is equal in efficacy to the repetition of a hundred other hymns put together' (Taraporewala 1965: 33). Thereafter, no one is ordinarily allowed to touch the body except professional body-bearers, who are to cleanse their own bodies by formal baths employing *gomez* (consecrated bull urine) before and after, and to wear special white apparel while performing their duties. The *Sachkar* ceremony (of bathing with *gomez* and water, and dressing the corpse) is described as 'elaborate' and of a nature demanding 'great fortitude' (Rustomjee 1965: 3). It is accompanied throughout by prayers, and completed when the *Sudreh* and *Kusti* (white undershirt and woven string girdling the waist—the external symbols of Parsi identity) have been put on and the body covered by used but freshly laundered white garments.

When the bearers have shifted the body to a low stone slab and described three circles around it with a metallic instrument, such as a nail, they temporarily retire. Twice during the shrouding of the body a dog is brought in to view the corpse. It is supposed to be four-eyed—that is, to have two eyelike spots above its eyes—but lack of a dog with such marks is the mother of frequent substitutions of any dog available . . . . The usual explanation . . . is the one favoured by Rustomjee, to the effect that a dog is 'infallible' in detecting whether or not the corpse is really and finally lifeless.[3] This 'viewing' [*sagdid*] is repeated at the beginning of each of however many of five periods (*Gahs*) of the Zoroastrian day pass before transfer of the body to a *dakhma*.

Fire, the Zoroastrian symbol par excellence, is brought in after the first *sagdid*. Fed by scented sandalwood, it is kept kindled by either priest or layman, until departure for the *dakhma*. The fire tender usually also recites prayers from the *Avesta*.

The principal ceremony is performed during the last hour that the body is in the *bungli*. The two bearers return and place an iron bier next to the body. Two priests then begin the *Geh-Sarna*, the recital of the *Gathas*. When they pause midcourse, the bearers lift the body over the bier; the priests complete the recital. Once more

[3] . . . [Of] the possible reasons for the *sagdid* the *Videvadat's* own explanation, to the effect that the four-eyed dog prompts *Nasu* (the corpse demon, feminine in gender) to fly away [may be noted].

the dog is brought in. Then assembled male relatives and friends proceed past the body and bow in respectful salute. The bearers cover the face of the deceased, strap the body to the bier, and deliver it to other bearers outside for final carriage to the *dakhma*. These bearers, who must work in pairs—one or more according to the weight to be carried—are of another class; their only business is that of rendering this nearly final service. The males who wish to follow do so in pairs and only if dressed in white. The body is put down outside the *dakhma* and another *sagdid* is performed. The company pays a last respectful look, and the initial bearers return to carry the bier inside the tower, where the body is then undressed and left partly if not entirely exposed for drawing the attention of vultures. The clothes are thrown into a pit to decompose.

Outside, the prayers first spoken when the person was dying or had just died arc repeated. All those present, after bathing any uncovered portions of their bodies with *gomez* and water, depart. After returning to their homes, it is expected that they will do what those who did not participate in the final procession have presumably done already—take an ordinary bath and resume their normal activities. Meanwhile, all participating bearers have been engaging in the rituals of their own purification.[4]

But this summary account is misleading as it stands. Reference must be made to concerns besides those humanitarian and hygienic. For example, there is the *paiwand* (a cloth such as a handkerchief or cotton tape), which must be held by two persons—the bearers who prepare the body, the two persons who must always be in attendance by a corpse until the final ceremony, the bearers who carry the body to the *dakhma*, and the pairs of persons joining the final procession. The usual explanation, that pairing and the use of the *paiwand* 'create a view of sympathy and mutual help' (Modi 1922: 64), obfuscates but does not conceal the survival of fear engendered by the *Videvdat* that

> corporeal defilement is just as much an abomination to Ahuramazda as the moral one; both are fully alike and equally punishable. Through contamination with unclean things, *e.g.*, a dead corpse, which is possessed by Ahriman [the evil spirit], this enemy of cleanliness acquires just as much domination over men, as through the perpetration of wicked deeds, and in consequence, the laws in reference to the purity of the body have just as

[4] Rustomjee (1965: 4) and Taraporewala (1965: 60n) agree that the bearers' clothing has to be discarded and never worn again. Clothing worn by family and friends during the rites may be cleansed and reworn, although not again for 'religious purposes'. See also Modi (1922: 73).

much weight as those in reference to the purity of the soul or to the moral deeds (observation by John G. Rhode, 1879, quoted by Cama 1970: 61). . . .

In any case, the confusion of the material with the spiritual shows in the notion of the *Karp* or astral body. As noted earlier, ceremonies continue into the morning of the fourth day of (or third day *after*) death, because the soul remains in the world for three nights before proceeding to *Chinvat*. The ceremonial fire and a light are kept burning at the place where the body had lain, and priests lead prayers at the beginning of each *gah*. A special ceremony called the *Afringan* is performed each night and another called the *Uthamna* on the morning of the fourth day. The effort is mainly to beseech and even strengthen *Sraosha* so that he 'will be able to save his [the departed's] soul from the hands of the demons for the three days' (Modi 1922: 78). Meanwhile, during the first half-hour the body lay in the *dakhma*, the sun and the supplementary action of the vultures helped the soul and its spiritual body, the *Karp*, to come out from the physical body. The heat of the ceremonial fire then protects the soul and *Karp* until they rise from the earth for a 'new location in God's unbounded Universe' (Rustomjee 1965: 6).

The inventory of prescriptions and proscriptions is still incomplete. The corpse when first laid out must not be in a position for its head to point northward because, according to tradition, the north is the direction from which proceed 'all kinds of dangers and evils [including] mental' (Modi 1922: 56). *Juddins* (non-Zoroastrians) may view the body before it is first bathed by bearers but not afterward; nor are they to join in the procession to the *dakhma* or touch any Zoroastrian until the *dakhma* ceremonies are completed, lest the protection afforded the believers by their prefuneral purificatory ceremony be vitiated. Even the language of the rituals is prescribed—as is the case for all Zoroastrian ceremonies—and this despite the fact that only the exceptional priest knows the Avestan and later Pahlavi period languages enough to translate what he first learned by rote and is now reciting. To translate texts into the vernacular for liturgical use 'would be revolting', according to one highly authoritative priest [Firoze Meherji Kotwal]; at the very least, the ritual in translation could not 'retain its mystic attraction and convincing efficacy' [according to the Parsi sociologist Jal F. Bulsara; both statements recorded during interviews].

The most pressing obligations, before any worshipful post-*dakhma* rituals are performed, are to cleanse the slab on which the corpse first lay and any utensils that may have touched the body at home or *bungli*. The agents are *gomez* and water, with the number of washings varying from one for gold to six for stone—the more porous, in other words, the more the cleansing required. Contaminated porcelain, however, and wood or clay as well, cannot be salvaged.

For the next three days, abstinence from meat and from cooking in the house where death occurred is generally observed. At the five *gahs* of each of these days a prayer of thanks to *Sraosha* (the *Sravosh-baj*)[5] and the prayer of repentance (the *Patet*) are said, along with the traditional *gah* prayers (one for each particular period), by two or more priests and the relatives. The *Afringan* ceremony, repeated at each nightfall, increases the honour paid to *Sraosha* by requiring the artifacts of fire, a metallic tray, water, and flowers, a special seating arrangement, and the priests' recitation of additional textual material, mainly Avestan. The family may wish also that certain higher liturgical services, useful for any occasion of need for aid from the heavenly hierarchy, be performed at a fire-temple coincidentally with the domestic rites. The *Uthamna* ceremony occurs after 3 pm on the third day. It is much like those of the other *gahs* except for announcing the donations relatives and friends will make to charity as memorials to the deceased. The soul, having thus received the protection and support of *Sraosha* for three days, proceeds to *Chinvat* for the judgment it will receive on the following morning.

Before dawn of the fourth day, the last and most ambitious of the funeral ceremonies, the *Cheharum*, should be performed. It consists of four *baj*, the first addressed to the *yazatas*, *Rashnu* and *Astad*; the second, to *Ram-Khvastra* (the *yazata* of rarified air through which 'the soul of a good pious man passes away to the higher regions'); the third, to *Ardafravash* ('the spirits of all the departed souls whose rank the particular deceased . . . has joined' [Modi 1922: 84–5]); and the fourth or final, to *Sraosha*, in gratitude for the protection he has given the soul during its ordeal.

There are still *Afringan-baj* ceremonies to be performed during the next *gah* of this fourth day. They will be expected again on the tenth day, the thirtieth day, then monthly, and after that, annually. The annual observances continue as long as the living descen-

[5] A *baj* is a brief ceremony consisting of 'words or prayers religiously recited in honour of particular beings, such as the Yazatas . . . and Fravishes . . .' with offering sometimes accompanying the recital (see Modi 1922: 354).

dants are willing and able to pay the fees for their performance. The presumption is that the arrangement is mutually rewarding. A soul, pleased by the righteousness of 'dear sons', can 'rest in peace and tranquillity', and the living may find themselves in turn assisted with 'an invisible helping hand' (Modi 1922: 85–6).

Sceptics may regard the anxieties which the ceremonies attempt to vanquish as arising from notions lacking validation from Zoroaster, reason, or nature; and there are members of the community, especially among *behdins*, who think just that. But, as noted earlier, the ceremonial answer seems equal to the magnitude of the problem as the majority view it, and the needs of particular persons, deceased and living, are apparently met. It is otherwise with respect to the fear of corporate extinction.

The Threat of Parsi Demise

This old fear undoubtedly arose when Persia fell to the Greeks and remained under a rule not strictly indigenous until Pars again supplied the ruling dynasty in the Sassanid era. At that time, however, it was only the religion, not the people, that languished. Hence the earliest analogue to the Parsis' present plight was occasioned by the Muslim conquest of Persia and final victory in AD 641.

Parsis differ when identifying the time of greatest trouble, but almost all affirm that the flight to India was occasioned not only by Muslim pressure to convert but also by the threat of death if they did not.[6] Actually, the history of the times as far as Zoroastrians are concerned is sketchy and difficult to authenticate. What has apparently locked the tradition of persecution firmly into the store of Parsi memories, making the fact if not the date important, is a Persian-language poem, *Kisseh-i-Sanjan*, composed by a priest of the Gujarati community in about AD 1600. It is the story of how that community came to be, according to the cumulative oral traditions of the time.

The Persian experience might still be recalled as a romantic example of heroism and its pain forgotten were it not that the Hindu

[6] I. J. S. Taraporewala has stood almost alone as a challenger of this off-parroted tradition. He is convinced that the Zoroastrian masses readily converted once given the occasion for choosing between their own decadent religion and the still fresh ideals of Islam, and that the period of persecution is to be placed later, in the ninth century, when the Muslim's evangelism had deteriorated into coercive fanaticism (see Taraporewala 1965: 70–3).

provincial rulers, who had given the Parsi pilgrims asylum, were overwhelmed in the late fourteenth and early fifteenth centuries by Muslim rulers already in India and ever seeking to increase the area of their hegemony. Once again the ancestors of today's Parsis are remembered as having found their lives as well as their faith in jeopardy. But another obscure era followed, and not until after the late seventeenth century, when a significant number of those disheartened by their fluctuating fortunes under the Moguls had begun their migration southward to the developing settlement of the English that is now Bombay can the threads of the story be picked up again.

Today, of course, the Parsis do not fear external persecution. But the memory of past instances is recalled to make real the fear of extinction for whatever reason, and this in the hope of persuading the living to man the barricades against the latest strategy of the prince of demons—racial suicide.

The problem, judging by the number and temper of pamphlets, tracts, articles, and chapters of books devoted to it, is serious and multifaceted. The Bombay Parsis who prospered, first as ambitious employees of English entrepreneurs and then as entrepreneurs themselves (so that theirs was the bellwether community of all Indian Parsi communities well into the twentieth century), are now suffering economic decline and demotion to lower rungs on the Indian social-political ladder.[7] With the economic pinch has come postponement of marriage and thus smaller families, not to mention increasing incidence of what is almost apostasy for males—bachelorhood by choice. The practice of endogamy is part of the syndrome. At the same time that the Parsis are shrinking in number, the youth are exercising more independence in choosing their own mates; finding fewer fellow Parsis to choose from, they tend more and more to marry exogamously or to honour endogamy in the breach by not marrying at all. The divorce rate, too, has risen sharply since 1936. Still other causes of concern, apparently justified by recent corroborating studies, are the signs among Parsis of deterioration in general health and a high incidence of genetically transmitted vulnerabilities.[8]

[7] See Wadia (1949: 4–9) for documentation of a marked slippage of Parsis from the professional and business ranks into the ranks of unskilled labour and the unemployed.

[8] Desai (1948: 87–112) cited tuberculosis, respiratory diseases, mental illness, and retardation as endemic among Parsis. [He also has data on divorce, postponement of marriage, unmarried adults, and smaller families.]

The net result of all interrelated factors is a steady decline in the Parsi population of India,[9] and most notably of its largest community, in Bombay, where the death rate is approximately 50 per cent higher than the birth rate. The danger of extinction is real and the intense concern about it is understandable.

Proposed Solutions

The concern is expressed again and again . . . by respected and articulate leaders of the Parsi community [and others]. In either case, views are more polarized than marked by moderation. Thus, at one extreme, counsel stresses rededication to the whole scriptural, theological, and cultic tradition, faithful cultic observance and retention of the liturgical languages (otherwise dead), respect for priestly authority, more religious education for the laity, strict endogamy, exclusion of prospective converts, and support of familiar types of charitable trusts and benevolence as means of promoting the Parsis' education, health, and social welfare. In contrast is the agenda of the reformers. They would depend almost exclusively upon the *Gathas* for foundations, and upon their interpretation in the light of modern knowledge for current guidance (thus denying the authority of the late Avestan and Pahlavi traditions). They would reform the cultus—by translating the liturgical texts, eliminating the elements of ritual deemed archaic, abandoning altogether such ritual acts as purport to supply religious remedy for physical pollution, and utilizing modern science to clarify and separate the traditionally and confusedly overlapping categories of hygiene, morality, and religion. There appears to be no demand for abandoning the hereditary principle with respect to the priesthood, but the reformers are generally in agreement that there can be no revision of the cultus without thoroughgoing reform of priestly education, the functions of the priestly office, and compensation for the profession. They would, in most cases, tolerate exogamy and endorse conversion to the faith. And, finally, they are concerned to devise new institutional agencies to combat the decline in fortunes and restore the Parsis' individual and corporate self-respect and well-being.

[9] Eckehard Kulke's inquiry yielded population figures of 110,000 Indian Parsis in 1951 but only 100,600 ten years later—a loss of 10 per cent. [The 1981 census figure is much lower at 72,000.].

Illustrative of the reformers' position is the advice of the sociologist P. A. Wadia that the community cease trusting in

> teachers who make a deliberate effort to teach dogmatics, to glorify the dead past and to instill in the minds of the young ideas which have become discredited. . . . It is infinitely better to leave boys and girls alone in these matters than to start them on ideas that can only breed a false religious pride . . . and . . . incline them to superstition and bigotry (1949: 77–8).
>
> Our own ancestors in India freely mingled by marriage and otherwise with the people of the land; and it was because we mingled that we managed to survive. Can we today by a different policy, a policy of rigid exclusivism and in-breeding . . . hope to survive (ibid.: 140)?
>
> Can our small community . . . with religious beliefs which do not penetrate beyond the surface . . . reasonably look forward to the future with courage and confidence? . . . self-righteous pride will not convert us into the strong ones of the Lord (ibid.: 141).

. . . Judging, however, by the tone of frustration in reformist literature, orthodox traditionalism—represented principally but by no means exclusively by the priesthood—is retaining its at least nominal authority over the Parsi community. As Dabu has written, in justification of leaving customs intact:

> Ceremonies are the pillars of Zoroastrian Faith. . . . If one is after fault-finding no custom or usage is foolproof or faultless (1967: 17).
>
> Parsis' . . . racial characteristics are hereditary, and preservation of their blood from getting mixed with that of other races is a necessity. . . . The admission to the Parsi community is impossible as an alien cannot change his blood . . . and . . . may not have the same reverence for fire in the Parsi Temples (1959: 15, 17).

Another venerable *ervad* (priest), the Dastur at Udvada (site of the oldest fire-temple in India), has located in divine and therefore eternally valid revelation the authority for traditional views:

> Our religion is the religion sent to us by Ahuramazda. Conversion and faith in Religion of Revelation are incongruous. God has given us our Religion under His own Laws of making up an appropriate set of beliefs of His own Choice and man takes birth in an environment best suited for him to carry out the allotted mission in life. Just as a man cannot change his parents he cannot change his religion. . . . It is our Prophet and our Ancestors who have put us in charge of our divine heritage. . . . Our Ancestors suffered a good deal . . . to preserve, promote and defend this divine heritage and pass it on to a succession of generations. We pray to God to help us fulfil our allotted mission (Mirza 1970: 33).

The word of an influential *behdin* [Professor Firoz C. Davar] on the issue of mixed marriages and their threat to the religion was widely circulated in 1970 for the support it gave to a custom of long standing.

> We emphatically maintain that our religion and culture deserve to survive and not be frivolously frittered away....
>
> Our boys were the first to set the bad example. Due notice was not taken of it by our community, in the belief that children born of a Parsi father... would after all be Parsis and admissible in the Parsi fold. Then Parsi girls followed the evil example....
>
> We maintain that mixed marriages are condemnable for Parsis (n.d.: 3, 4, 5).[10]

Although it is common to argue that traditions once based on revelation and religious insight are also validated today by science and common sense, Rustomjee and others are satisfied that the benefits of tradtional cultic observance are discernible and need no scientific explanation or demonstration.

> The 'Sudreh' [the identifying undershirt] has a magnetic effect upon the body, when it is worn next to the skin.... That effect is discernible by the soul....
>
> [It] helps to ward off the malefic influence of the inclement elements outside man....
>
> It will thus be noticed that man's full purpose of life is achievable through the force of the symbology of his sacred garment....
>
> Let us [also] therefore treat our valuable symbol, the 'Kusti', [the sacred girdle] our fortifying power, our help against the onslaught of evil... as... the protective spiritual weapon which can stand by us, giving us the hope of salvation for our soul (1971: 19–20, 21).

Conclusion

The myth and ritual that compose a cultus are living bread if they rescue life from banality and transmute death by explaining it as requisite to life's renewal. Zoroastrians have found their cultus functional in this sense for many centuries and thus without need of essential change. Like all people, they might face perils visible and material, invisible and spiritual, and not without fear and trembling; but anxiety met its match in the hope and assurance engendered by time-honoured forms of belief and cultic observance. In this century, however, declining fortunes and diminishing numbers have become a concern of the whole community. The establishment finds the basis for infidelity in the doubts and scepticism encouraged by modernity and, in turn, the cause of Parsi acceleration towards extinction. The accused have not been at

[10] [Firoz C. Davar's article, 'Parsis and Racial Suicide', first appeared in a Gujarati newspaper in 1970, and was reprinted four times, once as a pamphlet in English from which the quotation has been taken (see Davar n.d.)].

pains to deny that funeral rites in particular have their efficacious relevance, but they have replied that it is for want of reform measures in general that the community is dying.

Doubtless there are many nonreligious factors, favourable and unfavourable, having their bearing on the issue of survival. But the traditionalists and reformers alike believe that if their advice were taken, all the factors favourable to the preservation of the faith and the community would be called into play. Meanwhile, neither of the opposing convictions about what ought to be allays anxiety about what is. Communities of immigrant Zoroastrians in other hemispheres may evolve strategies of survival that prove successful. But in India, where the largest community of Zoroastrians has its home, if no stratagem old or new stems the present trend, the vultures may wheel omniously in the air, with no feast in sight.

References

Aggarwal, Partap

1971 *Caste, Religion and Power*. New Delhi: Shri Ram Centre for Industrial Relations.

Ali, M. Athar

1968 *The Moghul Nobility under Aurangzeb*. Bombay: Asia Publishing House.

Anon

n.d. *Śrī Sudhāras Stavan Saṅgrah*. Palitana: Kantilal D. Shah.

Babb, Lawrence A.

1988 Giving and giving up: the eightfold worship among Śvetāmbar Mūrtipūjak Jains. *Journal of Social Research* **44**: 67–86.

Banerji, Indubhusan

1962(1947) *Evolution of the Khalsa*, II. Calcutta: A. Mukherjee.

Barr, J.

1977 *Fundamentalism*. London: SCM Press.

Basham, A. L.

1954 *The Wonder that was India*. New York: Grove Press.

Bayly, C. A.

1975 *Local Roots of Indian Politics*. London: Oxford University Press.

Beck, Brenda F.

1972 *Peasant Society in Konku: A Study of the Right and Left Subcastes in South India*. Vancouver: University of British Columbia.

Berger, Peter L.

1963 Charisma and religious innovation: the social location of Israelite prophecy. *American Sociological Review* 28: 940–50.

1973 *The Social Reality of Religion*. Harmondsworth: Penguin.

Bhattacharya, Debiprasad

1969 *Indian Atheism: A Marxist Approach*. New Delhi: People's Publishing House.

Bhindranwale, Sant Jarnail Singh
1983 Address to the Sikh congregation. Transcript of a sermon at the Golden Temple in November 1983. Trans. by Ranabir Singh Sandhu, April 1985. Distributed by the Sikh Religious and Educational Trust, Columbus, Ohio.
1987 Excerpts of speeches in English translation. *In* Joyce Pettigrew, In search of a new kingdom of Lahore. *Pacific Affairs* 60: 1–25.

Bipan Chandra, *see* Chandra

Bose, N. K.
1968 *Calcutta: A Social Survey*. Bombay: Lalvani Publishers.

Boyce, Mary
1971 Zoroastrianism. *In* C. Jouco Bleeker and George Widengren, eds., *Historia Religionum*, Vol. 2, *Religions of the Present*. Leiden: E. J. Brill.

Bruner-Lachaux, Hélène, trans. & ed.
1977 *Somaśambhupaddhati, pt 3, Rituels occasionnels dans le tradition . . . II*. Pondicherry: Institut Francais d'Indologie.

Buchanan, Hamilton
1811–12 *Patna-Gaya Report*, Vol. 1 Patna: Bihar and Orissa Research Society.

Buddhisāgarsūrī, Ācārya
1925 *Jainsūtra mā Mūrtipūjā*. 3rd. printing. Bombay: Adhyatmak Jnan Prasarak Mandal.

Burgess, James
1869 *Notes of a Visit to Somnath, Girnar and Other Places in Kathiawad in May, 1869*. Reprinted 1976. Varanasi: Kishor Vidya Niketan.
1884 Papers on Śatruñjaya and the Jainas, VI: the Jaina ritual. *Indian Antiquary* 13: 191–6.

Caldwell, R
1886 On demonolatry in southern India. *Journal of the Anthropological Society of Bombay* 2: 91–105.

Cama, K. R.
1970 *The Collected Works of K. R. Cama*, Vol. 2. Bombay: K. R. Cama Oriental Institute.

Caplan, L.
1985 The popular culture of evil in south India. *In* D. J. Parkin, ed., *The Anthropology of Evil*. Oxford: Basil Blackwell.

Chadwick, Owen
1975 *The Secularization of the European Mind in the Nineteenth Century*. Cambridge: Cambridge University Press.

Chandra, Bipan
1984 *Communalism in Modern India*. Delhi: Vikas.

Chatterjee, Partha
1986 *Nationalist Thought and the Colonial World*. Delhi: Oxford University Press.

Chaudhuri, Nirad C.
1979 *Hinduism: A Religion to Live by*. London: Chatto and Windus.

Clarke, S.
1980 *Let the Indian Church be Indian*. Madras: Christian Literature Society.

Cole, W. Owen and Piara Singh Sambhi
1978 *The Sikhs: Their Religious Beliefs and Practices*. London: Routledge and Kegan Paul.

Coomaraswamy, Ananda K.
1908 *Mediaeval Sinhalese Art*. Broad Campden, Gloucestershire: Essex House Press. 2nd. edn., 1956. New York: Pantheon.
1978 *Spiritual Authority and Temporal Power in the Indian Theory of Government*. New Delhi: Munshiram Manoharlal.

Cort, John E.
1988 Review of Shah 1987: *South Asia in Review* 13: 12–13.
1989 *Liberation and Wellbeing*. Doctoral dissertation. Cambridge, MA: Harvard University.

Cox, Harvey
1965 *The Secular City: Secularization and Urbanization in Theological Perspective*. New York: Macmillan.

Dabu, Khurshed S.
1959 *Message of Zarathustra*, 2nd ed. Bombay: New Book Co. Pvt. Ltd.
1967 Ceremonies for Dead. *Parsiana* 3, 12 (Oct. 1967).

Daniel, J.
1980 *Another Daniel*. Madras: The Laymen's Evangelical Fellowship.

Das, Veena
1977 *Structure and Cognition: Aspects of Hindu Caste and Ritual*. Delhi: Oxford University Press.

Davar, Firoz C.
n.d. *Parsis and Racial Suicide*. Bombay: Dinar Printery.

Davis, Marvin
1976 A philosophy of Hindu rank from rural West Bengal. *The Journal of Asian Studies* 36: 5–24.

de Bary, Theodore, ed.
1970 *The Sources of Indian Tradition*, vol. 1. New York: Columbia University Press.

Desai, Sapur Faredur

1948 *A Community at the Cross-Road*. Bombay: New Book Co.

Dhalla, Maneckji Nusservanji

1963 *History of Zoroastrianism*. Bombay: K. R. Cama Oriental Institute.

Dhanagare, D. N.

1977 Agrarian conflict, religion and politics: the Moplah rebellions in Malabar in the 19th. and early 20th. centuries. *Past and Present* 74: 112–42.

Dube, S. C. and V. N. Basilov, eds.

1983 *Secularization in Multi-Religious Societies*. New Delhi: Concept.

Dumont, Louis

1962 The concept of kingship in ancient India. *Contributions to Indian Sociology*, 6: 48–77 Reproduced in Dumont 1970b.

1967 *Homo Hierarchicus: essai sur la système des castes*. Paris: Gallimard.

1970a* *Homo Hierarchicus: The Caste System and its Implications*. London: Widenfeld and Nicolson, Chicago: University of Chicago Press.

1970b *Religion, Politics and History in India: Collected Papers in Indian Sociology*. Paris: Mouton.

1980 *Homo Hierarchicus: The Caste System and its Implications*. Complete Revised Edition. Chicago: University of Chicago Press.

1983 A modified view of our origins: the Christian beginnings of modern individualism. *Contributions to Indian Sociology* (n.s.) 17: 1–26.

1986 *A South Indian Subcaste: Social and Religious Organization among the Pramalai Kallar*. Trans. by Michael Moffatt et al. Delhi: Oxford University Press.

1986a *Essays on Individualism*. Chicago: University of Chicago Press.

Dundas, Paul

1985 Food and freedom: the Jaina sectarian debate on the nature of the kevalin. *Religion* 15: 161–98.

Durkheim, Émile

1965(1915) *The Elementary Forms of the Religious Life*. Trans. by J. W. Swain. New York: The Free Press.

Eliade, Mircea

1959 *Cosmos and History: The Myth of the Eternal Return*. New York: Harper and Row.

* The reference to Dumont 1970 on pp. 79, 81, 84, 91, 94 and 163 is to Dumont 1970a.

Eliade, Mircea
1961 *The Sacred and the Profane*. New York: Harper and Row.

Elmore, W. Th.
1925 *Dravidian Gods in Modern Hinduism*. Madras.

Emeneau, Murray B.
1938 Toda culture thirty five years after—an acculturation study. *Annals of the Bhandarkar Oriental Research Institute* (Poona) 19: 101–31.
1974 *Ritual Structure and the Language Structure of the Todas*. Philadelphia: *Transactions of the American Philosophical Society* (NS) 64, 6.

Evans-Pritchard, E. E.
1937 *Witchcraft, Oracles and Magic among the Azande*. Oxford: Clarendon Press.
1956 *Nuer Religion*. Oxford: Clarendon Press.
1965 *Theories of Primitive Religion*. Oxford: Clarendon Press.

Fanon, Frantz
1963 *The Wretched of the Earth*. New York: Grove Press.

Ferreira, J. V.
1965 *Totemism in India*. Bombay: Oxford University Press.

Foucault, M
1980 *Power/Knowledge: Selected Interviews and Other Writings 1972–1977*. Ed. by C. Gordon. Brighton: Harvester.

Fuller, C. J.
1985 Initiation and consecration: priestly rituals in a south Indian temple. *In* R. Burghart and A. Cantlie, eds., *Indian Religion*. London: Curzon Press.

Gaborieau, Marc
1972 Muslims in the Hindu kingdom of Nepal. *Contributions to Indian Sociology* (n.s.) 6: 84–105.

Gandhi, M. K.
1940 *An Autobiography or the Story of My Experiments with Truth*. Ahmedabad: Navjivan.

Geertz, Clifford
1975 *The Interpretation of Cultures*. New York: Basic Books.

Geiger, see *Mahāvaṁsa*.

Geldner, Karl F.
1904 Avesta Literature. *In* Karl J. Trubner and Otto Harrassowitz, eds., *Avesta, Pahalvi and Ancient Persian Studies*, first series. Byculla: Bombay Education Society's Press.

George, T. C.
1975 *The Growth of Pentecostal Churches in South India*. M. A. Thesis in Missiology. California: Fuller Theological Seminary.

Gerth, H. H. and C. Wright Mills, eds.
1948 *From Max Weber: Essays in Sociology*. London: Routledge and Kegan Paul. See Weber 1958a.

Gilsenan, M.
1982 *Recognizing Islam: An Anthropologist's Introduction*. London: Croom Helm.

Gold, Ann Grodzins
1988 *Fruitful Journeys: The Ways of Rajasthani Pilgrims*. Berkeley: University of California Press.

Gonda, Jan
1969(1966) *Ancient Indian Kingship from the Religious Point of View*. Leiden: E. J. Brill.

Gopal, S., ed.
1980 *Jawaharlal Nehru: An Anthology*. Delhi: Oxford University Press.

Gould, Harold A.
1958 The Hindu jajmani system: a case of economic particularism. *Southwestern Journal of Anthropology* 14: 428–37.

Grigson, W. V.
1938 *The Maria Gonds of Bastar*. London: Oxford University Press.

Hall, S.
1981 Notes on deconstructing 'the popular'. *In* R. Samuel, ed., *People's History and Socialist Theory*. London: Routledge and Kegan Paul.

Harper, Edward E.
1964 Ritual pollution as an integrator of caste and religion. *The Journal of Asian Studies* 2: 151–97.

Hasan, Mushirul
1979 *Nationalism and Communal Politics in India*. New Delhi: Manohar.

Heesterman, J. C.
1957 *The Ancient Indian Royal Consecration*. The Hague: Mouton.

Heine-Geldern, R.
1942 Conceptions of state and kingship in South-east Asia. *Far Eastern Quarterly* II: 15–30.

Hertz, Robert
1960 *Death and the Right Hand*. London: Cohen and West.

Hill, C.
1983 Science and magic in seventeenth century England, *In* R. Samuel and G. Stedman Jones, eds., *Culture, Ideology and Politics*. London: Routledge and Kegan Paul.

Hocart, A. M.
1927 *Kingship*. London: Oxford University Press.
1931 *The Temple of the Tooth in Kandy*. Memoirs of the Archaeological Survey of Ceylon, Vol. IV. London: Luzac.
1936 *Kings and Councillors: An Essay in the Comparative Anatomy of Human Society*. Cairo: Printing Office. Reprinted 1970, Chicago: University of Chicago Press.
1950 *Caste*. London: Methuen.

Hollenweger, W. J.
1972 *The Pentecostals*. London: SCM Press.

Humphreys, Caroline
1985 Some aspects of the Jain puja: the idea of 'God' and the symbolism of offerings. *Cambridge Anthropology* 9: 1–19.

Inden, Ronald B.
1978 Royal authority and cyclic time in Hindu kingship. *In* J. F. Richards, ed., *Kingship and Authority in South Asia*. Madison: University of Wisconsin. South Asian Studies, Publication Series No. 3. 2nd. edn., 1981.

Iqbal, Muhammad
1980 *The Reconstruction of Religious Thought in Islam*. Delhi: New Taj Office. Reprint.

Iyer, Raghavan, ed.
1986 *The Moral and Political Writings of Mahatma Gandhi. Vol. 1: Civilization, Politics, and Religion*. Oxford: Clarendon Press.

Jain, Jyotindra
1977 Jains ritual and space. *In* Niels Gutschow and Thomas Sieverts, eds., *Beitrage und Studienmaterialien der Fachgruppe Stadt Nr. 11: Stadt und Ritual/Urban Space and Ritual*, 35–41. Darmstadt: Technisse Hochschule Darmstadt, 1977; and London: Art and archaeology research papers, 1978.

Jalal, Ayesha
1985 *The Sole Spokesman: Jinnah, Muslim League, and the Demand for Pakistan*. Cambridge: Cambridge University Press.

James, William
1985 *The Varieties of Religious Experience*. Cambridge, Mass: Harvard University Press.

Jigyasu, Chandrika Prasad
1968 *Sri 108 Svāmī Achchutānandjī: Jīvanī, Siddhānta, Bhāṣana aur Kavitāyen*. Lucknow: Janata Welfare Publications.

Jinnah, M. A.
1947–48 *Speeches as Governor-General of Pakistan*. Karachi: Pakistan Publications.

Jones, Kenneth W.
1976 *Arya Dharm*. New Delhi: Manohar.

Joshi, P. C.
1980 The economic background of communalism in India. *In* B. R. Nanda, ed., *Essays in Modern Indian History*. Delhi: Oxford University Press.

Juergensmeyer, Mark
1982 *Religion and Social Vision*. Berkeley: University of California Press.
1987 Non-violence. *In* Mircea Eliade, ed., *The Encyclopedia of Religion*. New York: Macmillan.

Kakar, Sudhir
1978 *The Inner World: A Psychoanalytic Study of Childhood and Society in India*. Delhi: Oxford University Press.
1982 *Shamans, Mystics and Doctors: A Psychological Inquiry into India and its Healing Traditions*. New York: Alfred Knopf.

Kapadia, Hiralal Rasikdas
1932 *Bhaktāmara-kalyāṇamandira-namiūṇa-stotra-trayam* Critical edn. Surat: Sheth Devchand Lalbhai Jain Pustakoddhar Fund Series, No. 79.

Kapur Singh, S.
1959 *Parasharprasna, The Baisakhi of Guru Gobind Singh*. Jullundur: Hind Publishers.

Kāśī Khaṇḍa (Skanda Purāṇa)
1961 Calcutta; Gurumandala Granthamalaya

Kāśī Rahasya (Brahmavaivarta Purāṇa Pariśiṣṭa)
1957 Calcutta: Gurumandala Granthamalaya.

Kasturi, N., ed.
n.d.a. *Sathya Sai Speaks*, Vol. 5. Prasanti Nilayam: Sanathana Sarathi Office.
n.d.b. *Sathya Sai Speaks*, Vol. 7. Bombay: Sri Sathya Sai Education Foundation.
n.d.c. *Sathya Sai Speaks*, Vol. 9. Tustin, Calif.: Sri Sathya Sai Baba Book Centre of America.

Kasturi, N., ed.

1975a *Sathya Sai Speaks*, Vol. 8. Tustin, Calif.: Sri Sathya Sai Baba Book Centre of America.

1975b *Sathyam, Śivam, Sundaram*, pt. 2, 3rd., edn. New Delhi: Bhagwan Sri Sathya Sai Seva Samithi.

1977 *Sathyam, Śivam, Sundram*, pt. 1, 4th. edn. Whitefield, India: Sri Sathya Sai Educational and Publication Foundation.

Khare, R. S.

1979 The untouchable elite (mimeo.). Charlottesville: University of Virginia.

Kiernan, J. P.

1982 Authority and enthusiasm: the organisation of religious experience in Zulu Zionist churches. *In* J. Davis, ed., *Religious Organisation and Religious Experience*. London: Academic.

Kosambi, D. D.

1962 *Myth and Reality: Studies in the Formation of Indian Culture*. Bombay: Popular Prakashan.

1965 *Culture and Civilization of Ancient India in Historical Outline*. London: Routledge and Kegan Paul.

Kosambi, Meera

1980 *Bombay and Poona: A Socio-ecological Study of Two Indian Cities 1650–1900*. Doctoral dissertation. Oslo: University of Stockholm.

Kothari, Rajni

1970 *Politics in India*. New Delhi: Orient Longman.

Kulke, Eckehard

1968 *The Parsees, A Bibliography on an Indian Minority*. Freiburg: Arnold-Bergstraesser Institute.

Kurien, G.

1981 *Mission and Proclamation: The Church in India Today and Other Pieces*. Madras: Christian Literature Society.

Kuśalcandravijay, Muni

1977 *Śrī-Nemi-Vijñān-Kastūrsūrī Smṛti Śreṇī*. Bombay: Prarthana Samaj.

LaBarre, Weston

1972 *The Ghost Dance: Origins of Religion*. London: Allen and Unwin.

Lévi-Strauss, Claude

1963 *Totemism*. Boston: Beacon Press.

1966 *The Savage Mind*. London: Weidenfeld and Nicolson.

Lewis, Bernard
1968 *The Emergence of Modern Turkey*. London: Oxford University Press.

Lingat, Robert
1973 *The Classical Law of India*. Berkeley: University of California Press.

Lowith, Karl
1982 *Max Weber and Karl Marx*. Trans. by H. Fantel. London: Allen and Unwin.

Luthera, V. P.
1964 *The Concept of the Secular State and India*. Calcutta: Oxford University Press.

Lynch, Owen M.
1969 *The Politics of Untouchability*. New York: Columbia University Press.

Macauliffe, M. A.
1909 *The Sikh Religion*, V. Oxford: Clarendon Press.

Macfarlane, A.
1985 The root of all evil. *In* D. J. Parkin, ed., *The Anthropology of Evil*. Oxford: Basil Blackwell.

Madan, T. N.
1989 Religion in India. *Daedalus* 118: 115–46.

Madan, T. N., ed.
1982 *Way of Life: King, Householder, Renouncer. Essays in Honour of Louis Dumont*. New Delhi: Vikas, Paris: Maison des Sciences de l'Homme.

Mahalingam, T. V.
1955 *South Indian Polity*. Madras: Madras University Press.

Mahar, Pauline M.
1959 A multiple scaling technique for caste ranking. *Man in India* 39: 127–47.

Mahāvaṁsa or the great Chronicle of Ceylon
n.d. Trans. by Wilhelm Geiger. Colombo: Ceylon Government Information Department.

Malik, Hafeez
1963 *Muslim Nationalism in India and Pakistan*. Washington, D. C.: Public Affairs Press.

Malinowski, Bronislaw
1974(1925) *Science, Magic and Religion, and Other Essays*. London: Souvenir Press.

Marglin, Frédérique Apffel
1985 *Wives of the God-King: Rituals of the Devadasis of Puri*. Delhi: Oxford University Press.

Marriott, Mckim
1955 Little communities in an indigenous civilization. *In* M. Marriott, ed., *Village India*. Chicago: University of Chicago Press.
1968 Caste ranking and food transactions: a matrix analysis. *In* Milton Singer and Bernard S. Cohn, eds., *Structure and Change in Indian Society*. Chicago: Aldine.
1976 Hindu transactions: diversity without duality. *In* Bruce Kapferer, ed., *Transaction and Meaning*. Philadelphia: Institute for the Study of Human Issues.

Marriott, Mckim and Ronald B. Inden
1973 Caste systems. *Encyclopedia Britannica* 3: 982–91.
1977 Towards an ethnosociology of South Asian caste systems. *In* Kenneth A. David, ed., *The New Wind*. Chicago: Aldine.

Marx, Karl
1959 *Economic and Philosophic Manuscripts of 1844*. Moscow: Progress Publishers.

Marx, Karl and Frederick Engels
1959 *Basic Writings on Politics and Philosophy*. Ed. by Lewis S. Feuer. New York: Doubleday, Anchor.
n.d. *The Indian War of Independence*. Moscow: Progress Publishers.

Mayer, A. C.
1960 *Caste and Kinship in Central India*. Berkeley: University of California Press.
1982 Perceptions of princely rule: perspectives from a biography. *In* T. N. Madan, ed., *Way of Life: King, Householder, Renouncer*. New Delhi: Vikas.

Mines, Mattison
1972 *Muslim Merchants: The Economic Behaviour of an Indian Muslim Community*. New Delhi: Shri Ram Centre for Industrial Relations.

Mirza, Hormazdiar Kaiyoji
1970 On Conversion and Converts in Zoroastrianism. *Parsiana* 6, 10 (Aug. 1970).

Mishra, Vikas
1962 *Hinduism and Economic Growth*. Bombay: Oxford University Press.

Modi, Jivanji Jamshedji
1922 *The Religious Ceremonies and Customs of the Parsees*. Bombay: British India Press.

Monier-Williams, Monier
1891 *Brahmanism and Hinduism*. London: John Murray.

Mueller, F. Max
1889 *Natural Religion*. London: Longmans.

Mukherjee, Ramkrishna
1973 Social background of Bangladesh. *In* K. Gough and H. P. Sharma, eds., *Imperialism and Revolution in South Asia*. New York: Monthly Review Press.

Murphet, Howard
1975 *Sai Baba: Man of Miracles*. Madras: Macmillan.

Mushir-ul-Haq
1972 *Islam in Secular India*. Simla: Indian Institute of Advanced Study.

Nadel, S. F.
1954 *Nupe Religion*. London: Routledge and Kegan Paul.

Nandy, Ashis
1985 An anti-secularist manifesto. *Seminar* 314: 14–24.

Nehru, Jawaharlal
1961 *The Discovery of India*. Bombay: Asia Publishing House.
1972–82 *Selected Works of Jawaharlal Nehru*. New Delhi: Orient Longman.
1980 *An Autobiography*. Delhi: Oxford University Press.

Nietzsche, Friedrich
1961(1884) *Thus Spake Zarathustra*. Trans. by R. J. Hollingdale. Harmondsworth: Penguin.

Norman, E.
1981 *Christianity in the Southern Hemisphere: The Churches in Latin America and South Africa*. Oxford: Clarendon Press.

Obeyesekere, Gananath
1981 *Medusa's Hair: An Essay on Personal Symbols and Religious Experience*. Chicago: University of Chicago Press.
1984 *The Cult of the Goddess Patini*. Chicago: University of Chicago Press.

Oppert, G.
1893 *On the Original Inhabitants of Bhāratvarṣa or India*. Westminister: Constable.

Östör, Ákos
1980 *The Play of the Gods: Locality, Ideology, Structure and Time in*

the Festivals of a Bengali Town. Chicago: University of Chicago Press.

Palaniappan, K.
1970(1963) *The Great Temple of Madurai*. Madurai: Sri Meenakshisundreswar Temple Renovations Committee.

Panikkar, K. N.
1979 Peasant Revolts in Malabar in the 19th. and 20th. Centuries. *In* A. R. Desai, ed., *Peasant Struggles in India*. Bombay: Oxford University Press.

Paranavitana, S.
1950 Sigiri abode of a good king. *Journal of the Royal Asiatic Society* (Ceylon Branch) n.s., I: 129–61.

Pate, H. R.
1917 *Tinnevelly District Gazetteer, Vol. I*. Madras: Government Press.

Pocock, D. F.
1973 *Mind, Body and Wealth: A Study of Belief and Practice in an Indian Village*. Oxford: Basil Blackwell.

Radcliffe-Brown, A. R.
1952 *Structure and Function in Primitive Society*. London: Cohen and West.

1964(1922) *The Andaman Islanders*. Glencoe, III.: The Free Press.

Rahman, Fazlur
1982 *Islam and Modernity*. Chicago: University of Chicago Press.

Rahula, W.
1956 *History of Buddhism in Ceylon*. Colombo: M. D. Gunasena and Co.

Rangachari, K.
1931 *The Sri Vaishnava Brahmans*. Madras: Bulletin of the Madras Government Museum (NS) 2, 2.

Rapoport, David
1984 Fear and trembling: terrorism in three religious traditions. *American Political Science Review* 78: 658–77.

Rapoport, David and Y. Alexander, eds.,
1982 *Morality of Terrorism*. New York: Pergamon Press.

Rivers, W. H. R.
1906 *The Todas*. London: Macmillan.

Rodinson, Maxime
1971 *Mohammad*. Harmondsworth: Penguin.

Rose, H. A., compiler
1911 & 1914 *A Glossary of the Tribes and Castes of the Punjab and the North*

West Province (3 vols.), II & III. Based on the Census Reports for the Punjab, 1883 and 1892. Lahore: Samuel T. Weston at the Civil and Military Gazette Press.

Roy, Sarat Chandra
1934, 1937, 1938 Caste, race and religion in India. *Man in India* 14, 2; 17, 4; 18, 2–3.

Rustomji, Framroz
1965 *Zoroastrian Ceremonies of the Dead*, 2nd. ed. Colombo: Nadarja Press.

1971 Distinguishing Symbols of the Parsees. *Parsiana* 7, 3 (Jan. 1971).

Saberwal, Satish
1976 *Mobile Men: Limits to Social Change in Urban Punjab*. New Delhi: Vikas.

1979 Inequality in colonial India. *Contributions to Indian Sociology* (n.s.) 13: 241–64.

Sagar, Sunderlal
1973(1965) *Hindū Samskṛti mein Varna Vyavasthā aur Jātibedha*. Lucknow: Janata Welfare Publications.

Sandeen, E.
1970 *The Roots of Fundamentalism: British and American Millenarianism 1800–1930*. Chicago: University of Chicago Press.

Sapir, Edward
1949 The meaning of religion. *In* D. G. Mandelbaum, ed., *Selected Writings of Edward Sapir in Language, Culture and Personality*. Berkeley: University of California Press.

Saran, A. K.
1963 Hinduism and economic development in India. *Archives de sociologie des religions* 15: 81–94.

Sargunam, E.
1974 *Multiplying Churches in Modern India*. Madras: Evangelical Church of India.

Sarkar, Sumit
1973 *The Swadeshi Movement in Bengal 1903–1908*. New Delhi: People's Publishing House.

Seneviratne, H. L.
1978 *Rituals of the Kandyan State*. Cambridge: Cambridge University Press.

Shah, K. J.
1982 Of *artha* and the Arthaśāstra. *In* T. N. Madan, ed., *Way of Life: King, Householder, Renouncer*. New Delhi: Vikas.

Shah, U. P.
1987 *Jaina-Rūpa-Maṇḍana*. Vol. 1. New Delhi: Abhinav.

Sharif-ul Mujahid
1981 *Quad-i-Azam Jinnah*. Karachi: Quad-i-Azam Academy.

Shaw, Bernard
1946 *Saint Joan*. Harmondsworth: Penguin.

Singer, Milton
1966 Religion and social change in India: the Weber thesis, 'phase three'. *Economic Development and Culture Change* 14: 497–505.
1972 *When a Great Tradition Modernizes: An Anthropological Approach to Indian Civilization*. New York: Praeger.

Smith, Donald Eugene
1963 *India as a Secular State*. Bombay: Oxford University Press.

Smith, Wilfred Cantwell
1962 *The Meaning and End of Religion*. New York: Mentor.
1976 Objectivity and the humane sciences: a new proposal. *In: Religious Diversity*. New York: Crossroads.

Smith, William Robertson
1927(1899) *Lectures on the Religion of the Semites*. New York: Macmillan.

Sprinzak, Ehud
1988 The politics of Zionist fundamentalism in Israel. *In* David Rapoport, ed., *Religious Terrorism*. New York: Columbia University Press.

Srinivas, M. N.
1952 *Religion and Society among the Coorgs of South India*. Oxford: Clarendon Press.

Stanner, W. E. H.
1967 Reflections on Durkheim and aboriginal religion. *In* Maurice Freedman, ed., *Social Organization*. London: Frank Cass.

Stevenson, H. N. C.
1954 Status evaluation in the Hindu caste system. *Journal of the Royal Anthropological Institute* 84: 45–65.

Stevenson, Margaret
1921 Worship (Jain). *In* J. A. Hastings, ed., *Encyclopaedia of Religion and Ethics*, Vol. XII: 799–802.

Stutley, Margaret and James Stutley
1977 *A Dictionary of Hinduism*. London: Routledge and Kegan Paul.

Subramaniam K.
1974 *Brahman Priests of Tamil Nadu*. New York: John Wiley.

Swallow, D. A.
1982 Ashes and powers: myth, rite and miracle in an Indian godman's cult. *Modern Asian Studies* 16: 123–58.

Tambiah, Stanley J.
1970 *Buddhism and the Spirit Cults in North-East Thailand*. Cambridge: Cambridge University Press.
1976 *World Conqueror and World Renouncer*. Cambridge: Cambridge University Press.
1981 *A Performative Approach to Ritual*. London: Proceedings of the British Academy. Included in Tambiah 1985.
1985 *Culture, Thought and Social Action: An Anthropological Perspective*. Cambridge MA: Harvard University Press.

Taraporewala, I. J. S.
1965 *The Religion of Zarathustra*, 2nd ed. Bombay: Bombay Chronicle Press.

Taylor, D.
1985 Theological thoughts about evil. *In* D. Parkin, ed., *The Anthropology of Evil*. Oxford: Basil Blackwell.

Teja Singh
1938 *Sikhism: Its Ideals and Institutions*. Calcutta: Longmans, Green & Co.

Thurston, Edgar (with K. Rangachari)
1909 *Castes and Tribes of Southern India*. 7 Vols. Madras: Government Press.

Timberg, Thomas A.
1978 *The Marwaris: From Traders to Industrialists*. New Delhi: Vikas.

Tully, Mark and Satish Jacob
1985 *Amritsar: Mrs Gandhi's Last Battle*. London: Jonathan Cape.

Turner, Victor
1967 *The Forest of Symbols: Aspects of Ndembu Ritual*. Ithaca: Cornell University Press.
1969 *The Ritual Process: Structure and Anti-Structure*. Chicago: Aldine.
1975 *Dramas, Fields and Metaphors*, Ithaca: Cornell University Press.

Turton, A.
1984 Limits of ideological domination and the formation of social consciousness. *In* A. Turton and S. Tanabe, eds., *History and Peasant Consciousness in South East Asia*. Osaka: National Museum of Planning.

Tylor, Edward B.
1913(1871) *Primitive Culture*. London: John Murray.

van den Dungen, P. H. M.
1968 Changes in status and occupation in nineteenth century Punjab. *In* D. A. Low, ed., *Soundings in Modern South Asian History*. London: Weidenfeld and Nicolson.
1972 *The Punjab Tradition*. London: Allen and Unwin.

van Gennep, A.
1960 *The Rites of Passage*. Trans. by M. B. Vizedom and G. L. Caffee. London: Routledge and Kegan Paul.

Vidyarthi, L. P.
1961 *The Sacred Complex of Hindu Gaya*. Bombay: Asia.

Wadia, P. A.
1949 *Parsis Ere the Shadows Thicken*. Bombay: n.p.m.

Weber, Max
1930 *The Protestant Ethic and the Spirit of Capitalism*. Trans. by Talcott Parsons. London: Allen and Unwin.
1947 *The Theory of Social and Economic Organization*. Trans. by A. M. Henderson and T. Parsons. New York: Oxford University Press.
1958a *From Max Weber: Essays in Sociology*. Trans. by H. H. Gerth and C. Wright Mills. New York: Oxford University Press.
1958b *The Religion of India: The Sociology of Hinduism and Buddhism*. Trans. by H. H. Gerth and Don Martindale. Glencoe, III: The Free Press.
1964 *The Sociology of Religion*. Boston: Beacon Press.

Wheatley, Paul
1967 *City as Symbol*. London: University College.
1971 *The Pivot of the Four Quarters: A Preliminary Enquiry into the Origins and Character of the Ancient Chinese City*. Chicago: Aldine.

White, Charles
1972 The Sai-Baba movement: approaches to the study of Indian saints. *The Journal of Asian Studies* 31: 863–78.

Whitehead, H. (Bishop R. R.)
1921 *The Village Gods of South India*. Calcutta.

Wilson, Bryan
1973 *Magic and the Millenium*. London: Paladin.

Worsley, Peter
1970 *The Trumpet shall Sound: A Study of Cargo Cults in Melanesia*. London: Paladin.

Zaehner, R. C.
1961 *The Dawn and Twilight of Zoroastrianism*. New York: Putnam.

Ziegenbalg, G.
1869 *Genealogy of the South Indian Gods*. Madras.

Index